Pro MSMQ: Microsoft Message Queue Programming

AROHI REDKAR, CARLOS WALZER, SCOT BOYD,
RICHARD COSTALL, KEN RABOLD, TEJASWI REDKAR

Apress®

Pro MSMQ: Microsoft Message Queue Programming
Copyright ©2004 by Arohi Redkar, Carlos Walzer, Scot Boyd, Richard Costall,
Ken Rabold, Tejaswi Redkar

ISBN 13 (pbk): 978-1-59059-346-2
ISBN 10 (pbk): 1-59059-346-4

Printed and bound in the United States of America (POD)

Lead Editor: Ewan Buckingham

Technical Reviewers: Yoel Arnon, Andrew Krowczyk

Editorial Board: Steve Anglin, Dan Appleman, Ewan Buckingham, Gary Cornell, Tony Davis, Jason Gilmore, Chris Mills, Steve Rycroft, Dominic Shakeshaft, Jim Sumser, Karen Watterson, Gavin Wray, John Zukowski

Assistant Publisher and Project Manager: Grace Wong

Copy Editor: Liz Welch

Production Manager: Kari Brooks

Production Editor: Ellie Fountain

Proofreader: Elizabeth Berry

Compositor: Molly Sharp, ContentWorks

Indexer: Valerie Haynes Perry

Artist: Kinetic Publishing Services, LLC

Cover Designer: Kurt Krames

Manufacturing Manager: Tom Debolski

In the United States: phone 1-800-SPRINGER, email orders@springer-ny.com, or visit http://www.springer-ny.com. Outside the United States: fax +49 6221 345229, email orders@springer.de, or visit http://www.springer.de.

For information on translations, please contact Apress directly at 2560 Ninth Street, Suite 219, Berkeley, CA 94710. Phone 510-549-5930, fax 510-549-5939, email info@apress.com, or visit http://www.apress.com.

The source code for this book is available to readers at http://www.apress.com in the Source Code section. You will need to answer questions pertaining to this book in order to successfully download the code.

To all those who have taught me something over the years.
—Scot Boyd

To Liz, Thomas and Oliver: I will always love you.
—Richard Costall

Dedicated to my wonderful wife Juli and my two boys,
Jordan and Alec. You mean the world to me.
—Ken Rabold

I dedicate this book to my parents, who taught me
the meaning of the word professionalism.
—Arohi Redkar

To my parents, thanks for being with me all the time.
—Tejaswi Redkar

Dedicated to the love of my life, Lauri.
—Carlos Walzer

Contents at a Glance

Contents

Foreword

No application is an island... In today's connected world, each and every professional developer must assume that his or her applications will need to communicate with other applications.

Distributed applications, however, present a large set of unique challenges, like, what do I do when the network is disconnected? How do I coordinate the actions of two separate applications? How do I handle peak times? How do I guarantee delivery? How do I upgrade my application without breaking the communication?

We at the Microsoft Message Queue (MSMQ) team have worked hard to provide an elegant solution to these questions and many others. This book will help you leverage this work by using MSMQ in your distributed applications so that you will be able to concentrate on the business logic rather than network problems.

What is MSMQ? MSMQ is message-oriented middleware (MOM) that comes as a standard component of Windows and allows applications to exchange messages among them using *queues*—outgoing queues for messages waiting to be sent, and incoming queues for messages waiting to be received. Queues—like dams—guarantee nice and controlled flow of information, even when the network is congested or suffers frequent disconnects.

Moreover, queues are a very natural programming metaphor. Most people would agree that working from a queue of to-do tasks is more effective than responding to requests on the spot. The same is true for computer programs. Programs that process queues of incoming messages tend to be simpler and more efficient than programs acting on interrupts.

The availability of powerful, yet simple, MOMs like MSMQ on millions of desktops and servers has changed the way programmers design and write distributed applications. The simple concepts of queue and message—along with powerful features like quality of service, transactions, and security—have enabled a new breed of distributed applications in a wide range of industries. In addition, MSMQ provides an excellent solution for integrating existing applications—for the Internet or for enterprise-wide systems like ERP.

Even after nine years on the MSMQ team, I am amazed to see the number of ways customers use this technology: in airlines and communication, financial services, e-retailers, traditional department stores, and even online games.

In addition to covering the essentials of MSMQ, this book is the first book covering the cool new features introduced in MSMQ 3.0 (which was released as part of Windows XP and Windows Server 2003)—features such as multicast, triggers, HTTP messages, and more. In addition, it is the first book covering the novel .NET MSMQ APIs: System.Messaging.

Today, MSMQ knowledge has become a standard requirement for a professional Windows developer, alongside such skills as Visual Basic, Visual C/C#, SQL/IIS/ADO/COM+, and others. Reading this book is a great way to get started.

If you consider yourself a professional Windows developer, and you know that no application is an island any longer, then this book is for you.

I am proud to be a part of the revolution MSMQ brought to the Windows application development world. I hope that you will enjoy using MSMQ as much as I—together with the other MSMQ team members—enjoyed developing it.

Yoel Arnon
Software Development Engineer
Microsoft Corporation

About the Authors

Scot Boyd

Scot Boyd was first introduced to MSMQ at Microsoft as a beta support engineer for MSMQ 1.0. In his seven years at Microsoft, he has also worked on Win32, COM/DCOM, MFC/ATL, Web Services, Messaging, and even Interactive TV. He currently works as an independent consultant and contractor based in the Seattle, Washington, area, where he enjoys the bright summers and rainy winters. Scot can be reached at scot@scotboyd.net.

Richard Costall

Richard Costall (MCSD, MCAD, MCSD.NET) has over 17 years' development experience and works for 1st, the U.K.'s leading software solution for financial advisers and intermediaries, designing and implementing Independent Financial Adviser applications in the financial services sector. Although mainly specializing in VB, XML/XSLT, COM, ASP, and MSMQ, Richard has now focused his attention on the world of .NET. Richard is also the Midlands regional coordinator for VBUG (Visual Basic User Group) and spends a fair amount of his time organizing and presenting at meetings.

When not in .NET land, Richard enjoys relaxing at home with his wife and two sons or ultimately jetting off to Walt Disney World, Florida, for a trip on the Tower of Terror. Richard can be contacted via http://www.costall.net.

Ken Rabold

Ken Rabold is a software engineering manager with Texas Instruments, where he works at enabling multimedia technologies on Microsoft Pocket PC and Smartphone platforms. Prior to joining TI, Ken was the senior software architect for BSQUARE Corporation, where he worked on various XML and MSMQ technologies for embedded devices.

A graduate of Seattle University and University of Washington, Ken is also a Microsoft Embedded MVP. You can reach him at kenrabold@hotmail.com.

Arohi Redkar

Arohi Redkar is a software designer. She has a master's degree in software engineering from National University. She has worked extensively in the .NET environment and has a passion for studying human aspects of user interface design. She gives special thanks to her husband, parents, brother, and son Aaryan for helping to make her dream a reality. You can reach her at arohig@hotmail.com.

Tejaswi Redkar

Tejaswi Redkar is a software architect and a consultant. He has a master's degree in enterprise software from San Jose State University.

He is currently working as a system architect at ViewCentral, Inc. He has experience in architecting service-oriented systems in the financial, telemetry, and e-commerce domains. He is an experienced .NET author and has contributed 3 books and more than 15 articles to the .NET community.

Tejaswi thanks his parents, his wife Arohi, and his son Aaryan for supporting him in whatever he does.

He can be reached at tejaswi_redkar@yahoo.com.

Carlos Walzer

Carlos Walzer is a software developer and consultant. He studied at the National Technological University in Argentina, where he was a professor for 5 years.

He now works with his partners in a consulting company called Vemn Systems, where he develops and performs architectural skills. He is an aspiring specialist in distributed applications and web development, and has extraordinary knowledge in .NET Framework.

He was awarded MVP (Most Valuable Professional) by Microsoft due to his .NET skills and his commitment to the developer community. He delivers conferences in DevDays and TechEd events, and writes articles for MSDN and ASPToday. You can reach him at carlosw@vemn.com.ar or via his web site at http://www.vemn.com.ar.

About the Technical Reviewers

Yoel Arnon

Yoel joined Microsoft in February 1995, and started working as the fourth developer in the "Falcon" project, which was later renamed MSMQ. He worked in MSMQ through its entire lifecycle—from the initial design through versions 1.0 (Windows NT 4, 1997), 2.0 (Windows 2000, 1999), and 3.0 (Windows XP and Windows 2003).

Yoel was responsible for the development of several MSMQ components, including the initial version of the MSMQ COM object, MSMQ cluster integration, and MSMQ Explorer and MSMQ MMC snap-in. In the last three years, he has worked in MSMQ sustained engineering, supporting existing customers through service packs and hotfixes, and giving MSMQ training and presentations.

Before joining Microsoft, Yoel worked at Intel Corporation (1992–1995) and Sterling Software (1987–1992).

Andrew Krowczyk

Andrew Krowczyk is a senior software architect currently working for a global insurance company near Chicago. His realm of expertise includes C# and .NET-related web and distributed systems. Holding both a bachelor's and a master's degree in computer science as well as Microsoft certifications, Andrew is always on the leading edge of Microsoft-related technologies.

Acknowledgments

Scot Boyd

I'd like to thank the folks at Apress for the opportunity to bring this material to a wider audience. I'd also like to thank all the coworkers who have taken time to educate me over the years, and the friends who have encouraged me to pursue my writing.

Richard Costall

Seven years ago, I had a job, but no career. I took a risk and checked in at the "Microsoft Hotel." Since then I have never looked back. Visual Basic 6 was cool, but .NET is awesome. Thanks, Microsoft, for a great technology, and roll on, Longhorn. Thanks also to my parents and my brother Stephen. Most of all, I have to thank my lovely wife Liz and my two fantastic sons, Thomas and Oliver, I will always love you. Thanks also to Birmingham Children's Hospital for giving Oliver the gift of life.

Ken Rabold

I'd like to thank my wife Juli and my sons, Jordan and Alec, for their patience and understanding during those late nights and weekends that were spent pulling this book together. I also want to acknowledge all the "road warriors" out there trying to develop cool applications for devices—I hope the chapter on MSMQ and Pocket PC will shed some light on the subject for you and inspire you to give it a try.

Arohi Redkar

I am thankful to my husband Tejaswi, my parents, my brother Amol, and my son Aaryan for supporting me in writing this book.

Tejaswi Redkar

Foremost, I thank my parents, my wife Arohi, and my son Aaryan for building a solid foundation around me. I also thank all my teachers, friends, and family who have supported me in whatever I do and also have provided healthy criticism. Finally, I am grateful to all the people at Apress for giving me the opportunity to contribute to this book.

Carlos Walzer

An author's dream is to write by the sea overlooking the waves and being inspired by the sky, thinking at his own pace and appreciating his work in the process. This is merely a dream. With my hectic schedule, the only time I could write was during vacation with the help of my lovely wife Laura and my sister-in-law Alejandra. At this time I'm truly thankful and grateful to my wife for all her assistance during this project. Thanks also goes to Nestor Portillo, Eddie Malik, my partners Daniel and Patricia, and my parents and sister.

Introduction

MICROSOFT PROVIDES A ROBUST, SCALABLE (and free) messaging solution for Windows, the Microsoft Message Queue Server (MSMQ). MSMQ is accessible to programmers of all skill levels, and offers APIs for .NET programmers, COM programmers, and Win32 programmers alike. *Pro MSMQ* is designed for programmers who want to begin taking advantage of what Microsoft Message Queueing has to offer.

The defining feature of most messaging systems is how messages are addressed and received; in Windows Sockets, for example, messages are sent to and received from a socket. In MSMQ, messages are sent to and received from a queue. A queue acts as a holding pen for messages, storing them in sequential order, where they can be viewed or removed at any time. Messages can be persistent, stored on disk in a queue where they can be read at any time. Messages can be sent as part of a transaction, ensuring that messages are received only once and in the order they were sent. For a higher level of security, messages can be authenticated and encrypted automatically.

Messaging applications can send messages across an enterprise network, between organizations, or to applications running on the very same computer. Indeed, a well-designed messaging application doesn't need to know how far the message has traveled, as long as it's delivered. In object-oriented programming, it's not important for the user of an object to know how the object is implemented; similarly, a messaging application does not need to know the layout of the messaging system to create powerful messaging applications. Message senders and receivers can be in different countries, or reside on the same computer, with little difference.

These capabilities in MSMQ allow programmers to create powerful decoupled applications for an enterprise network, or just improve existing applications with simple, reliable communications.

Chapter-by-Chapter Overview

Here are brief descriptions of the topics we cover in depth in this book.

Chapter 1: Introducing Message Queuing

This chapter introduces MSMQ, describes its advantages, and explains where it should be used. It starts with an overview of communication within distributed applications and the benefits of Message Queueing. It also examines the elements that are part of the MSMQ architecture, shows you how to use them in order to develop a Message Queuing–based application, and provides some architecture scenario examples of Message Queuing–based applications. Finally it compares and explains the changes introduced by each successive version of MSMQ, and gives a step-by-step guide of how to set up MSMQ.

This chapter provides the base for understanding the later chapters, which cover how to build MSMQ applications in detail.

Chapter 2: System.Messaging

With the advent of .NET Framework, MSMQ programming has taken a different turn from a programmer's perspective. In this chapter we explore the System.Messaging namespace from the .NET Framework and develop programs to interact with MSMQ from the .NET Framework.

Chapter 3: Administration

In this chapter, we discuss the administration of Message Queuing in detail. We start with typical administrative tasks, such as creating and deleting queues, and slowly proceed to building a Message Queuing network.

Chapter 4: Transactional Messaging

In this chapter, we discuss the internal and external transactions that MSMQ supports. We also develop programs that send and receive transactional messages from MSMQ.

Chapter 5: MSMQ Triggers

MSMQ Triggers enable specific actions to be performed on receipt of an incoming message in a queue. The action can take the form of the invocation of a method within a component/assembly or the running of a standard executable. This chapter explains what MSMQ Triggers are, where you can get them, how they work, and what they bring to the MSMQ party.

Chapter 6: MSMQ COM and Win32 API

This chapter explores COM and Win32 programming techniques in MSMQ using Visual C++, including new features in MSMQ 3.0 not directly available in the System.Messaging namespace. This chapter also demonstrates how to access the MSMQ COM API from within .NET using C#.

Chapter 7: MSMQ 3.0

This chapter covers the latest version of MSMQ included in Windows XP and Windows 2003. The most important feature introduced by MSMQ 3.0 is Internet Messaging, which provides support for sending and retrieving messages through Hypertext Transfer Protocol (HTTP). This chapter explains this feature in depth, providing an example of how to build a scalable MSMQ application over the Internet. It also explains the new Programmable Management COM interface, which provides several classes for managing queues and computers programmatically, and queue aliases, which are Active Directory objects used to reference queues by means of an alias. Finally, it shows how to send messages to multiple destinations using distribution lists, multicast addresses, and multiple-element format names.

As the majority features of MSMQ 3.0 are supported by the Message Queueing COM component, this chapter provides several examples coded in Visual Basic 6.0.

Chapter 8: MSMQ on Pocket PC

This chapter dives into how you can leverage the power of MSMQ messaging in the world of devices. Like the other chapters in this book, Chapter 8 shows you how you can program MSMQ on a Pocket PC using C++, VB, and C#, and describes the differences between MSMQ on the desktop and MSMQ for Windows CE. Additionally, this chapter discusses tips and tricks that will help you diagnose MSMQ problems that you may encounter with your device.

Who Should Read This Book?

This book is designed for programmers interested in learning messaging basics, and current MSMQ users who want a handy reference guide to MSMQ operations, including the System.Messaging API in .NET, and the latest features from MSMQ 3.0.

CHAPTER 1

Introducing Message Queuing

ONE OF THE BIGGEST CHALLENGES any organization faces is connecting disparate systems. **Microsoft Message Queuing (MSMQ)** is a middleware technology that allows applications running at different times in a distributed environment to communicate with one another either **synchronously** or **asynchronously**. Because MSMQ guarantees message delivery, it provides reliability even for networks and systems that are offline. **Message Queuing** is a protocol that allows multiple applications to exchange data in the form of **messages**; these messages are sent to **queues** on the remote server, where they can be read by the target application. One way to envisage MSMQ is as e-mail for applications: it allows the sending application to send a message to another application and then just go on with whatever it is doing, without waiting for a reply. The receiving application can even be offline.

In this chapter, we examine the elements that are part of the MSMQ architecture and learn how to use them in order to develop a Message Queuing–based application. We cover these topics in the following sections:

- The communication within distributed applications and the role of Message Queuing

- All the elements that form a Message Queuing environment

- Some architecture scenario examples of Message Queuing–based applications

- The changes introduced by each successive version of MSMQ

- How to set up MSMQ

This chapter introduces MSMQ, describes its advantages, and explains where it should be used. In addition, it provides the base for understanding the later chapters, which cover how to build MSMQ applications in detail.

Communications Within Distributed Applications

Message Queuing **middleware** offers a large number of benefits to help you build distributed applications:

- Asynchronous communication

- Decoupled applications

- Guaranteed processing of requests

- Scalability

- Reliability

- Fault tolerance

It basically helps you develop distributed applications running independently of one another, which means that the server need not be up when the client requests a service. The service is provided when the server comes up; at that point the client need not be up, and can accept the processed reply when it starts.

Asynchronous Applications

To spread the work within a distributed application, you must model a distributed environment, allowing tasks to run in different processes. However, you must consider the possibility that not all of the receiving applications will be up and running when you want them. If you are trying to connect in a synchronous or an asynchronous way, the applications have to be online. You also need availability, so you can't wait for one message to be processed before a second is sent. For this reason, you need a way of communicating between your applications asynchronously. In this section, we look at the difference between synchronous and asynchronous processes, and at the pattern suggested by Message Queuing: **asynchronous communication**.

Let's examine the way in which two people in an organization who work in different offices can communicate with each other, as an analogy illustrating the use of distributed applications. Our first actor, John, requires Mary to carry out a task and inform him of the result. For this purpose we will use UML activity diagrams. The UML activity diagram is a multipurpose flow diagram that enables us to model business workflow, illustrating the dynamic nature of a system by modeling the flow of control from activity to activity.

Synchronous Processes

In general, the term "synchronous" describes objects or events that are coordinated in time. In program-to-program communication, synchronous means that the process runs only as a result of some other process being completed or handing off an operation (see Figure 1-1).

As we stated, John needs Mary to carry out a task and inform him of the result. They communicate by telephone: John calls Mary, tells her what he needs, and holds on the telephone waiting for the answer.

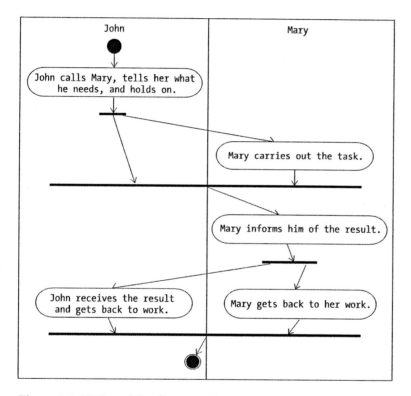

Figure 1-1. UML activity diagram of a synchronous process

Advantages

This system has the advantage that, although John doesn't know how to perform this task, he doesn't need to. Instead of worrying, he can count on Mary to do it for him. Translating it into a distributed environment, we are distributing logic and balancing load.

Disadvantages

However, by introducing this distributed system, we have also introduced a couple of disadvantages:

- John needs Mary to pick up the telephone in order to tell her what he needs. If Mary isn't available, John will not be able to continue with his work.

- As a result, John can't carry out another task until Mary solves his problem and communicates the result back to him. He needs her to complete the assignment before he can get back to work.

This process is similar to a synchronous call made by two applications. Both of them should be available to communicate synchronously. Unfortunately, while one works, the other one remains idle, as can be seen in the diagram.

Asynchronous Processes

The adjective "asynchronous" describes objects or events that are not coordinated in time. In terms of applications, an asynchronous operation is one where a process operates independently of other processes (see Figure 1-2).

Let's look at another situation. John telephones Mary, tells her what he needs, and hangs up. Mary carries out the task, and when she finishes it she calls him back to inform him of the result.

We have solved one problem:

- John can work while Mary carries out the task. If we translate it into a distributed environment, we are distributing processes.

However, a disadvantage remains:

- John needs Mary to pick up the telephone to communicate what he needs. If Mary isn't available, John can't get on with his work. Similarly, Mary needs John to pick up the phone to inform him of the result.

If John and Mary were applications, both of them should be online to communicate asynchronously.

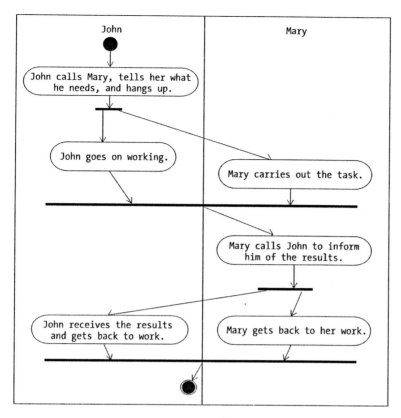

Figure 1-2. UML activity diagram of an asynchronous process

Asynchronous Communication

Finally, we arrive at the ideal situation proposed by Message Queuing. Working asynchronously, a process operates independently of other processes. Message Queuing adds a middleware component (a queue) to the communication between the applications to hold the interchanged messages. In this case John is capable of delivering an instruction to Mary, without needing her to be available, by sending an e-mail (a message) to an inbox (a queue) (see Figure 1-3). As soon as she is back at her workstation, she will get the instructions, create a report, and send it back to John by e-mail too.

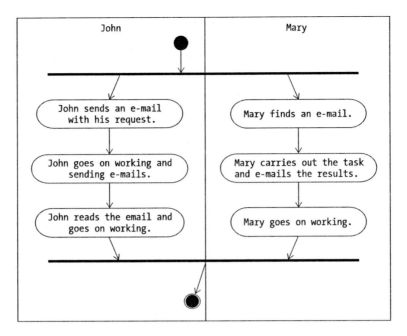

Figure 1-3. UML activity diagram of an asynchronous communication

We have solved all the problems considered earlier:

- John can work while Mary carries out the task.

- John doesn't need Mary to be available to tell her what he needs, and Mary doesn't need John to be available to inform him of the result.

- If Mary is unable to receive the request, any colleague at her office who finds it could carry out the task. In this case, there isn't just one person at your service: there is a whole team working for you!

If we translate this model into Message Queuing, the queues allow applications to communicate with one another even if they're not running, because a message is being placed in a shared "dropbox" and will wait until the proper party comes online to pick it up.

Message-Based Applications

Beyond having monolithic and isolated applications running on a machine, solutions become a group of applications distributed throughout your organization's entire network. These applications not only have to interact among themselves, but also have to communicate outside the boundaries of your organization. The most common way of communicating between applications is by sending messages.

Suppose that you have two isolated applications, each of which is running on a single machine, but now you need to connect them. Perhaps they need to share data or become part of a workflow process in your organization that could involve more applications than these two.

First, you need to provide them with a physical connection. Perhaps you can connect them to an existing network in your organization, or to the Internet. Then you need a common protocol. A protocol works as a language that each application should know in order to be able to understand the other applications. This is where Microsoft Message Queuing comes on to the scene, sitting on top of a networking protocol. Finally, you must upgrade your applications and code the functionality to enable communication between the applications. Once all these steps are complete, they will become message-based applications. How will they work? Application A sends a message to Application B. MSMQ takes care of the protocols they need to understand one another. The only thing that they need to solve is how to interpret the data transmitted by the message, which could be in any format (such as Extensible Markup Language, or XML).

Elements in a Message-Queuing System

In Figure 1-4, you see the component parts of the interaction between the two applications (a **sender** and a **receiver**) and the elements that form part of a queued message–based system.

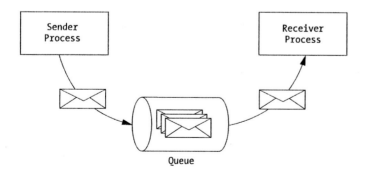

Figure 1-4. Elements involved in a queued message–based system

Therefore, you have two applications that interact via Message Queuing:

- **The sender:** Generally, the sender application sends a message in order to request a service from or pass some data to another application.

- **The receiver:** This retrieves messages from the queue and processes them.

 NOTE   *The sender and receiver could interchange their roles if a response is needed.*

There are two elements to a Message Queuing system that these applications use to communicate with one another:

- **Messages:** A message is like an envelope containing the data that the sender wants to submit, as well as further delivery information such as reply, routing, transactions, priority, destination, and correlation. This additional information allows Message Queuing to deliver the request.

- **Queues:** These are storage mechanisms that contain the exchanged messages. The sender creates a message, which is sent to the queue waiting for the receiver to attend to it. The two applications should come to an agreement on the name and location of the queue in which they will exchange the messages.

Decoupled Applications

Not all applications in a distributed environment might be online when you want them, and they don't need to know each other. Using queues as intermediate storage, the asynchronous communication pattern proposed by Message Queuing reduces the degree of coupling between applications.

Applications Decoupled by Time

In a queued messaging environment, there is no need to be online to process the messages. Applications only need to have access to queues to send and to retrieve the messages. Suppose that you have developed an application that performs batch processes at night, based on data provided by another application. The data application provider sends the messages all day long to be processed without caring whether the batch processing application is online: only the queue needs to be available. Then the batch processing application can be started at the end of a working day to process all the messages sent to the queues by the other applications. Message queuing offers a natural communication environment for distributed applications.

Applications Decoupled by Knowledge

Applications communicating asynchronously don't need to know each other. If an application sends a message to a queue, there can be two or more applications (of the same type) picking and processing messages. In this way, the sender application needs to know only the name and location of the intermediary, the queue, and does not need to know the name, location, or other details of the receiving application.

Benefits of the Message Queuing Middleware

While the messages are in transit between applications, MSMQ keeps messages in holding areas called queues. That's why Microsoft Message Queue Server is considered a Message Queuing middleware product. Message Queuing middleware adds some benefits that you should consider when designing your distributed environment.

Reliability

Message delivery is guaranteed. Using routing, transactions, and recoverable messages, MSMQ ensures that all messages will be properly delivered to their destination queue (see Figure 1-4). If the message can't reach the queue, there will be a copy of it somewhere. It is also possible to send express messages, with no guaranteed delivery but with high performance. In general, the designer should always make the trade-off between reliability and performance. We look at this in detail later in this chapter.

Scalability

You can increase the productivity of your systems, and allow them to scale in a simple way. All you have to do is run more processes that read messages from the same queue. You can achieve this by running more instances of the same receiving application on the same server or on a different machine. Distributing the reception to balance the load enables your system to scale with respect to both software and hardware (see "Receiving Only from Local Queues" section later).

MSMQ provides mechanisms such as message dealing and transactions to avoid the same message being processed by two different applications, as shown in Figure 1-5.

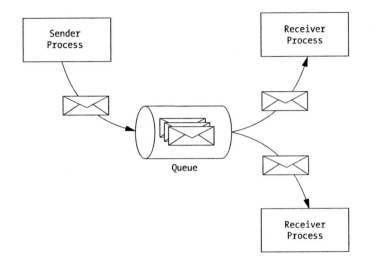

Figure 1-5. System scaled by parallel processes attending to the same queue

Fault Tolerance

Once you have two or more processes attending to the same queue, you are assured that all the messages will be processed (see Figure 1-6). If one process goes down, the other carries on processing messages. This guarantees that all the messages will be processed, unless both go down.

In MSMQ, a queue resides on a specific machine. If that machine goes down, there is no way to receive messages from the queue. One way to get fault tolerance in this case is to use the MCS cluster (Microsoft Cluster Services).

Guaranteed Processing of Requests

The sender application doesn't care whether the receiver is online or offline, because the messages will be processed at some point anyway. If the receiver application crashes, all messages will be stored up in the queue to be processed later (see Figure 1-7).

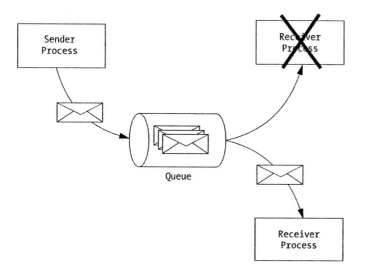

Figure 1-6. Fault tolerance provided by parallel processes attending to the same queue

Typically the queue resides on the receiving machine. So, if the machine running the queue crashes, all the sent messages will be lost unless Time to Be Received and Deadletter are set on the message, in which case the message is stored on the sender until actually read by the receiving application. The messages that were not sent are stored in an "outgoing queue" in the sending machine until the queue manager is able to deliver them to the receiver.

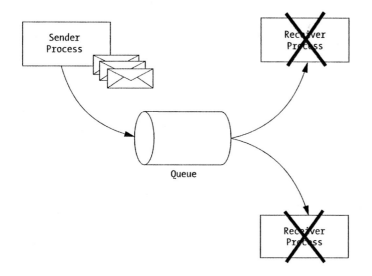

Figure 1-7. Undelivered messages waiting to be delivered

The MSMQ Architecture

The MSMQ architecture logically groups computers running MSMQ, helping administrators to manage thousands of computers in a simple way. Exploring MSMQ architecture in depth will help us to model distributed environments.

In this section, we examine the uses and properties of the MSMQ architecture, and explain how it can help you to organize communication between applications.

First, Microsoft provides you with three different **application programming interfaces (API)** to access Message Queuing programmatically:

- **The** System.Messaging **namespace** (covered in Chapter 2): The .NET Framework provides several classes to develop .NET queued messaging applications.

- **Message Queuing API** (covered in Chapter 6): A group of functions, properties, and structures, generally used in C++ applications.

- **Message Queuing COM component** (Chapter 6): A set of COM object classes with properties, methods, and events, typically used in Microsoft Visual Basic applications.

Because MSMQ is language independent, in this book you will find a mix of code in a number of languages: Visual Basic 6.0, Visual Basic .NET, C#, and C++. This variety provides you with a broad spectrum of functionality.

Keep in mind that all the features studied in this section are not available in every MSMQ version, and they may have different uses depending on the Message Queuing implementation. In this section, we treat them conceptually, but they will be covered in the later chapters.

MSMQ Enterprise

MSMQ architecture is based on a **Site/Enterprise Model**. An Enterprise represents an organization consisting of one or more sites. A Site is a group of computers in a physical location, such as a building. All the computers in an organization that are running MSMQ are part of the MSMQ Enterprise.

All the information about the MSMQ Enterprise is maintained by the **Directory Service**. A directory is an information source used to store hierarchical information about objects. A distributed computing system comprises many objects, such as printers, applications, databases, and other users. Administrators dictate the way the users use these objects.

In the case of MSMQ, every property for the machines and public queues that form part of the organization is stored in a distributed database called the Directory Service. The Directory Service also maintains security credentials, and is used by the MSMQ Service for routing purposes. Each server, workstation, and client has read/write access to the Directory Service and shares its data. The distributed Directory Service database is physically stored at every MSMQ Server computer.

The way the Directory Service is used depends on the version of MSMQ (more on versions in "MSMQ Versions" section later). MSMQ 1.0 uses the MSMQ Information Store (MQIS), which is implemented through a **SQL Server** database. On the other hand, in MSMQ 2.0 and higher the Directory Service is implemented through **Active Directory**.

Of course, you can also communicate with MSMQ-based applications running on computers that are operating in a **workgroup** environment or in offline mode, accessing the queues directly.

Obviously, these applications can't share the information stored in the Directory Service database. We'll look at this point in the section "Workgroup vs. Domain Mode" later in this chapter.

NOTE *The Directory Service database does not store messages. It stores only the information about every machine and every public queue in the Enterprise.*

MSMQ Servers

MSMQ Server is responsible for maintaining the distributed Directory Service database. In MSMQ 1.0, it stores the MQIS SQL Server database; in MSMQ 2.0 and higher, MSMQ Server can only be installed on servers that belong to an Active Directory domain. MSMQ Servers can also have routing purposes.

These are the roles to which MSMQ 1.0 Servers can belong:

- **Primary Enterprise Controller (PEC):** The PEC is in charge of maintaining the master Directory Service database, and must be defined when an MSMQ Enterprise is created. It stores information about the MSMQ Enterprise and the **certification keys** used to **authenticate** messages. The PEC allows message encryption.

- **Primary Site Controller (PSC):** The PSC has to be installed on every site, and maintains a copy of the Directory Service database. It keeps information about the machines and queues of its site. The Primary Enterprise Controller can act as a PSC for its site.

- **Backup Site Controller (BSC):** There can be zero or more BSCs installed in each site. They are used to reduce the site's failure risk. If the PSC is down and we have not installed a BSC, there will be no message queuing.

- **Routing Server:** This supports the routing of messages from one site to another. The Message Routing Server is the system that keeps the messages while they are moving from sender to receiver. The PEC, PSC, and BSC also perform routing tasks. The Routing Servers do not maintain a copy of the Directory Service database.

- **Connector Server:** This is a bridge between MSMQ and non-Microsoft queuing systems, acting as a translator between other middleware providers. The Connector Server provides the opportunity to interact with IBM's MQSeries and FalconMQ. The Connector Server must also be a Routing Server.

In MSMQ 2.0 (Windows 2000) and above, MSMQ uses the Active Directory Service Interface (ADSI) infrastructure to store machine and queue details. There is a requirement to install MSMQ on at least one domain controller that is also a global catalog in each site, and that domain controller appears like a PSC (for MSMQ 1.0 and 2.0 clients).

This requirement was lifted in MSMQ 3.0 (Windows XP and Windows 2003), where the clients access the ADSI infrastructure directly. MSMQ 3.0 clients work with the Active Directory and do not need MSMQ Servers; however, if you need to support MSMQ 1.0/2.0 clients, you must install MSMQ with down-level client support on a domain controller/global catalog in each site that contains such clients.

For further information, check the sections on "Installing MSMQ" and "MSMQ Versions" later in this chapter.

MSMQ Clients

MSMQ clients are typically installed on computers that run queued messaging applications. They provide all MSMQ APIs, allowing applications to send and receive messages, and to query the Directory Service database. MSMQ clients run a local queue manager.

Independent Clients

Independent clients supply applications with full MSMQ API access and local queue management services. They also maintain their own private queues.

Because they don't need to access the Directory Service database in order to send and receive messages, independent clients can send messages to and read them from local queues while they are disconnected from the network. Consequently, if the connection between the independent client and other machines on the network crashes, the sending application can continue sending messages as if it were online. The local queue manager temporarily stores the messages in an **outgoing queue** until the connection is reestablished. As soon as the independent client can access the Directory Service, it sends the buffered messages to their destinations.

NOTE *Independent clients can be detached from a site and attached to a site of the same organization through the Message Queuing icon in the Control Panel, or the Computer Management snap-in provided by MSMQ 3.0.*

Dependent Clients

Dependent clients are the thinnest MSMQ clients available. They require synchronous access to a Message Queuing server to perform all standard message queuing operations, such as sending messages, receiving them, and creating queues. The MSMQ Server maintains every queue created in a dependent client.

Choosing Between Dependent and Independent Clients

The connectionless model provided by independent clients is useful for environments where the network connections are poor or not always available; for example, mobile applications, or applications that are occasionally connected to the organization's network. As you will learn in Chapter 8, MSMQ is available for **Windows CE**, which is an operating system that was designed for devices that generally are disconnected from networks. For applications that run on laptops, you should also consider choosing an independent client connection model. This could be the case for a salesperson who is usually away from the office. He will be able to work with his laptop as if he were at his workstation, because as soon as he connects his notebook to the organization's network, all the messages will be delivered.

NOTE *If you have an isolated computer and you want to run a queued messaging application, you should install an independent client. Independent clients allow you to develop and test MSMQ-based applications without having to maintain an Active Directory installation.*

All the functionality provided by dependent clients can be achieved by using Distributed COM (DCOM) or COM+, because the dependent client uses a synchronous connection with its server. So, we recommend you use independent clients, because they can go on working through poor connections, even without any connections. Dependent clients already exist for backward compatibility reasons.

Machines

Every computer within an MSMQ Enterprise is called a machine, and is represented by a Machine object in the Directory Service. It can be either an MSMQ Server or an MSMQ Independent Client. Each Machine object that belongs to an MSMQ Enterprise is stored in the Directory Service database.

Each Message Queuing machine has properties that define the computer's messaging behavior. MSMQ is in charge of updating this information (which is read-only for applications). You can programmatically query these properties. The way you do this depends on the API we decide to use. In the following tables, you see the properties and methods available to Machine objects using generic names. Table 1-1 describes the properties of the Machine object, and Table 1-2 lists the methods.

Table 1-1. Available Information for a Message Queuing Machine

PROPERTY	DESCRIPTION
Path Name	The name of a machine.
Unique ID	Each machine within an MSMQ Enterprise has a **GUID**, or unique identifier.
Version	Specifies the version of MSMQ running on the computer. You can obtain the *Major, Minor,* and *Build number* components of the version number.

Table 1-1. Available Information for a Message Queuing Machine (continued)

PROPERTY	DESCRIPTION
Site Name	Identifies the site where the machine is located.
Directory Service Server Name	Returns the name of the current Directory Service server.
Active Queues	You can obtain the format names of all public, private, and outgoing queues (that are opened or hold messages) from a machine through this property.
Private Queues	Returns a list of all the private queues registered in a machine.
Bytes in all Queues	Returns the number of bytes in the messages currently stored in all queues on the machine.
Is Connected	Specifies whether the machine has been disconnected from the Directory Service.
Is DS Enabled	Indicates whether the Directory Service is available for Message Queuing. You can determine if MSMQ is running in **Workgroup** or **Domain mode** (see the section "Workgroup vs. Domain Mode" later in this chapter).

Table 1-2. Available Tasks for a Message Queuing Machine

METHOD	DESCRIPTION
Disconnect	Disconnects the machine from the network. From that moment, messages cannot reach the machine's queues.
Connect	Connects the machine to the network.
Register Certificate	You can register internal and external certificates to authenticate messages.

Message Queuing provides facilities to enable transfer of messages between the application that sends the message (*sender*) and the application that receives the message (*receiver*). It maintains channels called *queues* between the sender and the receiver.

Queues

Queues are intermediary container mechanisms used by Message Queuing to store messages. They provide a loosely coupled model. When sending applications send a message to a queue, they don't know when the message arrives in the queue or when the receiving application processes that message.

Although they are called queues, they don't have the First In, First Out (FIFO) behavior of a typical queue. The queue is reorganized continuously on receipt of new messages ordered by priority (and within the priority group, in the FIFO order). This is the dynamic nature of the queue.

They are mainly divided into two main categories: **application queues** and **system queues**.

Application Queues

Application queues are used primarily by applications for exchanging messages between senders and receivers. These queues can be created manually as well as programmatically. A sender places a message on the queue and a receiver receives the message from the queue. The four types of application queues are

- Destination queues

- Administration queues

- Response queues

- Report queues

Destination Queues

Destination queues are application queues that are used to store messages sent by the message's sender and to forward the message to the message receiver. The messages that travel through these queues are purely application-generated. There are two types of destination queues: public queues and private queues. These queues are used to exchange messages sent by applications.

Table 1-3 shows the common differences between public and private queues.

Table 1-3. Private and Public Queues

PRIVATE QUEUE	PUBLIC QUEUE
Private queues are registered on the local computer, not in Active Directory, and so cannot be replicated.	Public queues are queues that are published in Active Directory and hence replicated throughout the Windows 2000 or Windows .NET Server forest.
Properties of private queues cannot be obtained from a remote computer.	Any computer on the Windows 2000 or Windows .NET Server forest can access information about a public queue.
Private queues are the only option available in an MSMQ workgroup install.	Public queues cannot be created in a MSMQ workgroup installation.
To send messages to private queues in a workgroup install, it is not required to query Active Directory. Private queues are designated by direct format names (covered in the next chapter). This is the reason why private queues have less overhead, are faster, and have low latency. They are ideal for offline operations when the Directory Service is not available. However, a remote private queue in a domain, designated by a private format name in a call to send or receive a message, do require a directory lookup to convert the computer Globally Unique Identifier (GUID) to a computer name. The round-trip to Active Directory can be avoided by using direct format names to refer to the queues.	While sending a message to a public queue, the Directory Service is queried to get the location of the queue before placing the message on the queue. This can be avoided by using direct format names to refer to the queues.

NOTE   *Public queues cannot be created in a workgroup environment; they can only be created and managed in a domain environment.*

Administration Queues

These queues are used to store positive and negative acknowledgment messages generated by MSMQ. Administration queues cannot be transactional, so any nontransactional queue can be used as an administration queue. The MSMQ automatically generates acknowledgment messages and sends them to the specific administration queue. The acknowledgment message remains in the administration queue until it is received by the sender application. The sender application matches the original message to the message in the acknowledgment queue by comparing their identifier and correlation identifier, respectively. Acknowledgment messages are not generated by default; the sender application must set the `AdministrationQueue` property of the message to an instance of the `AdministrationQueue` (`MessageQueue` class) and the `AcknowledgmentType` property specifying the type of acknowledgment needed.

Response Queues

A queue where all the response messages are placed is called a *response queue*. The receiver and sender mutually agree on the name of the queue, and response messages are stacked in that queue. If a sender expects a response, the receiver sends a message to the response queue. The difference between response queues and administration queues is that administration queues contain messages generated by the Message Queuing system, whereas response queues contain responses sent by the message receiver application specifically for the message sender application. Administration queues and response queues can be combined into a single queue. This restricts the response queue to nontransactional messaging because the administration queue cannot be transactional.

Report Queues

Report queues are used to track the progress of messages as they are transmitted through the Message Queuing enterprise. These are public queues that contain the tracking information about the message from its source to the destination. Every time a message leaves from and arrives at a Message Queuing computer, a report message is generated and sent to the report queue. There can be only one report queue per computer, but one message can be tracked by multiple report queues along its path. Figure 1-8 shows typical report messages.

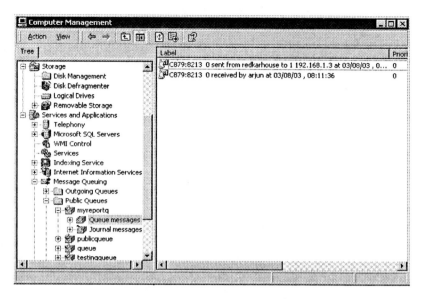

Figure 1-8. Report messages

Transactional and Nontransactional Queues

Queues can also be categorized by their transactional status:

- **Transactional queues** can only receive messages sent within a **transactional context**. When accessed locally, only transactional queues can take messages within a transactional context.

- **Nontransactional queues** can only receive messages that are sent outside of a transactional context.

NOTE *You have to specify whether a queue will be transactional when you create it, and this property is read-only.*

Messages sent in a transactional context are guaranteed delivery. If you send or receive a group of messages in a transactional context, those messages will be processed in the order in which they were sent, and they will all either be committed successfully or rolled back.

Chapter 4 examines transactional messaging in greater detail.

System Queues

System queues are generated by MSMQ during installation. MSMQ has four kinds of system queues:

- Journal queues

- Dead-letter queues

- Outgoing queues

- MSMQ private system queues

Journal Queues

Journal queues store copies of messages. In MSMQ, two types of journaling are available: queue journals and computer journals.

Queue Journals

Queue journals are created whenever application queues are created. Copies of messages are created in the journal queues by MSMQ whenever the messages are removed from the application queue by the message receiver. An important point to note is that messages that expire or are purged in the application queue are not copied to journal queues. Journaling is turned off by default. It can be turned on programmatically or even manually by using the Message Queuing user interface in the Computer Management console.

Computer Journals

A *computer journal queue* is created when MSMQ is installed. Computer journals store all the copies of messages sent by the computer. To use computer journaling, the sender application must set the journaling property of the message to true.

Dead-Letter Queues

Messages that cannot be delivered are held in the dead-letter queue. Messages become undeliverable when they expire, or perhaps the sender cannot get the proper authentication to add them in the queue, or the destination queue can't be found or is full. MSMQ maintains two dead-letter queues: one for transactional queues and the other for nontransactional queues. MSMQ automatically sends nondeliverable nontransactional messages to the dead-letter queues and nondeliverable transactional messages to the transactional dead-letter queue. The messages cannot go automatically to the dead-letter queues; the sending application should indicate it by setting the UserDeadLetterQueue property of the message to true.

One example of when the dead-letter queue is used is when a message's **timeout** expires. If this happens, MSMQ will change the class of the message and place it in the appropriate dead-letter queue. We cover these timers in the "Handling Timeouts" section later in this chapter.

Each time MSMQ addresses a message to a Dead-Letter queue, it sets a value to explain the rejection. For example, when a nonauthenticated message arrives in a queue that accepts only authenticated messages, MSMQ sets the value to MQMSG_CLASS_BAD_SIGNATURE in the Dead-Letter queue setting of the rejected message. This value is a class that warns the sender application. Remember that this process will have this behavior only if the sent message has previously explicitly requested negative acknowledgment messages.

Applications can query the system queues to find out the status of the distributed application. In critical environments, you can develop applications to monitor journal and dead-letter queues. This helps you track a message to know if it has reached its destination, and if not, why it didn't.

To learn more about transactions and transactional queues, see Chapter 4.

Outgoing Queues

Outgoing queues are system-generated queues created on an independent client. If a queued messaging application running on an independent client is disconnected from the network while sending a message, MSMQ will store the message temporarily in an outgoing queue. Once the connection is reestablished, the local queue manager sends the messages to the destination. Outgoing queues provide the level of disconnected reliability that we expect from a remote queue.

MSMQ Private System Queues

MSMQ creates five private system queues for administration purposes. These are private queues and are therefore not published with Active Directory. These queues are used by MSMQ internally and cannot be deleted. Table 1-4 lists the private system queues.

Table 1-4. Private System Queues

MSMQ PRIVATE SYSTEM QUEUE	DESCRIPTION
admin_queue$	Stores administrative messages.
msmqadminresp$	Stores administrative response messages (like MQPing messages).
mqis_queue$	Used for NT4 MQIS replications (in PEC, PSC, or BSC only).
notify_queue$	Stores notification messages. These messages list computer and queue property changes, including creation and deletion of queues.
order_queue$	Stores messages for tracking transactional messages that require in-order delivery.

Accessing Queues

Queues can be accessed in four main ways, each one of which is used for a specific activity: path names, format names, direct format names, and by using queue actions and properties.

Path Names

The Path name is used to reference the queue while creating, deleting, sending, and receiving messages. The queue name depends on where the queue physically resides.

Path names are restricted to application queues that belong to our organization and are location dependent. Format names are more efficient than path names, and using them saves an Active Directory round-trip when opening the queue.

Path names consist of a machine name and a queue name used to locate a queue. This syntax is covered in Chapters 2 and 6.

Format Names and Direct Format Names

Every time MSMQ needs to send a message to a queue, it uses a **format name**. In order to locate a queue, applications have to create a format name or query the Directory Service to obtain it.

The format name is used to reach the queues that belong to your MSMQ Enterprise. The **direct format name** is used to reach queues that belong (or don't belong) to your MSMQ Enterprise as well. In such a case, MSMQ will deliver the message directly to the target queue, bypassing any routing configuration, and will not be able to use encryption or authentication. Besides, opening a queue in such a way is very efficient because it does not require Active Directory access.

Format names reference public or private queues. They are used to

- Open a queue; once the queue is opened, the queue handle is used to send or receive.

- Set and retrieve the properties of a queue.

- Obtain the security descriptor of the queue.

A format name consists of a string that points to a queue. If Message Queuing detects a format name when sending or receiving a message, it doesn't need to refer to the Directory Service to obtain information about the queue, but uses it to look up routing information.

Direct format names reference public or private queues without accessing the directory. They can be used to

- Send messages directly to a computer

- Send messages to computers through the Internet

- Read and send messages in Workgroup or Domain mode

As format names and direct format names depend on the implementation, they are covered in Chapters 2, 6, and 7.

Queue Actions and Properties

You can create, delete, and manage queues programmatically as well as through the MMC snap-in. The way you code it depends on the API you decide to use. Table 1-5 contains properties and Table 1-6 contains methods using generic names.

Managing queues within the .NET Framework is covered in Chapter 2. Chapter 6 addresses the MSMQ API and the Message Queuing COM Component.

We have to know the queue's capabilities to take advantage of them.

Table 1-5. Generic Queue's Properties

PROPERTY	DESCRIPTION
Label	Provides a description for the queue.
ID	Contains the unique Message Queuing identifier. It is read-only and is generated by MSMQ.

Path Name	Specifies the machine where the queue is located, whether private or public, and its name. Examples are:
	`machineName\queueName`
	`machineName\Private$\queueName`

Format Name	Message Queuing uses the format name of the queue to identify which queue to open and how to access it.
Service Type GUID	Specifies the type of service provided by the queue. It consists of an application-generated GUID. We can group queues that provide the same service by setting the same Service Type GUID. Then client applications can reach them by querying the Directory Service without needing to know their physical location. This is a good mechanism for clustering. We can create a GUID with a program called `Guidgen.exe` or by using the integrated tool in Visual Studio .NET.
Quota	Specifies the maximum size (in kilobytes) of a queue. The default value is infinite (depending on the machine capacity).
Authenticate	This property indicates if the queue accepts only authenticated messages. Any nonauthenticated message sent to a queue that only accepts authenticated messages will be rejected.
Encryption required	Gets or sets a value indicating whether the queue accepts only private (encrypted) messages, nonprivate (nonencrypted) messages, or both.
Transactional	This property specifies whether the queue supports transactions.
Use Journal Queue	Message queuing will automatically send a copy of the retrieved message to the Journal message if this property is set to `true`.
Journal Quota	Specifies the maximum size (in kilobytes) of a journal queue. The default value is infinite.

Table 1-5. Generic Queue's Properties (continued)

PROPERTY	DESCRIPTION
Bytes in Queues	Returns the number of bytes of the messages located in a queue.
Message count	Returns the number of messages in a queue.

Table 1-6. Generic Tasks That Can Be Programmatically Done with a Queue

METHOD	DESCRIPTION
Create	Creates a new queue at the specified path on a Message Queuing machine. This method allows us to create application queues; they can be public or private, transactional or nontransactional.
Delete	Deletes a queue from a Message Queuing computer.
Refresh	Queries the Directory Service and retrieves a queue's properties, such as the security descriptor, label, service type GUID, etc.
Update	Updates the queue's properties to the Directory Service, allowing us to change them.
Open	Opens a queue for sending, peeking at, or retrieving messages. When we open a queue, we have to specify the action to be taken. When we open a queue for peeking or retrieving, we have to specify the share mode: whether the queue is available to everyone, or is limited to the running process.
Close	To release resources, we have to close the queue.
Peek	This method returns the first message in the queue, or waits for a message to arrive if the queue is empty. It only reads the message without deleting it. When peeking at a message, if we want we can read only its header without retrieving its body or its response queue, optimizing the speed of this operation. Remember that this method doesn't remove the message from the queue.

continued

Table 1-6. Generic Tasks That Can Be Programmatically Done with a Queue (continued)

METHOD	DESCRIPTION
Receive	Works similar to the Peek method but removes the message from the queue. Both the Peek and Receive methods use the FIFO model, so they will take the *First In* message. The priority with FIFO order will be taken into consideration when we look at Cursor-based scan later in this table.
Purge	Deletes all the messages contained in the queue. Messages purged from the queue are not sent to the dead-letter queue or the journal queue, so we cannot recover them. If the application needs to return negative acknowledgment messages or place the purged messages in the appropriate dead-letter queue, it should use the appropriate Peek or Receive method.
Cursor-based scan	We can traverse all messages that are in a queue sequentially forward or backward, using a cursor. This method is useful for reading messages ordered by priority.
Lookup ID–based scan	Lookups are 64-bit identifiers that are assigned to each message placed in the queue. (This is available only in MSMQ 3.0.)
Peek and Receive by ID	Each message located in any queue of the MSMQ Enterprise has a unique ID. Using these methods, we can peek or receive a specific message in a queue without going through all the messages. These methods are available only through the System.Messaging API: they use sequential search and can cause serious performance problems.
Peek and Receive by Correlation ID	Response messages that are correlated can be picked up using these methods. They scan the queue for you and return a message based on its correlation ID, working sequentially as Peek and Receive by ID do. Refer to the "Response Messages Based on Correlation Identifiers" section later in this chapter.

Remember that all these features are not available in every MSMQ version, and keep in mind that they have different usages, depending on the Message Queuing implementations.

Messages

Messages are stored in queues and travel through all the MSMQ Enterprise's machines. They are like **envelopes** containing the data sent by applications along with additional information needed by MSMQ to handle them.

Messages can be created by applications or by the system:

- **Application-generated messages:** Sent by queued messaging applications to distribute the data throughout the MSMQ Enterprise.

- **System-generated messages:** MSMQ can automatically create some messages in response to an application's requirements. They include

  - **Acknowledgment messages:** Generated in order to inform the sender whether the message has reached its destination.

  - **Report messages:** Generated by the queue manager when application-generated messages are routed through the MSMQ Enterprise. They are helpful for tracing purposes. Report messages are generated only by administrator's request.

Report messages can be logically classified as

- **Request messages:** Sent by an application that requires another application to accomplish a task and send it back the response/result.

- **Response messages:** Shipped by applications in response to a request message. They can carry correlated information.

- **Informative messages:** Sent by an application that requires another application to perform a task without needing a response.

Express and Recoverable Messages

The message is stored locally at every step along its route, until it is forwarded to the following destination. During this trip, messages can persist on disk or remain in memory:

- **Express messages:** These are stored in RAM memory during routing and delivery, providing better performance. However, they have one disadvantage: if the computer where they are located crashes, they get lost. This can be set by a property, as you will see in the "Message Properties" section.

- **Recoverable messages:** Recoverable messages are written on the disk, so they are guaranteed delivery. Although they are slower than express messages, they are the best choice when failures cannot be tolerated or when machine shutdowns are expected to occur while messages remain in queues.

We can find the recoverable messages on the machine's local disk. Figure 1-9 shows the Message Queuing Properties dialog box opened from Control Panel for all the local queues of the computer. We can set or retrieve the storage path for recoverable messages using this dialog box.

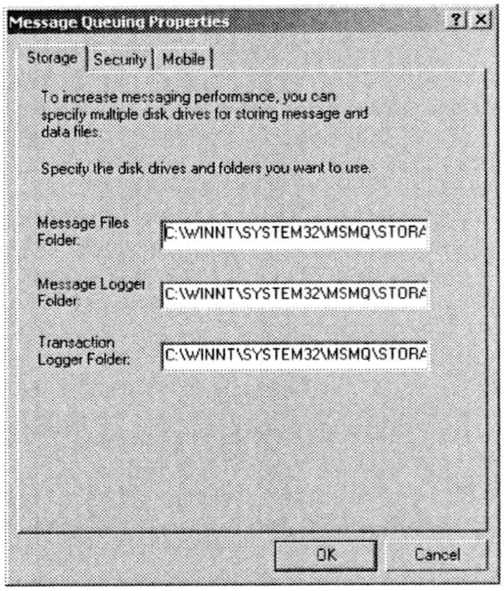

Figure 1-9. Message Queuing Properties dialog box opened from Control Panel

This dialog box allows you to specify multiple disk drives for storing messages, in three groups:

- **Message Files Folder:** Stores the messages contained in outgoing, public, and private queues

- **Message Logger Folder:** Stores the journal messages

- **Transaction Logger Folder:** Stores transactional dead-letter messages

Recoverable messages are recommended in cases where a message contains important data that can be resent, or in mobile applications that run on laptops.

If the user shuts down the computer while disconnected, the messages in the outgoing queue will be lost if they are sent in express mode.

Transactional and Nontransactional Messages

Message Queuing provides support for transactions when sending and retrieving messages from transactional queues.

In order to reach a transactional queue, a message (which has to be recoverable) should be sent in a **transactional context**. Transactional messages are guaranteed delivery. They can be coordinated with other operations, such as updates to data. Because of the overhead of transactions, they will slow down communications.

Message Priority vs. Lookup Identifiers

As you saw earlier in the "Queues" section, messages may not have the same FIFO behavior as queues. They are ordered by priority as they arrive in the queue. When messages with different priority levels arrive in a queue, MSMQ orders them based on the queue priority level and the message arrival time, so messages cannot be inserted at the end of the queue as they arrive.

The cursor-based scan is sequential and uses only FIFO messages. When we use a cursor-based scan on a queue, messages may be inserted before or after the cursor's position as they arrive in the queue.

Lookup ID can be used to re-access a message that was "peeked" before (read but not deleted from the queue). This method is useful for applications, such as a message browser, that peek part of the message's properties first, and then peek all the properties when the user selects the message. It is also useful for applications that first peek all the messages in the queue and then receive selected messages.

Encryption and Authentication

Message Queuing provides **security** tools that can be used to establish the distributed security that is common with distributed Remote Procedure Call (RPC) protocols such as DCOM. The sender application can provide message authentication and encryption, and the receiver application can request authenticated and encrypted messages (in order to accept them).

Authentication ensures that nobody can change the message content in transit. To authenticate messages, the sender applications have to set the authentication level of the message and the security certificate. The authentication is achieved through a digital signature, which is a combination of a message hash encrypted by the sending machine's private key and the receiver's use of a public key, which is used to verify the signature. Message Queuing allows you to use internal and external certificates.

Encryption protects the message against curious people or applications. MSMQ provides a secured channel for sending private messages, using 40-bit or 128-bit encryption with a symmetric key. Symmetric or secret encryption requires two copies of the same key (stored in the Directory Service database) to be shared to encrypt and decrypt a message. This ensures that the message body will be sent in encrypted form through the MSMQ Enterprise.

Message Properties

Messages are the data containers, and you need to know what information they transport. Table 1-7 contains properties that use generic names. Since there are quite a few, we'll categorize them into groups (see Tables 1-8 through 1-13).

Table 1-7. Generic Message's Properties

PROPERTY	DESCRIPTION
Label	Specifies a description defined by applications. They are useful to caption messages, either for applications or for administrative purposes.
Body	The body is the data container, and it can include, for example, a string, a number, an array of bytes, or a serialized object.
Body Type	Indicates the type of information that is stored in the message body.
Body Length	This property returns the size of the message body. Message size is limited to 4MB in all current versions of MSMQ. (The total size of all messages in a computer was up to 2GB in MSMQ 1.0 and 2.0 and increased in MSMQ 3.0.)
Formatter	To serialize or deserialize an object into a message body, the .NET Framework uses the Formatter property. If we want to send a persistent COM object, it has to implement the IDispatch and IPersist COM interfaces.
Type	Indicates whether it is a normal, acknowledgment, or report message.
Soap	MSMQ 3.0 supports **Internet Messaging**. Using this property, we can obtain the Simple Object Access Protocol (SOAP) format of an **HTTP message**. Internet Messaging is studied in Chapter 7.
Recoverable or Express	Indicates whether the message will persist during routing and delivering.

Table 1-7. Generic Message's Properties (continued)

PROPERTY	DESCRIPTION
Priority	Establishes the message priority between 0 and 7.
Application Specific	A value used by applications for filtering messages.
Extension	Additional application-defined information associated with the message. It is an array that should be interpreted by the sender and the receiver application.

Table 1-8. Generic Identification Message's Properties

PROPERTY	DESCRIPTION
ID	Each message in the MSMQ Enterprise has a unique ID, consisting of the machine GUID and a 4-byte serial number.
Correlation ID	This property is set on response, report, and acknowledgment messages. In a request-response model, it is used to correlate messages; in other words, it determines which message created the corresponding acknowledgment or report message.
Lookup ID	Lookup identifiers are 64-bit identifiers that are assigned to each message when the message is placed in the queue. They are used by applications to locate a message in a queue avoiding the priority order.

Table 1-9. Generic Message's Properties That Specify the Queues Associated with the Message

PROPERTY	DESCRIPTION
Use Journal Queue	Indicates whether a copy of the removed message has to be kept in the associated journal queue.
Use Dead-Letter Queue	Indicates if a copy of the message that could not be delivered should be sent to a dead-letter queue.
Response Queue	Can be used by a server application to send a response message (when you are working with a request-response model).
Destination Queue	Specifies the queue where the message has to be sent.

Table 1-10. Generic Time Message's Properties

PROPERTY	DESCRIPTION
Arrived Time	The time when the message reaches the queue.
Sent Time	The local time of the application that sends the message.
Time to Reach Queue	Determines the time limit in which a message has to reach the queue manager of the target queue.
Time to be Received	Specifies how long a message has to remain in the system, starting from the time the message is sent to the time it is removed from the target queue.

NOTE   *Times are adjusted to time zones.*

Table 1-11. Generic Message's Properties That Provide an Object's Transaction Context Information

PROPERTY	DESCRIPTION
Transaction ID	Retrieves the transaction context ID of the message.
Is first in Transaction	Is used for messages sent in-group within a transaction and indicates if the message was the first one sent within the transaction.
Is last in Transaction	For messages sent in-group within a transaction, indicates if it was the last message sent within the transaction. These two properties mark the beginning and the end of a group of messages sent in a transaction.

Table 1-12. Generic Acknowledgment and Tracing Message's Properties That Provide an Object's Transaction Context Information

PROPERTY	DESCRIPTION
Acknowledgment	Specifies whether a positive or negative acknowledgment should be sent indicating if the message reaches its destination. You have to specify the acknowledgment queue.
Use Tracing	Indicates if the route of the message should be traced and a report message should be generated.

Table 1-13. Generic Message's Properties That Give Information About the Sender

PROPERTY	DESCRIPTION
Sender ID	Identifies the sender of the message.
Sender Certificate	Retrieves the security certificate used to authenticate the sent message.
Source machine GUID	The GUID that identifies which machine sent the message.

Scope and Expanse

Although the boundaries are your MSMQ Enterprise, Microsoft Message Queuing gives you some tools to interact with other organizations and Message Queuing systems, perhaps even running on other operating systems. In this section, we'll take a look at some of these tools.

Connector Applications

In order to connect to another messaging system, such as IBM MQSeries, Tivoli, or Tibco, you need a **connector application**. A connector application acts as a bridge between the two messaging systems, translating message properties from one system to the other, and vice versa. You can use an existing connector or just develop a custom connector application. Within the Microsoft world, the most important application used to bridge between disparate systems is BizTalk Server. BizTalk uses MSMQ as a transfer protocol and provides a number of adapters for non-Microsoft messaging systems such as MQSeries.

We can take the MSMQ to MQSeries Bridge as an example of a connector application, which enables applications to easily interchange messages between IBM MQSeries MSMQ. The connector provides full format compatibility, which allows applications to manipulate messages using the native APIs of either MQSeries or MSMQ. MSMQ/MQSeries Bridge is part of Microsoft Host Integration Server 2000.

Internet Messaging

Microsoft Message Queue 3.0 version introduces Messaging over the Internet, providing support for sending messages through HTTP channels. This new feature enhances the intercorporate message delivery using the XML SOAP open protocol. You can even communicate with other nonqueued messaging systems if they are able to understand these XML SOAP messages sent via HTTP.

.NET Framework

Keep in mind that MSMQ is a feature of the operating system, and you don't have to install the .NET Framework to use it. The System.Messaging namespace included in the .NET Framework merely provides access to the MSMQ service.

Sending Messages Across Domains

What about sending messages across domains? In this situation, you have two Active Directory forests, probably with separate DNS servers in each forest, which do not replicate between them. Because applications can only query the Directory Service of the domain to which they belong, and the Directory Service of a domain has no information about queues on the other domain, the only way of sending messages across domains is to use direct format names.

An MSMQ Enterprise can span multiple domains in the same company, as long as you have a global catalog in each domain.

Architecture Scenarios

Now that we have looked at the MSMQ architecture, we will study some typical scenarios, which will help you to design your queued messaging distributed applications.

Service-Based Applications

N-tier applications have become the norm for building enterprise software. An n-tier application can be divided into discrete logical parts. The n-tier model provides a structured approach for creating applications with components that are separated into different functional groups. Breaking a large piece of software into smaller pieces makes it easier to build, reuse, and modify.

Message Queuing allows you to create n-tier applications, dividing and isolating logic in Queued Messaging Services and thus making your distributed application more reliable and scalable, and providing it with fault tolerance and load balancing. You can benefit from these features by incorporating message-based communication in the **middle tier**.

Using this feature, you can develop message-based applications that use Message Queuing to communicate with the layers in an asynchronous way, as shown in Figure 1-10.

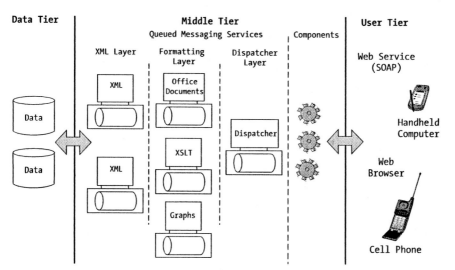

Figure 1-10. Scenario for Queued Messaging Service

Note in Figure 1-10 that the middle tier is divided into two sections:

- A **Queued Messaging Services section**, which divides the distributed application into more layers

- A **Components section**, which provides the User layer with the message queue communication functionalities

The components have access to a queued message–based **dispatcher** that distributes the requests through the next layer, which is in charge of formatting. Message requests may be **XML** formatted.

When the **formatting** layer requires data, its applications send a message to the XML layer, which is in charge of querying the databases. Note that there are two processes running in the XML layer, ensuring reliability and fault tolerance. The dispatcher layer waits for each response, passing the data to the **user** layer. Instead of waiting for every service to be completed, the dispatcher can present the data as it is resolved. The result seems faster to the user.

Starting from this scenario, you can generate your own architecture and upgrade your application to a distributed environment, achieving reliability, scalability, fault tolerance, and load balancing.

Response Messages Based on Correlation Identifiers

Let's look at a typical configuration model that involves some clients and a server. The clients running on different machines send request messages to the server, which has to send back response messages.

Two questions arise here:

- If the server receives several messages from different clients, how does it know which of the clients' queues it needs to send the response to?

- If the client sends several messages to the server, how does it know which of the request messages each response message corresponds to?

As we have seen earlier, a message is a sort of envelope that contains data in its body along with additional information. We use three message properties to correlate the requests and responses: Response Queue Info, ID, and Correlation ID.

How Does the Server Know Which Queue to Send the Response To?

The client sets the **Response Queue Info** property of the request message and sends it to the server. This property contains information about the queue where the client wants to receive the response message. The server receives the request message with the corresponding Response Queue Info property, so it already has the specifications to address the reply.

How Does the Client Know Which Request Corresponds to Each Response?

MSMQ assigns each message a unique identifier called **ID** when you send it. This ID consists of a **machine GUID** followed by an **identity number**, for example:

```
{ABE50E01-BC2F-437b-A801-6C864A8F3152}/7659862
```

The client application sends a request in a message to the server application and saves the ID in memory. The server application receives that message, processes the request, and sends a response message, setting its **Correlation ID** property with the received **message ID**. Then the client application looks up the message response in the response queue for the message response based on the **Request ID**. Figure 1-11 shows this process.

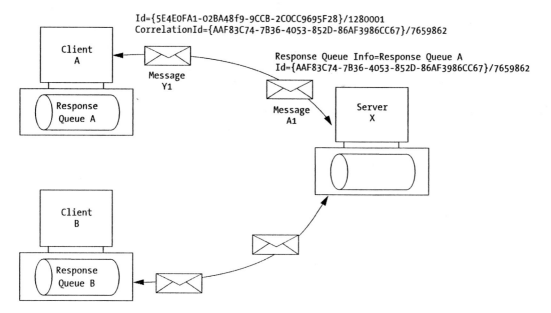

Figure 1-11. Correlated message-based communication

In Figure 1-11, we have several clients sending request messages to Server X, which has to respond to them. Let's study the interaction between Client A and Server X:

- Client A sends message A1 to Server X.

- When Client A sends the request message A1, it saves the message ID ({5E4E0FA1-02BA-48f9-9CC8-2C0CC9695F28}/7659862).

- Server X receives the request message A1 sent by Client A, reads its body, and carries out the process specified by the message. It also stores A1's message ID.

- Once the server finishes the process, it has to send the response back to Client A, so Server X creates a Message Y1, assigns A1's message ID to its Correlation ID property, and sends the response message Y1 to Response Queue A. Remember that Response Queue A was specified by message A1 in the Response Queue Info property.

- Client A, who is waiting for the response, will look for the message response in the Response Queue A, whose Correlation equals {5E4E0FA1-02BA-48f9-9CC8-2C0CC9695F28}/7659862.

Receiving Only from Local Queues

MSMQ allows us to develop applications that are independent from their location. This technique may result in performance and failure issues under some circumstances:

- Sending messages is based on TCP/IP, while receiving messages is based on RPC, which adds another layer.

- MSMQ cannot receive messages while disconnected from the queue's host computer. If you are receiving messages in a remote queue and the host computer crashes, a failure will occur.

- Transactional messages can be received only in local transactional queues.

In order to avoid this problem, you should receive messages in local queues.

Multiple Destinations and Response Queues

If you need to send the same message to several applications, you don't have to send it several times, because MSMQ 3.0 allows you to send a single message to multiple destinations. Message Queuing provides three mechanisms to accomplish this:

- Distribution lists

- Multiple-element format names

- Multicast addresses

When an application sends a single message to multiple destinations using distribution lists or multiple-element format names, the local queue manager duplicates the message, assigns them the same ID, and sends a copy to the specified destinations. Similarly, an application can send a request message, which specifies multiple response queues. We will see some further examples in Chapter 7.

For multicast messages, MSMQ sends the message only once to a multicast IP address, using the Pragmatic General Multicasting (PGM) protocol.

Handling Timeouts

Message Queuing provides two timers to help you to maintain better control of your messages:

- **Time-To-Reach-Queue:** This determines the time limit in which the message has to reach the destination queue. If this time has elapsed when the message arrives, it is discarded, saving the receiving application some unnecessary processing.

- **Time-To-Be-Received:** This specifies how long the message is allowed to remain in the target queue before being received by the receiving application, starting at the moment the message is sent to the time it is removed from the target queue. A message is not allowed to remain in the system longer than the time specified by the Time-To-Be-Received timer.

Suppose we have developed a critical application that has to get a query result in 2 minutes. We have distributed it into two processes, one that interacts with the user (the client application), and the other that queries the data (the server application). The client sends the message to the server and waits for the response message to show the query result to the user. This process should be performed within 2 minutes, so we send a message that specifies a timeout of 2 minutes. If the request message doesn't reach the destination queue or the receiver application can't read it in 2 minutes, then it would be better for the server not to process it. Thus, we are discarding unnecessary operations.

Meanwhile, what happens with the discarded messages? When a timer expires, Message Queuing discards the message. However, Message Queuing can send a copy of the discarded messages to the respective dead-letter queue if the deadletter property is set. It can send a negative acknowledgment message to an administration queue as well, if the administration queue is set for the message and the proper level of acknowledgment is requested. Negative acknowledgements contain the body of the original message.

NOTE *When we set both timers, the Time-To-Reach-Queue should be shorter than the Time-To-Be-Received; the message will expire once Time-To-Be-Received is reached, so Time-To-Reach-Queue will be meaningless in such a case. Keep in mind that the clocks of the two computers must be synchronized.*

Workgroup vs. Domain Mode

Active Directory is the directory service included with the Microsoft Windows 2000 and 2003 Server family, and has the advantages of being secure, distributed, partitioned, and replicated. It is designed to work in any size installation, from a single server with a few objects to thousands of servers and millions of objects. Active Directory maintains information about objects such as printers, applications, databases, users, and message queues. It also provides many features that make it easy to navigate and manage large amounts of information, generating savings for both administrators and end users.

Perhaps you are thinking that your organization is too small for it to be worth having an **Active Directory** installation, and you may be wondering whether you can use Message Queuing without Active Directory.

The answer is: yes, you can. You can run Message Queuing in **Workgroup** mode. You can have many **independent clients** installed throughout your network if your computers are installed in Workgroup mode. They act as if they were *offline from the Directory Service*. Dependent clients cannot be used for offline operations. Keep in mind that you will *not* be able to take advantage of all the features provided by the Directory Service, features such as

- A centralized and distributed database containing the MSMQ Enterprise information

- Public queues

- Routing

- Authenticated messages

- Encrypted messages

- Distribution lists

- Queue aliases

- MSMQ/MQSeries Bridge

 NOTE *You can use multicast in Workgroup mode.*

Workgroup mode MSMQ is restricted to the following tasks:

- Creating private queues on local computers

- Setting and obtaining the security descriptors for local queues

- Opening queues using direct format names to send and receive messages

In Workgroup mode, applications cannot do the following:

- Call a method that requires querying the Directory Service

- Create a public queue

Although applications that run in Workgroup mode can reach queues that belong to a Directory Service, they can't query the Directory Service database to discover their location. For these applications, those queues are just **remote queues**. In fact, applications are responsible for knowing a queue's location, and they have to use direct format names to send or receive messages.

NOTE *If you install MSMQ 3.0 on a computer requiring AD integration, Message Queuing can access Active Directory as long as the computer is part of an AD forest.*

MSMQ Versions

Let us go back in time and look at the history of MSMQ. In this section, we study the changes introduced by different versions of MSMQ across time. As you know, MSMQ runs as a Windows **service** called "Message Queuing." Microsoft has introduced new versions of MSMQ with new releases of the operating system:

- **MSMQ 1.0:** Windows NT 4.0, Windows NT Professional, Windows 98, and Windows 95

- **MSMQ 2.0:** Windows 2000 Server, Windows 2000 Professional, and Windows Millennium

- **MSMQ 3.0:** Windows 2003 Server, Windows XP Professional, and Windows XP Home Edition

NOTE *Although each version presents new features, they can all live together throughout the MSMQ organization. Always remember that an application running on a machine can only use the features provided by the version of MSMQ installed on it.*

There have been many changes between MSMQ 1.0, 2.0, and 3.0, but only two really major ones:

- MSMQ 2.0: Uses Active Directory

- MSMQ 3.0: Supports Internet Messaging

MSMQ 1.0

To install an MSMQ 1.0 Enterprise, you need to install SQL Server 6.5 or higher on every server, because the Directory Service database is implemented through a SQL Server database called Message Queue Information Store (MQIS). Every time you install a Primary Enterprise Controller, Primary Site Controller, or Backup Site Controller, MSMQ 1.0 creates a local SQL Server database named MQIS.

NOTE *We can set the replication time between the servers in order to keep the Directory Service database up-to-date.*

Installation of MSMQ 1.0 takes place through the Windows NT 4.0 Option Pack setup interface.

The Option Pack Installation wizard offers six types of installations:

- Primary Enterprise Controller

- Primary Site Controller

- Backup Site Controller

- Routing Server

- Independent Client

- Dependent Client

We covered these installation types in the "MSMQ Architecture" section earlier in this chapter.

MSMQ 1.0 also provides a tool called Message Queue Explorer (MQE), which is the main administrative tool. MQE was an independent application, instead of being a snap-in for the Microsoft Management Console (MMC). MSMQ version 2.0 solved this problem. Although it used to be the main administrative tool, nowadays we know that it has some limitations, such as the inability to create a private queue with it.

MSMQ 1.0 also has some restrictions in its Message Queuing COM component. Not all properties exposed by the Message Queuing API were available for the COM component model.

MSMQ 2.0

Since the arrival of MSMQ 2.0, Message Queuing supports Active Directory as its Directory Service. Active Directory replaces MQIS and thus allows the integration of MSMQ 2.0 with Windows 2000, permitting your MSMQ Enterprise automatically to encompass all Windows 2000 domains. Today your MSMQ Enterprise boundaries are the entire Active Directory domain enterprise.

MSMQ 2.0 servers use only the Active Directory infrastructure, but they mimic the client interface of MQIS. MSMQ 2.0 clients use the old MQIS interface.

An MSMQ 2.0 Server has to be installed on an Active Directory server. Therefore, a Primary Enterprise Controller should be installed on a domain controller. MSMQ 3.0 also uses Active Directory as a Directory Service.

Message Queuing allows you to communicate with computers within your MSMQ Enterprise even if they don't have the same MSMQ version installed. In fact, you can connect an MSMQ 2.0 client to an MSMQ 1.0 server that uses an MQIS as the Directory Service.

Currently, the main administrative tool is integrated into the **Microsoft Management Console** (MMC) as a snap-in. You can administer any computer of your MSMQ Enterprise using this tool.

Here is a list of the main features introduced in MSMQ 2.0:

- DNS path name support

- Ability to register certificates programmatically

- New digital signatures for authenticating messages

- 128-bit encryption support

- Multithreaded apartment (MTA) support for COM components

- Queued components

- Improved COM+ transactional support

- A COM component that wraps up the API completely

MSMQ 3.0

The main feature introduced by Windows 2003 Server and Windows XP for MSMQ 3.0 is Internet Messaging. MSMQ 3.0 provides support for sending and retrieving messages through HTTP. You can reference queues by their URLs, and send and read SOAP-formatted messages.

The following list shows the principal new features introduced in MSMQ 3.0:

- Direct messaging

- The ability to reference queues with a queue alias

- The ability to send messages to multiple destinations

- Specification of multiple response queues

- Queue and computer administration

- The ability to receive or peek at a specific message using lookup identifiers

- The ability to delete all messages from a queue

Chapter 7 treats all these topics in detail.

Although MSMQ triggers could be installed in Windows 2000, you can download the program from Microsoft's MSDN site (`www.microsoft.com/windows2000/ technologies/communications/msmq/default.asp`). Admin APIs can be found in the same place; they were integrated into the operating system by MSMQ 3.0.

We will study MSMQ triggers further in Chapter 5.

Installing MSMQ

Now that you have studied all aspects of MSMQ—its architecture, versions, and the scenarios for using it—you just need to know how to install it. In this section we look at the setup process for MSMQ 2.0; MSMQ 3.0 installation will be discussed in Chapter 7.

We have studied many types of MSMQ machines—servers, clients, and so forth—even though we don't need them all to have an MSMQ installation. That means you don't need several computers; you can have all their functionality in a single one. Even if you have a professional OS edition, you can just install MSMQ as an independent client.

MSMQ servers and routing servers can be installed on a Windows Server Family operating system. Running Active Directory is a prerequisite for installing MSMQ Server.

> **NOTE**   *MSMQ Server is not available for Workgroup mode.*

You can install either a dependent or an independent client on a Windows Professional or Home Edition operating system. When installing a client, you can automatically or manually access a Directory Service. This allows you to connect to another Directory Service: a domain controller or a PEC of an MSMQ 1.0 Enterprise.

> **NOTE**   *You can install an independent client only in Workgroup mode and not in domain mode.*

Beginning the Installation Process

Unlike Internet Information Server 5.0, the operating system setup process does not automatically install MSMQ. So, after installing the operating system, you have to run the MSMQ setup program. (MSMQ 3.0 setup process will be convered in Chapter 7. MSMQ 1.0 setup process won't be covered.)

You can launch the setup process through the Add/Remove Programs icon in Control Panel. From the open window, click the Add/Remove Windows Components button. This prompts the Windows Component Wizard, which allows you to add or remove Message Queuing Services, depending on whether it was installed (see Figure 1-12).

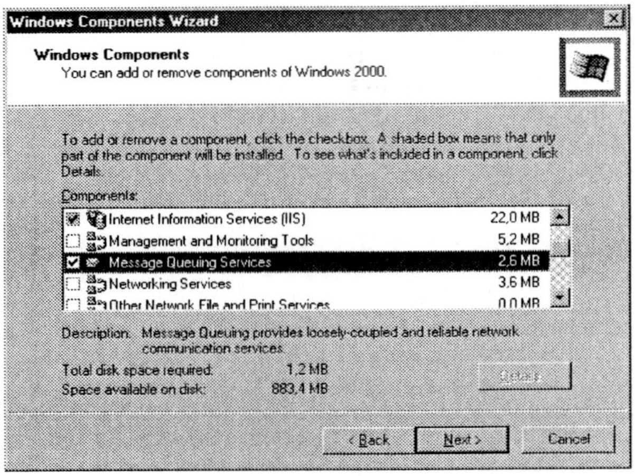

Figure 1-12. First window of the setup process wizard running in a Windows 2000 Server

Check the Message Queuing Services and begin the installation by clicking the Next button. The setup process will customize the screens depending on whether Active Directory is installed on this computer.

Server Installation

As you have seen, MSMQ Server needs Active Directory in order to run the Directory Service. When you run the setup on a computer with this specification, you'll see the screen shown in Figure 1-13.

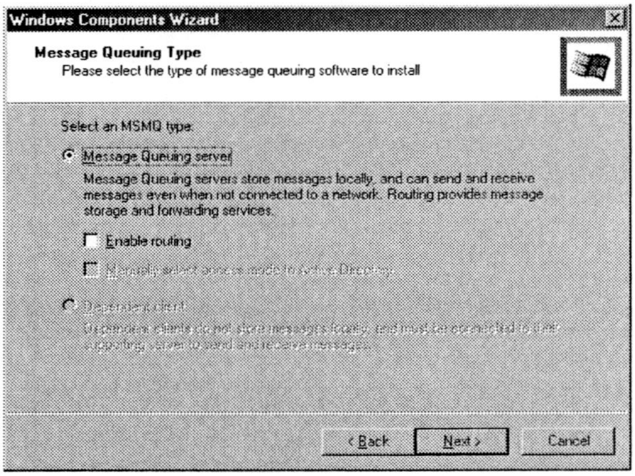

Figure 1-13. The server installation setup

As you can see, you have no choices to make. The only thing you can select is whether the running server will have routing capabilities by checking the Enable Routing check box, (which is not available in the Professional OS version). When you click Next, the installation process begins.

Independent Client Installation

Independent clients maintain their own queues, and can work disconnected from the MSMQ Enterprise. They can be installed in either Domain or Workgroup mode.

To install an independent client, you have to select the Message Queuing server option from the screen shown in Figure 1-14.

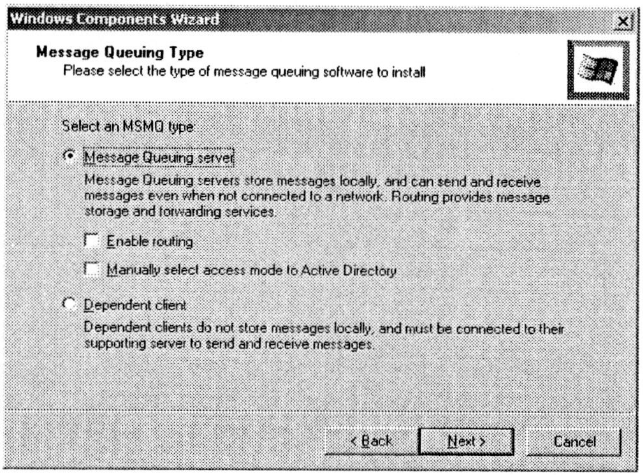

Figure 1-14. The independent client installation setup

The Enable Routing check box is only available on a Windows Server and turns that server into an MSMQ routing server. If during the installation process the setup program can't access the Directory Service automatically, you can specify it by checking the Manually Select Access Mode to Active Directory check box. This option is useful for installing an independent client connected to an MSMQ 1.0 Server that holds the MQIS database as well. Then click the Next button to continue.

If you previously checked the Manually Select Access Mode to Active Directory check box, the screen shown in Figure 1-15 will appear, which allows you to specify whether the independent client will be part of the MSMQ Enterprise. If you need to access a Directory Service, you have to select the Message Queuing Will Access a Directory Service option. Then you have to type the name of a domain controller running Message Queuing, an MSMQ 1.0 primary enterprise controller, or an MSMQ 1.0 primary site controller in order for the independent client to become part of the MSMQ Enterprise.

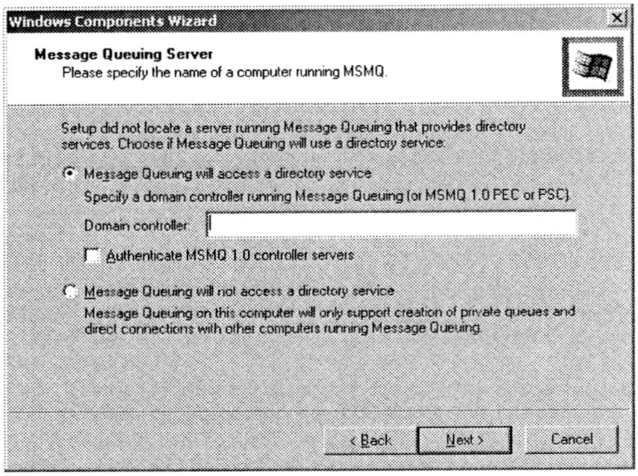

Figure 1-15. Selecting the server access for an independent client

If you don't need to access a Directory Service, or you are in Workgroup mode, you have to select the Message Queuing Will Not Access a Directory Service option.

When you click Next, the installation process begins.

Dependent Client Installation

Dependent clients require synchronous access to a Message Queuing server to perform all standard message queuing operations. You can only install a dependent client in Domain mode. To install a dependent client, you have to select the Dependent client option from the screen shown in Figure 1-16.

Then you specify a domain controller running MSMQ, an MSMQ 1.0 primary enterprise controller, or an MSMQ 1.0 primary site controller.

When you click Next, the installation process begins.

Completing the Installation Process

After you click the last Next button, the installation process begins; it takes a couple of minutes to complete. You'll see the screen shown in Figure 1-17 as you wait.

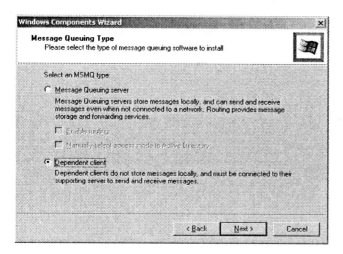

Figure 1-16. An independent client installation

Figure 1-17. The setup process wizard's final window

You don't need to reboot the system after finishing the installation process.

Checking the Installation

Once MSMQ is installed, you have a service process running. You can stop and start the MSMQ Service from the Computer Management console by enabling and disabling Message Queuing, as shown in Figure 1-18.

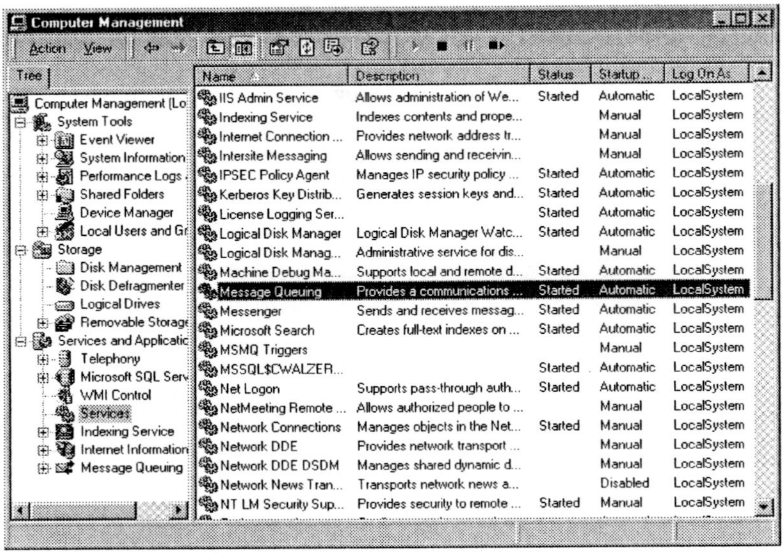

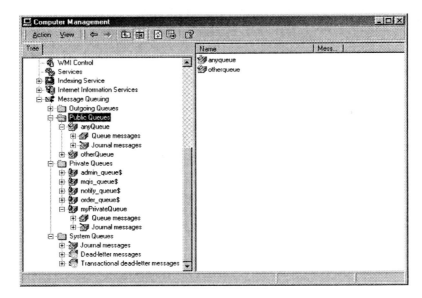

Figure 1-18. MMC snap-in tool for administrative purposes

The setup process automatically added an administrative tool, shown in Figure 1-19. We will study the MMC snap-in console tool for administrative processes in Chapter 3.

Figure 1-19. MMC administrative snap-in tool showing the PC's queues

Uninstalling MSMQ

Removing Message Queuing from a computer is easy. You only have to deselect the Message Queuing Services option from the Windows Component wizard screen. You can launch it by selecting the Add/Remove Programs icon from Control Panel, and clicking the Add/Remove Windows Components button. Before removing MSMQ, the setup will inform you that all the queues and messages hosted by the machine will be deleted.

Summary

This chapter has introduced you to the world of message based-distributed applications, using Microsoft Message Queuing. We looked at some of the issues involved with message-based applications, explained the elements that are part of a Message Queuing environment, presented some typical scenarios for queued message–based applications, looked at the new features introduced by each version of MSMQ, and explained how to install MSMQ.

The following chapters go into further detail on each of these topics. Because MSMQ is language-independent and cross-platform, this book uses a mix of Visual Basic 6.0 and the C# and C++ languages to provide you with the ability to develop a distributed message-based application using any platform and language available.

CHAPTER 2

System.Messaging

IN THIS CHAPTER, WE DISCUSS THE System.Messaging namespace in detail. You'll see how the commonly used classes are applied in some sample programs. The System.Messaging namespace is an integral part of the .NET Framework and is contained in the System.Messaging.dll assembly. The System.Messaging namespace provides classes that allow you to connect to, monitor, and administer message queues on the network and send, receive, or peek messages.

Apart from System.Messaging, Message Queuing has COM and C programming APIs. Both COM and C APIs run in an unmanaged environment, whereas System.Messaging is an integral part of the .NET Framework and thus runs in a managed environment. System.Messaging also gives the programmer a wide range of programming languages with which to program Message Queuing applications.

The System.Messaging namespace can be used by any language supported by the .NET Framework—for example, Visual Basic .NET, Visual J#, JScript .NET, and C#. In this chapter, we use C# as the programming language. Initially, we spend some time on MSMQ basics such as System.Messaging architecture and types of queues; then we examine the different paths and format names used to access these queues. We also highlight some of the new features that are available in MSMQ 3.0 from a programmer's perspective. Some of these new features are the ability to send messages to multiple destinations, Internet messaging, and multicast messaging.

System.Messaging gives you the option of receiving messages asynchronously as well as synchronously. This chapter shows you in detail when and how these two techniques can be applied in an enterprise application. One of the advantages System.Messaging gives you is the ability to add custom formatters to process the message body. In this chapter we also see how to develop custom formatters by implementing a Simple Object Access Protocol (SOAP) formatter to exchange SOAP messages between applications. In addition, you learn how to exchange complex messages like files and legacy COM objects between applications. At the end of the chapter, we discuss message properties such as priority, acknowledgments, and message enumerators.

System.Messaging Namespace Programming Architecture

With the growing popularity of the .NET Framework, Windows programming has taken a different turn and has become more object oriented. While programming, developers don't feel as if they are developing software using proprietary APIs.

The .NET Framework consists of namespaces that represent almost all the interfaces to the Windows API, and MSMQ is not an exception. The System.Messaging namespace in the .NET Framework interfaces directly with the MSMQ. Another invaluable feature of the Framework is its language independence. For developing an MSMQ application, a C# application uses the same base class library and namespaces as a Visual Basic .NET (VB.NET) application, Visual C++ (VC++) application, or even a Visual J# application. This helps increase developer productivity, as the developer does not have to learn multiple languages to program parts of the same application. Previously, MSMQ had two popular programming interfaces, C API and the COM API. Some features that were available in the C API were not available in the COM API. Therefore, if the developer were an expert in VB, he would have to learn C to develop some parts of the application that needed the C API features. The .NET Framework solves this problem by introducing a common namespace to the MSMQ that can be used by any language supporting the Framework.

In this section, we cover the System.Messaging API from a beginner's point of view. We examine some System.Messaging classes that are most often used for developing MSMQ applications. Figure 2-1 shows the most commonly used classes. Before going ahead, make sure you have the .NET Framework SDK 1.0 or later installed on your system.

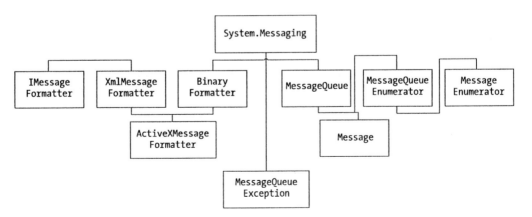

Figure 2-1. System.Messaging *namespace hierarchy*

Core Message Queuing Classes

Table 2-1 shows the most commonly used classes from the System.Messaging namespace.

Table 2-1. System.Messaging *Classes*

CLASS	DESCRIPTION
MessageQueue	This class provides interaction with the queue on the server using other methods in the class. An instance of this class represents a singleton instance of a queue that already exists in MSMQ.
Message	This class provides properties and methods that can be used on the message sent to the queue. It can be also used for peeking or receiving a message.
MessageEnumerator	This class is used to iterate over the messages in the queue.
MessageQueueException	An exception of this class is thrown when an internal exception occurs during message queuing.

Message Formatters

Message formatters are used to serialize and deserialize the body of a message from the queue while sending and receiving the message, respectively. While sending the message, the formatter serializes the message into a stream and inserts it into the body of the message. When receiving the message, the formatter deserializes the contents of the body of the message before the application receives it. A message formatter must implement the IMessageFormatter interface. Three built-in classes implement the IMessageFormatter interface, as shown in Table 2-2.

Table 2-2. Built-in Message Formatters

CLASS	DESCRIPTION
ActiveXMessageFormatter	Serializes or deserializes primitive data types and ActiveX objects to or from the body of a Message Queuing message.
BinaryMessageFormatter	Serializes or deserializes an object using the binary as a format.
XMLMessageFormatter	Serializes or deserializes an object using Extensible Markup Language (XML) as a format. This is a default formatter used when sending or getting a message.

Working with Queues

In this section, you'll learn how to create, delete, and purge queues (public and private) as well as how to send and receive messages synchronously and asynchronously.

Paths

The Path property of the queue is used to reference the queue while creating, deleting, sending, and receiving messages. The Path property value varies considerably depending on the type of queue used. The format name or the label of the queue may also be specified as the Path property. Table 2-5 shows different values for this property depending on the type of the queue used.

NOTE *If your machine is offline or is disconnected from the domain controller, you must use the* FormatName *because Active Directory is not available to the local Message Queuing server to resolve the path name of a queue to its format name. Using the direct* FormatName *avoids a round-trip to Active Directory and is recommended even when the machine is online.*

Table 2-5. Path Values to Access Queues Programmatically

QUEUE TYPE	SYNTAX	EXAMPLE
Public queue	`MachineName\QueueName`	`REDKARHOUSE\` `myfirstpublicq`
Private queue	`MachineName\Private$\` `QueueName`	`REDKARHOUSE\private$\` `myfirstprivateq`
Journal queue	`MachineName\QueueName\` `Journal$`	`REDKARHOUSE\` `myfirstpublicq\Journal$`
Machine journal queue	`MachineName\Journal$`	`REDKARHOUSE\Journal$`
(For workgroup installations use `FormatNames`.)		
Machine dead-letter queue	`MachineName\` `Deadletter$`	`REDKARHOUSE\Deadletter$`
(For workgroup installations use `FormatNames`.)		
Machine transactional dead-letter queue	`MachineName\` `XactDeadletter$`	`REDKARHOUSE\` `XactDeadletter$`
(For workgroup installations use `FormatNames`.)		

NOTE   *The name of the queue cannot contain the following special characters:*

\ (backslash)
; (semicolon)
CR (ASCII 13)
LF (ASCII 10)
+ (plus)
, (comma)
" (double quotation mark)
    It is also worth knowing the fact that the maximum size of a queue name is 124 Unicode characters and that using names longer than 64 Unicode characters may cause a slight reduction in performance and display in Active Directory.

Format Names

The `Path` property of the queue may also be the `FormatName` of the queue. MSMQ supports three types of `FormatNames`: public, private, and direct.

Public Format Names

Public format names are used to access public queues. They cannot be used on MSMQ workgroup installations. When the queue manager detects a public format name, it queries the Directory Service to get the name of the machine that the queue is hosted on and obtains the required information to route the message to the queue. The syntax for using public format names is

```
FormatName:PUBLIC=QueueGUID
```

For example:

```
FormatName:Public= 5A5F7234-AE9F-41E3-934d-845C2AFF9001
```

For journal queues, the syntax is

```
FormatName:PUBLIC=QueueGUID;JOURNAL
```

For example:

```
FormatName:PUBLIC= 5A5F7234-AE9F-41E3-934d-845C2AFF9001;JOURNAL
```

Private Format Names

Private format names are used to access private queues. They cannot be used on MSMQ workgroup installations. When the queue manager detects a private format name, it does not query the directory for the queue information, but it queries the Directory Service to convert the GUID to the host name of the machine for routing purposes. The syntax for using private format names is as follows:

```
FormatName:PRIVATE=MachineGUID\\private_queue_id
```

For example:

```
FormatName:PRIVATE= 5A5F7234-AE9F-41E3-934d-845C2AFF9001\\00000017
```

For journal queues, the syntax is

```
FormatName:PRIVATE = MachineGUID\\private_queue_id;JOURNAL
```

For example:

```
FormatName:PRIVATE = 5A5F7234-AE9F-41E3-934d-845C2AFF9002\\0000002E;JOURNAL
```

Direct Format Names

Direct format names are used to access queues without querying the Directory Service. Direct format names must be used to access private queues on a remote machine with a workgroup MSMQ installation. They must be used when working in an offline mode because the queue manager does not have to query the Directory Service.

The syntax for using direct format names for public queues is

```
DIRECT=AddressSpecification\QueueName
```

For example:

```
FormatName:DIRECT=IPX: 00000012:00a0234f7500\myfirstpublicq
FormatName:DIRECT=TCP:192.168.1.34\myfirstpublicq
FormatName:DIRECT=OS:redkarhouse.metrysoft.com\myfirstpublicq
FormatName:DIRECT=OS:redkarhouse\myfirstpublicq
```

NOTE *The IPX protocol is not supported in MSMQ 3.0 going forward.*

The syntax for using direct format names for private queues is

```
DIRECT=AddressSpecification\PRIVATE$\QueueName
```

For example:

```
FormatName:DIRECT=IPX: 00000012:00a0234f7500\PRIVATE$\myfirstprivateq
FormatName:DIRECT=TCP:192.168.1.34\PRIVATE$\myfirstprivateq
FormatName:DIRECT=OS:redkarhouse.metrysoft.com\PRIVATE$\myfirstprivateq
FormatName:DIRECT=OS:redkarhouse\PRIVATE$\myfirstprivateq
FormatName:DIRECT=HTTP://redkarhouse/msmq/myfirsthttpq (HTTP Messaging, MSMQ 3.0
only)
FormatName:DIRECT:OS:redkarhouse\myfirstq,
DIRECT:OS:redkarhouse\mysecondq (Multi-Destination queues, MSMQ 3.0 only)
```

NOTE *MSMQ 3.0 introduces multicast messaging, where a group of queues can be configured using the Multicast tab in the Microsoft Management Console (MMC) snap-in to listen to the same multicast address. To access these queues programmatically, the following path can be used:*

```
FormatName:MULTICAST=224.0.0.1:8001
```

For computer system queues (computer journal, dead-letter, transactional dead-letter), the syntax is

```
DIRECT=AddressSpecification\SYSTEM$;computersystemqueue
```

For example:

```
FormatName:DIRECT=OS:redkarhouse\SYSTEM$;JOURNAL;
FormatName:DIRECT=OS:redkarhouse\SYSTEM$;DEADLETTER;
FormatName:DIRECT=OS:redkarhouse\SYSTEM$;DEADXACT;
```

Labels

We may also specify a label to access a queue. If the label is not unique, an exception will be thrown. The syntax for using the Label is as follows:

```
Label:Label of the Queue
```

For example:

```
Label:MyFirstQLabel
```

> **TIP**   *Using* FormatNames *offers better performance because Message Queuing does not have to query Active Directory to resolve the name of the queue to the GUID of the queue. One drawback of using the ID value is that the value may change if the queue is deleted and/or re-created. So, hard-coding the* FormatName *of the queue in any application is not a good idea. One solution is to load the* FormatName *of the queue from an XML file or Active Directory.*

Creating a Queue Programmatically

The MessageQueue class has a static method, Create(), that is used to create queues. Create() has two overloads:

```
public static MessageQueue Create(string path);

public static MessageQueue Create(
    string path,
    bool transactional
);
```

The path parameter specifies the path of the queue, which can either be a Path property or a FormatName of the queue. The transactional parameter specifies whether or not the created queue will be transactional. Thus, the decision for marking a queue as transactional is made during the creation of the queue. Once a queue is created as a transactional queue, it cannot be changed to nontransactional, and vice versa. Transactional queues can receive messages only in the context of a transaction. We cover transactional queues and transactions in Chapter 4.

The following example illustrates how to use the Create() method:

```
class MessageQueueOperations
{
 public static void Main(string[] args)
 {
  if(args.Length == 2)
  {
   try
   {
    MessageQueue q = MessageQueue.Create
      (args[0], Convert.ToBoolean(args[1]));
   }
```

```
  catch(Exception ex)
  {
   Console.WriteLine
     ("Exception while creating the queue " + ex.Message);
  }

 }
 else
 {
  Console.WriteLine
    ("Usage:CreateQueue [Path of the queue]"
    + "[True/False for transactional/non-transactional]");
 }
 }
}
```

In the previous example, we ask the user to specify the path of the queue and a Boolean value to indicate whether the created queue will be transactional. Then we call the static `Create()` method of the `MessageQueue` class. Note that the `Create()` method returns a reference to the `MessageQueue` object that can be used for more interactions with the queue if required.

The output from the previous program with different parameters looks like this:

First run: Creating a private nontransactional queue:

```
>CreateQueue .\private$\myfirstprivatenontransactionalq false
```

Second run: Creating a private transactional queue:

```
>CreateQueue.\private$\myfirstprivatetransactionalq true
```

Third run: Trying to create the queue again:

```
>CreateQueue.\private$\myfirstprivatetransactionalq true
Exception while creating the queue Queue with the specified path name is already
registered in the DS
```

While we're trying to create the same queue again in the third run, an exception is thrown by the Framework, suggesting that the queue already exists. In order to avoid an exception being thrown, we can use another static method,

Exists(), from the MessageQueue class to check whether a queue with the same name exists in MSMQ:

```
public static bool Exists(
    string path
);
```

where path is the path of the queue whose existence needs to be checked. Exists() is an expensive method because it has to query Active Directory to get the existence of the queue. It is recommended that you use exceptions instead of this method. The following listing illustrates using the Exists() method of the MessageQueue class:

```
using System;
using System.Messaging;

class MessageQueueOperations
{
 public static void Main(string[] args)
 {
  if(args.Length == 2)
  {
   try
   {
    if(!MessageQueue.Exists(args[0]))
    {
     MessageQueue q = MessageQueue.Create
       (args[0], Convert.ToBoolean(args[1]));
    }
    else
    {
     Console.WriteLine
       ("MessageQueue " + args[0]
       + " already exists in MSMQ.");
    }
   }
   catch(Exception ex)
   {
    Console.WriteLine
      ("Exception while creating the queue "
      + ex.Message);
   }
```

```
  }
  else
  {
    Console.WriteLine
      ("Usage:CreateQueue [Path of the queue]"
      + "[True/False for transactional/non-transactional]");
  }
 }
}
```

In the preceding listing, before creating the queue we call the static `Exists()` method of the `MessageQueue` class to verify whether the queue already exists. The method returns a true Boolean value if the queue exists and returns false otherwise. In general, the `Exists()` method is an expensive operation to use in an MSMQ Enterprise because it has to query Active Directory to check whether the queue exists. But during the creation of the queue, performance may not be an issue because the queue will be created only once. It is advisable not to use the `Exists()` method all the time while referencing a queue to send or receive messages. Another thing worth trying is to run this program to do the following:

- Create a public queue in a workgroup environment.

- Create a public queue in a domain environment.

- Create a public queue on an offline machine in a domain environment.

Creating Queues Manually

Queues can also be created manually from the Message Queuing snap-in in the Computer Management console. Right-click on the My Computer icon on the Desktop and click on Manage to open the Computer Management console. Go to Services and Applications | Message Queuing. Depending on the type of queue to be created, right-click on either the Public or Private category and click on New ➤ Private Queue or Public Queue. This will open the dialog box shown in Figure 2-3. Specify a name for the queue and click OK to create the queue. If you want to create a transactional queue, select the Transactional check box. The newly created queue should be visible in the Public or Private category.

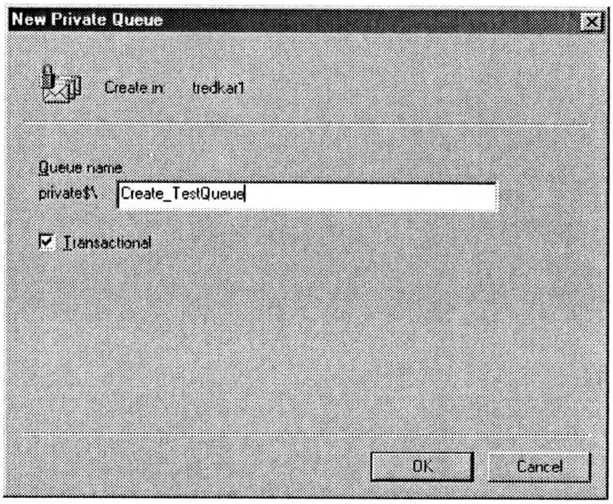

Figure 2-3. The Create Queue dialog box

Deleting a Queue Programmatically

The MessageQueue class has a static method Delete() that is used to delete queues:

```
public static void Delete(string path);
```

The path parameter specifies the path of the queue, which can either be a Path property or a FormatName of the queue. The following example shows the usage of the Delete() method:

```
using System;
using System.Messaging;

class MessageQueueOperations
{
 public static void Main(string[] args)
 {
  if(args.Length == 1)
  {
    try
    {
          MessageQueue.Delete(args[0]);
      }
```

```
    catch(MessageQueueException ex)
  {
      Console.WriteLine("Exception "
        + ex.Message);
          Console.WriteLine("Error Code "
          +   ex.MessageQueueErrorCode.ToString());
    }
  }
  else
  {
   Console.WriteLine
    ("Usage:DeleteQueue "
    + "[Path of the queue]");
  }
 }
}
```

In the example, we ask the user to specify the path of the queue to be deleted. Then we call the Delete() method of the MessageQueue class. In this code we introduce the MessageQueueErrorCode enum available in the System.Messaging namespace. The MessageQueueErrorCode enum pinpoints the type of MessageQueueException that was thrown. In the exception block, we print the string representation of the MessageQueueErrorCode—for example, if the queue to be deleted is not found, the MessageQueueErrorCode will have the value QueueNotFound. To run the example that we have looked at, run the DeleteQueue.exe file from the command prompt, as shown here:

```
> DeleteQueue \Private$\Create_testqueue
Queue deleted Successfully
```

Deleting a Queue Manually

Queues can also be deleted manually from the Message Queuing snap-in of the Computer Management console. To do so, right-click on any queue in either the Public or Private category of Services and Applications | Message Queuing in the console and select Delete to delete the queue. This opens the dialog box shown in Figure 2-4, asking you to confirm the queue to be deleted. Click Yes to delete the queue. The queue will be deleted from the Public or Private category.

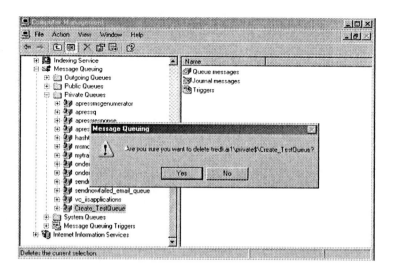

Figure 2-4. Confirm that you want to delete the queue.

Referencing Queues

We've seen how to invoke static members of the MessageQueue class. There are four ways to create an instance of the MessageQueue class that references a queue in MSMQ. Three of these ways involve using the constructors, and the fourth one takes place while creating the queue. When you create a queue using the Create() method, a reference to the MessageQueue object is returned.

Using Constructors

In this section, you'll see how to use the three constructors of the MessageQueue class.

Using the No Argument Constructor

When we instantiate this constructor, it does not reference any queue. When the Path property is set, the queue is referenced. When you set this property, the reference to the queue that the object is holding is reset to the new value:

```
String PATH_OF_THE_QUEUE = @".\private$\myfirstq";
MessageQueue mq1 = new MessageQueue();
mq1.Path = PATH_OF_THE_QUEUE;
```

Using the Constructor with the Path Argument

This constructor takes the Path of the queue as the parameter, and so we don't need to set the Path property:

```
MessageQueue mq2 = new MessageQueue(PATH_OF_THE_QUEUE);
```

Using Constructor Path and Boolean Arguments

This constructor accepts the path of the queue and a Boolean value of true/ false indicating whether the application creating this instance needs exclusive read access to the queue. With exclusive read access, no other application any-where on the network will be able to read messages from the queue:

```
MessageQueue mq3 = new MessageQueue(PATH_OF_THE_QUEUE, false);
```

Using the Create() Method

Here we get a reference to the created queue. We can use this method only if the queue does not already exist. If the queue exists, and we try to create one, this method will throw an exception and the value of the mq4 object will be null:

```
MessageQueue mq4 = MessageQueue.Create(PATH_OF_THE_QUEUE);
```

Purging Messages Programmatically

Purging is used to delete all the messages in a queue. Sometimes messages are accumulated in queues that do not have receiver applications. For example, journal queues or dead-letter queues continue to grow in size if there is no receiver application running to receive messages from these queues. As mes-sages are accumulated in these queues, the memory used by Message Queuing keeps on growing, which may further lead to *disk thrashing* (swapping disk space for memory). To avoid disk thrashing, periodically purge the queues that are susceptible to accumulation of messages.

NOTE   *In MSMQ 1.0 and MSMQ 2.0 there is a total limit of 2GB for all messages in the application and system queues combined. This limit was eliminated in MSMQ 3.0.*

The MessageQueue class has a method Purge(), which is used to delete messages programmatically:

```
public void Purge();
```

The following listing shows how to use the Purge() method:

```
using System;
using System.Messaging;

class PurgeQueue
{
public static void Main(string[] args)
{
        if(args.Length >= 1)
        {
                try
                {
                    if(!MessageQueue.Exists(args[0]))
        {
                Console.WriteLine("Queue does not exist");
        }
            MessageQueue q =  new MessageQueue(args[0]);
            q.Purge();
        Console.WriteLine("Messages deleted successfully");
        }
        catch(MessageQueueException ex)
        {
        Console.WriteLine("Exception " +     ex.Message);
        Console.WriteLine("Error Code " +
        ex.MessageQueueErrorCode.ToString());
        }

        }
        else
        {
```

```
                    Console.WriteLine("Usage:PurgeQueue "
            + "[Path of the queue]");
    }
  }
}
```

In the previous listing, we ask the user to specify the path of the queue, the messages of which are to be deleted. We then reference the queue by calling the MessageQueue class constructor, which accepts the path of the queue as the only parameter. If this instantiation is successful, we call the Purge() method of the MessageQueue class. If the instantiation is not successful (e.g., if the queue does not exist), a MessageQueueException is thrown.

To run the example, run PurgeQueue.exe from the command prompt, as shown here:

```
>PurgeQueue .\private$\myfirstq
```

Purging a Queue Manually

Queues can also be purged manually from the Message Queuing snap-in of the Computer Management console. To do this, select any one of the queues in the console and then right-click on Queue Messages ➤ All Tasks ➤ Purge. This opens the dialog box shown in Figure 2-5. Simply click Yes to delete all the messages in the queue.

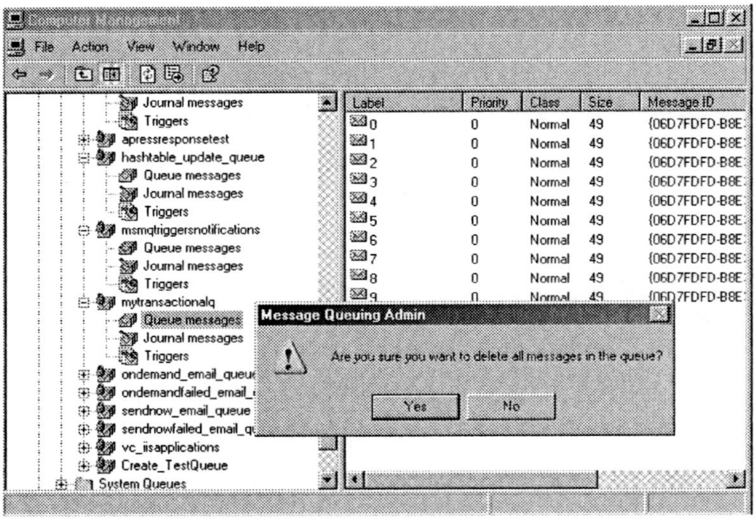

Figure 2-5. Purging messages

Interacting with Queues

In this section, we cover sending simple messages to the queue, receiving simple messages, using message formatters, and sending and receiving complex messages. *Simple* messages are sent using all the default properties, and complex messages are sent overriding the default properties.

Sending a Simple Message to a Queue

System.Messaging provides the Send() method in the MessageQueue class to send messages to the queue. The Send() method has the following overloads that we will use in this chapter:

```
public void Send(
    object obj
);
```

This is the simplest form of the Send() method. The object parameter can either be any object that you want to send or the System.Messaging.Message object. If any object is used, it will be sent using all the default properties of the System.Messaging.Message object; if the System.Messaging.Message object is passed, then its properties will take precedence over the default properties.

```
public void Send(
    object obj,
    string label
);
```

This method is similar to the first overload, with the exception that it takes a string parameter representing the label of the message. The object that is sent to the queue must be serializable and must have a no argument constructor. This is because the message formatter serializes the object into the body of the message when the Send() method is called.

The first overload of the Send() method is the simplest method for sending messages to the queue and requires the following steps:

1. Obtain a reference to the queue where the message needs to be sent:

   ```
   MessageQueue Mq = new MessageQueue(PATH_OF_THE_QUEUE);
   ```

2. Create the object that you need to send:

   ```
   String message = "Hello";
   ```

3. Invoke the Send() method by passing the created object as one of the parameters. Alternatively, you may also pass a string label for the message:

```
Mq.Send(message);
```

or

```
Mq.Send(message, "Message Label");
```

Using this Send() method, the object that is passed as the message is inserted into the body of the message. The message is sent using all the default properties of the System.Messaging.Message object.

The following listing shows how to send a message to the queue:

```
using System;
using System.Messaging;

class SendSimpleMessage
{
  public static void Main(string[] args)
  {
    if(args.Length >= 2)
    {
      try
      {
        //Check whether the queue exists or not
        if(!MessageQueue.Exists(args[0]))
        {
          MessageQueue.Create(args[0]);
          Console.WriteLine("Queue was not registered,"+
            "so new queue created for you");

        }
        MessageQueue q = new MessageQueue
          (args[0]);
        String message = args[1];
        //Check if the user provided a label
        if(args.Length == 3)
          q.Send(message, args[2]);
        else
          q.Send(message);
```

```
      Console.WriteLine("Message sent successfully");


    }
    catch(Exception ex)
    {
      Console.WriteLine
        ("Exception " + ex.Message);
    }


  }
  else
  {
    Console.WriteLine
      ("Usage:SendSimpleMessage [Path of the queue]"
      + "[Message Body] <Label (Optional)>");
  }
 }
}
```

In the preceding listing, we ask the user to input the path of the queue, the message to send, and optionally the label of the message. After checking the input, if the queue does not exist, we create the queue for the user. Finally, we check whether the user provided us with the label of the message. If the user provided the label, we call the Send() method that accepts a message and a label. If the user provided only the body, we call the Send() method that accepts only the body of the message. To run the sample, type

```
>SendSimpleMessage .\private$\myfirstq TestMessage
```

To view the messages sent, we can open the Message Queuing user interface from the Computer Management console and expand the tree to the user-specified queue to view the messages sent. Figures 2-6 and 2-7 show the messages sent and the body of the message.

In Figure 2-7, the body of the message is in XML format because the default formatter for any message sent is XmlMessageFormatter. A formatter serializes the message content into a stream and inserts it into the body of the System.Messaging.Message object. (We cover formatters in detail later in this chapter.) Other message formatters that are a part of the System.Messaging namespace are ActiveXMessageFormatter (for sending primitive data types or ActiveX objects) and BinaryMessageFormatter (for sending messages in binary form).

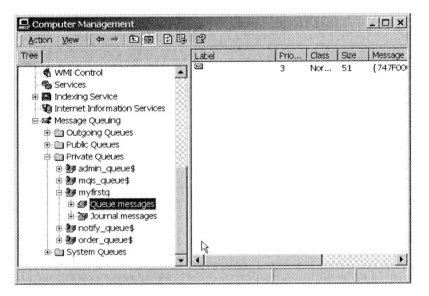

Figure 2-6. Message sent

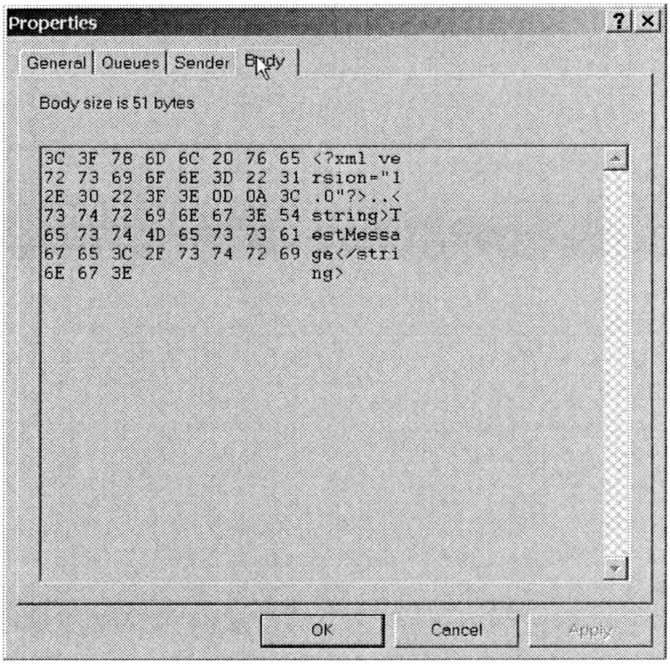

Figure 2-7. Body of the message

XmlMessageFormatter makes it easier to send an object to the queue because the serialization of the object to the XML form is taken care of by the XmlMessageFormatter and at the same time you can view the state of the serialized object visually. One more advantage of using the XmlMessageFormatter is that it enables a loosely coupled messaging channel between the message sender application and the message receiver application. The receiver of the message can be totally unaware of the version of the object and its binary representation on the sender side. The receiver can read the message as an XML string and parse it into whatever object it wants. The only disadvantage of XmlMessageFormatter is its low throughput, a result of the overhead required to parse each received message. In the following listing, we create a Thermostat class and then send a Thermostat object to the queue:

```
using System;
using System.Messaging;

public class Thermostat
{
  private double _currentTemperature;
  private double _setPointValue;
  private readonly String _id;
  public Thermostat()
  {
    this._id = System.Guid.NewGuid().ToString();
  }
  public double CurrentTemperature
  {
    get
    {
      return this._currentTemperature;

    }

    set
    {
      this._currentTemperature = value;

    }

  }
```

```csharp
      public double SetPointValue
      {
        get
        {
          return this._setPointValue;

        }
        set
        {
          this._setPointValue = value;

        }
      }

      public String ID
      {
        get
        {
          return this._id;

        }

      }

    }
    class SendObject
    {

      public static void Main(string[] args)
      {
       if(args.Length == 1)
       {
        try
        {
         if(!MessageQueue.Exists(args[0]))
         {
          MessageQueue.Create(args[0]);
          Console.WriteLine("Queue was not registered,"+
            "so new queue created for you");

         }
```

```
MessageQueue q = new MessageQueue
  (args[0]);

Thermostat message = new Thermostat();
  message.CurrentTemperature = 78.6;
  message.SetPointValue = 86.7;
  q.Send(message, message.ID);

Console.WriteLine("Message sent successfully");

}
catch(Exception ex)
{
Console.WriteLine
  ("Exception " + ex.Message);
}
}
else
{
Console.WriteLine
  ("Usage:SendObject [Path of the queue]");
}
}
}
```

In the preceding listing, we have a class called Thermostat with three instance variables: the current temperature (_currentTemperature), the set point value (_setpointValue), and the unique ID (_id). In the main method, we create an instance of a Thermostat object, specify its set point and current temperature values, and pass the object to the Send() method of the message queue. The serialization of the object is taken care of by the XmlMessageFormatter in the System.Messaging namespace. Note that we can view the state of the object visually, which would not have been possible if we had used the BinaryMessageFormatter or the ActiveXMessageFormatter. To run the sample, type the following at the command prompt:

```
>SendObject .\private$\myfirstq
```

Figure 2-8 shows the visual representation of the serialized Thermostat object.

```
ffd89955-f378-40d8-8a83-9e5fa888c97d Properties          ? X

General | Queues | Sender | Body |

Body size is 237 bytes

3C 3F 78 6D 6C 20 76 65    <?xml ve
72 73 69 6F 6E 3D 22 31    rsion="1
2E 30 22 3F 3E 0D 0A 3C    .0"?>..<
54 68 65 72 6D 6F 73 74    Thermost
61 74 20 78 6D 6C 6E 73    at xmlns
3A 78 73 64 3D 22 68 74    :xsd="ht
74 70 3A 2F 2F 77 77 77    tp://www
2E 77 33 2E 6F 72 67 2F    .w3.org/
32 30 30 31 2F 58 4D 4C    2001/XML
53 63 68 65 6D 61 22 20    Schema"
78 6D 6C 6E 73 3A 78 73    xmlns:xs
69 3D 22 68 74 74 70 3A    i="http:
2F 2F 77 77 77 2E 77 33    //www.w3
2E 6F 72 67 2F 32 30 30    .org/200
31 2F 58 4D 4C 53 63 68    1/XMLSch
65 6D 61 2D 69 6E 73 74    ema-inst
61 6E 63 65 22 3E 0D 0A    ance">..
20 20 3C 43 75 72 72 65      <Curre
6E 74 54 65 6D 70 65 72    ntTemper
61 74 75 72 65 3E 37 38    ature>78
2E 36 3C 2F 43 75 72 72    .6</Curr
65 6E 74 54 65 6D 70 65    entTempe

        OK          Cancel         Apply
```

Figure 2-8. The serialized Thermostat *object*

The following listing shows the state of a Thermostat object serialized by the XmlMessageFormatter:

```
<?xml version="1.0" ?>
<Thermostat
xmlns:xsd="http://www.w3.org/2001/XMLSchema"
xmlns:xsi="http://www.w3.org/2001/XMLSchema-instance">
        <CurrentTemperature>78.6</CurrentTemperature>
          <SetPointValue   >86.7</SetPointValue>
</Thermostat>
```

NOTE   *One requirement for successfully serializing objects while sending them to the queue is that the object must have a no argument or default constructor. The serialization will fail if the object does not have a no argument constructor and a runtime exception will be thrown.*

Receiving Messages Synchronously

In the previous section, we looked at how to send simple messages to the queue. Next, let's see how you can receive a message from the queue synchronously. In a synchronous receive, you call the Receive() method of the MessageQueue instance on demand and wait until the message arrives in the queue. Alternatively, you can specify a timeout value to end the wait. The Receive() method returns a reference to the Message object. To get the contents of the Message, you have to call its Body property. The overloads of the Receive() method that we will use in this chapter are

```
public Message Receive();
```

This method receives the first message from the queue. If the message queue is empty, the method waits indefinitely, blocking the current thread of execution, until a message arrives in the queue.

```
public Message Receive(
    TimeSpan timeout
);
```

This method receives the first message from the queue. If the message queue is empty, it waits for the timeout specified and returns. This is a much more elegant approach.

NOTE *Receiving a message deletes a message from the queue.*

Here are the steps to receive messages synchronously:

1. Obtain a reference to the proper MSMQ queue by instantiating the MessageQueue object:

    ```
    MessageQueue mq = new MessageQueue(PATH_OF_THE_QUEUE);
    ```

2. Specify the formatter for the messages that will be received. The System.Messaging.Message class also has a Formatter property, which takes precedence over the formatter of the MessageQueue class. Since you are using the default XmlMessageFormatter, you need to specify the list of possible data types that might be contained in the message. In this case, you are using only the String data type:

    ```
    mq.Formatter = new XmlMessageFormatter
    (new Type[]{typeof(System.String)});
    ```

Alternatively, to be more dynamic, you can also specify the types using simple strings:

```
mq.Formatter = new XmlMessageFormatter
(new string[]{"System.String"});
```

This method is more dynamic (and more error prone) because you can load the types at runtime. If you were to deserialize the Thermostat object, you could have instantiated the XmlMessageFormatter in the following way:

```
mq.Formatter = new XmlMessageFormatter
(new string[]{"Thermostat"});
```

3. Call the Receive() method on the MessageQueue instance to receive the first message from the queue:

```
Message msg = mq.Receive();
```

Alternatively, specify the formatter for the retrieved message to deserialize the message body. This formatter takes precedence over the formatter of the MessageQueue. It is a good programming practice to specify the formatter for the MessageQueue rather than on each message. Reflection of the data type happens only once for the MessageQueue formatter and not for each and every message that is received. Reflection reduces performance, as it is burdened with the overhead of determining and loading the instances dynamically at runtime.

```
 msg.Formatter = new XmlMessageFormatter
(new Type[]{typeof(System.String)});
```

4. Finally, use the Body property of System.Messaging.Message to retrieve the content of the message and cast it into the appropriate type:

```
String messageBody = msg.Body.ToString();
```

or

```
String messageBody = (System.String) msg.Body;
```

Figure 2-9 shows the MSMQUI Windows application that is used to receive messages synchronously. Table 2-6 lists the controls of the MSMQUI Windows application.

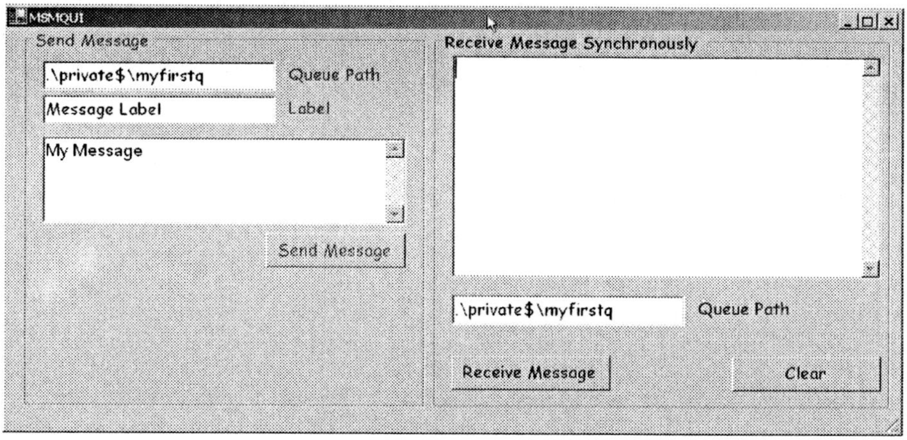

Figure 2-9. MSMQUI Windows application

Table 2-6. MSMQUI Controls

CONTROL NAME	CONTROL TYPE	EVENT OPERATION	DESCRIPTION
ReceiveMessage	Button	ReceiveMessage_Click	Calls the Receive() method of the MessageQueue class with a timeout value of 2 seconds. The body of the returned message is displayed in the Output TextBox.
ReceivePath	TextBox		The Path or FormatName of the queue.
Output	TextBox		Displays the body of the received message.

The following listing shows the code in the `ReceiveMessage_Click()` method:

```
private void ReceiveMessage_Click(object sender, System.EventArgs e)
{
statusBar1.Text = "";

try
{
        messageQueue1.Path = ReceivePath.Text.Trim();
        System.Messaging.Message msq =
            messageQueue1.Receive (new TimeSpan(0, 0, 2));
        msq.Formatter = new XmlMessageFormatter
            (new Type[]{typeof(System.String)});
        Output.AppendText((string)msq.Body);
        Output.AppendText("\r\n");
        statusBar1.Text = "FormatName = " +
        messageQueue1.FormatName;

}
catch(MessageQueueException ex)
{
            statusBar1.Text = "";
                statusBar1.Text = ex.Message;

}
catch(Exception ex1)
{
            statusBar1.Text = "";
            statusBar1.Text = ex1.Message;

}

}
```

In the preceding listing, we get the path of the queue and then call the `Receive()` method with a timeout of 2 seconds. Then we set the formatter of the returned message to `XmlMessageFormatter` with `String` as one of the expected data types of the message body. Finally, we cast the message body to a string and append it to the Output TextBox. We cast the message body to a string because we have specified `String` as the data type of the message body. When we call the `msg.Body` property, the `XmlMessageFormatter` takes over and deserializes the body of the message to a string. Thus, we can assume that the `msg.Body` property returns a string. Figure 2-10 shows the Receive Message functionality at work.

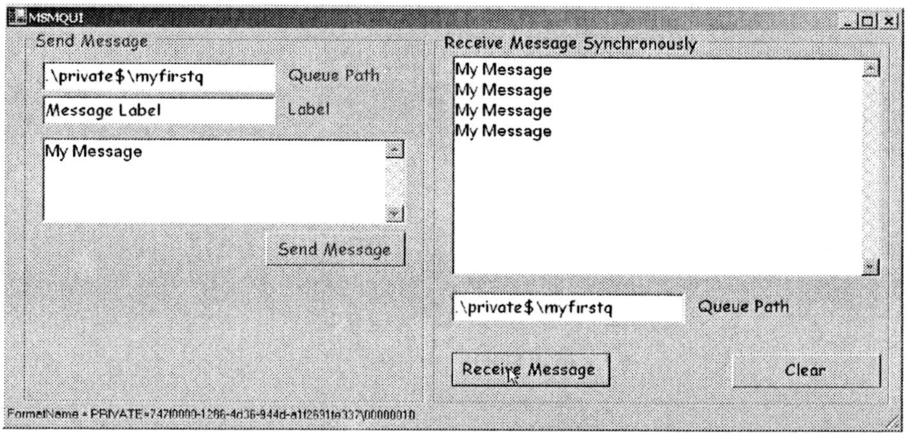

Figure 2-10. Using MSMQUI to receive messages

NOTE *The formatter used while sending a message must match the formatter used while receiving the message.*

Message Formatters

As we discussed earlier, message formatters are used to serialize and deserialize the message body when the message is sent or received from the queue. In the `System.Messaging` namespace there are three types of formatters:

- `XmlMessageFormatter`

- `ActiveXFormatter`

- `BinaryMessageFormatter`

85

XmlMessageFormatter

XmlMessageFormatter is the default message formatter for sending messages to the queue. It enables loosely coupled communication between the message sender and the receiver. This means that the message serialized by the message sender does not have to be compliant in type version with the message that is deserialized. This is because XML is just a string representation of an object and not a binary representation. XmlMessageFormatter has three constructors. If XmlMessageFormatter is initialized using this constructor

```
public XmlMessageFormatter();
```

the TargetTypeNames or the targetTypes property must be used to provide the XmlMessageFormatter with the data type of the object to be deserialized.

```
public XmlMessageFormatter(
    string[] TargetTypeNames
);
```

This constructor is used to initialize the XmlMessageFormatter by specifying the names of type of objects that this instance of the XmlMessageFormatter will deserialize. The TargetTypeNames parameter is a String array containing the fully qualified names of the type of objects to be deserialized. For example, if you want to deserialize an Order object using the XmlMessageFormatter, initialize the XmlMessageFormatter using this constructor in the following manner:

```
XmlMessageFormatter xFormatter = new XmlMessageFormatter(new
                        String[]{"Order"});
```

The advantage of using this constructor is that the types of the objects can be loaded at runtime and you can load objects dynamically without recompiling the application. For example, you can specify the type of the deserialized/serialized objects in an XML file and the application can read these names as strings and pass them to the XmlMessageFormatter constructor as the TargetTypeNames. The disadvantage is that there is no type checking at compile time.

```
public XmlMessageFormatter(Type[] TargetTypes);
```

This constructor is used to initialize the XmlMessageFormatter by specifying the types of objects that this instance of the XmlMessageFormatter will deserialize. The TargetTypes parameter is a Type array containing the type of object to be deserialized. For example, if you want to deserialize an Order object using the

XmlMessageFormatter, initialize the XmlMessageFormatter using this constructor in the following manner:

```
XmlMessageFormatter xFormatter = new XmlMessageFormatter
(new Type[]{typeof(Order));
```

The advantage of using this constructor is that the types of the objects are checked at compile time; the disadvantage is that the types of the objects cannot be loaded at runtime. The following shows how to deserialize an Order object from the queue:

```
IMessageFormatter formatter = new XmlMessageFormatter(new Type[]{
                              typeof(Order)});
```

ActiveXMessageFormatter

ActiveXMessageFormatter is typically used to serialize and deserialize either primitive data types or ActiveX objects. This makes ActiveXMessageFormatter capable of deserializing messages sent using the MSMQ COM API. ActiveXMessageFormatter is the ideal way to send objects that implement the IPersist interface, such as Office documents and Visual Basic COM objects. ActiveXMessageFormatter provides better performance and throughput than the XmlMessageFormatter because the objects are exchanged in native Windows format and do not need parsing. For example, a string will be sent as a plain string and not as an XML string. So, the size of the message is also smaller than the messages generated by XmlMessageFormatter.

BinaryMessageFormatter

The third type of formatter that comes packaged in the System.Messaging namespace is the BinaryMessageFormatter. This formatter deserializes and serializes objects or graphs of objects in binary format. Graphs of objects are objects related to one another with an object-oriented paradigm such as inheritance and composition. The advantage of using BinaryMessageFormatter is that the message is in binary format and the throughput is much higher than with the XmlMessageFormatter. The disadvantage is that the type version of the message sent must match the type version of the message received—that is, if a version 1.0 of an object is sent by a sender but the receiver is expecting a version 1.1, then the deserialization of the message will fail. Thus, binary compatibility between the object sent and the object received is absolutely necessary when you're using BinaryMessageFormatter. The following example shows a program that sends a message using all three formatters:

```
using System;
using System.Messaging;

class SendSimpleMessage
{
 public static void Main(string[] args)
 {
  if(args.Length == 2)
  {
   try
   {
    //Check whether the queue exists or not
    if(!MessageQueue.Exists(args[0]))
    {
     MessageQueue.Create(args[0]);
     Console.WriteLine("Queue was not registered,"+
       "so new queue created for you");

    }
    MessageQueue mq1 = new MessageQueue(args[0]);
    //Create a new XmlMessageFormatter
    IMessageFormatter formatter =
     new XmlMessageFormatter
    (new Type[]{typeof(System.String)});
    //Assign the formatter to the queue
    mq1.Formatter = formatter;
    String message = args[1];
    //Create a new Message object with body
    Message m1 = new Message(message);
    m1.Label = "XmlMessageFormatter";
    //Send the Message
    mq1.Send(m1);
    Console.WriteLine
    ("Message sent successfully using "
      + "XmlMessageFormatter");
    //Create a new ActiveXMessageFormatter
    formatter = new ActiveXMessageFormatter();
    //Create a new Message with body and formatter
    Message m2 = new Message(message, formatter);
    m2.Label = "ActiveXMessageFormatter";
```

```
    //Send the message
    mq1.Send(m2);
    Console.WriteLine
    ("Message sent successfully using "
      + "ActiveXMessageFormatter");
    //Create a new BinaryMessageFormatter
    formatter = new BinaryMessageFormatter();
    //Create a new Message with body and formatter
    Message m3 = new Message(message, formatter);
    m3.Label = "BinaryMessageFormatter";
    //Send the message
    mq1.Send(m3);
    Console.WriteLine
    ("Message sent successfully using "
      + "BinaryMessageFormatter");
    }

  catch(MessageQueueException ex)
  {
    Console.WriteLine
      ("Exception "
      + ex.Message);

    Console.WriteLine
      ("Error Code "
      + ex.MessageQueueErrorCode.ToString());
  }

  }
  else
  {
   Console.WriteLine
   ("Usage:ThreeFormatters [Path of the queue]"
     + "[Message Body]");
  }
 }
}
```

In the preceding listing, we ask the user to enter the path of the queue and the body of the message to be sent. Based on the path of the queue, we instantiate a MessageQueue object. Then, we instantiate an IMessageFormatter of type XmlMessageFormatter. Then, we create an instance of the System.Messaging.Message class with the body of the message and the formatter. Next, we set the Label property of the `System.Messaging.Message` object to the name of the formatter. We then send the message using the `Send()` method of the `MessageQueue` object. Similarly, we instantiate new `System.Messaging.Message` objects and set their formatters to `ActiveXMessageFormatter` and `BinaryMessageFormatter`, respectively, and send the messages. To run the sample, type the following at the command prompt:

```
>ThreeFormatters .\private$\myfirstq TestMessage
```

We can view the messages sent using the Message Queuing MMC snap-in, as shown in Figure 2-11.

Note that the `XmlMessageFormatter` message has the biggest size of the three messages.

In the preceding example, we introduced one new concept, the `System.Messaging.Message` class. This class represents an MSMQ message and offers properties for configuring the state of the message to be sent to the queue. In the previous listing, we set the body and the formatter of the `Message` object through its constructor and also set the label of the object by setting its `Label` property. One point worth noting is that while sending the message using `XmlMessageFormatter`, we set the formatter of the queue to the `XmlMessageFormatter`, but for the other two formatters, we just set the formatters of the individual messages through their constructors. Thus, the formatter of the `Message` object takes precedence over the formatter of the `MessageQueue`. We discuss the `System.Messaging.Message` class and its properties later in this chapter.

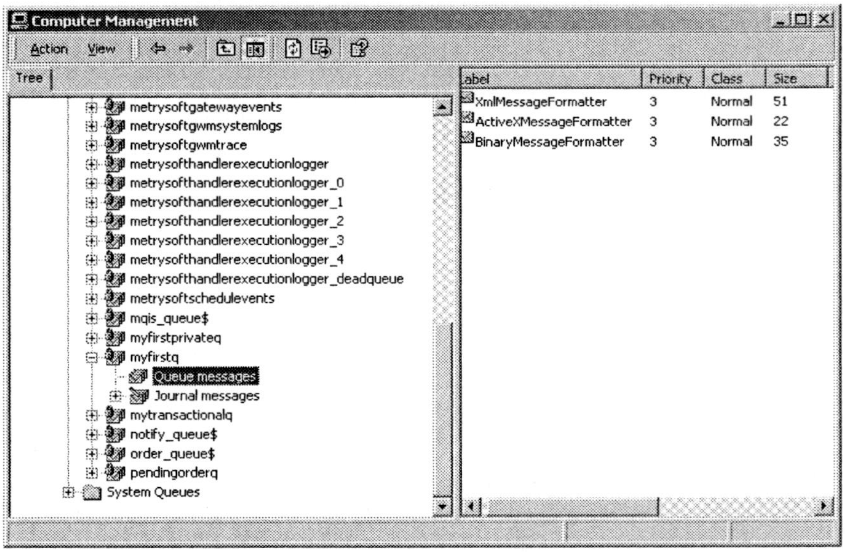

Figure 2-11. MessageFormatters in MMC

NOTE *The formatter of the* Message *object takes precedence over the formatter of the* MessageQueue.

Sending Complex Messages

Until now, in most of the examples we have been sending messages using the defaults. Complex messages are sent using the System.Messaging.Message class. This class allows us to exercise more control over the message that will be sent to the queue. When sending a simple message, in our examples we sent the object directly by calling the Send() method of the MessageQueue class. The Send() method can also accept a System.Messaging.Message object. During a simple send, a Message object is created and all the default properties are applied to it before sending it to the queue. Table 2-7 lists the properties of the Message class that are initialized to their default values when sending a simple message.

Table 2-7. Message Properties

PROPERTY	INITIAL VALUE (DEFAULT VALUE)	DESCRIPTION
AcknowledgeType	AcknowledgeType.None	Gets or sets the type of acknowledgment message requested from Message Queuing when a message arrives in the queue. If you want an acknowledgment when a message reaches or fails to reach the *queue* to which it was sent, set the property to FullReachQueue. If you want an acknowledgment when the message reaches or fails to reach the *destination application*, set the property to FullReceive. Note that this acknowledgment is generated by the queue manager rather than by the destination application. If you want an acknowledgment only if a message you send fails to reach the destination queue, set the property to NotAcknowledgeReachQueue. If you want an acknowledgment for a message you sent that cannot be retrieved by its destination application, set the property to NotAcknowledgeReceive. For this property to be effective, an administration queue must be specified using the AdministrationQueue property of the Message object.

continued

Table 2-7. Message Properties (continued)

PROPERTY	INITIAL VALUE (DEFAULT VALUE)	DESCRIPTION
AdministrationQueue	A null reference	The system can specify what went wrong (or right) during a Message Queuing operation. The administration queue receives the acknowledgment message for the message you send.
AppSpecific	0	The information generated by the application, such as single integer values or application-defined message classes. The default is 0.
AttachSenderId	true	Gets or sets a value indicating whether the sender ID is to be attached to the message. Set it to true if the SenderId is to be attached to the message; otherwise, false. The default is true.
Authentication ProviderName	Microsoft Base Cryptographic Provider, Ver. 1.0	The name of the cryptographic provider used to generate the digital signature of the message.
Authentication ProviderType	CryptoProvider Type.RSA_FULL	Gets or sets the type of cryptographic provider used to generate the digital signature of the message.
Body	A null reference (Nothing)	An object that specifies the message contents to be serialized, including string, date, currency, number, an array of bytes, or any managed object.
BodyStream	Stream.null	The BodyStream represents the body content after it has been serialized using the formatter specified in the Formatter property.
BodyType	0	The true type of the message body, such as string, date, currency, or number.

Table 2-7. Message Properties (continued)

PROPERTY	INITIAL VALUE (DEFAULT VALUE)	DESCRIPTION
ConnectorType	Guid.Empty	The ConnectorType property is required by the receiving application whenever the sender sets a property that is normally set by Message Queuing itself—for example, if the sender application sets any one of these properties: AuthenticationProviderName, AuthenticationProviderType, DestinationSymmetricKey, DigitalSignature, MessageType, SenderId.
CorrelationId	" " (empty string)	When Message Queuing generates an acknowledgment or report, it uses the CorrelationId property to specify the message identifier of the message that generated the acknowledgment or report. The application can then look at the CorrelationId property to find the message ID of the original message.
Destination SymmetricKey	A zero-length array of bytes	An array of type 8-bit unsigned integer, which specifies the destination symmetric key, used to encrypt the message.
DigitalSignature	A zero-length array of bytes	An array of type 8-bit unsigned integer, which specifies the Message Queuing 1.0 digital signature, used to authenticate the message.
EncryptionAlgorithm	Encryption Algorithm.RC2	One of the EncryptionAlgorithm values used to encrypt the message body of a private message.
Extension	A zero-length array of bytes	The Extension property is used to pass any application-specific information along with the message (e.g., a custom object). An array of 8-bit unsigned integers provides additional, application-defined information associated with the message.

continued

Table 2-7. Message Properties (continued)

PROPERTY	INITIAL VALUE (DEFAULT VALUE)	DESCRIPTION
Formatter	XmlMessageFormatter	The IMessageFormatter that produces a stream to be written to the message body.
HashAlgorithm	HashAlgorithm.MD5	One of the HashAlgorithm values that identify the hashing algorithm Message Queuing uses when authenticating messages.
Label	" " (empty string)	The label of the message.
Priority	MessagePriority. Normal	Priority affects how Message Queuing handles the message while it is in route, as well as its place in the queue. High-priority messages are given preference during routing, and inserted toward the front of the queue. Messages of equal priority are placed in the queue according to their arrival time. Priority can only be set for nontransactional messages, because transactional messages are always delivered in order, and therefore their Priority for transactional message is automatically set to 0.
Recoverable	false	Recoverable messages are stored on the disk in memory-mapped files, and thus can survive machine reboots or crashes. Until the message is received or is delivered to another computer, the message is stored on the disk.
ResponseQueue	A null reference (Nothing)	The MessageQueue to which application-generated response messages are returned. The default is a null reference (in Visual Basic, Nothing). Messages returned to the response queue are application-defined. That is, the application defines the content of the messages and action to take upon receipt.
SenderCertificate	A zero-length array of bytes	Specifies the security certificate used to authenticate messages.

Table 2-7. Message Properties (continued)

PROPERTY	INITIAL VALUE (DEFAULT VALUE)	DESCRIPTION
TimeToBeReceived	Message.Infinite Timeout	The time limit, in seconds, for the message to be retrieved from the target queue. The default is InfiniteTimeout. If the TimeToBeReceived interval expires before the message is removed from the queue, Message Queuing discards the message and sends it to the dead-letter queue if the message's UseDeadLetterQueue property is set to true. Message Queuing can also send a negative acknowledgment message to the sending application via the administration queue if the message's AcknowledgeType property is set accordingly and the message is not retrieved before the timeout expires.
TimeToReachQueue	Message.Infinite Timeout	Gets or sets the time limit for the message to reach the queue. If the TimeToReachQueue interval expires before the message reaches its destination, Message Queuing discards the message and sends it to the dead-letter queue if the message's UseDeadLetterQueue property is set to true.
TransactionStatus Queue	A null reference (Nothing)	Gets the transaction status queue on the source computer. This property is only used by connector applications when they receive transactional messages sent to a foreign queue. Connector applications use the transaction status queue to send positive (read receipt) or negative acknowledgment messages back to the sending application. The transaction status queue should receive these acknowledgments even if the sending application does not request other acknowledgments.

continued

Table 2-7. Message Properties (continued)

PROPERTY	INITIAL VALUE (DEFAULT VALUE)	DESCRIPTION
UseAuthentication	false	Gets or sets a value indicating whether a message must be authenticated. It is not possible to look at the properties of a message and determine whether a message failed authentication. Messages that fail authentication are discarded and are not delivered to the queue. Discarded messages are then sent to the dead-letter queues and a negative acknowledgement is sent to the administration queue.
UseDeadLetterQueue	false	Gets or sets a value indicating whether a copy of an undeliverable message should be sent to a dead-letter queue. When you store messages in a dead-letter queue, clear the queue periodically to remove messages that are no longer needed.
UseEncryption	false	Gets or sets a value indicating whether to encrypt messages.
UseJournalQueue	false	Gets or sets a value indicating whether a copy of the message should be kept in a machine journal on the originating computer. When you store messages in a journal queue, clear the queue periodically to remove messages that are no longer needed.
UseTracing	false	Gets or sets a value indicating whether to trace a message as it moves toward its destination queue. When a message is sent with tracing enabled, a report message is generated and sent to the system report queue each time the message passes through a Message Queuing routing server. Report queues are not limited to Message Queuing–generated report messages. Application-generated messages can be sent to report queues as well.

When sending a complex message, you can create an instance of the Message class and set the properties to the desired values to exercise more control over the message to be sent. The Body property of the message contains the content of the message.

The following example shows the use of the Message class for sending an Order object to the queue:

```
using System;
using System.Messaging;

namespace ComplexMessage
{
  [Serializable]
  public class Order
  {
    public String OrderId;
    public String CustomerName;
    public String CustomerLastName;
    public String OrderDate;
    public Order()
    {
      this.OrderDate = DateTime.Now.ToString();
    }
  }
    public class ComplexMessage
    {
      public static void Main(string[] args)
      {
        if(args.Length == 1)
        {
          try
          {
            if(!MessageQueue.Exists(args[0]))
            {
              MessageQueue.Create(args[0]);
              Console.WriteLine("Queue was not registered,"
                              + "so new queue created for you");
            }
            //Create an instance of the MessageQueue
            MessageQueue q = new MessageQueue(args[0]);
```

```
                    //Create a new BinaryMessageFormatter
                    IMessageFormatter formatter =
                    new BinaryMessageFormatter();
                    //Create a new Order object
                    Order o = new Order();
                    o.OrderId = System.Guid.NewGuid().ToString();
                    o.CustomerName = "Tejaswi";
                    o.CustomerLastName = "Redkar";
                    //Create an instance of the Message
                    System.Messaging.Message msg1
                    = new System.Messaging.Message();
                    msg1.Body = o;
                    msg1.Priority = MessagePriority.Highest;
                    msg1.Label = "Complex Message";
                    msg1.Recoverable = true;
                    msg1.Formatter = formatter;
                    //Send the message
                    q.Send(msg1);
                    Console.WriteLine("Message sent successfully");
                    Console.WriteLine("Waiting for Response.....");
                    //Receive the message
                    Message orderMsg = q.Receive(new TimeSpan(0, 0, 10));
                    orderMsg.Formatter = formatter;
                    Order oReceive = (Order)orderMsg.Body;
                    Console.WriteLine("Received Order Message");
                    Console.WriteLine("OrderId = "+ oReceive.OrderId);
                    Console.WriteLine("OrderDate = " + oReceive.OrderDate);
                    Console.WriteLine("First Name = "+ oReceive.CustomerName);
                    Console.WriteLine("Last Name = "
                                    + oReceive.CustomerLastName);
                }
            catch(Exception ex)
            {
                Console.WriteLine(ex.Message);
            }
        }
        else
        {
            Console.WriteLine("Usage:ComplexMessage "
                            + "[Path of the queue]");
```

```
                }
            }

        }
}
```

In the preceding example, we have an Order class that is marked as Serializable. As discussed earlier, every class sent to the queue must be Serializable. The Order class has four fields: OrderId, CustomerName, CustomerLastName, and OrderDate. The OrderDate is assigned to the current time in the constructor of the Order class. In the main function, we accept the path of the queue as the user input and create a reference to the MessageQueue object. After creating the BinaryMessageFormatter instance, we create the Order object and set its fields to appropriate values. We create an instance of the Message object and pass the Order object to the Body property of the message. Then we set the Priority of the message to the highest level. Then, we also set the message to be Recoverable so that the message survives reboots and system crashes. We also set the Formatter property of the message to the BinaryMessageFormatter. Once we have set all the required properties of the message, we just send the message by passing to the Send() method. The BinaryMessageFormatter takes care of serializing the object. Next, we receive the same message from the queue by calling the Receive() method. Before accessing the Body property of the message, we have to set the Formatter for the message, as the Read() method of the message formatter will be called when we call the Body property of the message. Finally we print the results to the console. To run the preceding example, type the following at the command prompt:

```
> complexmessage .\private$\myfirstq
```

Sending and Receiving Files

Message Queuing can be used to send and receive files using BinaryMessageFormatter. BinaryMessageFormatter serializes objects and object graphs into serialized streams, using binary format. The message body of the serialized object(s) is not human readable as in XmlMessageFormatter, but has a higher throughput than the XmlMessageFormatter class. BinaryMessageFormatter does not allow for loosely coupled messaging as does the XmlMessageFormatter. This means that the version of the object serialized by the sender application must match the version of the object deserialized by the receiver application. The following listing shows the use of BinaryMessageFormatter in sending a file to MSMQ:

```
FileInfo fInfo = new FileInfo("Thermostat.xml");
FileStream fStream = fInfo.OpenRead();
byte[] b = new byte[fStream.Length];
fStream.Read(b, 0, b.Length);
MemoryStream mem =
  new MemoryStream(b, 0, b.Length, false);
//Create an instance of the MessageQueue
MessageQueue q = new MessageQueue
  (args[0]);
//Create a new BinaryMessageFormatter
IMessageFormatter formatter =
  new BinaryMessageFormatter();
//Create an instance of the Message
System.Messaging.Message msg1
  = new System.Messaging.Message(mem, formatter);
//Set the Label of the
//Message to the file name
msg1.Label = fInfo.Name;
//Send the message
q.Send(msg1);
```

In the preceding listing, we open the file Thermostat.xml and open the file for read access only by using the OpenRead() method of the FileInfo class. The OpenRead() method returns a FileStream object associated with the file. Then, we create a byte array and read the contents of the file into a byte array. We then create an instance of a MemoryStream by passing the byte array, to store the contents of the file. The false parameter of the MemoryStream constructor indicates that the MemoryStream object does not support writing.

NOTE MemoryStream *inherits from the* Stream *class and has memory as its backing store.*

After creating an instance of the MessageQueue and BinaryMessageFormatter classes, we create an instance of the System.Messaging.Message class and pass the

MemoryStream as the body of the message and BinaryMessageFormatter as the formatter for the body. Under the hood, BinaryMessageFormatter serializes the entire MemoryStream into the body of the message. Then, we set the label of the message to the name of the file to identify it visually from the MMC. Finally, we send the message object to the queue by calling the Send() method of the MessageQueue class. In the preceding example, we could have sent the FileStream object directly as the body of the message instead of the MemoryStream object, but the FileStream object is not serializable whereas the MemoryStream object is. So, if you try to send a FileStream object, a System.Runtime.Serialization.SerializationException will be thrown complaining that the System.IO.FileStream is not marked as Serializable. To run the sample, type the following at the command prompt:

```
>FileSender .\private$\fileq
```

Make sure that the Thermostat.xml file is in the same directory as the FileSender.exe executable.

Now that we have the message sitting in the queue, we need to write a receiver to receive the message containing the file, and then re-create the file locally to the receiver. The following listing shows the receiver for receiving the file from the queue:

```
//Create an instance of the MessageQueue
MessageQueue q = new MessageQueue
  (args[0]);
//Receive the file with a timeout of 3 seconds
System.Messaging.Message m =
  q.Receive(new TimeSpan(0, 0, 3));
m.Formatter = new BinaryMessageFormatter();
MemoryStream mem = (MemoryStream)m.Body;
FileStream fStream =
  new FileStream(m.Label,
  FileMode.Create, FileAccess.ReadWrite);
mem.WriteTo(fStream);
mem.Close();
fStream.Close();
```

In the preceding listing, we follow exactly the reverse procedure in comparison with the FileSender application. We create an instance of the MessageQueue class and then receive the message from the queue by calling the Receive()

method with a timeout value of three seconds. The timeout value prevents the Receive() method from blocking indefinitely and waits for the message to arrive in the queue. After the message is received, we assign the BinaryMessageFormatter to the message. In the FileSender application, we sent a MemoryStream containing the contents of the Thermostat.xml file as the body of the message. So, we must receive a MemoryStream from the body of the message. We cast the body of the message to a MemoryStream object. We also know that the Label of the message was set to the name of the file. So, we create a FileStream object with the Label of the message (though not necessary) as the name of the file, file mode set to Create, and access set to ReadWrite. Then we write the contents of the MemoryStream to the FileStream by calling the WriteTo() method of the MemoryStream. Finally, we close the MemoryStream and the FileStream. To run the sample, type the following at the command prompt:

```
>FileReceiver .\private$\fileq
```

After the FileReceiver.exe completes its execution, a file named Thermostat.xml will be created in the same directory as FileReceiver.exe. The contents of the created Thermostat.xml file should match the contents of the Thermostat.xml file sent by the FileSender application.

Interoperating with COM Objects

ActiveXMessageFormatter is used for serializing primitive data types and COM objects that implement the IPersistStream OLE interface. This formatter is interoperable with applications written in the MSMQ COM API or the MSMQ C API. This means that we can have a Visual Basic 6.0 application as a message sender and a .NET message receiver (or vice versa), provided the .NET message receiver uses the ActiveXMessageFormatter to deserialize the message. The ActiveXMessageFormatter is good for protecting the existing investment in MSMQ COM components. Figure 2-12 describes a typical interoperability scenario where a Visual Basic 6.0 sends a Thermostat COM object to the queue and a .NET application receives it.

NOTE *The Runtime Callable Wrapper, or RCW, is the glue between unmanaged and managed code. RCW is responsible for handling all interactions between .NET components and COM/ActiveX components.*

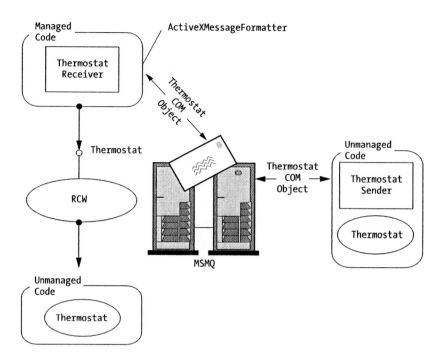

Figure 2-12. Sending the COM object

For the .NET application to interoperate with a COM/ActiveX DLL, we have to first create a wrapper (RCW) using either Visual Studio .NET or tlbimp.exe.

To create an RCW for a COM/ActiveX DLL using Visual Studio. NET, follow these steps:

1. Register the COM/ActiveX DLL using regsvr32.exe.

2. From the Project menu, select References.

3. Select the COM tab.

4. Select the Type Library from the list or browse to the DLL/ type library.

5. Click OK.

To Create an RCW for a COM/ActiveX DLL Using tlbimp.exe

Type Library Importer, or tlbimp.exe, is a command-line tool for creating an RCW for a COM/ActiveX DLL. Here's how you'd use tlbimp.exe:

```
>tlbimp VBThermostat.dll /out:NETVBThermostat.dll
```

The /out: switch is used to specify the name of the RCW. If /out: is not specified, an RCW with the same name as the original DLL is created and may cause confusion.

To demonstrate interoperability, let's first develop a Visual Basic 6.0 Thermostat object that is persistable. To make an object persistable, we have to set the Persistable property of the ActiveX DLL to Persistable, as shown in Figure 2-13.

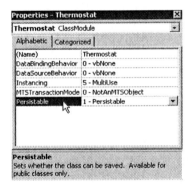

Figure 2-13. The ActiveX Persistable *property*

The Thermostat Visual Basic 6.0 class module that we'll develop has three properties: ID, CurrentTemperature, and SetPoint. The following listing shows the code for Thermostat class module:

```
Option Explicit
Private tID As String
Private CurrTemp As Double
Private SetPt As Double
Public Property Get ID() As String
    ID = tID
End Property
```

```
Public Property Let ID(ByVal ThermostatID As String)
    tID = ThermostatID
End Property
Public Property Get CurrentTemperature() As Double
    CurrentTemperature = CurrTemp
End Property
Public Property Let CurrentTemperature(ByVal temperature As Double)
    CurrTemp = temperature
End Property
Public Property Get SetPoint() As Double
    SetPoint = SetPt
End Property
Public Property Let SetPoint(ByVal TemperatureSetPoint As Double)
    SetPt = TemperatureSetPoint
End Property
Private Sub Class_ReadProperties(PropBag As PropertyBag)
  ID = PropBag.ReadProperty("ID", "")
  CurrTemp = PropBag.ReadProperty("CurrTemp", "")
  SetPt = PropBag.ReadProperty("SetPt", "")
End Sub
Private Sub Class_WriteProperties(PropBag As PropertyBag)
  PropBag.WriteProperty "ID", ID
  PropBag.WriteProperty "CurrTemp", CurrTemp
  PropBag.WriteProperty "SetPt", SetPt
End Sub
```

The name of the DLL that is generated by compiling the previous listing is named VBThermostat.dll. Once we have a persistable ActiveX object, we should register it using regsvr32.exe. We can now develop a Visual Basic 6.0 application to create and send the object to the queue. For this, we need to know the MSMQ COM API, which is significantly different than the System.Messaging API. (We discuss the MSMQ COM API in later chapters.) The following listing shows the code snippet that creates an instance of the Thermostat object and sends it to the queue:

```
Private Sub cmdSendThermostat_Click()
On Error GoTo SendError
  Dim qi As MSMQQueueInfo
  Set qi = New MSMQQueueInfo
  qi.PathName = txtQueuePath.Text
  Dim q As MSMQQueue
  Set q = qi.Open(MQ_SEND_ACCESS, MQ_DENY_NONE)
```

```
    Dim msg As MSMQMessage
    Set msg = New MSMQMessage
    Dim Thermo As Thermostat
    Set Thermo = New Thermostat
    Thermo.Id = txtID.Text
    Thermo.CurrentTemperature = txtCurrTemp.Text
    Thermo.SetPoint = txtSetPt.Text
    msg.Body = Thermo
    msg.Send q
Exit Sub
SendError:
    MsgBox "Error sending Thermostat object to the queue."
    Exit Sub
End Sub
```

In the previous listing, we create a new MSMQQueueInfo reference and then set the PathName property of the queue to the value specified in the TextBox by the user. We then open the MSMQQueue by calling the Open() method of the MSMQQueueInfo with a send access. The MQ_DENY_NONE parameter specifies that we are opening the queue with a nonexclusive access. Now that we have opened the queue successfully, we create a new MSMQMessage object, and then create a new Thermostat object and set its properties to the values specified by the user. Then, we set the Body property of the MSMQMessage to the Thermostat object. Finally, we send the MSMQMessage by calling the Send() method of the MSMQMessage class.

NOTE *Do not forget to add reference to the VBThermostat.dll using the References command from the Project menu in Visual Basic 6.0 before you compile.*

Figure 2-14 shows the user interface for running our application.

The next step is to develop a message receiver in .NET. Before we start coding, we need to create an RCW for the VBThermostat.dll so that we can use it from our .NET application. The easiest way to create the RCW is to add a reference to VBThermostat.dll in Visual Studio .NET. Once the RCW is created, it should be visible as VBThermostat in the References section of the Solution Explorer. Figure 2-15 shows the Object Browser view of the Thermostat RCW.

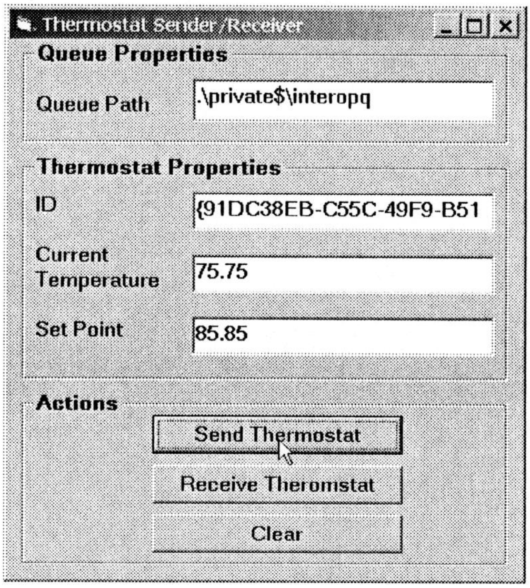

Figure 2-14. Sending the Thermostat *object*

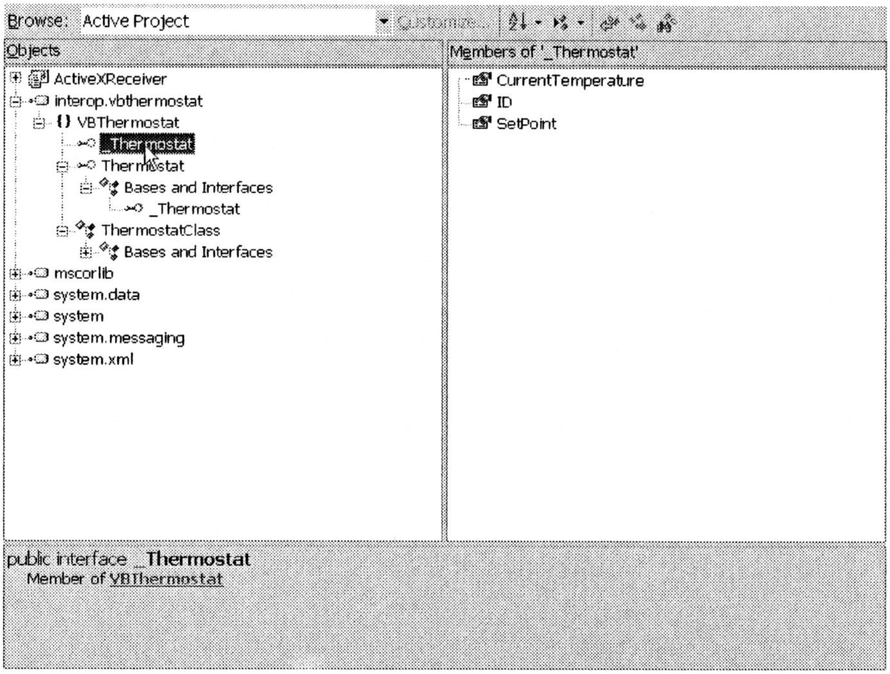

Figure 2-15. The Thermostat RCW in the Object Browser

The following listing shows the code for receiving the `Thermostat` object from the queue:

```
//Create an instance of the MessageQueue
MessageQueue q = new MessageQueue
  (args[0]);
//Receive the file with a timeout of 3 seconds
System.Messaging.Message m1 =
  q.Receive(new TimeSpan(0, 0, 3));
//Set the Formatter to ActiveXFormatter
m1.Formatter = new ActiveXMessageFormatter();
//Cast the Body to the ThermostatClass
VBThermostat.ThermostatClass thermostat =
  (VBThermostat.ThermostatClass)m1.Body;
Console.WriteLine("Received Thermostat");
PrintThermostat(thermostat);
//Now change the thermostat and send it back
thermostat.ID = System.Guid.NewGuid().ToString();
thermostat.CurrentTemperature = 80.5;
thermostat.SetPoint = 70.5;
System.Messaging.Message m2 =
  new System.Messaging.Message(thermostat);
m2.Formatter = new ActiveXMessageFormatter();
q.Send(m2);
```

In the previous listing, we create an instance of the `MessageQueue` that stores the `Thermostat` objects sent by the Visual Basic 6.0 ActiveXSender application. Then, we call `Receive()` on the `MessageQueue` object to receive the `System.Messaging.Message` object. Now we know that we have the `Thermostat` in the body of the `System.Messaging.Message` object. To retrieve the `Thermostat`, we have to first specify the formatter for deserializing it. So, we specify `ActiveXMessageFormatter` as the formatter for deserializing the body of the message. After specifying the formatter, we can safely cast the body of the message to the `ThermostatClass` object. After casting, we change the properties of the `ThermostatClass` and send it back to the same queue to see if reverse interoperability works. Here are the steps to run the sample:

1. Start the ActiveXSender.exe Visual Basic 6.0 application.

2. Click the Send Thermostat button.

3. Run the ActiveXReceiver.exe .NET application from the command prompt with the following parameters: `>ActiveXReceiver .\private$\interopq`.

4. Click the Clear button on the ActiveXSender.exe application.

5. Click the Receive Thermostat button to check reverse interoperability with .NET.

 NOTE *If the* Persistable *object implements the* IPersistStreamInit *interface instead of the* IPersistStream *interface, the* public static void InitStreamedObject(object streamedObject); *method should be used to help initialize the ActiveX/COM object. The* streamedObject *parameter represents the ActiveX/COM object to be initialized.*

Using BodyStream

In the previous sections, we were using the Body property of the System.Messaging.Message class to send messages to the queue. When we set the Body property of a System.Messaging.Message, the contents of the body are serialized in the BodyStream property of the System.Messaging.Message. It is possible to set the BodyStream property directly instead of the Body property. This is particularly useful when you need more control over serialization of the object.

In this section, you'll learn how to use the BodyStream along with System.Xml.Serialization.XmlSerializer class to control the serialization of a System.Data.DataSet object. The XmlMessageFormatter uses XmlSerializer to serialize an object into XML format. In this section, we bypass the XmlMessageFormatter and serialize the object directly to the BodyStream of the Message. One of the benefits of bypassing the XmlMessageFormatter is that we can control the character encoding of the DataSet by using a System.Xml.XmlTextWriter. The following listing shows the code to serialize a DataSet into the BodyStream property of the System.Messaging.Message object:

```
using System;
using System.Messaging;
using System.Xml;
using System.Data;
using System.Xml.Serialization;
using System.Text;

class SerializeDataSet
{
  public static void Main(string[] args)
```

```
{
  if(args.Length == 1)
  {
    try
    {
      if(!MessageQueue.Exists(args[0]))
      {
        MessageQueue.Create(args[0]);
        Console.WriteLine("Queue was not registered,"+
          "so new queue created for you");
      }
      DataSet ds = new DataSet("ThermostatDataSet");
      ds.ReadXml("Thermostat.xml");
      //Create an instance of the MessageQueue
      MessageQueue q = new MessageQueue
        (args[0]);
      //Create an instance of the Message
      System.Messaging.Message msg1
        = new System.Messaging.Message();
      //Set the Label of the Message
      //to the formatter name
      msg1.Label = "XmlSerializer DataSet Message";
      //Create an XmlSerializer
      XmlSerializer ser = new XmlSerializer
        ( typeof(DataSet) );
      //Create an XmlTextWriter with BodyStream
      // as its storage stream and UTF-8 encoding.
      XmlTextWriter writer = new XmlTextWriter
        ( msg1.BodyStream, Encoding.UTF8);
      //Serialize the DataSet to the XmlTextWriter
      // and hence to the BodyStream.
      ser.Serialize( writer, ds );
      //Send the message
      q.Send(msg1);
      Console.WriteLine("XmlSerialized DataSet "
        + "Message sent successfully");
    }
    catch(Exception ex)
    {
      Console.WriteLine
        ("Exception " + ex.StackTrace);
    }
  }
```

```
    else
    {
      Console.WriteLine
        ("Usage:SerializeDataSet [Path of the queue]");
    }
  }
}
```

In the preceding listing, initially we create an instance of the MessageQueue and then the Message. Then, we create an instance of a DataSet class and name it **ThermostatDataSet**. Next, we read the Thermostat.xml into the DataSet. To serialize a DataSet using the XmlSerializer, we have to initialize the XmlSerializer with the Type DataSet. XmlSerializer needs a Stream, XmlWriter, or TextWriter. We could pass the BodyStream of the Message to the XmlSerializer, but this won't allow us to control the character encoding of the DataSet. XmlTextWriter, which inherits from the XmlWriter, gives us an option to specify the character encoding. So, we create an instance of the XmlTextWriter with the BodyStream of the message as its storage backing and the character encoding of UTF-8. The Encoding class in the System.Text namespace contains different types of encoding.

Now that we've set up the XmlTextWriter, we call the Serialize() method on the XmlSerializer and pass XmlTextWriter and the ThermostatDataSet as its parameters. The Serialize() method will serialize the ThermostatDataSet into XML and pass it to the XmlTextWriter for writing to a storage stream. Because we have specified the BodyStream of the message as the storage backing for our XmlTextWriter, the XmlTextWriter writes the serialized XML to the BodyStream of the message. Finally, we send the message to the queue. When the character encoding of the serialized DataSet is specified as UTF-8, the serialized XML will have UTF-8 in the XML start tag, like <?xml version="1.0" encoding="utf-8"?>.

Now, we need a message receiver that will receive the ThermostatDataSet message and deserialize it correctly. Because we have to consider the character encoding of the serialized DataSet while deserializing, we have to deserialize the BodyStream directly by bypassing the XmlMessageFormatter. The following listing shows the code required for deserializing the message from BodyStream:

```
using System;
using System.Messaging;
using System.Xml;
using System.Data;
using System.Xml.Serialization;
using System.Text;
using System.IO;
```

```
class DeserializeDataSet
{
  public static void Main(string[] args)
  {
    if(args.Length == 1)
    {
      try
      {
        //Create an instance of the MessageQueue
        MessageQueue q = new MessageQueue
          (args[0]);
        //Receive DataSet with a timeout of 3 seconds
        System.Messaging.Message m =
          q.Receive(new TimeSpan(0, 0, 3));
        //Create an XmlSerializer
        XmlSerializer ser = new XmlSerializer
          ( typeof(DataSet) );
        //Deserialize the DataSet
        DataSet ds = (DataSet)ser.Deserialize
          (m.BodyStream);
        Console.WriteLine(ds.GetXml());
      }
      catch(Exception ex)
      {
        Console.WriteLine
          ("Exception " + ex.Message);
      }
    }
    else
    {
      Console.WriteLine
        ("Usage:DeserializeDataSet [Path of the queue]");
    }
  }
}
```

This listing is the reverse process of the SerializeDataSet application. First, we initialize the queue and receive the message. We then initialize the XmlSerializer with DataSet Type. Deserializing the DataSet is much easier since the XmlSerializer has a Deserialize() method that accepts any System.IO.Stream as its parameter. The BodyStream inherits from the System.IO.Stream abstract class. So, we can directly pass the BodyStream property to the Deserialize() method. The return value of this method is an object, and we need to cast it to the DataSet Type. Finally, we print the XML contents of the DataSet to the console. To exercise the character encoding, a good test would be to specify some Unicode characters like Ã© in the ID property of the Thermostat.xml file and play around with the character encoding in the System.Text.Encoding class while sending the message.

We did not have to set the Formatter property of the received message to XmlMessageFormatter because we bypassed the formatter altogether by directly deserializing the BodyStream.

To run the sample listings, follow these steps:

1. Run >SerializeDataSet .\private$\myfirstq at the command prompt to send the message.

2. Run >DeserializeDataSet .\private$\myfirstq at the command prompt to see the message received.

Custom Formatters (SoapMessageFormatter)

System.Messaging also gives you the liberty to implement your own message formatter. Sometimes you might need to write your own message formatter—for example, when dealing with legacy applications to send messages to the queue in some proprietary format, you may have to write a custom formatter to deserialize the legacy message. The rules for implementing message formatters are as follows:

- All message formatters must implement the IMessageFormatter interface.

- The message formatter must implement the Write() method of the IMessageFormatter interface for serializing the object into the body of the message.

- The message formatter must implement the Read() method of the IMessageFormatter interface for deserializing the object from the body of the message.

- The message formatter must implement the CanRead() method of the IMessageFormatter interface and return a Boolean value indicating whether the formatter can deserialize the object from the body of the message.

- As the IMessageFormatter interface implements the ICloneable interface, the message formatter must also implement the Clone() method of the ICloneable interface.

In this section, we implement a custom formatter that will serialize any serializable object into SOAP (Simple Object Access Protocol) format. As a result, we will be able to send and receive SOAP messages between applications using Message Queuing. The SOAP format is widely used in web services and is gaining popularity due to its communication protocol independence. SOAP messages can be sent using any communication medium of choice (e.g., HTTP, SMTP, IIOP). In this section, we use Message Queuing as our communication medium to send SOAP messages. For this purpose, we use the SoapFormatter from the System.Runtime.Serialization.Formatters.Soap namespace. The SoapFormatter exposes an instance method called Serialize(); when invoked it serializes an object to any stream. The corresponding method Deserialize() allows us to reconstruct a stateful .NET type from the stream by passing the object to be serialized and the Stream where the serialized object will be written. In this case, we can pass the BodyStream of the Message object as the Stream to write the serialized object to. Similarly, to deserialize the object, we need to call the Deserialize() method by passing the BodyStream as the Stream containing the data to be serialized. The following example shows the implementation of the SoapMessageFormatter class:

```csharp
using System;
using System.Messaging;
using System.IO;
using System.Runtime.Serialization.Formatters.Soap;

namespace MyFormatters
  {
    [Serializable]
    public class SoapMessageFormatter : IMessageFormatter
    {
      public SoapMessageFormatter()
        {

        }
      public object Clone ()
      {
        return this.MemberwiseClone();
      }

    public bool CanRead (Message message)
    {
      bool isValid = false;
      try
      {
        SoapFormatter soap = new SoapFormatter();
```

```
      object obj = soap.Deserialize(message.BodyStream);
      if(obj != null)
        return true;
    }
    catch(Exception)
    {
      isValid = true;
    }

    return isValid;
  }

  public object Read (Message message)
  {
    try
    {
      SoapFormatter soap = new SoapFormatter();
      return soap.Deserialize(message.BodyStream);
    }
    catch(Exception ex)
    {
      throw ex;
    }
  }

  public void Write (Message message,
    object obj)
  {
    try
    {
      SoapFormatter soap = new SoapFormatter();
      message.BodyStream = new MemoryStream();
      soap.Serialize(message.BodyStream,
        obj);

    }
    catch(Exception ex)
    {
      throw ex;
    }

  }
 }
}
```

Here, we implement the Read(), Write(), and CanRead() methods of the IMessageFormatter class. In the Write() method we call the Serialize() method of the SoapFormatter object and pass it the object to serialize to the BodyStream of the message. In the Read() method, we call the Deserialize() method of the SoapFormatter object and return the deserialized object back to the application. Thus, now we can develop applications that can exchange SOAP messages using MSMQ.

NOTE *The* Write() *method of the message formatter is called implicitly, after the* Send() *method of the* MessageQueue *is called. The* Read() *method of the message formatter is called implicitly, after the* Body *property of the* Message *object is accessed.*

The following example shows how to use the SoapMessageFormatter when sending and receiving messages:

```
//Create a new SoapMessageFormatter
IMessageFormatter formatter =
  new SoapMessageFormatter();

//Create a new Order object
Order o = new Order();
o.OrderId = System.Guid.NewGuid().ToString();
o.CustomerName = "Aaryan";
o.CustomerLastName = "Redkar";
//Create an instance of the Message
System.Messaging.Message msg1 = new System.Messaging.Message
                                    (o, formatter);
//Send the message
q.Send(msg1);
//Receive the Message
Message orderMsg = q.Receive(new TimeSpan(0, 0, 10));
orderMsg.Formatter = formatter;
Order oReceive = (Order)orderMsg.Body;
```

In this example, we initialize the SoapMessageFormatter and then just pass the formatter object to the constructor of the Message class. Then, we send the Order object using the Send() method. The Write() method of the SoapFormatter is called implicitly by the .NET Framework, after we call the Send() method. After we receive the message from the queue, we set the Formatter property of the received message to the SoapFormatter object.

The output of the SoapMessageApplication is shown in Figure 2-16.

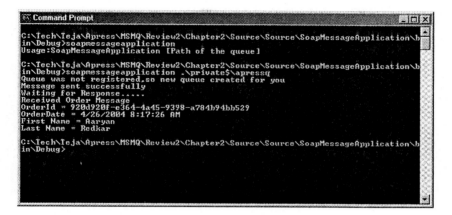

Figure 2-16. The SoapFormatter console application

Receiving Messages Asynchronously

Up to this point we've been calling the Receive() method of the MessageQueue class on-demand to receive the message from the queue. This type of method call, in which you call the Receive() method on the MessageQueue and wait for the message to be retrieved from the queue, is called a *synchronous* approach. The synchronous approach is not very scalable since the thread running the Receive() method blocks and, if there is a timeout specified, quits only after the timeout has been reached and the message has still not arrived in the queue. In a real-world application, you would also have to include a timer in the application to periodically check the queue for new messages. Instead, it would be good if Message Queuing notified you if there is a new message in the queue. This is called an *asynchronous*, or *event-based*, approach. You register the application as an event handler with the Message Queuing and give Message Queuing a delegate to be called when a message arrives in the queue. Then, you call the BeginReceive() method to start the asynchronous processing. When the message arrives in the queue, Message Queuing calls the delegate of your application. From the parameters of the delegate, you get the MessageQueue and retrieve the message from the queue. In asynchronous messaging the application is not tied up and can continue its usual process while this task is being completed. In this type of message interaction, it works on the task without waiting for a result. The following example shows the program for receiving messages asynchronously:

```
using System;
using System.Messaging;
using System.Threading;
```

```
class AsyncReceiver
{
  private System.Messaging.MessageQueue messageQ;
  private static bool STOPPED = true;
  public AsyncReceiver(String path_of_the_queue)
  {
    this.messageQ = new MessageQueue(path_of_the_queue);
    //Create the Event Handler
    this.messageQ.ReceiveCompleted +=
    new System.Messaging.ReceiveCompletedEventHandler
    (this.messageQ_ReceiveCompleted);
    //Add a Formatter
    messageQ.Formatter = new XmlMessageFormatter
                         (new String[]{"System.String"});
    //Start receiving the message
    messageQ.BeginReceive(new TimeSpan(0,0,3));

  }

  public void messageQ_ReceiveCompleted(object source,
    System.Messaging.ReceiveCompletedEventArgs asyncResult)
  {
    MessageQueue tempMessageQ = null;
    try
    {
      // Connect to the queue.
      tempMessageQ = (MessageQueue)source;
      // End the asynchronous receive operation.
      System.Messaging.Message m =
        tempMessageQ.EndReceive(asyncResult.AsyncResult);
      // Process the message here.
      Console.WriteLine();
      Console.WriteLine("*******************");
      Console.WriteLine(m.Body.ToString());
      Console.WriteLine("*******************");
      Console.WriteLine();

    }
    catch(MessageQueueException)
    {

    }
```

```
    catch(Exception ex)
    {
      Console.WriteLine(ex.Message);
    }
    finally
    {
      //Call this to continue processing
      this.messageQ.BeginReceive(new TimeSpan(0,0,3));
    }
  }

  static void WaitThread()
  {
    try
    {
      while(!STOPPED)
      {
        //Sleep for 5 seconds
        Thread.Sleep(5 * 1000);
      }
      STOPPED = true;
    }
    catch(Exception)
    {}
  }

  [STAThread]
  static void Main(string[] args)
  {
    if(args.Length == 1)
    {
      if(!MessageQueue.Exists(args[0]))
      {
        MessageQueue.Create(args[0]);
        Console.WriteLine("Queue was not registered,"
          + "so new queue created for you");
      }
      AsyncReceiver ml =
        new AsyncReceiver(args[0]);
      Thread t =
        new Thread(
        new ThreadStart(AsyncReceiver.WaitThread));
```

```
        STOPPED = false;
        t.Start();
        Console.WriteLine
          ("Started Async Receiver Application");
            t.Join();


    }
    else
      Console.WriteLine
        ("Usage: AsynchronousReceive.exe [Path of the MSMQ]");


  }
}
```

- Get a reference to the MessageQueue object. We create a new MessageQueue object by passing in the path of the queue to the constructor.

  ```
  MessageQueue messageQ = new MessageQueue(path_of_the_queue);
  ```

- Create an event handler on the ReceiveCompleted event and pass a delegate that will receive the callback events:

  ```
  messageQ.ReceiveCompleted += new
  ReceiveCompletedEventHandler (messageQ _ReceiveCompleted);
  ```

- The delegate messageQ _Received is automatically called when a new message arrives in the queue. The method signature of the delegate is

  ```
  public static void messageQ _ReceiveCompleted
  (Object sender, ReceiveCompletedEventArgs args){}
  ```

- Call the MessageQueue's BeginReceive() method to start listening for messages. TIMEOUT indicates the time to wait for a message to become available:

  ```
  messageQ.BeginReceive (TIMEOUT);
  ```

- In the delegate method messageQ _ReceiveCompleted, the sender parameter should be cast to the MessageQueue object:

```
MessageQueue tempMessageQ = (MessageQueue)sender;
```

- Call the EndReceive() method of the MessageQueue to get a reference to the System.Messaging.Message object:

```
System.Messaging.Message message =
MessagemqTemp.EndReceive(args.AsyncResult);
```

- Call the BeginReceive() method of the messageQ object to start the asynchronous processing again. If the BeginReceive() method is not called, the processing stops after the delegate function returns:

```
messageQ.BeginReceive (TIMEOUT);
```

To run the preceding example, type the following at the command prompt:

```
>asynchronousreceive .\private$\myfirstq
```

Peeking Messages

Peeking is the process of reading messages from the queue without removing them. Receiving the message from the queue removes the message from the queue. The MessageQueue class has a Peek() method that returns a copy of the first message from the queue without removing it from the queue. Consecutive calls to the Peek() method return the same message unless another application receives it or a message with a higher priority is inserted into the queue. The following shows how to use the Peek() method:

```
MessageQueue q = new MessageQueue(@".\private$\apressq");
Message msg = q.Peek (new TimeSpan(0, 0, 3));
msg.Formatter = new XmlMessageFormatter(new Type[]{typeof(System.String)});
String s = (String) msg.Body;
```

Like the Receive() method, the peek operation can also be carried out asynchronously. Similar to the BeginReceive() and EndReceive() method calls, there are BeginPeek() and EndPeek() methods in the MessageQueue class. Another method in the `MessageQueue` class that supports peek operation is `GetAllMessages()`, as shown here:

```
public Message[] GetAllMessages();
```

This method returns a static snapshot of all the messages from the queue. This method, like other peek operations, does not remove messages from the queue:

```
MessageQueue mq = new MessageQueue(@".\private$\apressq");
Message[] messages =mq.GetAllMessages();
```

NOTE *If you want to delete all the messages after calling* `GetAllMessages()`, *you might call the* `Purge()` *operation. But the disadvantages of using this method are that the messages that have arrived between the* `GetAllMessages()` *and the* `Purge()` *methods will also be deleted by* `Purge()`, *and the deleted messages will not appear in the journal queue even if the journaling for that queue is enabled. So, it is recommended you call* `Receive()` *for each message returned by calling* `GetAllMessages()`.

Message Timeouts

As you've seen, when a message is sent to a queue it remains in the queue until a receiver receives it or the queue is purged. But what if the message is time sensitive and the receiver does not receive the message on time? An example is a stock quote application that sends stock quotes to a queue every two minutes. The receiver application receives the quotes and displays them to the user. Suddenly, the receiver application machine crashes or is temporarily unreachable for about an hour. After the receiver application comes online, the stock quote application must have fed 30 stock quotes (once every two minutes). When the receiver application receives the messages, it has to have the intelligence to handle these numerous messages at the same time and figure out which is the most recent one to be displayed to the user. To solve this problem, `System.Messaging.Message` has two timeout properties: `TimeToReachQueue` and `TimeToBeReceived`.

The `TimeToReachQueue` property determines the time required by the message to reach the queue manager and thus the queue of the destination machine.

If the time required is greater than the `TimeToReachQueue` value, the message is discarded by MSMQ. For logging purposes, if we set the `UseDeadLetterQueue` property of the message to `true`, the expired message will be sent to the dead-letter queue of the machine that could not deliver the message.

The `TimeToBeReceived` property represents the time required by the message to be received from the destination queue. This includes the time required to reach the destination queue and the time the message stays in the destination queue until it is received. So, typically, `TimeToBeReceived` must be greater than `TimeToReachQueue`. If `TimeToBeReceived` is less than `TimeToReachQueue`, then `TimeToBeReceived` takes precedence. If the message is not received by the receiving application, MSMQ discards the message, and if the `UseDeadLetterQueue` property of the message is set to `true`, MSMQ places the message in the dead-letter queue.

NOTE *Expired messages due to* `TimeToReachQueue` *and* `TimeToBeReceived` *timers do not appear in the journal of the destination. For logging expired messages, the dead-letter queue is used. That queue is MSMQ-generated so we do not need to create one. If the journaling at the source machine was turned on, then the message would appear in the source machine's journal queue if it satisfied the* `TimeToReachQueue` *criteria but failed the* `TimeToBeReceived` *criteria.*

The following listing illustrates both of the message timers:

```
using System;
using System.Messaging;

class MessageTimers
{
  public static void Main(string[] args)
  {
    if(args.Length == 1)
    {
      try
      {
        if(!MessageQueue.Exists(args[0]))
        {
          MessageQueue.Create(args[0]);
          Console.WriteLine("Queue was not registered,"+
            "so new queue created for you");
```

```
        }
        //Create an instance of the Message Queue.
        MessageQueue q = new MessageQueue
          (args[0]);
        //Create an instance of the Message
        System.Messaging.Message msg1
          = new System.Messaging.Message("TestMessage");
        //Set the TimeToReachQueue to 20 seconds
        msg1.TimeToReachQueue = new TimeSpan(0, 0, 20);
        //Set the TimeToBeReceived to one minute
        msg1.TimeToBeReceived = new TimeSpan(0, 1, 0);
        //Set the UsesDeadLetterQueue property to true
        // to send the expired message to the dead-letter
        msg1.UseDeadLetterQueue = true;
        //Send the message
        q.Send(msg1);
        Console.WriteLine("Message sent successfully");
      }
      catch(Exception ex)
      {
        Console.WriteLine
          ("Exception " + ex.Message);
      }
    }
    else
    {
      Console.WriteLine
        ("Usage:MessageTimers [Path of the queue]");
    }
  }
}
```

In this listing, we set the TimeToReachQueue property to 20 seconds and the TimeToBeReceived property to 60 seconds. We also set the UsesDeadLetterQueue property to true so that the expired messages are sent to the dead-letter queue. To run the sample, type the following at the command prompt:

```
>MessageTimers .\private$\myfirstq
```

Because we don't have any message receivers to receive the message, the message will time out after one minute and will be sent to the dead-letter queue. We can view the contents of the dead-letter queue from the Message Queuing

MMC interface, as shown in Figure 2-17. Note that the body of the expired message in the dead-letter queue has the same contents as the original message sent.

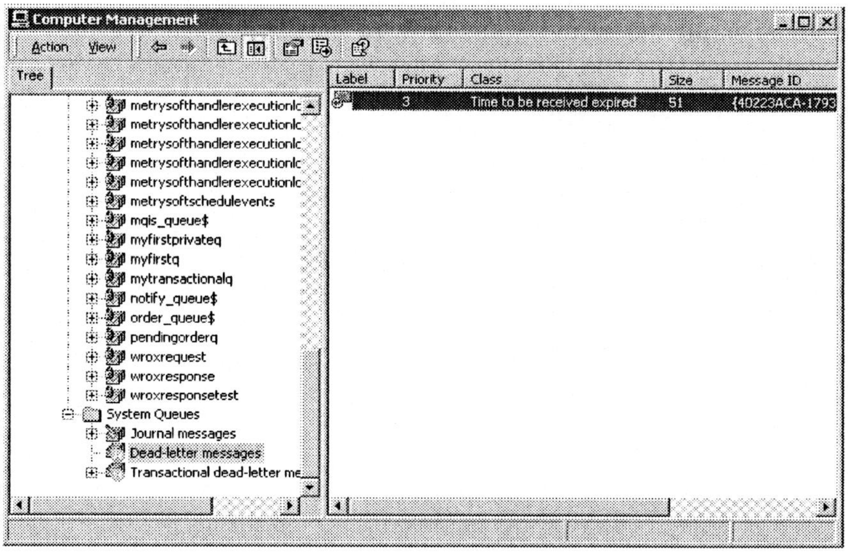

Figure 2-17. The dead-letter message

To access the dead-letter queue programmatically, you must use specific Path values. For instance, if you are working offline, you must use FormatName:

```
FormatName:DIRECT=TCP:ipaddress_of_your_machine\SYSTEM$;DEADLETTER
```

or

```
DIRECT=OS:name_of_machine\SYSTEM$;DEADLETTER
```

or (on a local machine)

```
DIRECT=OS:.\SYSTEM$;DEADLETTER
```

If you are connected with the domain controller, use

```
MachineName\Deadletter$
```

where MachineName is the name of the machine. You can use . for a local machine.

Recoverable Messages

Recoverable messages are messages that are written to the disk and can survive system failures and reboots. By default, all the messages are sent in express mode. Messages in express mode cannot survive reboots and system failures because they are stored in the memory (RAM). Because the messages are not written to the disk, the performance is higher for express mode. With recoverable mode, the performance is significantly lower than express mode, but the advantage is that the messages can survive system reboots and failures. Typically, recoverable messages are used where the content of the message has precedence over the performance of the system.

The Message class has a Boolean property named Recoverable that can be set to true to make the message recoverable—for example, message.Recoverable = true;.

Request-Response Messaging

Message Queuing supports request-response messaging via the ResponseQueue property of the Message class. In request-response messaging, the sender sends the message to a queue and waits for a response from the message receiver. The sender sets the ResponseQueue property representing a response queue and waits for a response to arrive in this queue. The message receiver reads this property after receiving the message and sends a response message to the response queue. The mapping between the sent message and the response message is done using the Id and CorrelationId properties of the Message object. When the sender sends a message to the queue, it saves the Id property of the message. The message receiver gets the Id property of the received message and assigns it to the CorrelationId property of the response message. The sender that is waiting for a response message can call the ReceiveByCorrelationId() method on the response queue to get the response message for the original sent message.

CAUTION ReceiveByCorrelationId() *and* ReceiveById() *must be used with extreme caution because these two methods use serial search on the queue to locate the message, and may be highly inefficient with lots of messages in the queue.*

Figure 2-18 depicts the request-response messaging scenario.

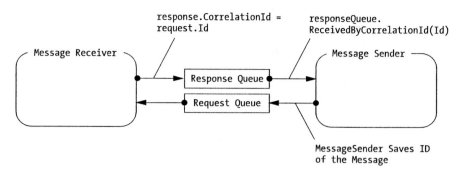

Figure 2-18. Request-response messaging

In Figure 2-18, the request queue contains the original message (request). The message sender sends the message to the request queue and saves the ID of the message. The message receiver receives the message from the request queue and creates a new response message to be sent to the response queue. The message receiver then sets the CorrelationId of the response message to the ID of the request message and sends the message to the response queue. The message sender, which is listening on the response queue for responses, receives the message from the response queue by calling the ReceiveByCorrrelationId() method and passing the Id property value of the original message that it had saved.

The following listing shows the program for the sender:

```
//Create an instance of the MessageQueue
 MessageQueue q = new MessageQueue
    (args[0]);
 String message = "Test Message";
 //Create an instance of the Message
 System.Messaging.Message msg1
    = new System.Messaging.Message
    (message);
 if(!MessageQueue.Exists(RESPONSE_QUEUE))
    MessageQueue.Create(RESPONSE_QUEUE);
 //Create an instance of the ResponseQueue
 MessageQueue response = new MessageQueue
    (RESPONSE_QUEUE);
 //Assign the ResponseQueue property
 msg1.ResponseQueue = response;
 //Send the message
 q.Send(msg1);
```

```
//Get the Id of the sent message.
String corrId = msg1.Id;
Console.WriteLine(corrId);
Console.WriteLine("Message sent successfully");
//Receive the message and send the response to the
// response queue
q.Formatter = new XmlMessageFormatter
   (new String[]{"System.String"});
Message receiveMsg = q.Receive(new TimeSpan(0, 0, 2));
//Get the response queue from the receiveMsg
response = receiveMsg.ResponseQueue;
//Set the CorrelationId of the message to the
//Id of the original message
receiveMsg.CorrelationId = corrId;
//Send the response message to the response queue
response.Send(receiveMsg);

Console.WriteLine("Waiting for Response.....");
//Receive the Response message by mapping
//the CorrelationId to the ID of the
//Original message
Message responseMessage =
   response.ReceiveByCorrelationId(corrId,
   new TimeSpan(0, 0, 30));
responseMessage.Formatter =
   (new XmlMessageFormatter
   (new Type[]{typeof(System.String)}));
Console.WriteLine(responseMessage.Label);
Console.WriteLine
("Received Response from Response Queue");
Console.WriteLine
   (responseMessage.Body.ToString());
```

As you can see, we set the ResponseQueue property of the Message object, which will be sent to the request queue, to the path of a ResponseQueue. Then, once we call the Send() method, we save the Id value of the message into the corrId variable. The message receiver application processes the message and sends the response to the response queue with the CorrelationId of the message equal to the Id value of the original message. The message sender application waits for the receiver to process the message with a timeout of 30 seconds and then receives the message by calling the ReceiveByCorrelationId() method on the response queue object. Figure 2-19 shows the output.

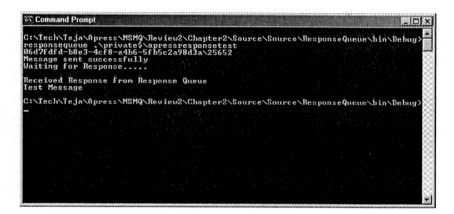

Figure 2-19. Request-response messaging

To run the example, type the following at the command prompt:

```
>ResponseQueue .\private$\apressresponsetest
```

For simplicity, in the preceding example the sender and the receiver are the same application. In a real-world scenario, the sender and the receiver will be two different applications and may be on two different machines using public queues for request-response messaging.

Prioritizing Messages

Message Queuing stacks messages into the queue based on their priority. Messages with higher priority are stacked at the front of the queue. By default, all the messages sent to the queue are assigned a priority level of 3 (Normal). The System.Messaging namespace has a MessagePriority enumeration that defines eight levels of priority supported by Message Queuing. Table 2-8 lists all the priority levels.

Table 2-8. Message Priorities

PRIORITY LEVEL	DESCRIPTION
Highest (7)	This is the highest priority and will have the utmost preference.
VeryHigh (6)	This priority has second-level preference.
AboveNormal (4)	Above normal priority.
Normal (3)	This is the default level of priority.
Low (2)	Low priority.
VeryLow (1)	Very low priority.
Lowest (0)	Lowest priority.

The `Priority` property of the `Message` class can be assigned any of the values listed in table 2-8. The following shows how to assign priority to a message before sending it to the queue:

```
Message msg = new Message(BODY);
msg.Priority = MessagePriority.High;
```

Using Acknowledgments

An *acknowledgment* is used to find out if the message has reached its destination queue and/or been successfully retrieved from the queue by the appropriate application. There are two types of acknowledgments; one is positive and the other negative. A positive acknowledgment is sent when your message reaches the desired destination queue successfully. Similarly, a negative acknowledgment is returned when the message fails to reach the desired destination queue or application. There are cases where the message cannot reach the destination due to the timeout period, where the time expires and a negative acknowledgment is received. Acknowledgment is received with the message header having the desired information; the body of the message is empty.

Requesting Acknowledgment Messages

Acknowledgment requires the creation of a queue to receive the confirmation of the message. Such queues must be nontransactional. Administration queues are used for receiving acknowledgments. Acknowledgments are generated by

Message Queuing and not by the application. Using the AdministrationQueue property of the System.Messaging.Message class, you can let Message Queuing know the AdministrationQueue so that acknowledgment messages can be automatically sent to it. The types of acknowledgments supported by Message Queuing are listed in the System.Messaging.AcknowledgmentTypes enumeration.

The property settings for AcknowledgmentTypes are as follows:

- FullReachQueue lets you know the success and failure of delivery to the queue.

- FullReceive is used to indicate the receipt of the message by the receiver application before the TimeToBeReceived timer expires.

- NegativeReceive is used when the message fails to be retrieved from a queue.

- NotAcknowledgeReceiveQueue is used when the message fails to be delivered to the queue.

- NotAcknowledgeReceive is used when the message fails to be retrieved.

- PositiveArrival is used when an acknowledgment is needed after the message reaches its destination.

- PositiveReceive is used when an acknowledgment is needed after the message is successfully retrieved by its destination.

The following listing shows the Acknowledgment process:

```
using System;
using System.Messaging;

class AckMessages
{
  public static void Main(string[] args)
  {
    if(args.Length >= 1)
    {
      try
      {
        if(!MessageQueue.Exists(args[0]))
        {
```

```
            MessageQueue.Create(args[0]);
            Console.WriteLine("Queue does not exist,"
                  + "so new queue created for you");
        }
      if(!MessageQueue.Exists(@".\Private$\AdminQueue"))
      {
        MessageQueue.Create(@".\Private$\AdminQueue");
        Console.WriteLine("Admin queue does not exist,"
                   + "so new queue created for you");
      }
      MessageQueue msgQ= new MessageQueue(args[0]);
      msgQ.DefaultPropertiesToSend.AdministrationQueue=
              new MessageQueue(@".\Private$\AdminQueue");
      msgQ.DefaultPropertiesToSend.AcknowledgeType=
      AcknowledgeTypes.FullReachQueue|AcknowledgeTypes.FullReceive;
      msgQ.Send("Sample");
      Console.WriteLine("Message sent successfully");
      //Receive Message
      Message msg;
      msg= msgQ.Receive(new TimeSpan(0));
      Console.WriteLine("Message Received {0}", msg.Id);
      }
      catch(Exception ex)
      {
            Console.WriteLine("Exception " + ex.Message);
      }
    }
    else
    {
      Console.WriteLine("Usage: AckMessages [Path of the Queue]");
    }
  }
}
```

In this example, we create a reference to the MessageQueue based on the user input and pass the AdministrationQueue to the DefaultPropertiesToSend.AdministrationQueue property of the MessageQueue. By setting this property, we ensure that all the messages sent to the queue will have the same AdministrationQueue. Then we set the AcknowledgeType property to FullReachQueue and FullReceive. Next, we send and then receive the message. The whole operation should generate two acknowledgment messages in the AdministrationQueue, first for the message reaching the queue message and the second for successful receipt of the message. The administration messages can be viewed using the Message Queuing MMC snap-in, as shown in Figure 2-20.

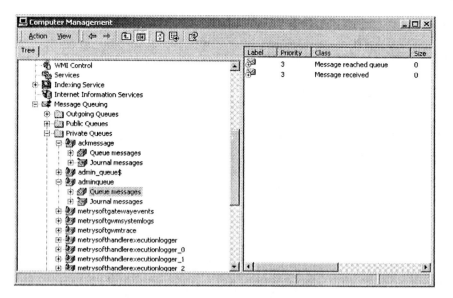

Figure 2-20. Administration messages

To run the preceding example, type the following at the command prompt:

```
>ackmessages .\private$\AckMessage TestMessage
```

Message Enumerator

The MessageQueue class has a method called GetMessageEnumerator(), which
returns a MessageEnumerator object. MessageEnumerator is a dynamic pointer to the
messages in the queue. The MessageEnumerator supports the MoveNext() method
to iterate over the messages in the queue. Let's see an example that uses the
GetMessageEnumerator() method:

```
System.Messaging. MessageEnumerator en =
        q.GetMessageEnumerator();

        q.MessageReadPropertyFilter
          .Label = true;
        q.MessageReadPropertyFilter
          .Body = true;
        q.MessageReadPropertyFilter
          .Priority = true;
```

```
//String source_queue_path = null;
while(en.MoveNext())
{
    Console.WriteLine("Message Label + en.Current.Label);
    Console.WriteLine("Message Body "
        + en.Current.Body.ToString());
    Console.WriteLine("Message Priority "
        + en.Current.Priority.ToString());
}
```

Here, we call the enumerator for the queue q and then set the MessageReadPropertyFilter for Label, Body, and the Priority properties so that only these properties will be imported from the message. Then, in the while loop, we traverse the enumeration using the MoveNext() method of the MessageEnumerator and display the three imported properties. Figure 2-21 shows the output.

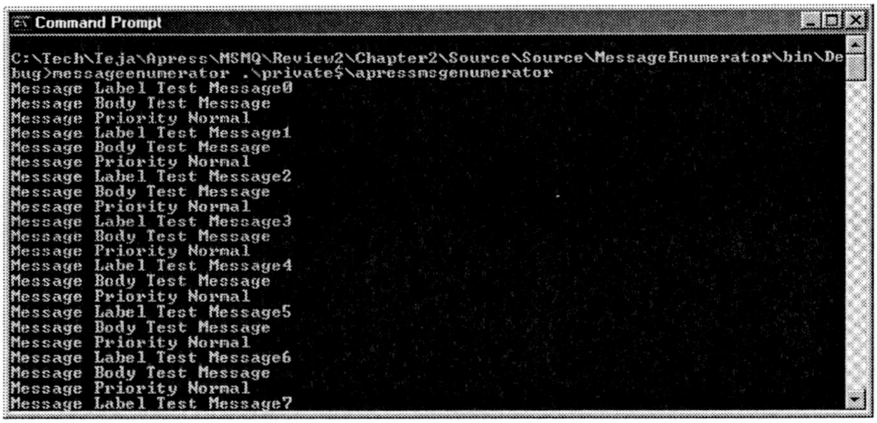

Figure 2-21. The message enumerator

The MessageQueue Enumerator

The MessageQueue class also supports methods for enumerating over the queue in Message Queuing. Table 2-9 lists these methods and their descriptions.

Table 2-9. MessageQueue Enumerators

ENUMERATOR	DESCRIPTION

`public static MessageQueueEnumerator`
`GetMessageQueueEnumerator();`
`public static MessageQueueEnumerator`
`GetMessageQueueEnumerator(`
`  MessageQueueCriteria criteria`
`);`
	This method returns a dynamic view of all the public queues in the Message Queuing network. The `MessageQueueCriteria` is the filter for retrieving queues. This filter is based on category, creation time, modification time, label, and machine name.

`public static MessageQueue[]`
`GetPrivateQueuesByMachine(`
`    string machineName`
`);`
	This method returns a static snapshot of all the private queues on the specified machine.

`public static MessageQueue[]`
`GetPublicQueues();`
`public static MessageQueue[]`
`GetPublicQueues(`
`    MessageQueueCriteria criteria`
`);`
	This method returns a static snapshot of all the public queues on the system. The difference between a static and a dynamic view is that, if any of the queues is modified, the static view does not reflect the changes, whereas a dynamic view does reflect the changes. This method also accepts a `MessageQueueCriteria` filter based on the category, creation time, modification time, label, and machine name.

`public static MessageQueue[]`
`GetPublicQueuesByCategory(`
`    Guid category`
`);`
	This method returns a static snapshot of all the public queues based on the category.

`public static MessageQueue[]`
`GetPublicQueuesByLabel(`
`    string label`
`);`
	This method returns a static snapshot of all the public queues based on the label.

`public static MessageQueue[]`
`GetPublicQueuesByMachine(`
`    string machineName`
`);`
	This method returns a static snapshot of all the public queues on the specified machine.

Summary

In this chapter, you learned how to use the System.Messaging namespace to interact with Message Queuing. You saw how to send simple and complex messages and how to receive messages from the queue synchronously as well as asynchronously. One important thing to keep in mind is how to write custom formatters by writing a SoapMessageFormatter that can be used to serialize and deserialize any serializable object. Finally, you saw how to use request-response messaging, journaling, and message enumerators. From all these examples, you can safely conclude that the System.Messaging namespace makes MSMQ programming easier than ever.

CHAPTER 3

Administration

IN THIS CHAPTER, WE DISCUSS the administration of Message Queuing in detail. We start with typical administrative tasks, such as creating and deleting queues, and slowly proceed to building a Message Queuing network. Along the way you'll learn about the various management interfaces that can be used to manage Message Queuing. We also touch on more advanced topics like message tracking, Message Queuing connectivity, message backup, encryption, firewall configuration for Message Queuing connectivity, and how to monitor Message Queuing performance.

In this chapter, we also highlight some of the new features added to Message Queuing 3.0 from an administrator's perspective—features such as improved management and deployment and an increase in the message store size to more than 2GB. Another benefit you'll learn about is that Message Queuing Server no longer must be set up on a domain controller. In addition, we cover some of the programmatic functions from the System.Messaging namespace in the .NET Framework that can be used to automate administrative tasks.

As you'll see, the administrator decides on the server setup and the specific role that each server plays in a Message Queuing network. Only local computer administrators can work on client installations of Message Queuing, and enterprise administrators (domain administrators) can work on domain controller installations. An administrator plays an important role in maintaining and controlling the Message Queuing network.

NOTE *Only administrators can install MSMQ, but other users may have privileges to do some or all of the administrative tasks.*

Here are some of the typical administrative tasks in a Message Queuing network:

- Creating queues

- Deleting queues

- Testing Message Queuing connectivity

- Monitoring the performance and throughput of the Message Queuing network

- Maintaining high availability of the Message Queuing network

- Monitoring the dead-letter queues for communication and transactional failures

- Securing the Message Queuing system

Interfaces for Managing a Message Queuing Network

There are four interfaces for managing a Message Queuing network:

- Using the Microsoft Computer Management Console (MMC) snap-in on a local machine

- Using the Active Directory Users and Computer snap-in on the domain controller

- Using the Active Directory Sites and Services snap-in on the domain controller

- Programmatically, using the System.Messaging API or the MSMQ COM Admin API

Let's take a closer look at the management tasks that can be performed using each of these interfaces.

Using the Microsoft Computer Management Console (MMC) Snap-In on a Local Machine

This interface is used to perform tasks on the Message Queuing installation. The MMC snap-in gives a single-machine view of a Message Queuing installation. MMC can also be used to manage Message Queuing on remote machines. Message Queuing tasks that can be performed using the MMC snap-in include managing

- Queues (Create Queues, Delete Queues, Purge Queues, Change Queue Properties, etc.)

- Message Queuing messages on the local computer

- Security for private and public queues

Using the Active Directory Users and Computer Snap-In on the Domain Controller

This interface allows the domain administrator to perform administrative actions on a domain-based Message Queuing installation. These actions include

- Managing public queues in a Message Queuing network

- Managing Active Directory users that will use Message Queuing

- Managing public and private queues on computers in the Message Queuing network

- Managing messages in the Message Queuing network

Using the Active Directory Sites and Services Snap-In on the Domain Controller

This interface is used for managing routing links and sites for a domain-based Message Queuing network. The tasks that can be performed using this interface are

- Creating, deleting, and managing routing links between Message Queuing computers

- Creating, viewing, and deleting foreign sites

- Creating foreign computers

- Setting the default lifetime or TimeToBeReceived property of messages exchanged in the Message Queuing network. If the messages are not received by the receiving application in the specified amount of time, the messages are marked as expired and removed from the queue

Programmatically Managing the Message Queuing System

The programmatic API (System.Messaging, COM Admin, and the MSMQ Admin API) of the Message Queuing system can be used to perform the following tasks:

- Creating, deleting, and purging public and private queues

- Setting queue properties

- Setting message properties

- Setting message queue security properties

- Setting message security properties

- Monitoring dead-letter and transaction dead-letter queues

Managing Queues

Once a distributed system is developed, management and deployment of the system dictate the success of the system. Queues are the heart of a Message Queuing system. They form a virtual FIFO channel between the message sender and the message receiver. They also play an important role in the overall performance of the Message Queuing system.

Types of Queues

We discussed types of queues in Chapter 2 from a programmer's perspective. In this section, we discuss these queues from an administrator's perspective. Queues are FIFO channels maintained by Message Queuing between the message sender and the message receiver. The sender sends a message to the queue and MSMQ forwards the message to the recipient. In Message Queuing 2.0, you can have only one message receiver for a message. If two or more recipients are registered with a particular queue, only one of them will receive the message. Message Queuing 3.0 extends this model from one-to-one to one-to-many.

Before you dive into managing queues, it is important to know the different types of queues supported by Message Queuing, since they form the backbone of a Message Queuing system. The types of queues in MSMQ are divided into two categories: application queues and system queues.

Application Queues

Queues that are created for the applications are known as application queues. These queues may be created manually using the MMC or programmatically. Depending on the application requirements, application queues can be public or private, and they can be transactional or nontransactional. There are four types of application queues: destination queues, administration queues, response queues, and report queues.

Destination Queues

Destination queues are application queues that are used to store messages sent by the sender and to forward the message to the message receiver. The messages that travel through these queues are purely application generated. Figure 3-1 shows a typical destination queue scenario.

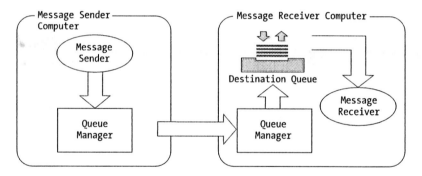

Figure 3-1. Destination queue

Destination queues can be private or public, and they can be transactional or nontransactional. The decision to make a queue public, private, transactional, or nontransactional is made during the creation of the queue.

Administration Queues

Administration queues store system-generated acknowledgment messages for sent messages. These queues are typically specified programmatically while sending messages. MSMQ generates system messages indicating whether a message arrived at its destination queue, whether it was retrieved from the destination queue, or both. The acknowledgment message contains information describing what triggered the acknowledgment. Administration queues cannot be transactional, so any nontransactional queue can be used as an administration queue.

Response Queues

Response queues are used by the receiving application to send response messages to the sending application. The sending application and the receiving application must understand the contents of the message. The decision to use a response queue is made by the sending application while sending messages to the receiving application. In MSMQ 3.0, you can define multiple response queues. Response queues can be transactional or nontransactional, depending on the application requirements. The functionality of the administration queue and response queue can be combined into a single queue. In this case, the response queue must be transactional because the administration queue cannot be transactional.

Report Queues

Report queues are public queues that contain routing information about the message from its source to the destination. Report queues can be used only if the administrator on the source computer enables message-route tracking and tracing is requested by the sending application. A report message is generated every time a message leaves or arrives at the Message Queuing computer. There can be only one report queue per computer, but one message can be tracked by multiple report queues along its path. The TypeID (GUID) for report queues is constant and must have the following values:

TypeID (GUID): {55EE8F32-CCE9-11CF-B108-0020AFD61CE9}

A report queue can be created either manually using the Active Directory User Interface or programmatically as long as the Label and TypeID have the specified constant values. Figure 3-2 shows the tracking of a message using report queues.

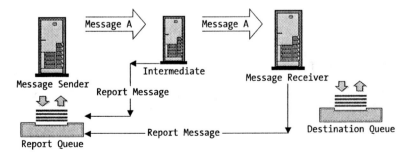

Figure 3-2. Report queues

In Figure 3-2, when Message A is sent from the Message Sender machine via the Intermediate machine to the destination queue on the Message Receiver machine, report messages are sent to the Message Sender machine.

System Queues

System queues are generated by MSMQ. They include the following types of queues:

- Journal queues

- Dead-letter queues

- MSMQ private system queues

Journal Queues

Journal queues store copies of messages. In MSMQ, two types of journaling are available: queue journals and computer journals.

Queue Journals

Queue journals are created whenever application queues are created. Copies of messages are created in the journal queues by MSMQ whenever the messages are removed from the application queue by the message receiver. Journaling can be turned on manually using the Message Queuing MMC snap-in, as shown in Figure 3-3.

NOTE   *It is always a good idea to limit the journal storage to some specified amount to save the disk space because in MSMQ 1.0 and MSMQ 2.0 there is a total limit of approximately 2GB on total size of all the messages in the Application and System queues combined. This limit was lifted in MSMQ 3.0.*

Figure 3-4 shows a queue with its journal queue. When journaling is enabled for the queue myfirstq queue, all the messages removed by the receiving application will be copied to the myfirstq journal queue.

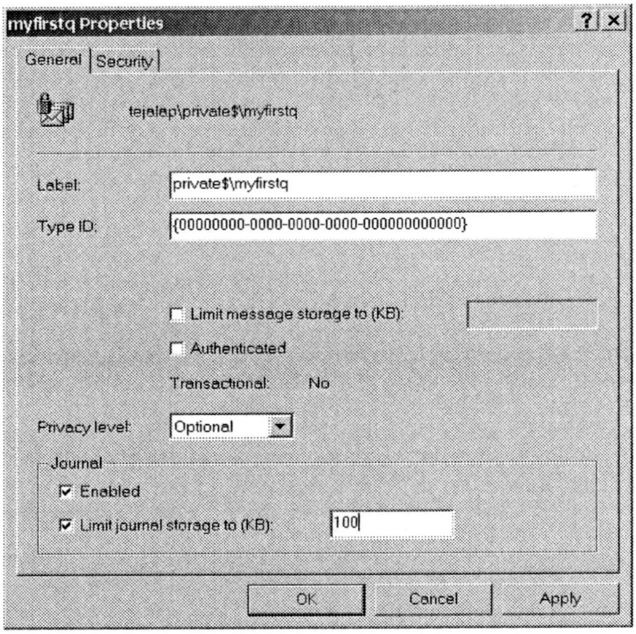

myfirstq Properties

General | Security

tejalap\private$\myfirstq

Label: private$\myfirstq

Type ID: {00000000-0000-0000-0000-000000000000}

☐ Limit message storage to (KB):

☐ Authenticated

Transactional: No

Privacy level: Optional ▾

Journal
☑ Enabled
☑ Limit journal storage to (KB): 100

OK | Cancel | Apply

Figure 3-3. Enable Journaling

- WMI Control
- Services
- Indexing Service
- Internet Information Services
- Message Queuing
  - Outgoing Queues
  - Public Queues
  - Private Queues
    - admin_queue$
    - mqis_queue$
    - notify_queue$
    - order_queue$
    - myfirstq
      - Queue messages
      - Journal messages
  - System Queues

Figure 3-4. Journal queue

Computer Journals

A computer journal queue is created when MSMQ is installed. Computer journals store all the copies of messages sent by the computer. To use computer journaling, the sending application must set the journaling property of the message to true. Figure 3-5 shows the location of the computer journal queue.

Figure 3-5. Computer journal queue

Dead-Letter Queues

Dead-letter queues are used to store messages that could not be delivered and if the sender of the message has set the UseDeadLetterQueue property of the message to true. MSMQ stores a message into a dead-letter queue on the machine where the message expired or from where the message could not be delivered. This machine can be the source, destination, routing server, or any intermediate machine along the path of the message. Two types of dead-letter queues are created by MSMQ: transactional and nontransactional. A transactional and a nontransactional dead-letter queue are created by MSMQ for one machine during installation. Messages stored in both these queues are recoverable, that is, they can survive system reboots.

Nontransactional Dead-Letter Queue

Nontransactional messages that could not be delivered or have expired are stored in a nontransactional dead-letter queue.

Transactional Dead-Letter Queue

Transactional messages that could not be delivered or have expired are stored in a transactional dead-letter queue. MSMQ stores a transactional message in the dead-letter queue if the queue manager on the source machine receives a negative acknowledgment message or does not receive any confirmation from the destination queue manager regarding successful delivery of the message. The presence of a message in the transaction dead-letter queue confirms that the message sent by the sending application was not retrieved by the receiving application on the destination machine. Figure 3-5 shows the location of the transactional and nontransactional dead-letter queues.

MSMQ Private System Queues

MSMQ creates five private system queues for administration purposes. These are private queues and hence not published with the Active Directory. These queues are used by MSMQ internally and cannot be opened or deleted by applications. Table 3.1 shows the list of MSMQ private system queues.

Table 3-1. MSMQ Private System Queues

MSMQ PRIVATE SYSTEM QUEUE	DESCRIPTION
admin_queue$	Stores administrative messages.
msmqadminresp$	Stores administrative response messages (like MQPing messages).
mqis_queue$	Used for NT4 MQIS replications (in PEC, PSC, or BSC only).
notify_queue$	Stores notification messages. These messages list computer and queue property changes, including creation and deletion of queues.
order_queue$	Stores messages for tracking transactional messages that require in-order delivery.

Using the MMC Snap-In on a Local Machine

The MMC snap-in on a local machine can be started by right-clicking on My Computer and clicking Manage to open the Computer Management console. Expand the Services and Applications tree node to get to the Message Queuing node, as shown in Figure 3-6.

Typically the local MMC snap-in will be used to monitor private and public queues on the local machine. By default, the Computer Management snap-in points at the local machine, but it is also possible to connect to a remote computer. To manage a remote computer, right-click Computer Management and then choose Connect to Another Computer. This will open the Select Computer dialog box, where you can specify the computer you want to connect to, as shown in Figure 3-7. You can then manage the messages and queues by expanding the Services and Applications tree node to the Message Queuing node.

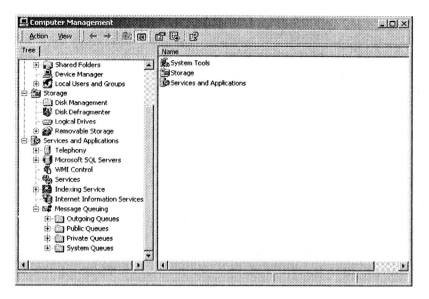

Figure 3-6. The Message Queuing MMC snap-in

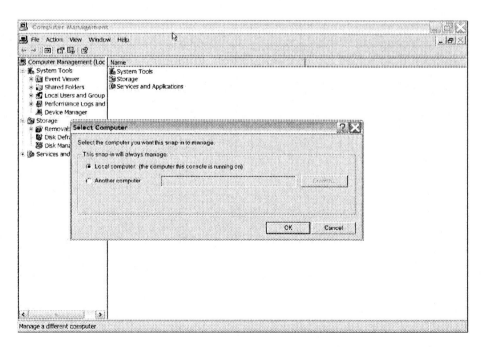

Figure 3-7. Managing remote machines with MMC

Creating Queues Manually

Queues can also be created manually from the Message Queuing snap-in of the Computer Management console. Right-click the My Computer icon on the desktop and click Manage to Open the Computer Management Console. Go to Services and Applications | Message Queuing. Depending on the type of queue to be created, right-click either the Public or Private category and click New ➤ Private Queue or Public Queue. This will open the Create Queue dialog box, as shown in Figure 3-8. Specify a name for the queue and click OK to create the queue. Select the Transactional check box if you want to create a transactional queue. The newly created queue should be visible in the Public or Private category.

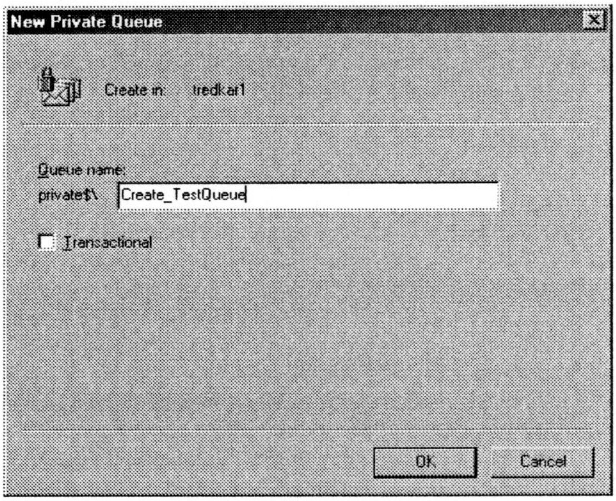

Figure 3-8. Creating a queue manually

Deleting Queues Manually

Queues can also be deleted manually from the Message Queuing snap-in of the Computer Management console. Right-click the My Computer icon on the desktop and click Manage to Open the Computer Management console. Go to Services and Applications | Message Queuing. Depending on the type of queue to be deleted, right-click either the Public or Private category and then select

Queue ➤ Delete. This will open the dialog box shown in Figure 3-9, asking you to confirm the queue to be deleted. Click Yes to delete the queue. The queue will be deleted from the Public or Private category.

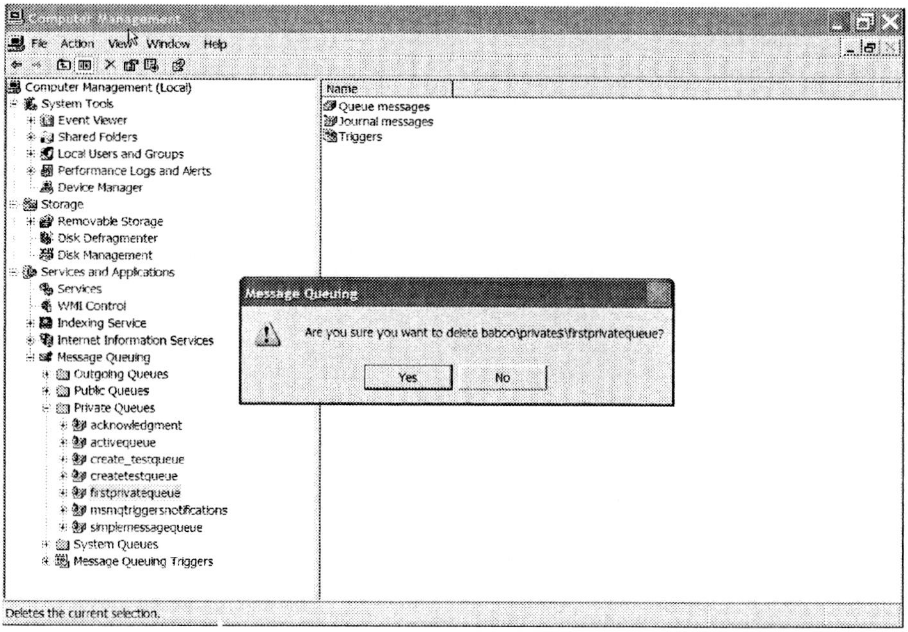

Figure 3-9. Confirming the deletion

Purging Queues Manually

Queues can also be purged manually from the Message Queuing snap-in of the Computer Management console. Right-click the My Computer icon on the desktop and click Manage to Open the Computer Management Console. Go to Services and Applications | Message Queuing. Depending on the type of queue to be deleted, right-click either the Public or Private category and double-click the queue; then select Queue Messages ➤ All Tasks ➤ Purge. This will open the dialog box shown in Figure 3-10, asking you to confirm if all the messages are to be deleted. Click Yes to delete all the messages. The messages will be deleted from the Public or Private category.

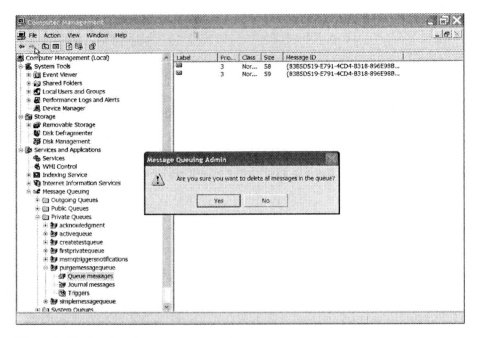

Figure 3-10. Purging the queue manually

The Label Property

The Label property of a queue is used to identify the queue in a Message Queuing network (see Figure 3-11). The property need not be unique. It can be used as a search criterion for querying public queues in a Message Queuing network. Such a query will return messages with the same label. The queue's properties dialog box allows you to set the Label property. For example, you could group all the queues that are used by an order processing system by setting their labels to OrderProcessingQueues. Then whenever you want to query the Message Queuing network programmatically or manually to retrieve only the queues involved in order processing, you can use this label as the query parameter.

Type ID

Type ID represents a GUID that can be used to categorize a queue. Typically Type ID is used to group queues that offer same services or functions. For example, all the queues that are used for testing a Message Queuing network must have a Type ID of {55EE8F32-CCE9-11CF-B108-0020AFD61CE9}, and all the queues that are used for sending test messages from the domain controller must have a Type ID of {55EE8F33-CCE9-11CF-B108-0020AFD61CE9}. Typically Type IDs are assigned to queues when they are created programmatically to eliminate the need to manually assign a Type ID to each queue, which can be time consuming.

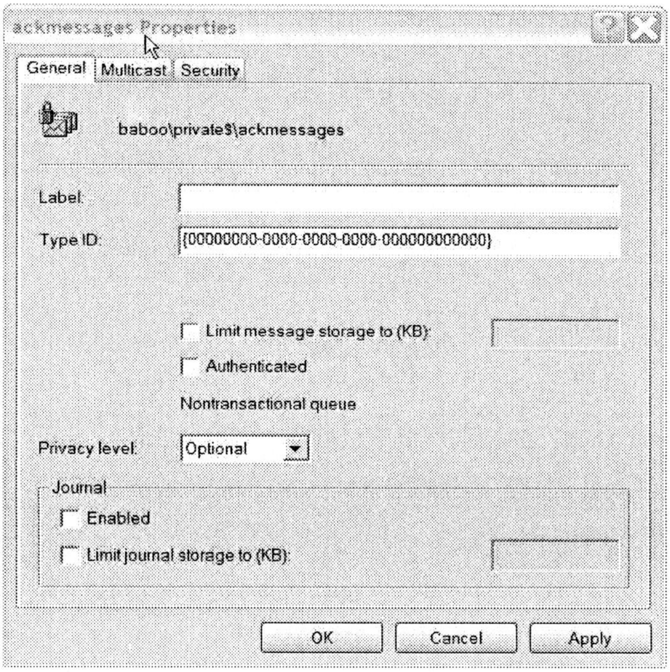

Figure 3-11. The Label property

Setting Journal Storage Size for Queues

As discussed earlier in the chapter, journaling stores copies of messages that are received by the receiving application. By default, journal storage has no upper limit, so if journaling of messages is not controlled, the journal messages will keep accumulating. We can limit the size of the journal by setting the journal storage size of the queue. When the journal storage limit is reached, journal messages can no longer be sent to the journal queue. You can set the journal storage for queues manually under the journal settings. Click on the check box as appropriate and type in the storage limit needed for all the journal messages that need to be stored in the queue.

Setting Message Storage Size for Queues

Practically, message storage has a limit, which is directly related to the available disk space on the local machine. (In MSMQ 1.0 and 2.0, this limit is no larger than 1.6GB. In MSMQ 3.0, this limit was raised to 8TB or the maximum disk space on the message storage disk. Note that even express messages consume disk space.) You can set the storage for queues manually in the properties dialog box by selecting the Limit Message Storage option and then typing the total size in kilobytes.

Allowing Only Authenticated Messages on Queues

When using authenticated messages, Message Queuing creates a digital signature and uses it to sign the message while sending it to queue. The receiving application also authenticates the message before receiving it. If an unauthenticated message is sent to a queue that accepts only authenticated messages, it will be rejected when it reaches the queue. You can enforce authentication of queue by opening the General tab and clicking on the Authenticated check box. Authentication and encryption are discussed in detail in the "Security" section later in this chapter.

Changing the Privacy Level for Queues

The default privacy level is Optional. A queue with the default (Optional) privacy level will accept both encrypted and unencrypted messages. A queue with the Body privacy level will accept only encrypted messages and will reject unencrypted messages. A queue with the None privacy level will accept only unencrypted messages. In short, if the message privacy level does not match the queue privacy level, the message will be rejected. If the message sending application has requested a negative acknowledgment for the sent message, a negative acknowledgment is sent to the sending application.

Using the Active Directory Snap-in

The Active Directory Users and Computer MMC snap-in is available on the domain controller installation of Message Queuing. To open this snap-in, go to Start ➤ Programs ➤ Administrative Tools under Active Directory Users and Computers. If the MSMQ node is not visible, click Users, Groups, and Computers as Containers in the View menu in the console, and then click Advanced Features. Figure 3-12 shows the Active Directory Users and Computer snap-in.

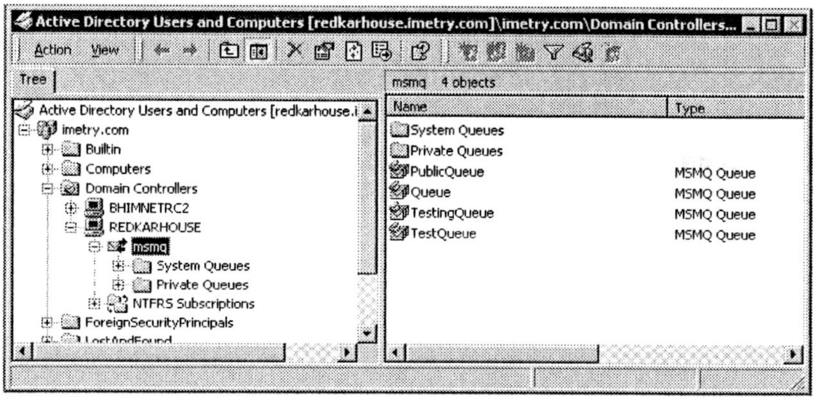

Figure 3-12. Active Directory Users and Computers

The Active Directory Users and Computers interface shows all the system, private, and public queues on all the computers in the Message Queuing network. Machines that have the Workgroup installation of Message Queuing are not listed in this interface, since they are not a part of the Active Directory database. Here are the queue management tasks that can be completed using the Active Directory Users and Computers snap-in:

- View all Message Queuing computers and the queues on those computers.

- Create, view, delete, and find all public queues and set queue properties.

- View and delete private queues and set queue properties for a local computer.

- View message properties and purge messages from queues.

Creating and Deleting Queues

Figure 3-13 shows how to create queues using the Active Directory Users and Computers interface.

To create a queue, right-click the appropriate folder (msmq for a public queue and Private Queues for a private queue), and click New ➤ MSMQ Queue. This will open the Queue Name dialog box, where you specify the name of the queue and choose whether it is transactional. To delete a queue, right-click the queue and click Delete. Note that only public queues can be created in this manner.

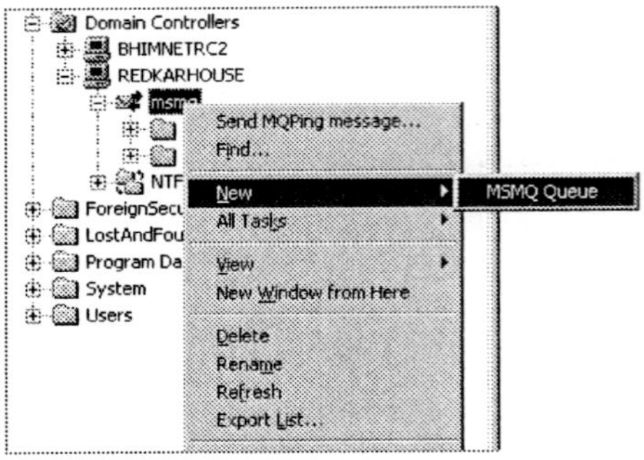

Figure 3-13. Creating a queue in the Active Directory Users and Computers interface

Finding Queues

You can also find public queues using the Active Directory Users and Computers interface. Right-click a folder and click Find. In the Find dialog box, choose the MSMQ queue, type the Label and/or Type ID of the queue you want to find, and click Find Now. If you don't specify the Label or Type ID, all the queues will be displayed.

You will see the result in the list box display. You can click a queue to view its details, as shown in Figure 3-14.

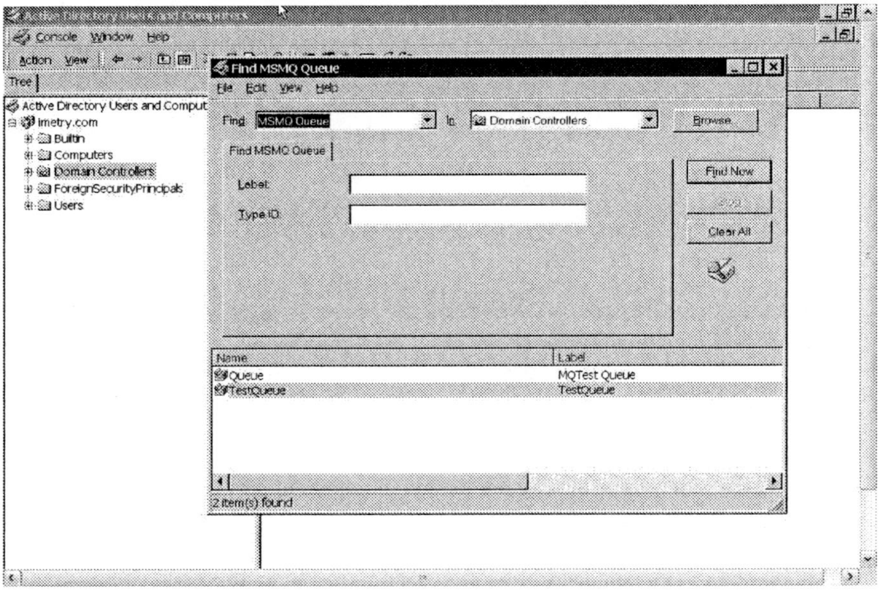

Figure 3-14. Finding a queue in the Active Directory Users and Computers interface

Changing the Queue's Properties

To view the properties of a queue, right-click the queue and click Properties to open the Properties dialog box, shown in Figure 3-15.

PublicQueue Properties

General | Object | Security |

REDKARHOUSE\PublicQueue

Label: PublicQueue

Type ID: {00000000-0000-0000-0000-000000000000}

ID: {5F238728-7159-40BC-A6CB-965438B485A3}

☐ Limit message storage to (KB):

☐ Authenticated

Transactional: No

Privacy level: Optional ▼   Base priority: 0

Journal
☐ Enabled
☐ Limit journal storage to (KB):

OK   Cancel   Apply

Figure 3-15. A queue's Properties dialog box in the Active Directory Users and Computers interface

From this interface, it is possible to change the Label, Type ID, Message Storage, Authentication, Privacy Level, Base Priority, and Journal properties of a queue. All the properties except Base Priority are similar to the ones that we saw earlier in this chapter.

The base priority of a public queue is used to route messages through the network. For example, if a message M1 is sent to a public queue Q1 with base priority 2, and if another message M2 is sent to a public queue Q2 with base priority 1, the message M1 will be routed before the message M2 through the network because Q1 has a higher priority than Q2. The base priority of the queue is not the same as the priority of the messages. The base priority does not have any effect on the priority of the messages or the order of the messages in the queue. The base priority value of public queues can range from -32768 to 32767. The default setting is 0.

NOTE   *Private queue messages are not routed in a Message Queuing network and so do not support base priority.*

Purging Queues

To purge a queue using the Active Directory Users and Computers interface, just right-click the queue messages for a queue and click All Tasks ➤ Purge, as shown in Figure 3-16.

Figure 3-16. Purging a queue using the Active Directory Users and Computers interface

Managing Queues Programmatically Using the System.Messaging API

The System.Messaging API in the .NET Framework offers classes and functions that let you perform operations on queues and messages in a Message Queuing system. We discuss some of these operations in this section. We'll keep the discussion short because some of these topics are covered in other chapters.

Creating Queues

The MessageQueue class has a static method Create() for creating queues. The Create() method has two overloads:

```
public static MessageQueue Create(
    string path
);
public static MessageQueue Create(
    string path,
    bool transactional
);
```

The path parameter is the path of the queue and the transactional Boolean value specifies whether the created queue is transactional or not. The transactional property of a queue cannot be changed once the queue is created. The path parameter depends on the type of queue being created. Also note that the Create() method returns a reference to the created queue. In the following listing the MessageQueueOperations class shows how to create a queue programmatically:

```
class MessageQueueOperations
{
 public static void Main(string[] args)
 {
  if(args.Length == 2)
  {
   try
   {
    MessageQueue q = MessageQueue.Create
     (args[0], Convert.ToBoolean(args[1]));
   }
   catch(Exception ex)
   {
    Console.WriteLine
     ("Exception while creating the queue " + ex.Message);
   }

  }
  else
  {
   Console.WriteLine
    ("Usage:MessageQueueOperations [Path of the queue]"
    + "[True/False for transactional/non-transactional]");
  }
 }
}
```

In this code, we accept the path of the queue and the transactional Boolean value as the input from the user and create the queue using these parameters. Output from the above program with different parameters is as follows:

- First run: Creating a private nontransactional queue

  ```
  C:\ >Listing01 .\private$\myfirstprivatenontransactionalq false
  ```

- Second run: Creating a private transactional queue

  ```
  C:\ >Listing01 .\private$\myfirstprivatetransactionalq true
  ```

- Third run: Trying to create the queue again

```
C:\ >Listing01 .\private$\myfirstprivatetransactionalq true
Exception While Creating the Queue with the Specified⤶
Path Name Is Already Registered in the DS
```

While we were trying to create the same queue again in the third run, an exception was thrown by the Framework, suggesting that the queue already exists. To avoid an exception being thrown, we can use another static method, Exists(), from the MessageQueue class to check whether a queue with the same name exists in MSMQ :

```
public static bool Exists(
    string path
);
```

where path is the path of the queue whose existence needs to be checked. Exists() is an expensive operation because it has to query the Active Directory to learn the existence of the queue. It is recommended you use exceptions instead of this method. The following listing shows how to use the Exists() method of the MessageQueue class:

```
using System;
using System.Messaging;

class MessageQueueOperations
{
 public static void Main(string[] args)
 {
  if(args.Length == 2)
  {
   try
   {
    if(!MessageQueue.Exists(args[0]))
    {
     MessageQueue q = MessageQueue.Create
      (args[0], Convert.ToBoolean(args[1]));
    }
    else
    {
     Console.WriteLine
      ("MessageQueue " + args[0]
      + " already exists in MSMQ.");
```

```
    }
  }
  catch(Exception ex)
  {
   Console.WriteLine
     ("Exception while creating the queue "
     + ex.Message);
  }

 }
 else
 {
  Console.WriteLine
    ("Usage:MessageQueueOperations [Path of the queue]"
    + "[True/False for transactional/non-transactional]");
 }
 }
}
```

In this listing, before creating the queue we call the static `Exists()` method of the `MessageQueue` class to verify whether the queue already exists. The method returns a true Boolean value if the queue exists and false otherwise. If the queue already exists, it notifies the user. Other tasks worth trying include running this program to do the following:

- Create a public queue in a workgroup environment.

- Create a public queue in a domain environment.

- Create a public queue on an offline machine in a domain environment.

Deleting Queues

The `MessageQueue` class has a static `Delete()` method that can be used to delete a queue:

```
public static void Delete(
    string path
);
```

where path is the path or the format name of the queue to be deleted. This listing shows the how to use the Delete() method of the MessageQueue class:

```csharp
using System;
using System.Messaging;

class MessageQueueOperations
{
 public static void Main(string[] args)
 {
  if(args.Length == 3)
  {
   try
   {
    //Check whether it's create or delete
    int operation = Convert.ToInt32(args[0]);

    if(operation == 1)
    {
     //Check whether the queue exists or not
     if(!MessageQueue.Exists(args[1]))
     {
      //Create the queue
      MessageQueue q = MessageQueue.Create
        (args[1], Convert.ToBoolean(args[2]));
     }
     else
     {
      Console.WriteLine
        ("MessageQueue " + args[1]
        + " already exists in MSMQ.");
     }
    }
    else
    {
     MessageQueue.Delete(args[1]);
    }
   }
   catch(Exception ex)
   {
    Console.WriteLine
      ("Exception while creating the queue "
      + ex.Message);
```

```
        }

    }
    else
    {
      Console.WriteLine
        ("Usage:MessageQueueOperations "
        + "[1 or 2 (1-Create, 2-Delete)]"
        + "[Path of the queue]"
        + "[True/False for transactional/non-transactional]");
    }
  }
}
```

We modified the previous listing by adding the delete functionality. Now we ask the user to enter an input parameter for determining which operation (Create() or Delete()) needs to be performed. If the user enters 2, we execute the delete operation; if the user enters 1, we execute the create operation.

Apart from Create(), Delete(), and Exists() methods, there are other useful static methods in the MessageQueue class; let's take a look. The first one is GetMachineId(), shown here:

```
public static Guid GetMachineId(
    string machineName
);
```

where machineName is the name of the machine. The GetMachineId() returns the GUID for the machine that MSMQ creates when a machine is added to the enterprise.

The next method is GetMessageQueueEnumerator():

```
public static MessageQueueEnumerator GetMessageQueueEnumerator();
 public static MessageQueueEnumerator GetMessageQueueEnumerator(
    MessageQueueCriteria criteria
);
```

This method returns an enumerator object for enumerating over all the public queues on the MSMQ network. The MessageQueueEnumerator returned is a dynamic snapshot of the public queues, that is, it will list the queues that were created after this method was called. MessageQueueCriteria is used as a filter for getting the queues and supports the following filters: Category or Type ID, CreatedAfter, CreatedBefore, Label, MachineName, ModifiedAfter, ModifiedBefore. The MessageQueueEnumerator allows us to enumerate over the returned MessageQueue objects one by one.

The GetPrivateQueuesByMachine() method shown here

```
public static MessageQueue[] GetPrivateQueuesByMachine(
    string machineName
);
```

retrieves an array of MessageQueue objects representing all the private queues on the given machine.

The GetPublicQueues() method

```
public static MessageQueue[] GetPublicQueues();
public static MessageQueue[] GetPublicQueues(
    MessageQueueCriteria criteria
);
```

returns a static snapshot of all the public queues on the MSMQ network. MessageQueueCriteria is used as a filter for getting the queues and supports the following filters: Category or Type ID, CreatedAfter, CreatedBefore, Label, MachineName, ModifiedAfter, ModifiedBefore.

The method shown here

```
public static MessageQueue[] GetPublicQueues();

public static MessageQueue[] GetPublicQueues(
    MessageQueueCriteria criteria
);
```

returns a static snapshot of all the public queues on the MSMQ network. MessageQueueCriteria is used as a filter for getting the queues. The MessageQueueCriteria supports the following filters: Category or Type ID, CreatedAfter, CreatedBefore, Label, MachineName, ModifiedAfter, ModifiedBefore.

The GetPublicQueuesByCategory() method

```
public static MessageQueue[] GetPublicQueuesByCategory(
    Guid category
);
```

gets a static snapshot of all the public queues on an MSMQ network belonging to the given Category or Type ID.

The GetPublicQueuesByLabel() method

```
public static MessageQueue[] GetPublicQueuesByLabel(
    string label
);
```

gets a static snapshot of all the public queues on an MSMQ network having the same label.

Finally, the GetPublicQueuesByMachine() method

```
public static MessageQueue[] GetPublicQueuesByMachine(
    string machineName
);
```

gets a static snapshot of all the public queues on the given machine on the MSMQ.

To show you how to use all the static methods from the MessageQueue class, I have developed a Windows application, as shown in Figure 3-17.

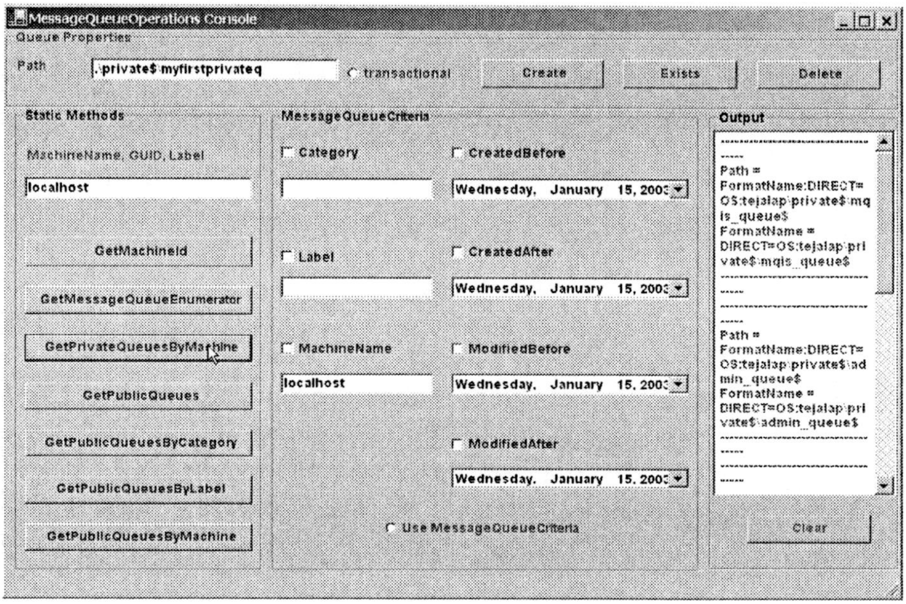

Figure 3-17. MessageQueueOperations Console

Table 3-2 lists some important components of the MessageQueueOperations application and their significance.

Table 3-2. MessageQueueOperations Controls

CONTROLNAME	CONTROL TYPE	EVENT OPERATION	DESCRIPTION
Path	TextField		User enters the Path, FormatName, or Label of the queue in this TextBox.
Transactional	RadioButton		User checks this radio button to specify whether the queue being created is transactional or not.
Create	Button	Create_Click	User clicks this button to create a new queue specified in the path.
Exists	Button	Exists_Click	User clicks this button to check whether the queue specified in the path exists or not.
Delete	Button	Delete_Click	User clicks this button to delete the queue specified in the path.
Output	TextBox		Displays the output from all the method invocations.
Input	TextBox		Accepts input for all the static methods listed in the Static Method group box.
GetMachineId	Button	GetMachineId_Click	Calls the MessageQueue.GetMachineId() method and displays the output in the output TextBox.
GetMessageQueue Enumerator	Button	GetMessageQueue Enumerator_Click	Calls MessageQueue.GetMessage QueueEnumerator() and displays the format names of the returned queues in the output TextBox. If the Use MessageQueueCriteria radio button is checked, then the criteria from the MessageQueueCriteria group box are taken as input.

Table 3-2. MessageQueueOperations Controls (continued)

CONTROLNAME	CONTROL TYPE	EVENT OPERATION	DESCRIPTION
GetPrivateQueues ByMachine	Button	GetPrivateQueues ByMachine_Click	Calls `MessageQueue. GetPrivate QueuesByMachine()` and displays the format names of all the returned private queues in the output TextBox.
GetPublicQueues	Button	GetPublic Queues_Click	Calls `MessageQueue. GetPublicQueues()` and displays the format names of the returned queues in the output TextBox. If the Use MessageQueueCriteria radio button is checked, then the criteria from the MessageQueueCriteria group box are taken as input.
GetPublicQueues ByCategory	Button	GetPublicQueuesBy Category_Click	Calls `MessageQueue. GetPublic QueuesByCategory` and displays the format names of the returned queues in the output TextBox. The input parameter for this method is the Category or the Type ID that is specified in the Input TextBox.
GetPublicQueues ByLabel	Button	GetPublicQueuesBy Label_Click	Calls `MessageQueue. GetPublic QueuesByLabel()` and displays the format names of the returned queues in the output TextBox. The input parameter for this method is the Label of the queue that is specified in the Input TextBox.

continued

Table 3-2. MessageQueueOperations Controls (continued)

CONTROLNAME	CONTROL TYPE	EVENT OPERATION	DESCRIPTION
GetPublicQueuesBy Machine	Button	GetPublicQueuesBy Machine_Click	Calls `MessageQueue.GetPublic QueuesByMachine()` and displays the format names of the returned queues in the output TextBox. The input parameter for this method is the Label of the queue that is specified in the Input TextBox.
Category_Check	CheckBox		If this CheckBox is checked, the Category_Value TextBox must contain the value for the Category of the queue. This value will be included in the MessageQueueCriteria.
Category_Value	TextBox		Contains the Category or TypeID of the queue to be included in the Message-QueueCriteria.
Label_Check	CheckBox		If this CheckBox is checked, the Label_Value TextBox must contain the value for the Label of the queue. This value will be included in the Message-QueueCriteria.
Label_Value	TextBox		Contains the Label of the queue to be included in the MessageQueueCriteria.
MachineName_ Check	CheckBox		If this CheckBox is checked, the MachineName _Value TextBox must contain the value for the MachineName of the queue. This value will be included in the MessageQueueCriteria.
MachineName _ Value	TextBox		Contains the MachineName of the queue to be included in the MessageQueueCriteria.

The MessageQueueOperations Windows application is a nice little toy you can use to play with the queues in the MSMQ network. One interesting operation in the MessageQueueOperations Console is GetMessageQueueEnumerator_Click(), which inputs the MessageQueueCriteria from the parameters specified in the controls in the MessageQueueCriteria group box. The following listing shows the implementation of some of the methods:

```
private void GetMessageQueueEnumerator_Click(object sender, System.EventArgs e)
  {
   try
   {
    this.output.Clear();
    this.statusBar.Text = "";
    MessageQueueEnumerator en;
    if(this.UseMQCriteria.Checked)
    {
     MessageQueueCriteria mqc = this.GetMessageQueueCriteria();
     en = MessageQueue.GetMessageQueueEnumerator(mqc);
    }
    else
     en = MessageQueue.GetMessageQueueEnumerator();

    this.EnumerateOverMessageQueueEnumerator(en);
   }
   catch(Exception ex)
   {
    this.statusBar.Text = ex.Message;
   }
  }

private MessageQueueCriteria GetMessageQueueCriteria()
  {
   MessageQueueCriteria mqc = new MessageQueueCriteria();

   if(this.Category_Check.Checked)
    mqc.Category = new System.Guid(this.Category_Value.Text.Trim());

   if(this.Label_Check.Checked)
    mqc.Label = this.Label_Value.Text.Trim();

   if(this.MachineName_Check.Checked)
    mqc.MachineName = this.MachineName_Value.Text.Trim();
```

```
    if(this.CreatedAfter_Check.Checked)
     mqc.CreatedAfter = this.CreatedAfter_Value.Value;

    if(this.CreatedBefore_Check.Checked)
     mqc.CreatedBefore = this.CreatedBefore_Value.Value;

    if(this.ModifiedAfter_Check.Checked)
     mqc.ModifiedAfter = this.ModifiedAfter_Value.Value;

    if(this.ModifiedBefore_Check.Checked)
     mqc.ModifiedBefore = this.ModifiedBefore_Value.Value;

    return mqc;


  }


private void
EnumerateOverMessageQueueEnumerator(MessageQueueEnumerator en)
  {

    while(en.MoveNext())
    {
    MessageQueue mq = en.Current;
    this.output.AppendText("------------------");
    this.output.AppendText("\r\n");
    this.output.AppendText(mq.FormatName);
    this.output.AppendText("\r\n");
    this.output.AppendText("------------------");
    this.output.AppendText("\r\n");


    }

  }
```

In this listing, we cover three methods from the MessageQueueOperation Console application: GetMessageQueueEnumerator_Click(), GetMessageQueueCriteria(), and EnumerateOverMessageQueueEnumerator(). In GetMessageQueueEnumerator_Click(), we check if the RadioButton Use MessageQueueCriteria is checked or not. If it is, we call the GetMessageQueueCriteria() method, which gets the value of each of the criteria specified in the controls in the MessageQueue criteria group box. These criteria values include the Category or Type ID of the queue, the Label of the queue, and the MachineName of the queue, as well as the CreatedAfter, CreatedBefore, ModifiedAfter, and ModifiedBefore DateTime values. The CreatedAfter DateTime value is used to get queues created after this date. Similarly, the CreatedBefore DateTime value is used to get queues created before this date. The ModifiedAfter DateTime value is used to get queues that were modified after this date, and the ModifiedBefore DateTime value is used to get queues modified before this value.

After setting the values of the MessageQueueCriteria object, we return the object to be passed to the MessageQueue.GetMessageQueueEnumerator() method. This method returns a MessageQueueEnumerator object. We pass this object to the EnumerateOverMessageQueueEnumerator() method to traverse the enumerator and display the FormatName of each of the returned queues in the output box. We can traverse the MessageQueueEnumerator by calling its MoveNext() method. The Current property of the MessageQueueEnumerator represents a MessageQueue object.

Managing Messages

Message administration is required for efficient functioning of the Message Queuing network. To manage messages in a queue, an administrator should be able to set and get properties of the queue, view the message properties, change the message property column, purge messages in the queue, and set the default lifetime for messages.

Viewing Message Properties from the Computer Management Console

To view properties of the messages in a queue, right-click on the queue in the Computer Management console and click on Properties. A dialog box showing the properties will appear as shown in Figure 3-18; you can click on the tab and view the properties of the messages.

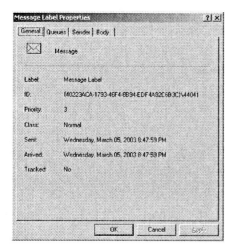

Figure 3-18. Viewing message properties from Console Management

Viewing Message Properties

To view the properties of a message, double-click on that message in the appropriate queue and click on View ➤ Add/Remove Columns.

You can add more columns as needed by clicking the Add button or remove columns by highlighting the columns in the display box and then clicking the Remove button.

If you want to change the order of display, move the columns by clicking on the Move Up or Move Down button, as shown in Figure 3-19.

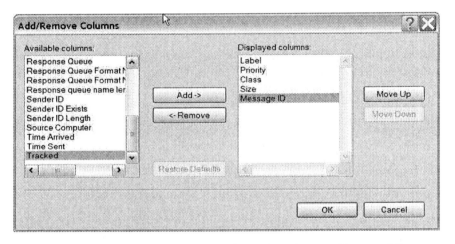

Figure 3-19. Managing messages using the Active Directory Users and Computer MMC snap-in on the domain controller

Changing the Default Lifetime of Messages

The default lifetime of a message is the default value of the TimeToBeReceived property of the messages. If the messages stay in a queue longer than the TimeToBeReceived value, they are considered expired and are removed from the queue. If the UseDeadLetter property of the message is true, it will be sent to the appropriate dead-letter queue. The message itself can override the default lifetime value if the sending application set the TimeToBeReceived property to a value different from the default value. To change the default lifetime of the messages in the network, open Start ➤ Programs ➤ Administrative Tools ➤

Active Directory Sites and Services. Expand the Service tree node and right-click MsmqServices ➤ Properties to open the MsmqService Properties dialog box, as shown in Figure 3-20.

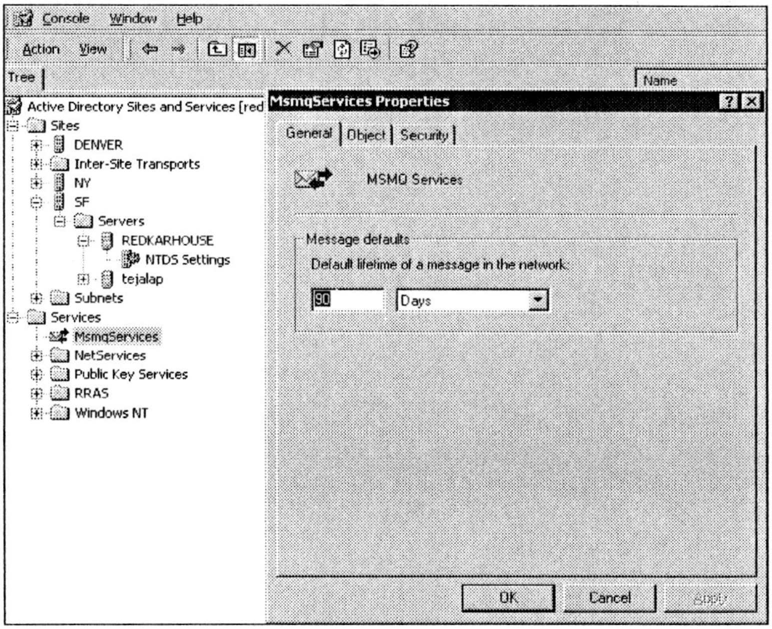

Figure 3-20. The MsmqService Properties dialog box

Monitoring Dead-Letter and Transactional Dead-Letter Queues

The dead-letter queue contains expired messages that were not delivered to the receiving application. Similarly, the transactional dead-letter queue contains transactional messages that were not delivered to the receiving application. A message is considered to be expired when its TimeToBeReceived property is set by the sending application and it is not received by the receiving application in that specified amount of time. So, to keep track of expired messages, you should monitor these queues. Figure 3-21 shows the dead-letter and transactional dead-letter queues.

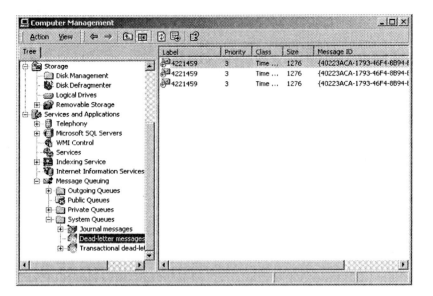

Figure 3-21. The dead-letter queue

The dead-letter and transactional dead-letter queues can also be monitored programmatically. The following path values are used to access these queues:

Dead-Letter Queue Path

```
FormatName:DIRECT=TCP:[IPAddress]\SYSTEM$;DEADLETTER
```

or

```
FormatName:DIRECT=OS:<machine name>\SYSTEM$;DEADLETTER
```

For example:

```
FormatName:DIRECT=TCP:10.1.48.67\SYSTEM$;DEADLETTER
```

or

```
FormatName:DIRECT=OS:redkarhouse\SYSTEM$;DEADLETTER
```

Transaction Dead-Letter Queue Path

FormatName:DIRECT=TCP:[IPAddress]\SYSTEM$;DEADXACT

or

FormatName:DIRECT=OS:<machine name>\SYSTEM$;DEADXACT

For example:

FormatName:DIRECT=TCP:10.1.48.67\SYSTEM$;DEADXACT

or

FormatName:DIRECT=OS:redkarhouse\SYSTEM$; DEADXACT

Message Tracking

Report queues can be used to track messages in a Message Queuing network. Report queues are public queues that contain routing information about the message from its source to the destination. Report queues can be used only if the administrator on the source computer enables message-route tracking and tracing is requested by the sending application. A report message is generated every time a message leaves or arrives at the Message Queuing computer. There can be only one report queue per computer, but one message can be tracked by multiple report queues along its path. The TypeID setting (GUID) for report queues is constant and must have the following value:

TypeID (GUID): {55EE8F32-CCE9-11CF-B108-0020AFD61CE9}

Report queues can be created using the Computer Management or the Active Directory Users and Computers interface. To create a report queue, open the Active Directory Users and Computers console, create a queue named **MyReportQ**, and change its Label and Type ID to the values shown in Figure 3-22.

Once you've created the report queue, you can then set up message route tracking from the Active Directory Users and Computers interface. Open this interface and right-click on the msmq node under the source machine. Then click Properties to open the Properties window. In the Properties window, click on the Diagnostics tab, as shown in Figure 3-23.

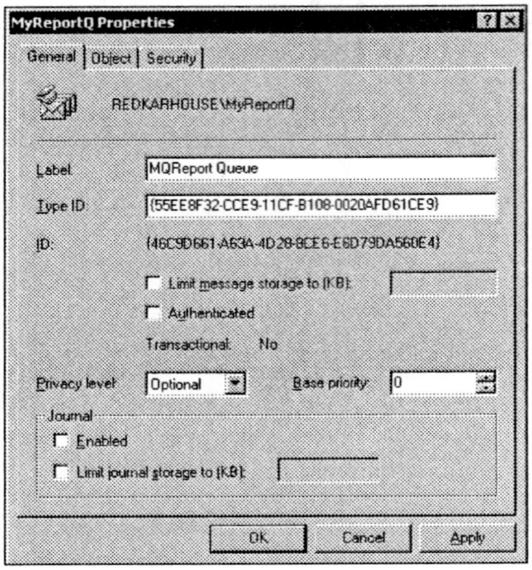

Figure 3-22. Report queues

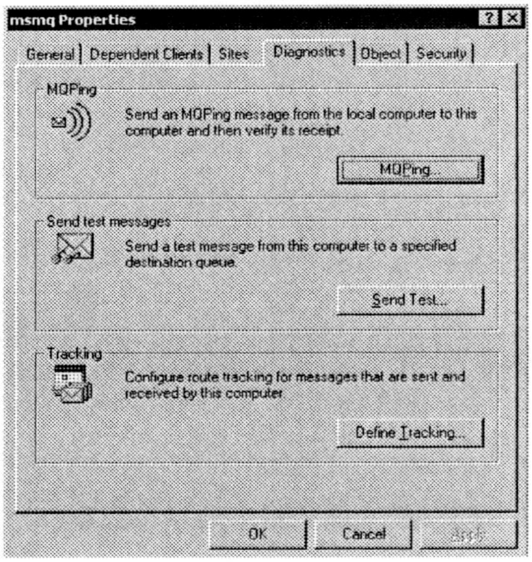

Figure 3-23. msmq diagnostics

Click the Define Tracking button to open the Message Route Tracking dialog box, shown in Figure 3-24.

From the drop-down list, choose the myreportq that you just created. If myreportq does not show up in the list, check the Label and Type ID of the queue that you created. Choose the Track Only Test Messages option to track only messages with the Use Tracking property set to true.

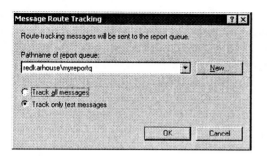

Figure 3-24. Message Route Tracking

Now create another public queue on another machine on the network using the Active Directory Users and Computers interface. In this example, I have created a queue named reporttest on a machine named ARJUN in the same domain. Then, send a message to the reporttest queue on ARJUN from the source machine (where the report queue is created, e.g., redkarhouse), as shown in Figure 3-25.

NOTE   *For Message Route Tracking to work, the sent message must have the Use Tracking property set to true (if you specified Track Only Test Messages).*

If you selected Track All Messages instead, remember to reset the setting once you are done with your tests; otherwise, any message leaving the machine will create report messages regardless of the status of the tracking setting. This can slow down the machine considerably and overfill the report queue.

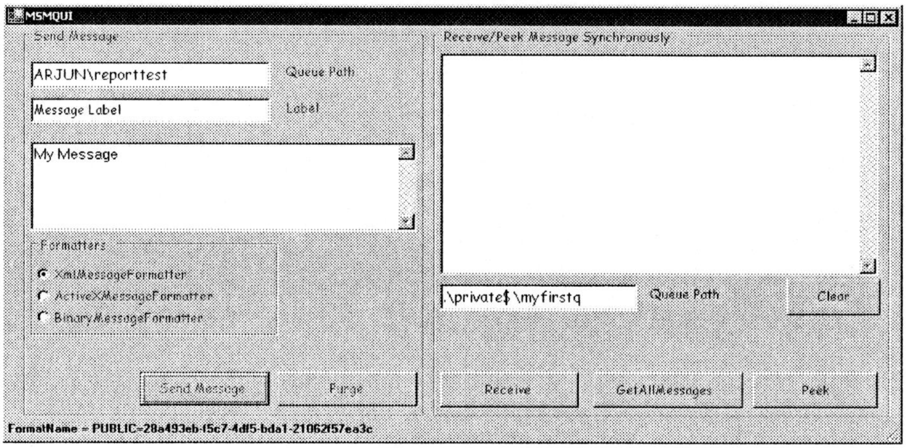

Figure 3-25. Sending messages to a public queue

Two report messages will be created in the myreportq queue on the source machine. One report message indicates that the message was sent from the source machine (e.g., redkarhouse), and the second message specifies that the message was received by the destination machine (e.g., ARJUN). Figure 3-26 shows the two report messages from the Computer Management console. It is also possible to create a report queue on the destination machine. In that case, the report queue on the destination machine will contain only one report message specifying that the message was received.

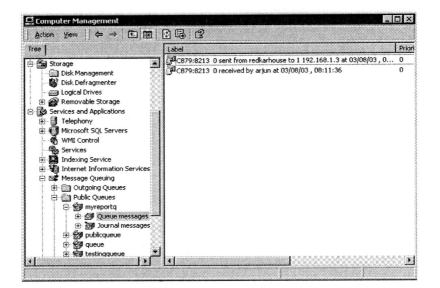

Figure 3-26. Report messages

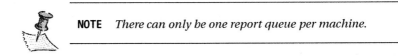

NOTE   *There can only be one report queue per machine.*

The format of the label of the report messages is as follows:

```
gggg:dddd:hh sent from <computer> to <address> at <time>
gggg:dddd:hh received by <computer> to <address> at <time>
```

where *gggg* consists of the first four hexadecimal digits of the GUID of the source queue, *dddd* is the internal message identifier, and *hh* is the hop count.

The format of the body of the report messages is shown in Figure 3-27.

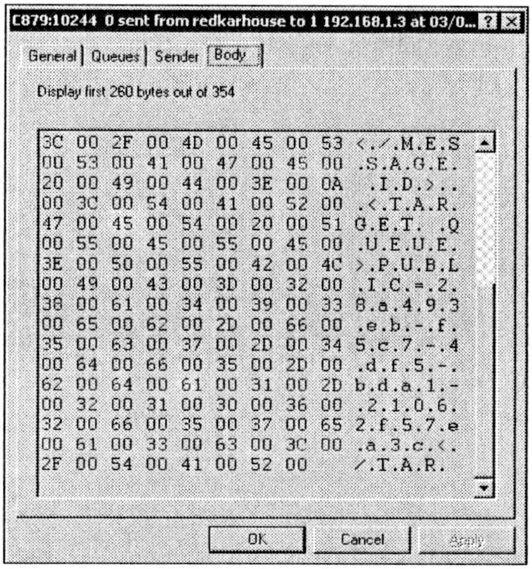

Figure 3-27. Report message body

The body of the message contains the message identifier of the original message and the format name of the target queue. The message may also contain the IP address of the machine to which the message is sent as well as the hop count. The report message body is in XML-like format, as shown here:

```
<MESSAGE ID>The Message Identifier</MESSAGE ID>
<TARGET QUEUE> Format Name of the destination queue</TARGET QUEUE>
<NEXT HOP> IPAddress of the machine to which the message is sent</NEXT HOP>
<HOP COUNT>integer</HOP COUNT>
```

Monitoring Message Queuing

In this section you'll learn how to view Message Queuing events and monitor performance. Monitoring Message Queuing performance is essential to achieving optimal performance.

Viewing Message Queuing Events

Message Queuing automatically logs all the information into event logs, which you can view in the Event Viewer accessed from Administrative Tools, under Application Log and Security Log (Figure 3-28). Under the Source column, you can see MSMQ listed in both logs. To view the MSMQ event, you will have to scroll down the column. You can get the details of the log entry by double-clicking on it.

Type	Date	Time	Source	Category	Event	User	Computer
Warning	10/12/2002	2:42:02 AM	MsiInstaller	None	1015	N/A	REDKARHO...
Warning	10/12/2002	2:55:53 AM	MsiInstaller	None	1015	N/A	REDKARHO...
Information	11/8/2002	5:05:26 PM	MSMQ	Kernel	2028	N/A	REDKARHO...
Information	11/4/2002	5:36:27 PM	MSMQ	Kernel	2028	N/A	REDKARHO...
Information	11/10/2002	8:16:16 AM	MSMQ	Kernel	2028	N/A	REDKARHO...
Information	10/5/2002	11:12:02 PM	MSMQ	Kernel	2028	N/A	REDKARHO...
Information	11/4/2002	12:21:47 ...	MSMQ	Kernel	2028	N/A	REDKARHO...
Information	11/24/2002	7:18:53 AM	MSMQ	Kernel	2028	N/A	REDKARHO...
Information	12/12/2002	5:13:34 AM	MSMQ	Kernel	2028	N/A	REDKARHO...
Information	12/24/2002	6:42:19 AM	MSMQ	Kernel	2028	N/A	REDKARHO...
Information	2/3/2003	2:41:51 AM	MSMQ	Kernel	2028	N/A	REDKARHO...
Information	1/14/2003	3:30:05 PM	MSMQ	Kernel	2028	N/A	REDKARHO...
Information	2/9/2003	3:30:02 AM	MSMQ	Kernel	2028	N/A	REDKARHO...
Information	9/2/2002	11:41:51 PM	MSMQ	Kernel	2028	N/A	REDKARHO...
Information	1/6/2003	5:23:35 AM	MSMQ	Kernel	2028	N/A	REDKARHO...
Information	12/24/2002	6:27:20 AM	MSMQ	Kernel	2028	N/A	REDKARHO...
Information	11/8/2002	5:34:28 AM	MSMQ	Kernel	2028	N/A	REDKARHO...
Information	12/9/2002	7:48:03 AM	MSMQ	Kernel	2028	N/A	REDKARHO...
Information	11/20/2002	10:05:01 PM	MSMQ	Kernel	2028	N/A	REDKARHO...
Information	11/16/2002	4:53:34 AM	MSMQ	Kernel	2028	N/A	REDKARHO...
Information	1/6/2003	3:10:50 AM	MSMQ	Kernel	2028	N/A	REDKARHO...
Information	10/20/2002	4:45:25 PM	MSMQ	Kernel	2028	N/A	REDKARHO...
Information	1/4/2003	11:07:26 PM	MSMQ	Kernel	2028	N/A	REDKARHO...
Information	1/14/2003	9:18:10 AM	MSMQ	Kernel	2028	N/A	REDKARHO...
Information	10/1/2002	2:15:15 AM	MSMQ	Kernel	2028	N/A	REDKARHO...
Information	8/28/2002	2:58:37 AM	MSMQ	Kernel	2028	N/A	REDKARHO...
Information	1/14/2003	9:02:28 AM	MSMQ	Kernel	2028	N/A	REDKARHO...
Information	9/14/2002	6:09:29 PM	MSMQ	Kernel	2028	N/A	REDKARHO...
Information	12/11/2002	1:36:12 AM	MSMQ	Kernel	2028	N/A	REDKARHO...
Information	11/10/2002	7:28:44 PM	MSMQ	Kernel	2028	N/A	REDKARHO...
Information	10/27/2002	2:59:13 AM	MSMQ	Kernel	2028	N/A	REDKARHO...
Information	10/8/2002	2:49:09 AM	MSMQ	Kernel	2028	N/A	REDKARHO...
Information	9/18/2002	4:16:32 AM	MSMQ	Kernel	2028	N/A	REDKARHO...
Information	1/3/2003	4:15:50 AM	MSMQ	Kernel	2028	N/A	REDKARHO...
Information	1/14/2003	6:02:20 AM	MSMQ	Kernel	2028	N/A	REDKARHO...

Figure 3-28. Message Queuing events

Monitoring Message Queuing Transactions

Message Queuing can participate in external Microsoft Distributed Transaction Coordinator (MSDTC) transactions—which means that Message Queuing can enlist itself in the context of a global transaction that may include multiple resource managers, like SQL Server or any other transaction database. Transactions are combinations of two or more actions and detail the failure or success status of the actions. Using the MSDTC, an action is either executed or not, depending on its commit or rollback.

NOTE *Message Queuing's internal transactions cannot be viewed using the MSDTC interface because they are internal to Message Queuing and are not coordinated by MSDTC.*

To view the transaction, you will need to select Administrative Tools ➤ Component Services. In the window that opens go to Component Services | Computers | My Computer | Distributed Transaction Coordinator and click on Transaction Statistics, as shown in Figure 3-29.

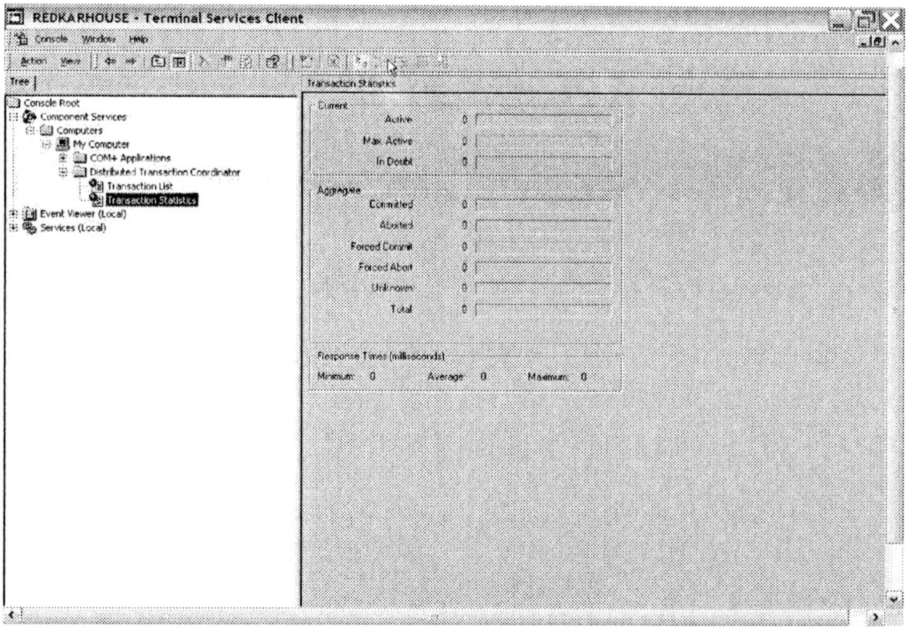

Figure 3-29. Monitoring Message Queue transactions

Transaction statistics gives the real-time transaction information. The Current section displays the number of active transactions, the maximum number of active transactions, and the transactions that are in doubt. The Aggregate section displays aggregate results. It presents the number of Committed, Aborted, Forced Commit, Forced Abort, Unknown, and Total transactions. The Response Times section shows the Minimum, Average, and Maximum response times for global transactional operations. Because multiple distributed components are involved in an external transaction, it carries a lot of overhead compared to a Message Queuing internal transaction. It is recommended that you use external transactions only if absolutely necessary due to the overhead associated with it.

Monitoring Message Queuing Performance

Performance viewing is used to keep a check on services, which can be monitored. The Message Queuing service provides performance counters specifically for monitoring. The System Monitor can be used to view these counters. The performance counters offered by Message Queuing are grouped under the following objects:

- MSMQ Service

- MSMQ Queue

- MSMQ Session

- MSMQ IS (NT4 MQIS Server—PEC, PSC, or BSC—or W2K DC, or W2K3 DC with downlevel service only)

- MSMQ Incoming HTTP Traffic (MSMQ 3.0 only)

- MSMQ Outgoing HTTP Session (MSMQ 3.0 only)

- MSMQ Outgoing Multicast Session (MSMQ 3.0 only)

- MSMQ Incoming Multicast Session (MSMQ 3.0 only)

The MSMQ Service Performance Object

This object helps in monitoring incoming and outgoing messages in Message Queuing and sessions in Message Queuing. Table 3-3 shows the counters available in this object for performance monitoring.

Table 3-3. MSMQ Service Performance Object

COUNTER	DESCRIPTION
Incoming Messages/sec	This counter monitors the rate of incoming messages handled by the Message Queuing service.
Outgoing Messages/sec	This counter monitors the rate of outgoing messages handled by the Message Queuing service.
Sessions	This counter monitors the total number of open network sessions.

Table 3-3. MSMQ Service Performance Object (continued)

COUNTER	DESCRIPTION
IP Sessions	This counter monitors the number of open IP sessions in Message Queuing.
IPX Sessions	This counter monitors the number of open IPX sessions in Message Queuing.
MSMQ Incoming Messages	This counter monitors the total number of incoming messages handled by the Message Queuing service.
MSMQ Outgoing Messages	This counter monitors the total number of outgoing messages handled by the Message Queuing service.
Total bytes in all queues	This counter monitors the total number of bytes (sum of bytes of all the messages) in all the Message Queuing queues.
Total messages in all queues	This counter monitors the sum of all the messages in all the Message Queuing queues.

Figure 3-30 shows the Add Counters dialog box, which displays a list of the MSMQ service counters.

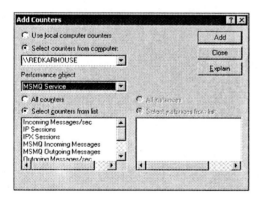

Figure 3-30. MSMQ service performance counters

The MSMQ Queue Performance Object

This counter is used to monitor individual queues that are available to the local machine for performance monitoring. Table 3-4 displays the counters that this object offers for performance monitoring.

Table 3-4. MSMQ Queue Performance Object

COUNTER	DESCRIPTION
Bytes in Journal Queue	This counter monitors the total number of bytes (sum of bytes of all the messages) in the journal queue of the selected queue. If the Computer Queues is selected, this counter will monitor the total number of bytes in the computer journal queue.
Bytes in Queue	This counter monitors the total number of bytes (sum of bytes of all the messages) in the selected queue. If the Computer Queues is selected, this counter will monitor the Dead-Letter queue.
Messages in Journal Queue	This counter monitors the total number of messages in the journal queue of the selected queue. If Computer Queues is selected, this counter will monitor the total number of messages in the computer journal queue.
Messages in Queue	This counter monitors the total number of messages in the selected queue. If Computer Queues is selected, this counter will monitor the total number of messages in the dead-letter queue.

Figure 3-31 shows the Add Counters dialog box displaying the MSMQ queue performance object counters.

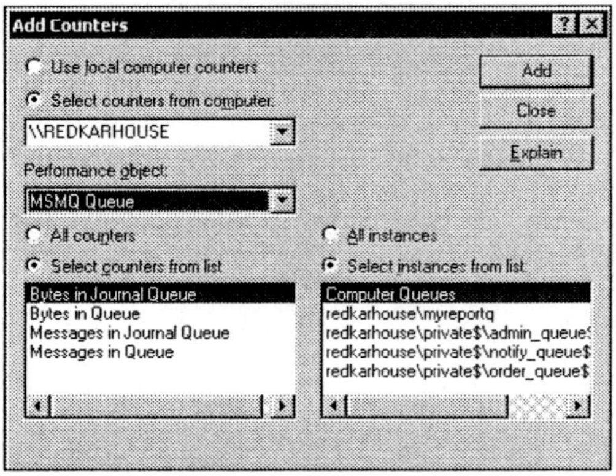

Figure 3-31. MSMQ queue performance counters

Figure 3-32 shows some of the performance counters in action on a busy Message Queuing system.

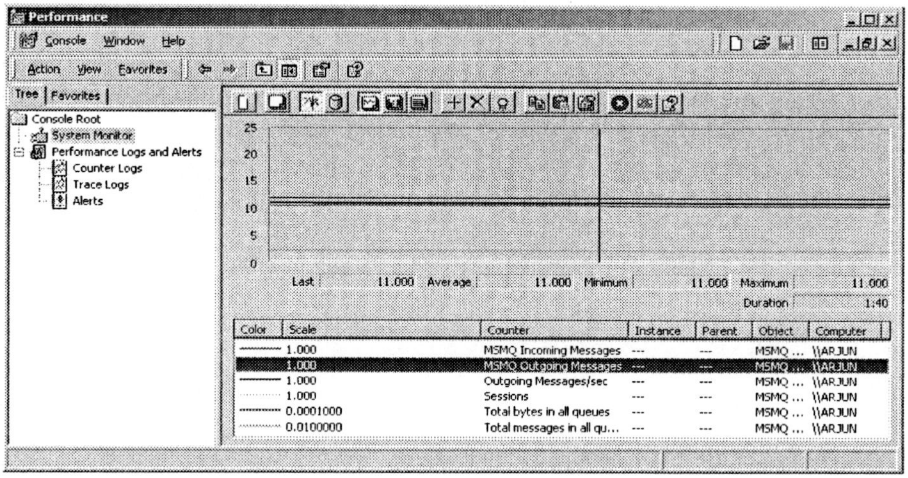

Figure 3-32. Message Queuing performance monitoring

Given that Message Queuing performance is not limited by the processor, here are some recommendations for improving its performance:

- Spread out the storage files for Message Queuing over multiple disks. This can be done using the Message Queuing Control Panel Utility (discussed later in this chapter).

- Purge all the journal queues regularly. Once the journaling is turned on for a queue for debugging purposes, the administrator often forgets to turn it off when the job is done. As a result, messages accumulate and ultimately the memory consumption goes up, leading to disk thrashing (swapping memory with the hard disk). It is also recommended that you limit the journal storage to a certain amount of bytes, so that even if the administrator forgets to turn the journaling off, the messages do not accumulate after the limit is reached.

- Monitor the dead-letter, transactional dead-letter, response, administration, and report queues constantly. Often messages accumulate in these queues, which leads to an increase in memory consumption and disk thrashing. It is recommended that you automate the task of removing messages from these queues and storing in a database for future reference.

Testing Queues

The testing of the connectivity between all the Message Queuing computers is an important factor to ensure the performance of a Message Queuing network. Let's test Message Queuing connectivity using MQPing and see how to send a test message.

Using MQPing

MSMQ has a tool called MQPing that can be used to test the connectivity of an MSMQ client or a server. Here are the steps for using MQPing from a domain controller:

1. Click Start ➤ Programs ➤ Administrative Tools ➤ Active Directory Users and Computers.

2. On the View menu, click Users, Groups, and Computers as Containers, and then click Advanced Features to view MSMQ.

3. Traverse the console tree to Active Directory Users and Computers | Our Domain | Computer or Domain Controller | Computer Name | MSMQ.

4. Right-click MSMQ to view the properties.

5. Click on the Diagnostics tab, as shown in Figure 3-33.

6. Click the MQPing button. If the operation is successful, you will see a successful ping message box, as shown in Figure 3-34.

MQPing sends a special MSMQ message to the target and gets the result using MSMQ. Therefore, it tests your MSMQ connectivity across sites and routing servers.

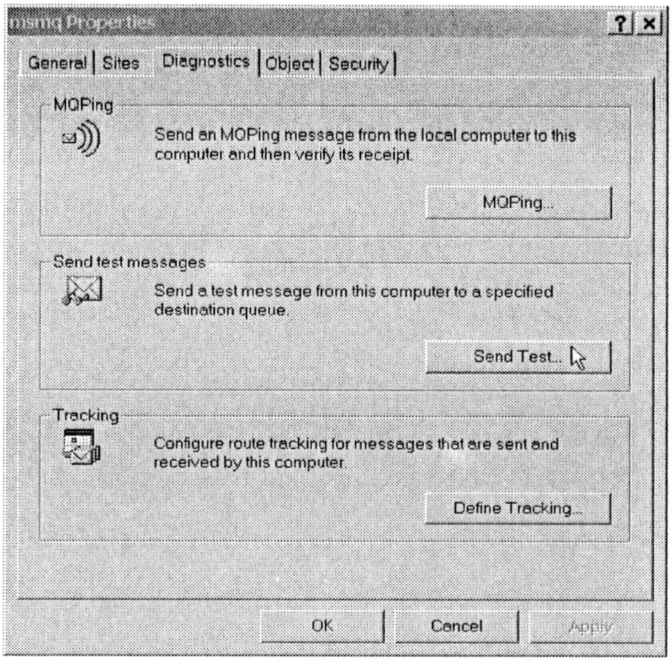

Figure 3-33. The MSMQ Diagnostics tab

Figure 3-34. MQPing Results

Sending Test Messages

Using the Diagnostics tab, you can also send test messages from any machine to queues on local or remote computers. Before sending the test message, you must first create a test queue.

NOTE *Sending test messages involves three parties:*
    1. The monitor—the machine that runs Active Directory Users &
Computers
    2. The sender—the machine whose properties are displayed
on Active Directory Users & Computers
    3. The receiver—the queue that receives the test messages
    The test messages are sent from the sender to the receiver by the
order of the monitor. All test messages are sent with the trace bit
turned on, so they can be tracked using the report feature.

The steps for creating a test queue are

1. Click Start ➤ Programs ➤ Administrative Tools ➤ Active Directory Users
    and Computers.

2. On the View menu, click Users, Groups, and Computers as Containers,
    and then click Advanced Features to view MSMQ.

3. Traverse the console tree to Active Directory Users and Computers | Our
    Domain | Computer or Domain Controller | Computer Name | msmq.

4. Right-click msmq, select MSMQ Queue from the New submenu, as
    shown in Figure 3-35.

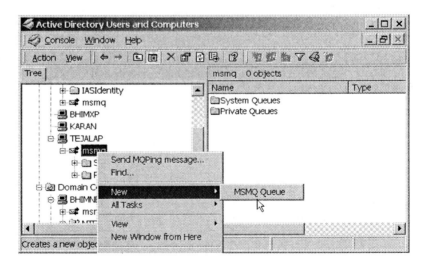

Figure 3-35. Creating a new test queue

5. Name the queue, as shown in Figure 3-36, and click OK. Make sure that you don't check the Transactional check box because test queues cannot be transactional.

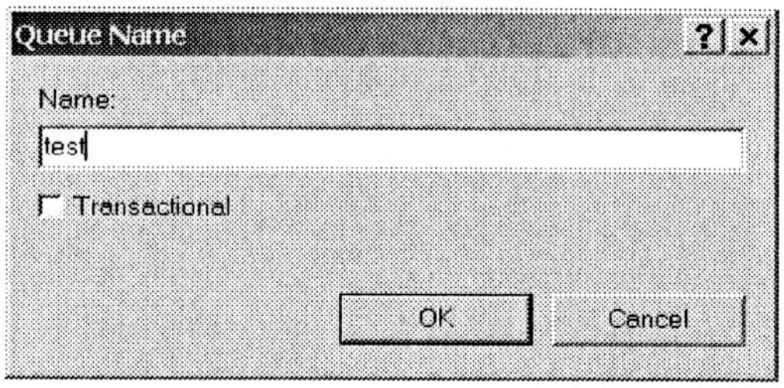

Figure 3-36. Naming the test queue

6. Right-click on the created test queue and open its Properties window.

7. Change the Type ID of the test queue to {55EE8F33-CCE9-11CF-B108-0020AFD61CE9}, as shown in Figure 3-37.

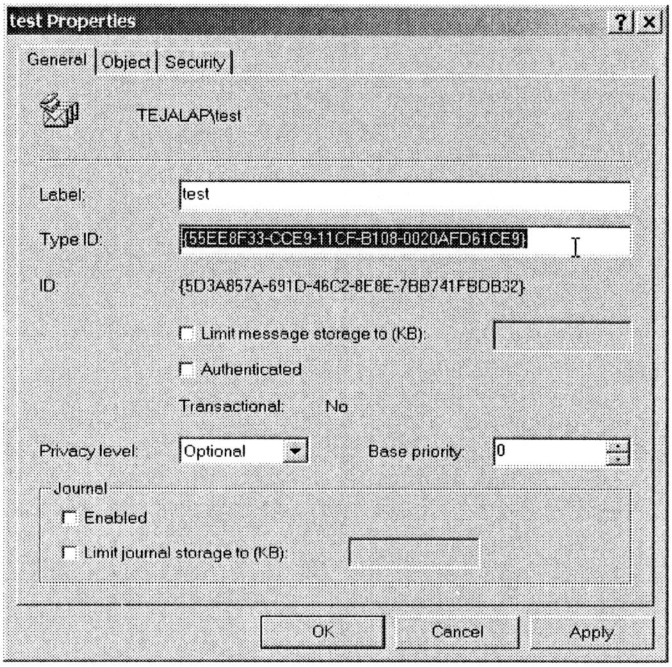

Figure 3-37. Test queue properties

8. Now go to the domain controller and click the Diagnostics tab as you did when sending MQPing, for the machine on which you created the test queue.

9. Click the Send Test button to open the Send Test Messages dialog box.

10. You should see the test queue in the drop-down list. (If you don't, double-check the Type ID of the test queue.) Choose the test queue from the drop-down list.

11. Click Send, as shown in Figure 3-38.

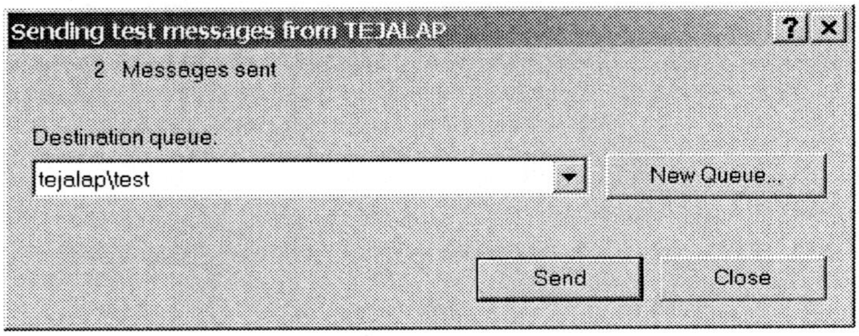

Sending test messages from TEJALAP ? ✕

　　　2　Messages sent

Destination queue:

tejalap\test ▾　　　New Queue...

　　　　　　　　　　　　　Send　　　Close

Figure 3-38. Sending the test message

NOTE *You can create test queues using this dialog box, without having to remember the test queue Type ID GUID, by clicking New Queue.*

12. Now you can view the test messages from the Computer Management console of the local machine, as shown in Figure 3-39.

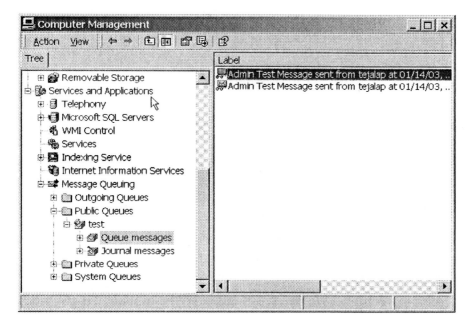

Figure 3-39. Viewing test messages

Security

Message Queuing integrates tightly with the Windows operating system security. Message Queuing uses access control lists (ACLs), authentication, encryption, and auditing for security.

Access Control Lists (ACL)

ACL is used to restrict user access to Message Queuing objects in Active Directory as well as locally (for a workgroup install). To access the security description for a particular queue, open the Message Queuing MMC snap-in on the local machine, right-click on the desired queue, and click Properties. Figure 3-40 shows the Security tab in the Properties window.

If you click the Advanced button, you will see the dialog box shown in Figure 3-41.

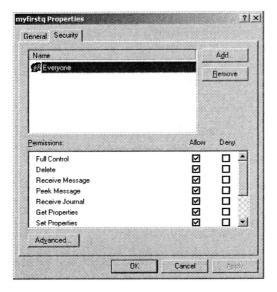

Figure 3-40. The ACL security interface

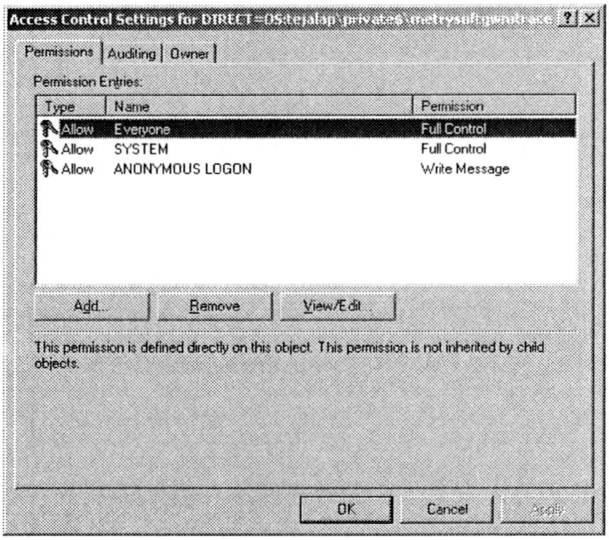

Figure 3-41. The advanced security options

Using the options in this window, you can change the permissions by adding and removing users from the Permissions tab. The Auditing tab is used to add users for recording access events. The Owner tab lets you change the ownership of the queue. When a queue is created manually, typically the queue will have Full Control for everyone. But if the queue created by the System account (e.g., a Windows service running under the System account), then other users are not allowed to access the queue. Only the System account has permission to access the queue. Even if you log in as the administrator and try to access the queue manually, you will be denied access to the queue. Therefore, you will have to first take the ownership of the queue from the System using the advanced security properties interface. Once ownership is transferred from the System account to the administrator, the administrator can then add itself as a user of the queue, using the Permissions tab.

The permissions can also be changed programmatically using the System.Messaging API from the .NET Framework. The following shows how to give Full Control to the Everyone account:

```
MessageQueue tempq = MessageQueue.Create

(@".\private$\myfirstq");
tempq.SetPermissions↵
(new MessageQueueAccessControlEntry↵
(new Trustee("Everyone"),↵
MessageQueueAccessRights.FullControl));
```

Here, we've created a new queue and then set its permissions using the SetPermissions() method of the MessageQueue class. This method takes a MessageQueueAccessControlEntry object. So, we've created a MessageQueueAccessControlEntry object and pass it to the SetPermissions() method. The MessageQueueAccessControlEntry accepts a Trustee object and the MessageQueueAccessRights enum. Simply create a Trustee object for the Everyone account and give it full control.

Authentication

Authentication allows the receiver to verify the sender's identity and integrity of the message. A digital signature is used to check whether the message has been tampered with during transmission across the network. Because Message Queuing is an asynchronous messaging system, the sender and receiver do not have to be online to verify each other's authenticity.

The authentication process is based on the asymmetric key protocol that is linked to internal as well as external certificates. Certificates, which are used for authentication of the identity of the sender and receiver, are issued by the certificate authorities. The internal certificate is generated by MSMQ and the external certificate is issued by external certificate authorities such as VeriSign.

Here are the steps that the Message Queuing client on the source computer follows for authenticating a message:

1. Message Queuing creates a hash value for a message using the digital signature and a hash algorithm.

2. Message Queuing then encrypts the hash value using the private key of the source computer.

3. Message Queuing then attaches the digital signature, security ID (SID), and the user certificate to the message.

User certificates can be managed using the Message Queuing Control Panel utility.

On the destination computer, the Message Queuing service does the following:

- Using the public key contained in the user certificate, the Message Queuing service decrypts the hash value of the message using the public cryptographic key.

- It recalculates the hash value of the message locally and compares it with the hash value of the message.

- If the calculated hash value matches the hash value of the message, the Message Queuing service locates the user certificate in Active Directory and verifies that the user who registered the certificate matches the senderID contained in the message and also verifies that the message was not tampered with during delivery.

Encryption

Using encryption, Message Queuing encrypts the message on the source computer and decrypts the message on the destination computer.

Here are the steps that Message Queuing takes while encrypting and decrypting messages:

1. Obtains public key of the destination computer

2. Creates a secret key

3. Encrypts the message body using the secret key

4. Encrypts the secret key using the public key of the destination computer

5. Attaches the encrypted secret key to the encrypted message

Message Queuing decrypts the encrypted message on the destination computer in the following manner:

- Decrypts the secret key attached to the message using its private key

- Decrypts the message body using the secret key

Backing Up and Restoring Message Queuing Storage Files

Message Queuing comes with a command-line utility, mqbkup.exe, located in C:\winnt\system32, that can used to back up and restore message storage files, log files, transaction log files, and Registry settings against computer failure. To back up the files on the local machine, run the mqbkup.exe application from the command prompt as follows.

1. First, create a directory for storing the backup files (e.g., C:> mkdir msmqbackup).

2. Run the mqbkup.exe command from the command prompt, as shown in Figure 3-42.

Figure 3-42. mqbkup application

The syntax of the mqbkup.exe utility is

```
mqbkup {-b backupfolderpath | -rrestorefolderpath | -?}
```

where

```
-b backupfolderpath   backs up the files to the specified folder
-rrestorefolderpath   restores the files from the specified folder
-? displays help for the utility
```

NOTE   *Using backup/restore on one machine only is usually meaningless and may lead to inconsistencies and loss of messages. Backup/restore is only meaningful when a snapshot of all the machines involved in MSMQ communication is taken and restored at the same time.*

The Message Queuing Control Panel Utility

The Message Queuing Control Panel utility can be used to perform the following local administrative tasks.

NOTE   *All the MSMQ Control Panel tasks were moved to the Computer Management snap-in in MSMQ 3.0.*

Managing Message Queuing Storage Files

The files where messages are stored can be found using the Control Panel Message Queuing utility. Click Start ➤ Settings ➤ Control Panel ➤ Message Queuing utility. Figure 3-43 shows the user interface of this utility.

The Message Files folder holds files containing Message Queuing messages, the Message Logger folder contains log messages, and the Transaction Logger folder contains transaction log messages. To improve the performance of the Message Queuing system and to reduce the I/O on a single disk, you can specify different disks for storing data files.

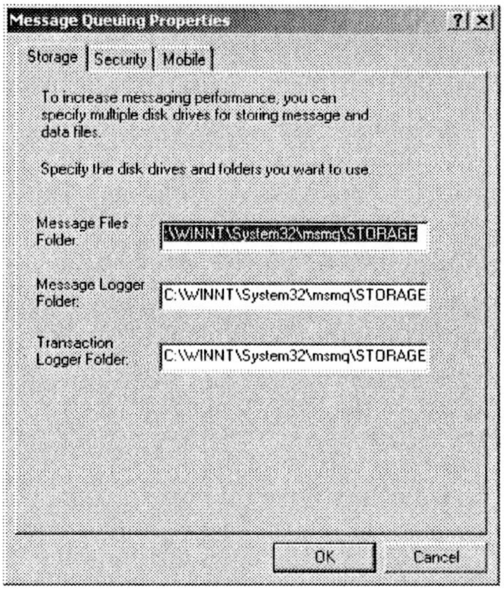

Figure 3-43. Message Queuing Properties

Managing User Certificates

You can register, view, remove, and renew user certificates on the Security tab, as shown in Figure 3-44.

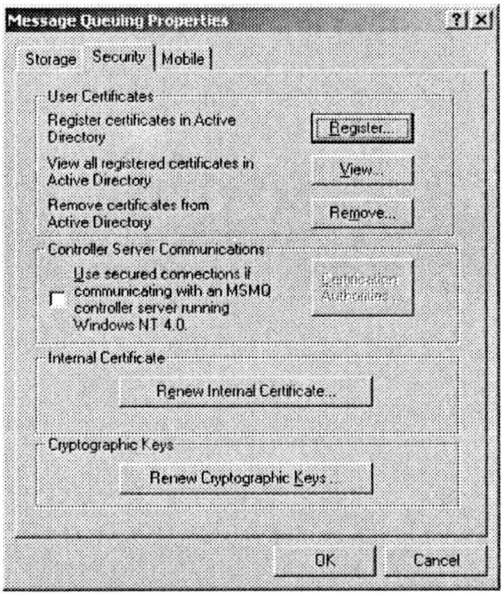

Figure 3-44. Registering the user certificate

From the Security tab, you can register a user certificate that will be registered with the Active Directory and can be used in Message Queuing applications. The interface also allows you to view and remove user certificates.

Cryptographic keys are public/private keys automatically generated during the Message Queuing installation. This user interface allows us to renew the cryptographic keys. The user should be aware that the messages that were sent using the previous cryptographic keys couldn't be decrypted. This occurs only until the public keys are replicated across the Active Directory and all the source computers start using it. The cryptographic key feature is not available to dependent clients because dependent clients rely on their Message Queuing server for most of the services.

Changing the Message Queuing Site for Mobile Clients

The Mobile tab is used to specify a new site for mobile Message Queuing clients, as shown in Figure 3-45.

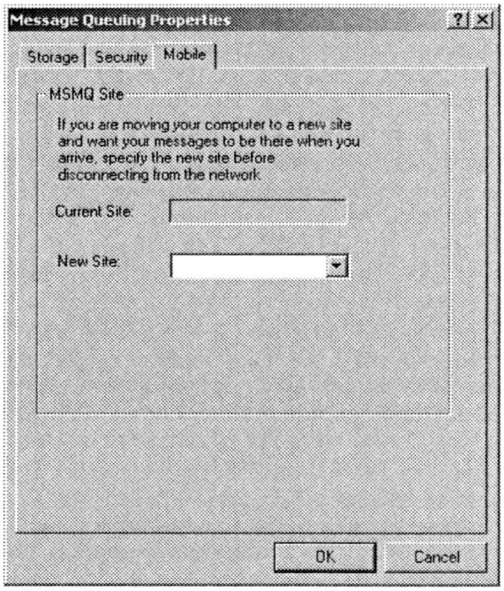

Figure 3-45. Changing the Message Queuing site

Using the MSMQ site interface, you can change the current site to a new one. This feature is used for forwarding messages to the new site if the mobile client is planning to move to a new site.

Administering a Message Queuing Network

In this section, we create a pseudo Message Queuing network that will help you understand how to administer a Message Queuing network. We include some terminology that is important to understand while administering a Message Queuing network.

MSMQ Servers

The MSMQ server forms the backbone of the MSMQ infrastructure and has the following features:

- Runs the MSMQ service

- Hosts queues

- Stores messages locally

- Sends and receives messages by default

- Supports dependent clients

The MSMQ 2.0 server comes with Windows 2000 Server and Windows 2000 Advanced Server, and the MSMQ 3.0 server comes with Windows XP and Windows 2003 servers.

If installed with routing services enabled, the MSMQ server can provide message routing and intermediate store-and-forward MSMQ. This kind of server can route messages between MSMQ clients not directly connected to each other.

Independent/Dependent Clients

When installing MSMQ clients, it is important to decide beforehand whether you need a dependent client or an independent client.

Independent clients do not need an active connection with the MSMQ server to send messages, whereas a dependent client cannot function without an active connection with MSMQ.

Independent Clients

An independent client has the following features:

- Runs the MSMQ service.

- Hosts queues.

- Stores messages locally.

- Sends and receives messages by default.

- Can operate in a disconnected network.

- Does not require a live connection with the MSMQ server.

- Independent clients do not provide access to the Active Directory for MSMQ 1.0 or 2.0 clients, but for MSMQ 3.0, all clients speak directly to the Active Directory infrastructure, and there is no need for an Active Directory server unless downlevel client support is requested.

- Independent clients is the recommended way to install MSMQ on a client OS, mobile or not.

Dependent Clients

Dependent clients have the following features:

- They require a live connection with an MSMQ server.

- They do not host queues or store messages locally, and they cannot send and receive messages on their own. They rely on the supporting MSMQ server to perform these functions.

- Queue access for dependent clients is slower than for independent clients because they (dependent clients) use RPC connections. For these reasons, a dependent client install is the least recommended install.

One more point to note is that older versions of MSMQ do not support newer versions of dependent clients. MSMQ 1.0 does not support dependent clients on MSMQ 2.0, and similarly, MSMQ 3.0 does not support dependent clients of MSMQ 1.0 or MSMQ 2.0 dependent clients.

NOTE *An independent client provides superior performance and connectivity than a dependent client, and when a client/server architecture is required for some reason, sometimes an EnterpriseServices/COM+ based solution will work better.*

The Domain Environment

In order to serve MSMQ 2.0 and 1.0 clients, MSMQ must be installed on at least one domain controller (DC) that is also a global catalog in each site. MSMQ 2.0 installed on such DCs supports Directory Service (DS) clients automatically. For MSMQ 3.0 (Windows 2003) server to support downlevel clients, you will need to select the appropriate option when installing MSMQ on the DC.

MSMQ 3.0 (XP or Windows 2003) clients do not require MSMQ to be installed on any DC, since they can talk with the Active Directory infrastructure directly. They do require, however, that at least one DC in their site also be a global catalog.

A domain controller that houses a global catalog of the Active Directory must be the first MSMQ installation in the enterprise. Installing clients before the domain controller MSMQ install can lead to the following error: "Failed to find MSMQ servers on domain controllers." As discussed earlier, in MSMQ 3.0 this is not a requirement—you can install clients before installing the MSMQ server. The reason for this is that in previous versions, the MSMQ clients would make RPC calls to the MSMQ server to handle configuration and create queues, and the server would do those things for the client. In MSMQ 3.0, the client has the capability to do these things.

NOTE *An MSMQ 2.0 install on a domain controller must always be the first installed in an MSMQ 2.0 network or enterprise. MSMQ 3.0 does not have this restriction because if all the clients are MSMQ 3.0, then installing the MSMQ 3.0 server on a domain controller is not a requirement.*

Sites

A large-scale MSMQ domain installation consists of multiple MSMQ sites interconnected with each other using routing links. Sites map to the physical topology of the network, and domains map to the logical structure of the organization. For example, there can be an MSMQ site in San Francisco and another site in New York. Even though they are two physically separate MSMQ sites, they can still belong to the same domain. On the other hand, if the network operations center of our company is located in Denver, there can be more than one MSMQ domain server hosted in Denver. In that case, Denver is a site hosting multiple domains. In short, domains and sites are two separate entities.

Domain controllers use the Active Directory DS to replicate configuration and status information across multiple sites using site links. In an Active Directory directory, all the domain controllers can read from and write to the objects stored.

Routing Links and Site Gates

Routing links are used by MSMQ servers to route messages between sites with the help of MSMQ servers that function as routers between sites. These MSMQ servers are called *site gates*. Site links are totally different from routing links and are used by domain controllers to replicate Active Directory information between sites. Site gates are MSMQ routers used for creating logical communication links between two MSMQ sites.

In Figure 3-46, there are two sites, A and B. Site A has the domain controller hosting an MSMQ 2.0 server, and Site B has a secondary domain controller hosting another MSMQ 2.0 server. Both the sites have site gates that can connect to the other site through a routing link.

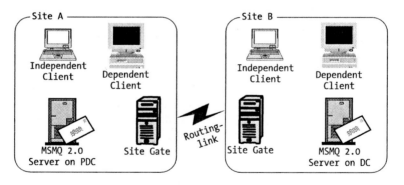

Figure 3-46. Site gates

Workgroup Install

In a workgroup installation, MSMQ is not a part of any domain, nor does MSMQ communicate with any other MSMQ server on the network.

The local MSMQ will serve as the server as well as the client, and the local queue manager will maintain all the created queues. In a Workgroup environment, a server cannot be a routing server or DS server.

We can create only private queues in a workgroup install. In Workgroup mode we can only send messages using the direct format name, which does not use any lookups or connectivity required for an Active Directory domain controller. And because of that, private queues are the only available queues. It is possible to access the private queues on the workgroup MSMQ server from a remote machine by using direct format names.

To route messages from a workgroup MSMQ install, direct connectivity with the destination computer is required. We cannot route messages using any MSMQ server on the network, as it requires access to the Active Directory.

The workgroup environment is the recommended environment for developing MSMQ applications where the developer may not have access to an Active Directory and the network connectivity is not guaranteed all the time. Sometimes in a small-scale deployment, when there are only few machines involved in a Message Queuing network, it is advantageous to use workgroup installs to avoid administration intricacies associated with Active Directory.

NOTE *All the MSMQ features exist in a workgroup environment, except*
- *Queue discovery (public queues)*
- *Routing*
- *Encryption*
- *Authentication*
- *Centralized access control*
- *Bridging*

Imetry Sample Network

To understand the administration process more clearly, let's create a pseudo network. Figure 3-47 shows the topology of our pseudo network covering most of the possible MSMQ installs.

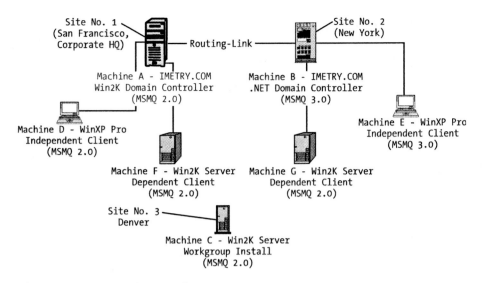

Figure 3-47. An MSMQ network

In Figure 3-47, we have three sites. Site No. 1 is located in San Francisco, Site No. 2 is located in New York, and Site No. 3 is located in Denver. Site No. 1 is our corporate headquarters, where the main MSMQ server runs and where all the MSMQ messages finally end up. Site No. 1 and Site No. 2 both host a domain controller each for the domain IMETRY.COM. Machine D is connected as an independent client to Server A. Machine F is connected as a dependent client to Server A. Machine E is connected as an independent client to Server B, and Machine G is connected as a dependent client to Server B. Site No. 3 just hosts a workgroup install of the MSMQ server. B is installed with routing services enabled and routes messages from client E and G to A. The operating systems involved in this architecture are as follows:

MSMQ Domain Servers

- Machine A – Windows 2000 Server (MSMQ 2.0)

- Machine B – Windows 2003 Server (MSMQ 3.0)

Workgroup Installation

- Machine C – Windows 2000 Server (MSMQ 2.0)

Independent Clients

- Machine D – Windows XP Professional (MSMQ 3.0)

- Machine E – Windows XP Professional (MSMQ 3.0)

Dependent Clients

- Machine F – Windows 2000 Server (MSMQ 2.0)

- Machine G – Windows 2000 Server (MSMQ 2.0)

Important administrative tasks required for maintaining the above network are creating a new site, adding servers to sites, creating a routing link between machines, configuring site gates for a routing link, and configuring firewalls.

Creating a New Site

1. To create a new site, open active Directory Sites and Services.

2. If the MsmqServices node is not visible, on the View menu, click Show Services Node.

3. Right-click on MsmqServices ➤ New Foreign Site.

4. The created site will appear under the Sites node, as shown in Figure 3-48.

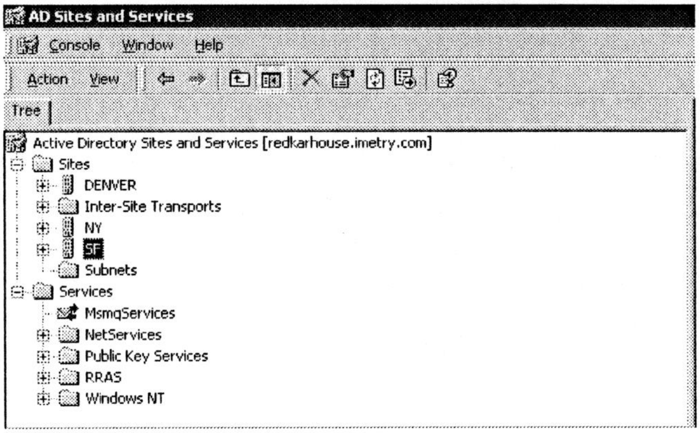

Figure 3-48. Creating a site

Adding Servers to Sites

1. To add servers to sites, expand the applicable site node.

2. Right-click on the Servers node to create a new server, as shown in Figure 3-49.

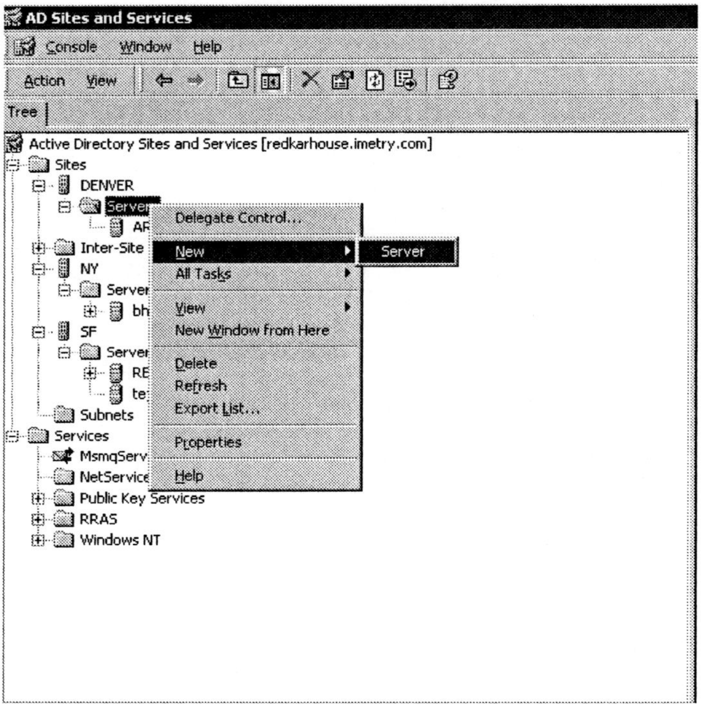

Figure 3-49. Adding a new server to a site

Creating a Routing Link Between Machine B and A

1. Open Active Directory Sites and Services.

2. In the console tree, right-click MsmqServices.

3. Click New ➤ MSMQ Routing Link to display the dialog box shown in Figure 3-50.

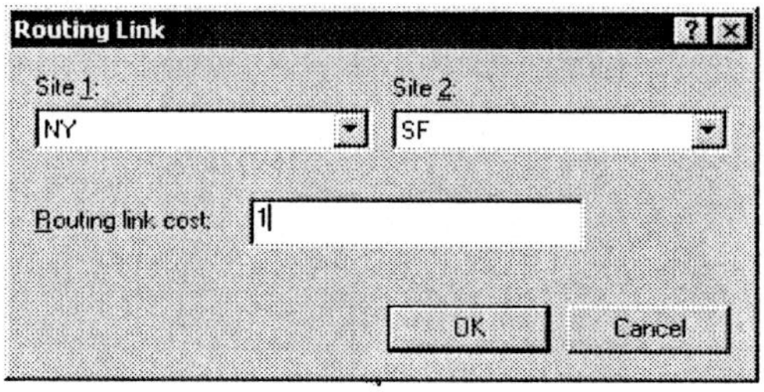

Figure 3-50. Routing a link between New York and San Francisco

4. The cost of a routing link ranges from 1 to 4,294,967,295. The default value of a routing link is 1. A cost of zero indicates that the two sites are not connected to each other at all. The routing link cost is changed only if there are multiple routing links in the network. For example, if we add one more site, London, to the above network that is connected to site SF by a low-speed link, then you can define the cost between London and SF as 2.

Configuring Site Gates for a Routing Link

1. Open Active Directory Sites and Services and click on the MsmqServices node.

2. In the details pane, you will see the created routing link.

3. Right-click on the applicable routing link and choose Properties to open the dialog box for the routing link properties, as shown in Figure 3-51.

4. Select the Site Gates tab and choose the site gates for this routing link, as shown in Figure 3-52. Then click OK.

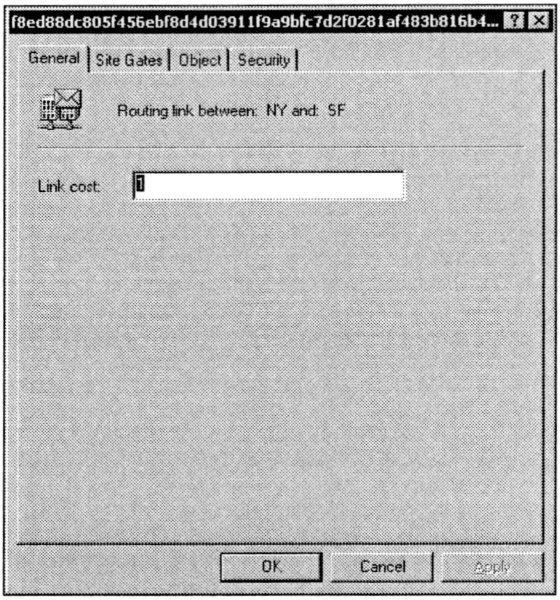

Figure 3-51. Routing link properties

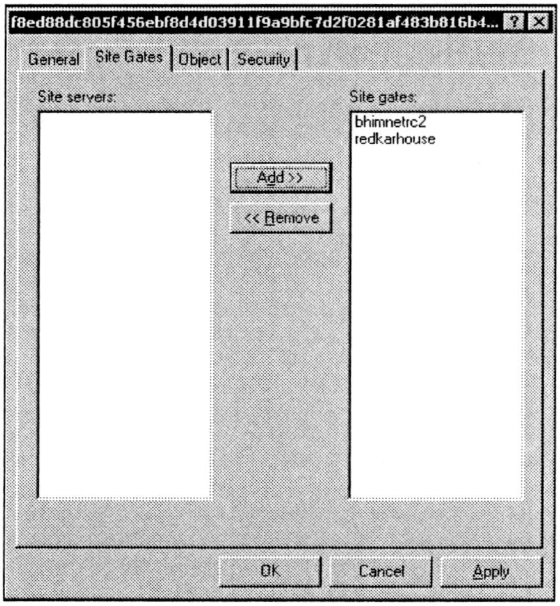

Figure 3-52. Selecting site gates

Configuring Firewalls

Most of the real-world enterprise applications have to be deployed behind fire-walls to keep them safe against hacker attacks. For Message Queuing to function across firewalls, selected service ports need to be opened in the firewall to allow Message Queuing traffic. Here are the ports that need to be opened in the firewall:

- TCP Port **1801** is the main port for sending MSMQ messages. Opening this port will allow only remote clients to connect to a destination message queuing server on the internal network.

- TCP Port **2101** is used for RPC calls, typically for queue creation and directory service functionality, like a lookup function that will happen over a Port 2101. TCP port **135** is used for handshaking between a remote client and a Message Queuing server. Opening these two ports permits remote clients access to the Active Directory.

- If the firewall is enabled to pass multicast network packets, UDP port **1801** also permits remote clients to send a broadcast message to automatically determine their site.

- UDP port **3527** is MSMQ's internal ping mechanism. Prior to sending messages, the queue managers try to ping each other over this port to make sure they can communicate, and then begin sending messages.

- TCP ports **2103** and **2105** also permits remote clients to make RPC calls to access queues and read messages on Message Queuing servers located on the internal network.

Troubleshooting Tips

Following are some troubleshooting tips to be read before installing any MSMQ:

- Follow the golden rule of thumb for installing an MSMQ 2.0 server on domain controllers as the first install in the enterprise. The error message "Failed to find MSMQ servers on domain controllers" should be a clear signal that you did not install MSMQ 2.0 on the domain controller before installing the MSMQ clients.

- If you see any errors containing "Access Denied," make sure that you have logged in using an appropriate account for installing.

- Before installing the MSMQ client (independent or dependent client), make sure the MSMQ 2.0 service on the domain controller is running. Also make sure that the domain controller is reachable from the client machine. If the setup is unable to locate a domain controller, it might prompt you to enter the name of the domain controller running the MSMQ 2.0 server.

- Sometimes you may see a "No Connection with Active Directory" or "Cannot Contact Message Queue Information Store" error (c00e0013 error code) after installing MSMQ successfully. This error means that the MSMQ on that machine is not able to connect to the information data store. Our information store on Windows 2000 and Windows 2003 Server is Active Directory. Common causes for this error are DNS errors where the client is not able to resolve the computer name for the MSMQ server that has been installed. Remember that certain ports are used for MSMQ to perform the install; if any of these ports are blocked, that could also cause this error. (See the next list for some of the ports used by MSMQ.)

- Check Firewall Settings if the Message Queuing server is behind a firewall.

Microsoft's Support web site is also a good resource for researching troubleshooting information. Here is a list of some of the MSMQ support articles from Microsoft's support web site (http://support.microsoft.com):

- "Q178517 TCP, UDP, and RPC Ports Used by MSMQ"

- "Q191989 Error Message: Error 0xc00e0013, No Connection with the Sites Controller"—Discusses in-depth troubleshooting of the common c00e0013 error or "No Connection with Sites Controller." In Windows 2000, that error would be "No Connection with Active Directory."

- "Q317329 MSMQ Installation Options for Windows XP Professional"— Describes the installation options for MSMQ on Windows XP Professional. It also includes different setup errors and recommended procedures for installing MSMQ in a mixed environment.

- Another very good resource for finding troubleshooting information on MSMQ is the MSMQ newsgroup microsoft.public.msmq.programming.

- A detailed FAQ document is available on the MSMQ web site (www.microsoft.com/msmq). This document contains useful troubleshooting information.

Summary

In this chapter, you saw how an administrator interacts with Message Queuing, and how to view, manage, and test the message queues in a Message Queuing network. You also saw how you can utilize the performance monitor to view real-time as well as archived performance of Message Queuing. Finally, you saw what a deployed Message Queuing network looks like and how the administrator can create routing links and site gates for efficient message routing. In the next chapter, you will learn how Message Queuing can participate in internal as well as external (MSDTC) transactions.

CHAPTER 4

Transactional Messaging

IN AN ENTERPRISE SYSTEM, maintaining the integrity of data across various applications, message queues, databases, and machines is critical. Regardless of the scope of the application, at least some aspects of transaction processing have to be implemented to guarantee the integrity of the data. Transaction processing systems are the backbone of nearly all data processing systems. These systems process the transactions that drive the modern business world, including banking, airline reservation systems, retail systems, and stock exchanges. The typical consumer encounters transaction processing systems dozens of times each day, from using the telephone to accessing bank accounts to the ATM. In this chapter you will learn about the transaction support in Message Queuing. As you will see, Message Queuing supports internal as well as external transactions.

Transaction Processing Fundamentals

A transaction is a unit of work in which either all the work is completed or all the work is rolled back. In short, the work entirely succeeds or it entirely fails. Modern transaction systems guarantee data integrity by organizing modifications to the resource (database, message queuing, etc.) into one single *transaction*. For example, a transaction might move $1000 from a person's savings account to his checking account. During this process, if the computer crashes or the transaction is otherwise interrupted, certain data integrity features of the transaction processing system ensure that the $1000 in the savings account remain intact and at the same time makes sure that an extra $1000 is not added to the checking account. The two most commonly used transaction models are Online Transactional Processing (OLTP) and Queued Transactions in the form that Message Queuing supports.

A transaction takes the general simple form

```
<begin transaction>
statement
statement
statement

procedure
statement
<commit transaction>
```

Each statement or procedure is either an SQL statement, which eventually may result in some change to the database; a Message Queue send operation; or a call to some legacy procedure that can contribute to a transaction.

If the transaction is interrupted before *commit transaction*, no permanent change is made to the resource; this is called *rollback*.

Resource managers (RMs), such as databases, and message queues are designed so that transactions have four properties that preserve data integrity. These properties are known as the ACID properties:

Atomicity: All changes that were made as part of the transaction are either completely committed or completely rolled back. For example, if there are two updates to be made to two different databases in a single transaction, if one of them fails, the entire transaction is rolled back and the database returns to its original state; that is, both the database updates appear as a single unit of work.

Consistency: The effects of a transaction preserve invariant (uniform) properties. This means that the transaction will leave the system's state consistent after a transaction completes.

Isolation: Isolation means concurrently executing transactions can't see each other's incomplete results. Isolation allows multiple transactions to write to a database without knowing about each other.

Durability: The effects of a transaction are persistent; that is, they continue indefinitely into the future. They are never lost even in case of a system failure.

Message Queuing Transactions

Message Queuing supports internal as well as external transactions. In internal transactions, single or multiple messages can be sent within a single transaction; in external transactions, Message Queuing can participate in a global transaction coordinated by Microsoft Distributed Transaction Coordinator (MSDTC) that may include other RMs like MS SQL Server. There is a semantic contradiction between transactions and asynchronous messaging. The sending and the receiving applications are interested in guaranteed message delivery, but the transaction cannot guarantee it because the ACK round-trip time for asynchronous technology in general is unpredictable. So, in case of MSMQ, the transaction is always local and includes separate acts of sending, separate acts of receiving, or separate actions of other RMs. For example, let's consider an application that is responsible for synchronizing two databases in which the message sender begins a transaction, updates the first database, and sends a message to the queue, and the receiver receives the message, updates the second database, and then commits the entire transaction. This transaction is not possible because of the asynchronous nature of MSMQ. A point to be noted here is that in case of external transactions, MSMQ does not propagate transactional context between the sender and the receiver. In a typical MSDTC transaction involving MSMQ, there are three units of work: the sender sending a message to MSMQ (Unit 1), the message ordering in MSMQ (Unit 2), and the receiver receiving the message (Unit 3). All the three units of work are independent of one another. MSMQ guarantees Unit 2 by providing exactly one delivery of the messages and ordering of the messages in the order in which they were received from the sender.

To send and receive transactional messages, the queue must be a transactional queue. The decision of specifying a queue as transactional is made during the creation of the queue. When creating the queue manually from the Message Queuing MMC snap-in, you click the transactional check box, as shown in Figure 4-1.

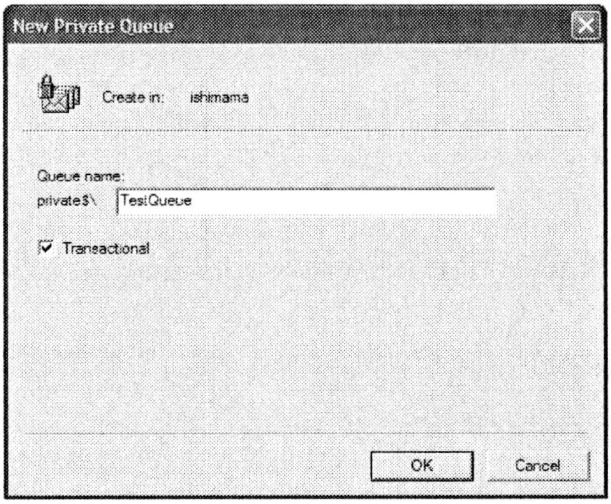

Figure 4-1. Creating a transactional queue

When you're creating a transactional queue programmatically, the `Create()` function accepts a Boolean value that must be set to `true`, as shown here:

```
MessageQueue.Create("@.\private$\mytransactionalqueue", true);
```

In Message Queuing, transactions enable multiple sends and receive within the context of the transaction. The advantage of this is that if one send or receive operation fails, none of the other operations in the same transaction succeed. Transactional messaging also guarantees that if multiple messages are sent to the same queue within the transaction, they will be received in exactly the same order in which they were sent. This is achieved by sending all the messages in a transaction using a single message stream. Each message in the stream carries a sequence number and the sequence number of the previous message (previous number). Before the message is sent to the queue, it is required to have a message with the previous number present in the queue. The first message will always have the previous number of zero.

NOTE *Only transactional messages can be sent to and received from a transactional queue. A* MessageQueueException *with the "Wrong Transaction Usage" message is thrown if the message is not transactional. An exception to this is if the sender application is using direct format names, the message is rejected, and a NACK (negative acknowledgement message) is sent (if it was requested by the sender).*

In general, transactional messaging guarantees the following:

Ordered delivery: This means that if the transaction is committed successfully, Message Queuing guarantees that all the messages encompassed in the transaction are received in the same order in which they were sent. None of the messages are sent if the transaction aborts. Because of guaranteed ordered delivery, the priority of the message does not play any part in transactional messaging. All the messages in a transaction have to have the same priority to guarantee ordered delivery.

Guaranteed delivery: Message Queuing guarantees the delivery of transactional messages to the destination once, at most.

Successful retrieval: Message Queuing ensures that transactional messages are retrieved by the destination. If the transactional messages are not retrieved successfully by the receiving application, the messages are sent to a transactional dead-letter queue.

NOTE *MSMQ stores a transactional message into the dead-letter queue if the queue manager on the source machine receives a NACK or does not receive any confirmation from the destination queue manager regarding successful delivery of the message. The presence of a message in the transaction dead-letter queue confirms that the message sent by the sending application was in doubt and may not have been retrieved by the receiving application on the destination machine.*

Internal Transactions

Internal transaction is the simplest form of transaction where there is only one resource, which is the Message Queuing server. Internal transactions are only limited to Message Queuing and cannot span other resources, like databases. Because of this, internal transactions have less overhead and are much faster than external transactions coordinated by MSDTC. To use internal transactions, you need to create a MessageQueueTransaction object, begin the transaction, carry out the Message Queuing action (Send(), Receive(), etc.), and then commit or abort the transaction. The Send() and Receive() methods of the MessageQueue class are overloaded to accept the MessageQueueTransaction object. The following code shows how to use the MessageQueueTransaction object to send multiple messages to a transactional queue:

```
MessageQueue q = new MessageQueue
  (args[0]);
using(MessageQueueTransaction mTx =
        new MessageQueueTransaction())
{
  mTx.Begin();
  try
  {
    for(int i = 0 ; i < 10 ; i++)
    {
      q.Send("Message " + i, i.ToString(), mTx);
    }
    mTx.Commit();
    Console.WriteLine("Messages sent successfully");

  }
  catch(MessageQueueException mx)
  {
    mTx.Abort();
    Console.WriteLine
      ("Exception while sending transactional messages, "
      + "aborting transaction. Error Code = "
      + mx.MessageQueueErrorCode.ToString()
      + ". Error Message " + mx.Message);

  }
```

In the preceding listing, we create an instance of the MessageQueue class based on the parameter passed by the user. Then, we create an instance of the

MessageQueueTransaction class and begin the transaction by calling the Begin() method on the MessageQueueTransaction object. After beginning the transaction, we send ten messages by calling the Send() operation in a for loop. Note that we pass the MessageQueueTransaction object as the second parameter to the Send() operation. If the Send() method is successful, we call the Commit() method on the MessageQueueTransaction object (mTx), but if an exception is thrown, we call the Abort() method on the MessageQueueTransaction object.

NOTE   *The* MessageQueueTransaction *object implements the* IDisposable *interface, so we can use it in a* using *code block.*

Figure 4-2 shows how to run the InternalTransactionSend application.

Figure 4-2. Running the internal transaction sending application

We can view the sent messages from the Message Queuing MMC snap-in, as shown in Figure 4-3. Note that the priority of the messages is 0 and not the default (3).

To deliberately abort a transaction, we can add the following line of code in the for loop of the previous application:

```
if(i == 9)
  q.Send("M");
```

When the counter is equal to 9, the nontransactional Send() operation will be called on a transactional queue and a MessageQueueException will be thrown. Abort() will be called in the exception block, and as a result, none of the messages will be sent to the queue. Thus, in a transaction, either everything succeeds or everything fails.

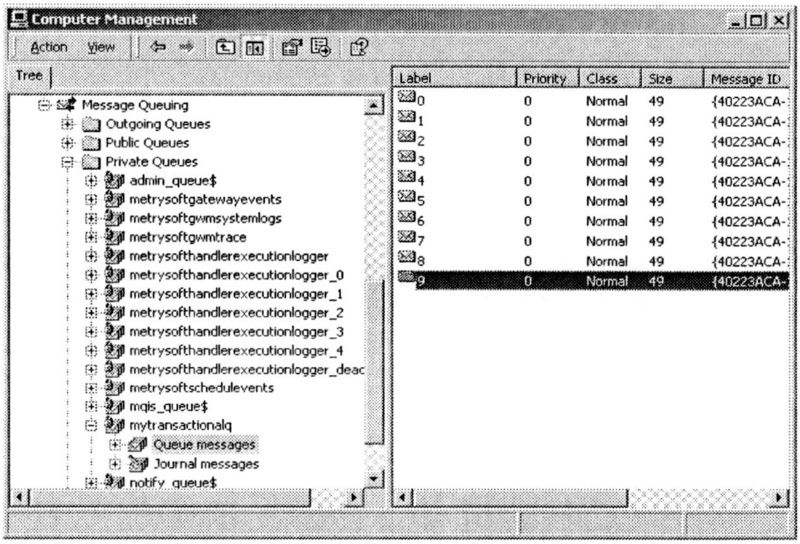

Figure 4-3. Viewing transactional messages

To receive the messages from a transactional queue, you need to call the Receive() method of the MessageQueue object within a transaction block. The following listing shows how to receive the messages sent in the preceding application:

```
try
     {
        MessageQueue q = new MessageQueue
          (args[0]);
        q.Formatter = new XmlMessageFormatter
          (new String[]{"System.String"});

        using(MessageQueueTransaction mTx =
                new MessageQueueTransaction())
        {
          mTx.Begin();
          try
          {
             for(int i = 0 ; i < 10 ; i++)
             {
```

```
            Message m = q.Receive
              (new TimeSpan(0, 0, 3), mTx);
              Console.WriteLine(m.Label + " " + m.Body);
        }
        mTx.Commit();
    }
    catch(MessageQueueException mx)
    {
        mTx.Abort();
        Console.WriteLine
            ("Exception while receiving transactional messages, "
            + "aborting transaction. Error Code = "
            + mx.MessageQueueErrorCode.ToString()
            + ". Error Message " + mx.Message);

    }
```

In the preceding listing, we create an instance of the MessageQueue class based on the path passed by the user. Then, we set the formatter for the queue to the XmlMessageFormatter, which is the default formatter when sending messages. Then, we create an instance of the MessageQueueTransaction class and begin the transaction by calling the Begin() method. Next, we call the Receive() method in a for loop to receive all the messages in the same transaction. The first parameter to the Receive() method is a TimeSpan object that specifies a timeout to wait on the Receive() method for a message to arrive in the queue. The second parameter is the MessageQueueTransaction object. Figure 4-4 shows how to run the receiving application.

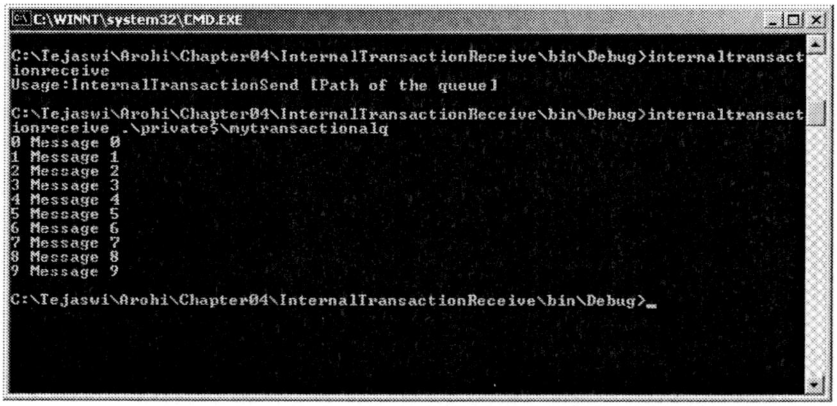

Figure 4-4. Running the InternalTransactionReceive application

In case the transaction aborts, none of the messages will be received by the application. To verify this, we can call mTx.Abort() in the for loop after some messages have been received and then check the messages in the queue from the MMC snap-in.

Note that it is possible to do nontransactional receives on transactional queues. The drawback of doing this is that if the transaction is aborted, the received message is not rolled back to the queue.

Internal transactions are also called single transactions. To send and receive a message as a single transaction, it is easier to use the overloaded Send() and Receive() methods, respectively, which accept the MessageQueueTransactionType as one of their parameters. For example, to send a transactional message in a single transaction, use this code:

```
q.Send("Message " + i, i.ToString(), MessageQueueTransactionType.Single);
```

To receive a message in a single transaction, use this code:

```
Message m = q.Receive(MessageQueueTransactionType.Single);
```

Transactional Dead-Letter Queue

When a transactional message is not successfully received by the receiving application, the message is sent to the transactional dead-letter queue. This can happen when the messages sent to a transactional queue have a receive time-out associated with them. So, if the messages are not received by the receiving application in the specified amount of time, the messages expire. Expired messages are removed from the destination queue and sent to the transactional dead-letter queue. To set the receive timeout for a message, you need to set its TimeToBeReceived property to a TimeSpan object representing the timeout value. By default, an expired transactional message is not sent to the transactional dead-letter queue; it will be sent only if the UseDeadLetterQueue property of the message is set to true. The following listing shows how to use the TimeToBeReceived and UseDeadLetterQueue properties of the message object:

```
System.Messaging.Message m =
new System.Messaging.Message("Message " + i);
m.TimeToBeReceived = new TimeSpan(0, 0, 3);
m.UseDeadLetterQueue = true;
q.Send(m, i.ToString(), mTx);
```

You can either view the expired messages in the transactional dead-letter queue from the Message Queuing MMC snap-in or programmatically by calling the Receive() or Peek() method on the transactional dead-letter queue. The FormatName used to access dead-letter queues follows the format

```
FormatName:DIRECT=AddressSpecification\SYSTEM$;DEADXACT
```

where AddressSpecification can be one of the following:

```
TCP:IPAddress
OS:<computer_name>
HTTP://<DNS_name>/msmq
```

For example:

```
FormatName:DIRECT=TCP:10.1.48.67\SYSTEM$;DEADXACT
```

NOTE *If you use the* DeadLetterQueue, *make sure you clean it by either receiving the messages or purging the queue at regular intervals.*

External Transactions

In this section, you'll see how Message Queuing can participate in a global MSDTC transaction. In an MSDTC transaction, there may be more than one resource, such as a SQL Server database, along with Message Queuing. To understand MSDTC or any global transactions, you need to first grasp the fundamentals of distributed transaction processing (DTP).

Distributed Transaction Processing (DTP) Fundamentals

Corporations have widely embraced distributed computing systems, using networks of Windows-based desktop computers to connect to servers running the UNIX and Windows NT/2000 operating systems. Most new mission-critical applications under development are distributed applications.

A distributed application is one in which the application logic is divided among two or more computers on the network. A client/server application is a typical example of a distributed application.

Distribution makes it possible to handle very large, very complex systems with many small, inexpensive computers.

The DTP Model

The X/Open Company has defined a standard for DTP systems called the DTP Reference model. The model has four key components:

- Transaction Manager (TM)

- Resource Manager (RM)

- Application Program (AP)

- Communications Resource Manager (CRM)

Transaction Manager (TM) (e.g., MSDTC)

- Defines scope of the transaction.

- Assigns a unique transaction identifier (XID).

- Coordinates with the RM/CRM to drive the completion of a transaction.

- Typically part of a larger transaction monitor.

Resource Manager (RM) (e.g., Microsoft SQL Server, Message Queuing)

- Maintains recoverable resources.

- Each RM is independent.

- Registers with the TM to receive notifications.

- TM notifies RM of transaction creation and synchronization.

- The file system, queue managers, session managers, or the print server can all be an RM as long as they support transactions with ACID properties.

Application Program (AP) (COM+ or MTS transactional component)

- AP is the user-provided code that contains custom business logic.

- Initiates start and completion of transaction in coordination with the TM.

- Directly interacts the RM for a specific transaction to manipulate the resource managed by the RM.

- More than one RM may be invoked by the AP in the context of the same transaction.

- A transaction that interacts with more than one RM is called a global transaction.

Communications Resource Manager (CRM)

- A special kind of resource manager.

- Supports standard transport protocols such as TCP/IP, APPC, and OSI as well as proprietary protocols.

- Coordinates transactions that span more than one node.

- The TM notifies the CRM when a transaction begins in its node.

- The CRM notifies the TM when a transaction leaves its node or when it arrives in the node.

- The interface for completion of transaction is achieved via a two-phase commit protocol.

Figure 4-5 shows a high-level view of a typical DTP system.

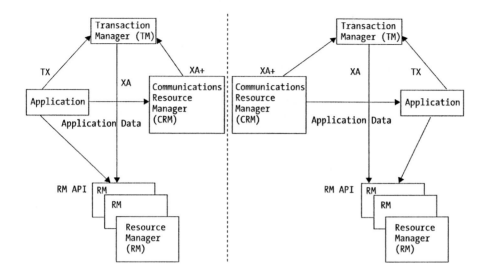

Figure 4-5. The DTP model

Two-Phase Commit Protocol

The two-phase commit protocol, or 2PC, allows for many TMs and RMs to participate in a transaction across a deployment. If any participant votes that the transaction should abort, all participants should roll back.

The following are the properties of a two-phase commit protocol:

1. There is one master transaction manager called Distributed Transaction Coordinator (DTC). This master DTC coordinates operations between other transaction managers.

2. The transaction coordinator sends a *prepare to commit* message to each TM involved.

3. Each TM propagates this message to its RM.

4. Each TM reports back to the transaction coordinator the outcome of the prepare. If everyone agrees to the commit operation, the operation is logged.

5. Finally, the transaction coordinator tells each TM to commit the transaction with its RM. If anything goes wrong, the log entry from Step 4 can be used to reapply the transaction.

Figure 4-6 shows a typical two-phase commit protocol action. The figure only shows what happens after the commit is issued:

- AP is the application program.

- TM is the transaction manager.

- RM1 is Resource Manager 1 (e.g., Microsoft SQL Server 2000 or Message Queuing).

- RM2 is Resource Manager 2 (e.g., another instance of Microsoft SQL Server 2000 or Message Queuing).

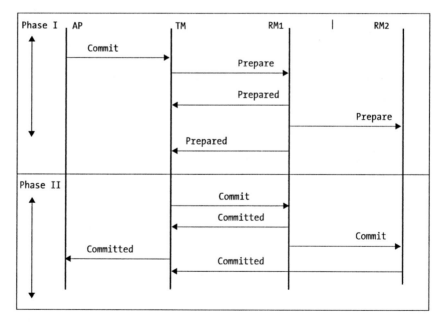

Figure 4-6. The two-phase commit protocol

Figure 4-7 describes an entire two-phase commit transaction:

- AP is the application program.

- TM is the Transaction Manager (e.g., MSDTC).

- RM1 is Resource Manager 1 (e.g., Microsoft SQL Server 2000 or Message Queuing).

- RM2 is Resource Manager 2 (e.g., another instance of Microsoft SQL Server 2000 or Message Queuing).

- TX is the protocol between the application program and the transaction manager.

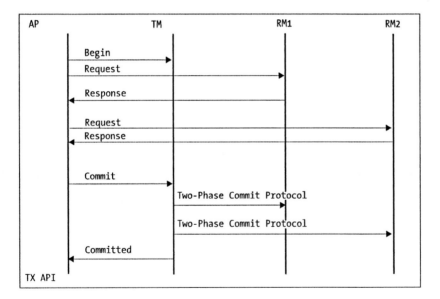

Figure 4-7. Two-phase commit transaction

The TX API

TX (see Figure 4-8) is a unidirectional API used by the application to communicate with the TM.

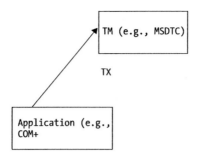

Figure 4-8. The TX API

The XA API

XA is a bidirectional API used for communication between a TM and an RM.
Figure 4-9 shows an overview of the XA API.

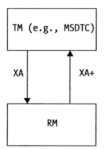

Figure 4-9. The XA API

Message Queuing External Transactions in Action

To learn how to use MSDTC transactions, let's develop a small part of an order-processing system, as shown in Figure 4-10.

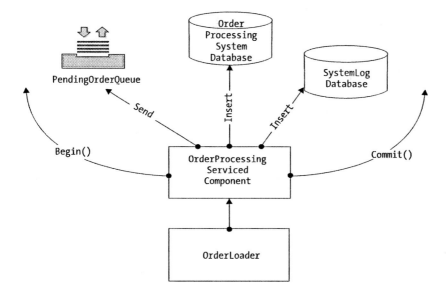

Figure 4-10. An order-processing application using external transactions

In Figure 4-10, we have two databases, the Order Processing System and the SystemLog. The Order Processing System has an Orders table that stores orders, and the SystemLog database has an OrderLog table that stores logs for each order inserted. There is also a transactional queue named PendingOrderQueue that stores all the orders that are pending. The OrderProcessing component is a Serviced Component, which is the .NET version of a COM+ component. The ServicedComponent class is in the System.EnterpriseServices namespace. It supports attributes that define the transactional behavior of the component. Table 4-1 lists the transaction attributes available for our OrderProcessing Serviced Component.

Table 4-1. Transaction Attributes

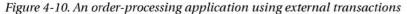

TRANSACTION OPTION	DESCRIPTION
Disabled	Any transaction in the context is ignored. For example, if a client starts a transaction and the server component does not support it, the transaction is ignored. [Transaction(TransactionOption.Disabled)]
NotSupported	The component is created without any governing transaction, i.e., the component cannot participate in any transaction. [Transaction(TransactionOption.NotSupported)]

continued

Table 4-1. Transaction Attributes (continued)

TRANSACTION OPTION	DESCRIPTION
Required	If a client is the root of the transaction, then the component participates in the transaction; otherwise, the component itself starts a new transaction. [Transaction(TransactionOption.Required)]
RequiresNew	The component always starts a new transaction regardless of the client. [Transaction(TransactionOption.RequiresNew)]
Supported	If the client starts a transaction, then the component participates in it, or it does not. [Transaction(TransactionOption.Supported)]

In our application, the OrderProcessing Serviced Component uses the Required transaction option to participate in a transaction. Figure 4-11 shows the sequence diagram for our order-processing application.

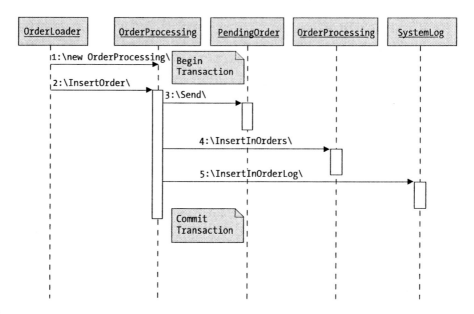

Figure 4-11. Order processing sequence diagram

The OrderLoader invokes a method on the OrderProcessing Serviced Component and passes the order information. The OrderProcessing component initiates a transaction (we will be using automatic transactions), inserts the Order object into the PendingOrderQueue message queue by calling its Send() method, then inserts the order information into the Orders table in the OrderProcessing database. Finally, the component inserts a log into the OrderLog table of the SystemLog database. All three operations occur as a part of the single transaction; therefore, if any one operation fails, all three are rolled back.

The following listing shows the code for the OrderProcessing component:

```
using System;
using System.EnterpriseServices;
using System.Data.SqlClient;
using System.Data;
using System.Messaging;

namespace OrderProcessingComponent
{
  [Transaction(TransactionOption.Required)]
      public class OrderProcessing : System.EnterpriseServices.ServicedComponent
        {
    private String _orderConStr =
"server=(local);uid=order;pwd=pass;database=OrderProcessingSystem";
    private String _logConStr =
      "server=(local);uid=order;pwd=pass;database=SystemLog";
    private MessageQueue _q;
    private String _qPath = @".\private$\pendingorderq";
    public OrderProcessing()
  {
      if(!MessageQueue.Exists(this._qPath))
    this._q = MessageQueue.Create(this._qPath, true);
    else
      this._q = new MessageQueue(this._qPath);
  }

    [AutoComplete()]
    public void InsertOrder
      (String orderID, String customerName, String item, int quantity)
    {
      System.Messaging.Message or = new System.Messaging.Message
        (new Wrox.Order(orderID, customerName, item, quantity));
       this._q.Send(or, orderID, MessageQueueTransactionType.Automatic);
      SqlConnection order = new SqlConnection(this._orderConStr);
      SqlConnection log = new SqlConnection(this._logConStr);
      try
      {
```

```
            order.Open();
            log.Open();
            SqlCommand insertOrder  = new SqlCommand();
            SqlCommand insertLog = new SqlCommand();
            DateTime dt = DateTime.Now;
            insertOrder.CommandType = CommandType.StoredProcedure;
            insertOrder.CommandText = "InsertOrder";
            insertOrder.Connection = order;
            insertOrder.Parameters.Add
               (new SqlParameter("@OrderID_1", orderID));
            insertOrder.Parameters.Add(new SqlParameter
               ("@CustomerName_2", customerName));
            insertOrder.Parameters.Add(new SqlParameter
               ("@OrderTime_3", dt));
            insertOrder.Parameters.Add(new SqlParameter
               ("@Item_4", item));
            insertOrder.Parameters.Add(new SqlParameter
               ("@Quantity_5", quantity));
            int status = 1;
            insertOrder.Parameters.Add(new SqlParameter
               ("@Status_6", status));
            insertOrder.ExecuteNonQuery();
            insertLog.CommandType = CommandType.StoredProcedure;
            insertLog.CommandText = "InsertOrderLog";
            insertLog.Connection = log;
            insertLog.Parameters.Add
               (new SqlParameter("@OrderID_1", orderID));
            insertLog.Parameters.Add(new SqlParameter
               ("@OrderReceivedTime_2", dt));
            insertLog.ExecuteNonQuery();
          }
          finally
          {
            order.Close();
            log.Close();
          }
        }
      }
    }
```

In the preceding code, the OrderProcessing component inherits from the ServicedComponent class. The TransactionOption.Required attribute is applied to the entire class, so that if a client is the root of the transaction, the component participates in the transaction; otherwise, the component itself will start a new transaction. Also note that we have applied the `AutoComplete` attribute to the `InsertOrder()` method. This attribute provides automatic transactional behavior for the method in the absence of exceptions. This means that, if the transaction is successful, it automatically calls the `ContextUtil.SetComplete()` method, and if an exception is thrown from the method, it calls the `ContextUtil.SetAbort()` method to abort or roll back the transaction associated with the entire method call.

NOTE `ContextUtil.SetComplete()` *and* `ContextUtil.SetAbort()` *are used to set the consistent bits of a COM+ context. They are used in manual transactions where we need to explicitly commit or roll back the transaction.*

In the `InsertOrder()` method, we carry out three transactional tasks:

- Send a transactional message to the pending order queue:

```
this._q.Send(or, orderID, MessageQueueTransactionType.Automatic);
```

Note that we pass the `MessageQueueTransactionType.Automatic` enum value to the `Send()` method so that Message Queuing automatically enlists itself into the associated transaction. If we don't pass the `MessageQueueTransactionType` value to the `Send()` method, a `MessageQueueException` with a "Wrong transaction usage" message will be thrown and the entire transaction will be rolled back.

- Insert a record into the `Orders` table of the `OrderProcessingSystem` database:

```
insertOrder.ExecuteNonQuery();
```

- Insert a record into the `OrderLog` table of the `SystemLog` database:

```
insertLog.ExecuteNonQuery();
```

The following listing shows the code for OrderLoader application:

```
try
    {
        OrderProcessingComponent.OrderProcessing order =
            new OrderProcessingComponent.OrderProcessing();
        string orderid ="1";
        if(args[0].Length > 0)
            orderid = args[0];
```

```
    order.InsertOrder
        (orderid, "TestCustomer", "TestItem", 1);
}
catch(Exception ex)
{
    Console.WriteLine(ex.Message);
}
```

In the preceding code, we accept the OrderID from the user. This is done on purpose since OrderID is the primary key in the database table, and inserting a duplicate OrderID should throw an exception that will allow us to see a rolled-back distributed transaction. After creating an instance of the OrderProcessing component, we call its InsertOrder() method and pass the appropriate values. All other parameters are kept constant for easier understanding of the distributed transaction concept. Figure 4-12 shows how to run the application.

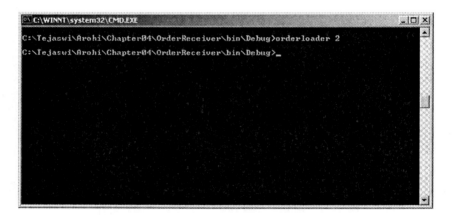

Figure 4-12. Running OrderLoader

If the transaction succeeds, we should be able to see a message in the pendingorderq Message Queue, a record in the Orders table of the OrderProcessingSystem database with the specified OrderID, and a record in the OrderLog table of the SystemLog database. To roll back the transaction, we can pass a duplicate OrderID. If the transaction gets rolled back, even if the message queue message is sent before an exception is thrown from the InsertOrder() method, we should not see any of the three transactional methods succeed.

That is, we should not see a message for this `OrderID` in the pendingordersq message queue, or a record in the `Orders` table, or a record in the `OrderLog` table.

The transactional integrity between Enterprise Services/COM+, Message Queuing, and the SQL Server database is coordinated by the MSDTC. You can view the MSDTC transaction statistics from the Component Services console, as shown in Figure 4-13.

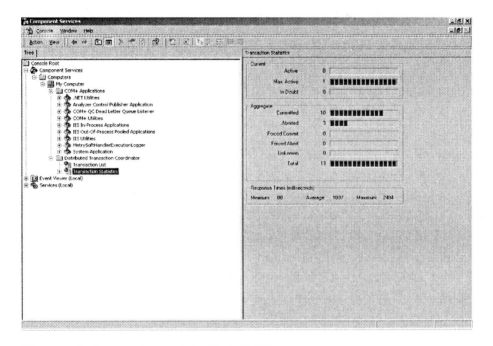

Figure 4-13. Transaction statistics for MSDTC

External transactions carry a lot of overhead in comparison to Message Queuing internal transactions, because the transactional integrity has to be maintained between multiple resource managers (e.g., Message Queuing, the SQL Server database) by MSDTC. In internal transactions, on the other hand, Message Queuing is the only RM and so MSDTC does not participate. Message Queuing itself maintains the integrity of the Message Queuing messages. If only the ordering of messages is important, use a single or internal transaction. Use an external transaction only if it is absolutely necessary to maintain transactional integrity between multiple RMs.

Summary

Transactional messaging offers a lot of benefits, such as message integrity and message order, over nontransactional messaging, but the performance price you pay for using transactional messaging is huge. Use internal transactions only if it is absolutely essential to maintain the order of messages in the queue. External transactions offer the benefit of propagating the transaction context across multiple resource managers. Such transactions are useful when there is a large-scale distributed system with multiple databases and message queues, and the transactional integrity between the messages exchanged between these resource managers is critical. The overhead incurred while using external transactions is significantly more than the one incurred by internal Message Queuing transactions. For most applications, transactions are not needed at all. There is a tendency to overuse transactions and affect the performance of the entire system unnecessarily. Before deciding to use transactions, analyze the ACID properties requirement of the entire system and the resulting performance impact.

MSMQ Triggers

IF YOU'VE REACHED THIS CHAPTER, you should now have a good appreciation of the value that MSMQ adds to your architecture. This excellent middleware tool enables applications to communicate with each other in an orderly and reliable manner. If a receiving application is not running, its messages are queued until it is started.

MSMQ triggers emerged alongside MSMQ 2.0 and became available as a separate download (see http://www.microsoft.com/windows2000/technologies/communications/msmq/default.asp; this download could also be applied to MSMQ 1.0 on Windows NT). With the launch of Windows XP Professional, both MSMQ 3.0 and triggers became a part of the operating system.

This chapter is devoted to MSMQ triggers, and we cover the following topics:

- What exactly MSMQ triggers are

- How triggers access the message queues

- Installing triggers under Windows 2000 and Windows XP

- Creating and using triggers

Introducing Triggers

Triggers are a supplementary feature, empowering MSMQ to perform a specific action upon receipt of an incoming message in a queue. The action can take the form of the invocation of a method within a COM component or running a standard executable.

Let's take a step back from this and consider the typical MSMQ application setup without the aid of triggers. A common architectural design would use a "Service" application on the receiving end of the queue that's constantly polling for new messages. When new messages arrive, it simply reads them from the queue and performs whatever processing that it's supposed to do. However, if the receiving application is not running, the message resides on the queue until the application is executed or restarted.

This architecture raises the following questions:

- Who is responsible for ensuring that the receiving application is running?

- Should the receiving application be an application or a Windows Service?

- How configurable is the application?

- How extensible or maintainable will the application be?

- What happens when the business logic changes?

Role of Triggers

Triggers essentially detach the business logic in your component from the process of monitoring and subsequently receiving messages from the message queue. It is possible to use triggers to take an existing component and invoke a specific method based on the attributes of the message and the queue it arrives on. A trigger consists of a set of **rules**, which are made up of *conditions* and *actions*. When a message is received on a monitored queue (that is, a queue with a trigger against it), the **Windows Trigger Service** uses the rules and conditions to determine which action to take, if any.

Triggers are bound to a queue at creation time. They can be attached to public or private user queues, one of the MSMQ dead-letter queues (for expired or undelivered messages), or the computer journal queue (for auditing outgoing messages onto a remote machine). One single queue can also have more than one trigger (subject to message processing type restrictions, which are discussed in the next section). In effect, you could have several triggers on a queue, each of which performs a separate task. Triggers can be attached to queues located on a remote computer as well as the local computer. We discuss the rules behind defining and invoking triggers in detail in this section.

Triggers Service

Triggers rely on a Windows Service running behind the scenes, as shown in Figure 5-1. This service monitors all the queues that have triggers associated with them and invokes the method call or runs the executable.

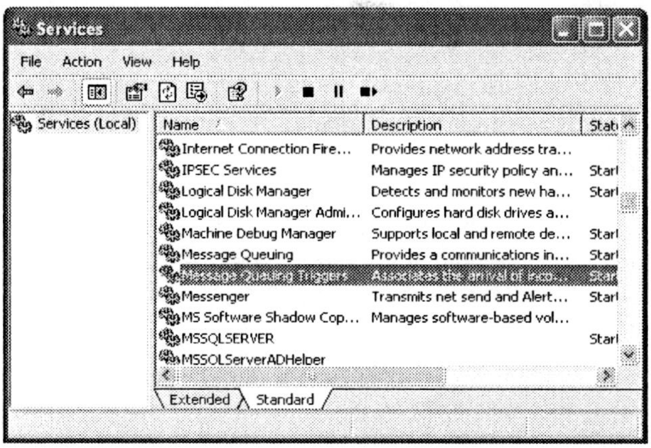

Figure 5-1. The Message Queuing Triggers Service

Rules

A single trigger can have many rules; each one is made up of conditions and actions. The first stage of using triggers involves creating a rule, providing it with a unique name and a description, and completing the conditions and actions. Rules are also created independently of the actual trigger, as they can belong to many triggers.

If you have created two rules that run executables, and want to attach them to the same queue using triggers, should you attach them to a single trigger or to two triggers?

Attaching Two Rules to One Trigger: When you attach two rules to one trigger, the Windows Service will run the first rule and wait until the execution is completed, or closed down, before executing the second one.

This execution is preferred when you want to perform all the rules against a trigger in a strict sequence. The last rule may want to consume the MSMQ message or perform some kind of notification that the trigger was executed and a message has been processed.

Each Rule as a Separate Trigger: In a multiple-triggers scenario, both rules will be processed independently of one another.

This execution would be preferable where the sequence in which the triggers execute is not critical, or where one of the rules involves a long-running process and other rules are not dependent on that completing first.

Conditions

Conditions make up the first part of a rule. Incoming messages have condition checks performed against them to determine whether or not the action is appropriate, based on whether the condition has been met. All checks must be passed for an action to be taken. It is also worth noting that conditions are case sensitive.

Conditions are similar to the WHERE clause in SQL statements; for example:

```
Message Label contains "Purchase Order" AND Message Priority is less than 2
```

In this example, the condition is made up of two clauses, both of which have to be true for the trigger to invoke the assigned action. Don't let the syntax for these conditions put you off, as the rule wizard will generate it all for you. The AND clause is the only option available for linking conditions, as there is no facility to create an OR clause.

```
Message body does not contain "IGNORE" AND Message Priority does not equal 7
```

Conditions are fixed and can only be based around limited message-specific data. For example, you cannot create a condition based on whether the Registry contains a certain entry or a specific file exists on a network share. Following is a list of the message-based fields and the associated conditions that can be attached:

- **Message Label:** Contains or does not contain

- **Message Body:** Contains or does not contain

- **Message Priority:** Equal, not equal to, less than or greater than

- **Message AppSpecific information:** Equal, not equal to, less than, or greater than

- **Message Source Machine ID:** Contains or does not contain

Actions

The second part of the rule is the action to be taken when all of the conditions are true. These actions can take one of two forms.

Invoking an ActiveX Method

One of the most powerful features of triggers is the ability to invoke a method in an ActiveX DLL (or .NET assembly through COM Interop). This means that your business components do not need to contain any MSMQ queue monitoring and message retrieval logic inside them. When creating the action against the rule, you simply provide the `ProgID` and method name for the component. Additionally, parameters can be passed to the method call that are either extracted from the message itself or hardwired.

Let's now consider the scenario where you have a component method that takes a string parameter in the form of an XML document. You can now invoke it, passing the message body (containing XML) into the parameters of the method call using triggers. This technique saves the overhead of having to write a monitoring application, a user interface, and all the MSMQ code to read and poll the queue for that component.

NOTE *These method calls are invoked from within the Triggers Service, and as a result, any value passed back from the method to the service will be ignored. This includes both function return values and values passed into the function by reference.*

Using triggers to invoke your method gives you a great degree of flexibility: you can change the rules, invoke an alternative method, or invoke two or more methods on receipt of one message.

Execution of Windows EXEs

Triggers also enable you to run a stand-alone executable. This can be run as a hidden process, or to interact with the desktop (for example, an alert), parameters can be passed to executables as arguments. Both COM-based and .NET-based executables can be run.

Limitations

It is worth mentioning the limitations that triggers impose; although there are not many, they are worth considering before designing your application.

- **Passing back values:** When invoking an ActiveX method, the Triggers Service will discard any return values or values passed by reference in your method call. It is not enforced that all method calls have to be a subroutine, or all parameters are passed by value; it's just that no one is listening to catch any of them (just like a queued component).

- **Mapping the message body into method parameters:** You cannot pass as a method parameter a section of the message body, or an XML element or attribute value—it's all or nothing.

- **.NET assemblies:** As triggers run inside the Windows Service, you cannot directly call a .NET assembly. However, you can use .NET COM Interop to get around this. This is explained later in the section "Creating Triggers."

- **Message removal (Windows 2000 only):** Triggers under MSMQ 2.0 have no facility for removing messages processed in the queue. The service tracks its current position in the list of messages, but if the service is restarted, all messages are processed again. To remove the message from the queue, you would have to pass the message ID as a parameter into your method call and programmatically remove it from the queue.

How Does the Service Know When Triggers Are Updated?

When the Triggers Service is running, how does it know when a trigger is created, updated, or deleted? The service itself uses MSMQ to keep track of any changes to the triggers. When triggers are initially installed, a private queue is created called **msmqtriggersnotifications**. Whenever a trigger is created, modified, or deleted, a message is sent to this queue; the service can then identify which trigger has changed and make the necessary adjustments.

You can see these messages by stopping the service, adjusting the triggers, and looking at the queue. Remember to refresh the queue if you had previously looked at it; otherwise you will not see any messages. Start the service and watch them disappear.

Are Triggers Just Queued Components?

This is a question that often comes up in discussions about triggers. Queued components, introduced in COM+, allow you to invoke a COM+ component method asynchronously within code. Trigger components do not have to reside in COM+; it is only when a message arrives on a monitored queue that the trigger is invoked.

Queued components use the MSMQ message body to hold serialized data, including the parameters and the ProgID of the class. Triggers are activated by the Triggers Service for any message arriving on a monitored queue that passes all the conditions.

You now have an overall view of the structure of MSMQ triggers—how rules, constraints, and actions are related to each other, and the advantages and disadvantages to MSMQ.

Message Access

How triggers read incoming messages plays an important part in their implementation, management, and debugging. It is only a matter of time before you ask yourself why some of the messages have been processed twice or why the messages are not being removed from the queue after being processed. This section answers these two inevitable questions; in addition, we describe how multiple triggers on one queue are managed.

Serialization

Each trigger contains a **serialized** flag that denotes the order in which the triggers will process messages on the queue:

- Serialized triggers are processed in a strict sequence of all triggers, being applied to the first MSMQ message, prior to moving on to the next message. This is invariably slower than nonserialized triggers.

- Nonserialized triggers process faster, because the service processes multiple triggers against different MSMQ messages on the same queue at the same time. This model can be used where the sequence in which the triggers fire is not critical.

NOTE *If you have multiple triggers against a queue, you cannot guarantee the sequence in which they will fire, regardless of whether or not they are serialized. If you wish to control the flow of triggers, make them serialized.*

Message Retrieval

In Windows 2000, and by default in Windows XP, messages are peeked by the Triggers Service rather than consumed. Basically, **peeking** means that the message will stay on the queue, since it is not deleted. This can lead to the following situations where messages are processed more than once.

Trigger Service Restarted

When the MSMQ Triggers Service is restarted, all message queues with triggers against them will have their messages processed again, and the trigger actions will fire again.

Machine Restart

In the event of a machine restart, any message that was sent as unrecoverable (those stored in memory) will have been lost, but the recoverable messages will be processed for a second time.

High-Priority Message Arrival

Messages arrive on the queue in a **FIFO (First In, First Out)** sequence. The exception to this is when a message with a priority higher than some of the existing messages arrives on the queue. This message will appear on the queue after messages of an equal priority but before those of a lesser priority. In this situation, this message will be processed for a second time, followed by all the subsequent messages being processed.

NOTE *Message priorities in MSMQ range from 0, which is the lowest priority, up to 7, which is the highest priority.*

The following listing shows a text file output from a peeking trigger attached to a message queue. Initially, six messages arrive (two very high, two medium, and two of low priority). The seventh message to arrive is a high-priority message. The trigger then proceeds to reprocess all the messages of a lower priority.

```
Message: Message 1 Received: 20/01/2003 13:23:31 Priority 7
Message: Message 2 Received: 20/01/2003 13:23:36 Priority 7
```

```
Message: Message 3 Received: 20/01/2003 13:23:41 Priority 3
Message: Message 4 Received: 20/01/2003 13:23:46 Priority 3
Message: Message 5 Received: 20/01/2003 13:23:55 Priority 1
Message: Message 6 Received: 20/01/2003 13:23:58 Priority 1

Message: Message 7 Received: 20/01/2003 13:24:22 Priority 6
Message: Message 3 Received: 20/01/2003 13:23:41 Priority 3
Message: Message 4 Received: 20/01/2003 13:23:46 Priority 3
Message: Message 5 Received: 20/01/2003 13:23:55 Priority 1
Message: Message 6 Received: 20/01/2003 13:23:58 Priority 1
```

The four messages (3 through 6) are processed for a second time when message 7 appears on the queue. Processing messages more than once is okay for our demonstration, but what if this were debiting a bank account or creating orders?

Although this seems somewhat strange, it is normal MSMQ behavior for a higher priority message to "jump" the queue. Triggers keep track of the last message processed, but when this higher-priority message appears, the trigger cursor is repositioned. While this is slightly annoying, it's nothing you cannot handle in code, as will be explained later, or by setting the message processing type in MSMQ 3.0.

Access Method

When using triggers under Windows 2000 (MSMQ 2.0) you can only peek at messages on the queue, and therefore some programmatic intervention is required. This takes the form of passing the message ID as a parameter to the method to invoke, and then programmatically reading through the queue until the message is identified and consumed.

For Windows XP (MSMQ 3.0) we now have a choice of three ways of consuming the message against the trigger:

- **Peeking:** Messages passing all the conditions will have the action performed but are not removed from the queue (as in Windows 2000). Using peeking for message consumption enables multiple triggers to be attached to one queue. Peeking is the default option when creating triggers.

- **Retrieval:** Messages passing all the conditions will be processed and subsequently removed from the queue. Retrieval message consumption will allow only one trigger to be attached to an individual queue (Windows XP only).

- **Transactional:** Messages are returned to the queue if the Triggers Service encounters problems for some reason while attempting to retrieve the messages from the queue. This could be due to the fact that another application may have retrieved the message at the same time or there was an exception while the triggers rules were being processed. Transactional message consumption will allow only one trigger to be attached to an individual queue and can be used only on a queue marked as transactional (Windows XP only).

Installing Triggers

Installing triggers is a fairly simple procedure; the only obvious requirement is that you install, or have installed, MSMQ on the local machine.

Windows 2000 (MSMQ 2.0)

Triggers can be freely downloaded from the Microsoft web site; two downloads are provided. The downloads can also be used to install triggers on Windows NT:

- The MSMQ Triggers installer (`MSMQTrigger.exe`)

- MSMQ Triggers Documentation (`MSMQTriggersDoc.zip`)

Running the installer will install MSMQ Triggers, which consists of the following files:

- Triggers Service (`trigserv.exe`)

- Triggers Service COM DLL (`trigobjs.dll`)

- MMC snap-in for maintaining triggers (`trigsnap.dll`)

- Triggers Monitor utility (`trigmon.exe`)

Windows XP Professional (MSMQ 3.0)

Under Windows XP, triggers are a part of the operating system setup and are installed using Add/Remove programs in Control Panel.

1.   Click the Start button.

2.   Select Control Panel.

3.   Double-click Add or Remove Programs.

4.   Select Add/Remove Windows Components on the left menu bar.

5.   Scroll down and check the box next to Message Queuing.

6.   Click Details toward the bottom of the form and make sure triggers are checked. (Triggers should be checked by default, as shown in Figure 5-2.)

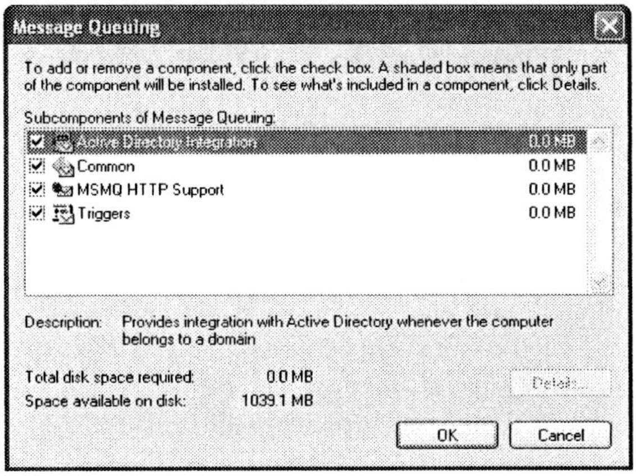

Figure 5-2. Add/Remove Windows Components MSMQ selection dialog box

7.   Click Next and complete the install.

8.   The installer will install the following files:

- Triggers Service (`mqtgsvc.exe`)

- Triggers Service COM DLL and its type library (`mqtrig.dll`, `mqtrig.tlb`)

- Clustered triggers component (`Mqtgclus.dll`)—used on Windows 2003 only

If you are having trouble finding the Administrative Tools in Windows XP, you will be pleased to know they are still there but are just hidden by default. To bring up that familiar Administrative Tools folder and start bar menu entry:

1. Right-click on the Start menu and select Properties.

2. On the Start menu tab select Customize.

3. Select the Advanced tab.

4. Scroll down to the bottom of the Start menu items.

5. Under System Administrative tools, select Display on the All Programs menu and Start menu.

6. Click OK and then Apply.

Triggers Service Configuration

Once you've installed the Triggers Service, there are a few configuration settings that you can change. Although the defaults seem fine, it is always worth being aware of what control you have over a service when it comes to fine-tuning servers. The Message Queuing Triggers Properties dialog box in Computer Manager (Figure 5-3) contains these configurable properties:

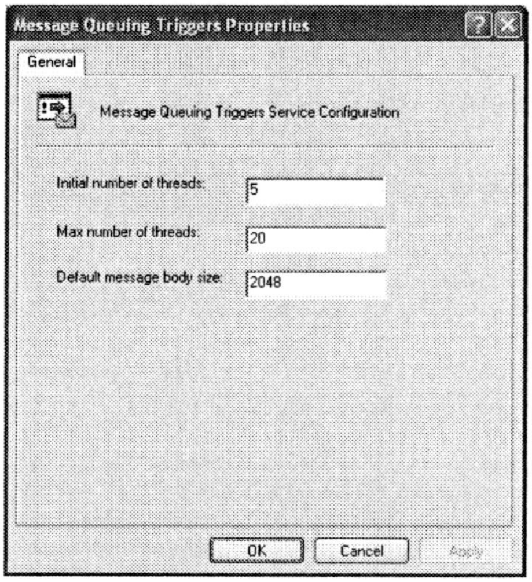

Figure 5-3. Message Queuing Triggers Properties box

- **Initial number of threads:** This property determines the initial number of threads that will be created by the Triggers Service that will be devoted to the processing of triggers. The default value for this is 5.

- **Max number of threads:** This property sets the maximum number of threads that can be created by the Triggers Service during an influx of messages. The default value is 20. Once the maximum number of threads has been reached, incoming messages will have to wait until a thread becomes free before being processed. Increasing this value will increase the throughput of messages, but will also be consuming valuable resources.

- **Default message body size:** This setting determines the amount of memory that will be allocated to incoming messages. The default for this is 2048. This helps the Triggers Service allocate memory efficiently and should be set so that about 80%–90% of all messages are smaller than this setting.

- **Write to log queue:** This check box option appears in Windows 2000 only. When it is selected, the Triggers Service will write tracing messages to a private message queue called MSMQTriggersLog. These messages can then be retrieved using the trigmon.exe utility, which we will look at shortly. It is the user's responsibility to clean up these log queues.

In addition those listed here, there is a setting, **Initialize timeout**, that cannot be configured from within the management console but that can be configured within the Registry. When the Triggers Service starts up, it initializes all the triggers, rules, and queues to monitor on the machine. If this process takes a long time, the service will fail to start. This setting specifies the number of milliseconds before the service will time out. The default is 300000 (which equates to 5 minutes).

The Registry entry for this setting is InitTimeout and can be found at HKEY_LOCAL_MACHINE\SOFTWARE\Microsoft\MSMQ\Triggers.

NOTE *If you change any of these configuration settings, the Triggers Service will need to be restarted in order for the change to take effect.*

Triggers Monitor

Triggers for Windows 2000 contains a utility, not available for XP, called trigmon.exe. This application takes tracing information from the MSMQTriggersLog queue and presents it to the user.

The Triggers Service writes information about the number of threads in use and status changes in the service's lifetime, as shown in Figure 5-4.

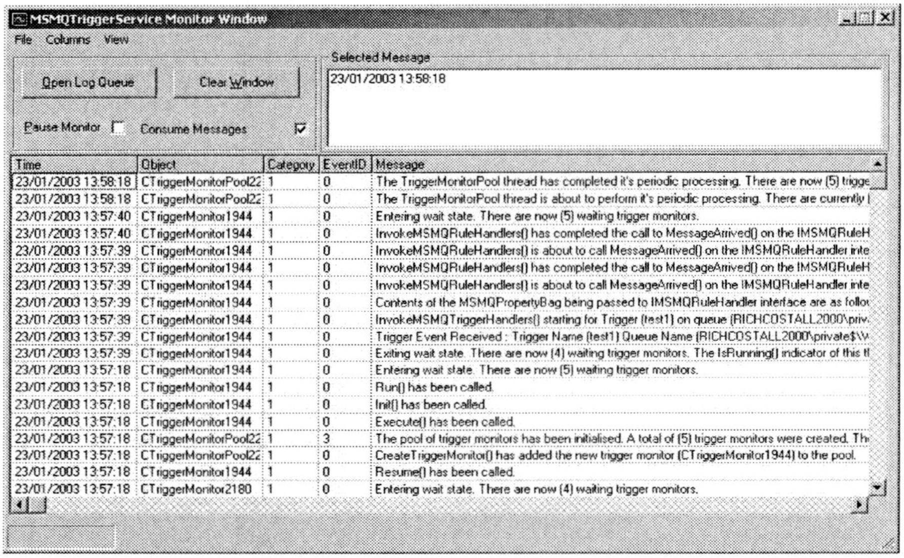

Figure 5-4. Trigmon, the triggers monitor

In order to catch this trace information, the Write to log queue check box must be ticked in the Message Queuing Triggers Properties dialog box in Computer Manager. For more extensive tracing, the Registry entry ProduceTraceInfo found at HKEY_LOCAL_MACHINE | SOFTWARE | Microsoft | MSMQ | Triggers needs to be set to 1 to be enabled or 0 for tracing to be disabled.

The look and feel of this application gives me the impression that it was written to aid the triggers' initial development, which could explain why it is no longer part of the XP triggers installation.

If triggers don't appear to be behaving themselves, the Event Viewer is the best place to start the investigation. It will normally log a trigger failure.

Trigger Service

The last thing we need to do now is to check that the MSMQ Triggers Service is running. Look in Services and ensure that the service has started. An example of this can be seen in Figure 5-1.

Now we have all the trigger theory out of the way, we can get on with the practical side of things and create our first trigger application.

Creating Triggers

For the first example, let's create a trigger that fires from a private queue and that will run an executable. The executable will be visible on the desktop after the trigger runs and serves as a good introduction. If you can see it, then it worked.

> **NOTE**   *We have already covered creating queues in detail in the previous chapters, so all I will say is we will be using a private queue called* .\private$\exedemoqueue. *As long as we attach the trigger to the correct queue, any one will do.*

Test Harness

In order to send some messages to the queue, we'll create a simple .NET Windows Forms application, shown in Figure 5-5.

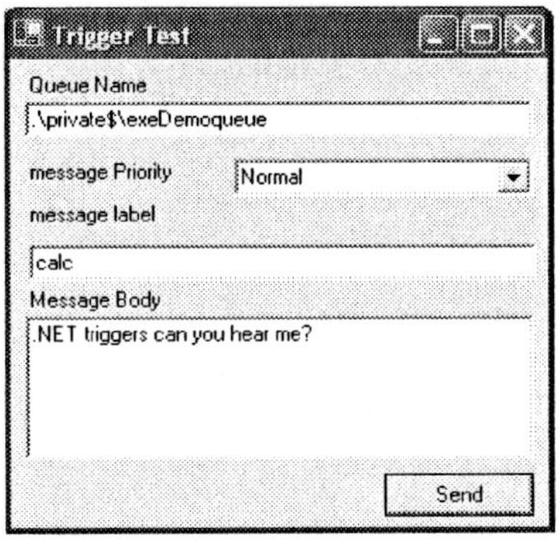

Figure 5-5. Triggers Test Harness application

The code within the Send button click event is

```
System.Messaging.Message myMessage = new System.Messaging.Message();

// Set the body from the textboxes
myMessage.Body = txtBody.Text;

// Set the priority from a combobox
myMessage.Priority = (MessagePriority)CmbPriority.SelectedIndex;

// Send message format
myMessage.Formatter = new ActiveXMessageFormatter();

// Create the queue
MessageQueue q = new MessageQueue(txtQueue.Text);

// Send the message
q.Send(myMessage, txtLabel.Text);
```

One point to note in the above example is that the `ActiveXMessageFormatter` object is being passed into the message's `Formatter` property. In the scenario where .NET is used at the sending and receiving end, this line is not required. Things become more complex when we are talking to a COM object, and indeed in our second example, which communicates through a service, then through a COM Interop layer, and finally back into .NET. Messages sent in .NET are in XML format by default (which is quite a surprise when you first send and view a .NET MSMQ message).

The body of this message is formatted in UTF-8 and will have to be converted by the receiving application. Fortunately, those nice people at Microsoft provided us with the `ActiveXMessageFormatter` for communicating in a format that is compatible with ActiveX components.

NOTE *When MSMQ 1.0 was released, programming against it was seen to be a dark art, requiring an in-depth understanding of the object model and a few lines of code just to send a message. We can now achieve the same effect in Visual Basic .NET with about three lines of code.*

Calculator Invasion

This demonstration will run the calculator tool whenever a message is received in our private queue whose label contains the word "calculator." In order to achieve this, we have to perform the following steps in the Computer Management administration tool:

- **Create the rule:** This rule will contain the condition to check the contents of the message label and define the action of running the calculator executable (`calc.exe`).

- **Create the trigger:** The trigger will be created against our private queue. We will use the `peek()` method in this instance to demonstrate how messages remain on the queue after processing.

- **Attach the rule to the trigger:** The rule is created independently of the trigger, and must therefore be assigned separately.

Create the Rule

1. In Computer Management, expand Services and Applications.

2. Expand Message Queuing.

3. If triggers are installed, the entry Message Queuing Triggers will exist. Expand this, as shown in Figure 5-6.

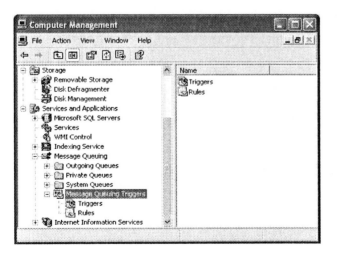

Figure 5-6. Creating triggers within Computer Management

4.   Right-click on the Rules entry and select New and then Rule.

5.   You are now prompted to enter a rule name and description. Use exeDemoRule as the name, as shown in Figure 5-7, and add a useful description.

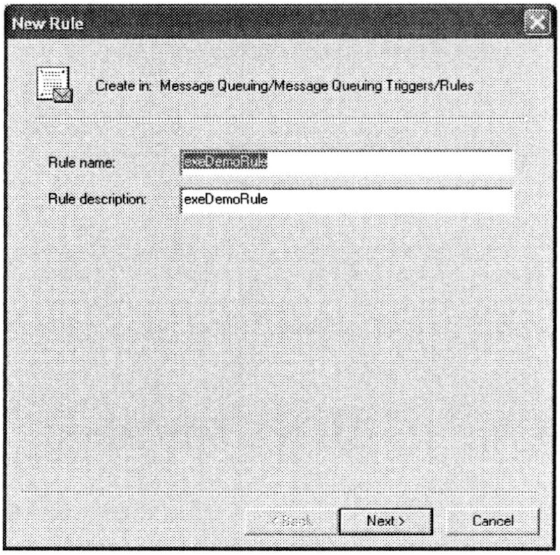

Figure 5-7. Rule description

6.   Click Next to move on to the condition page of the wizard. Under New condition, select Message label contains from the drop-down list and type **calculator** in the text box directly beneath it. Click the Add button to add the condition to the list, as shown in Figure 5-8. You can also remove conditions by highlighting the required item and then clicking the Remove button.

7.   Clicking the Next button takes you to the action page of the wizard (Figure 5-9), where you can choose between invoking a COM method and running a stand-alone executable. In this example, you want to run the calculator executable. Enter or browse to the executable name and remember to select the Interact with desktop check box, which ensures that you'll see the calculator application running and that it doesn't get left with a background process consuming resources. Click Finish to complete the creation of your new rule.

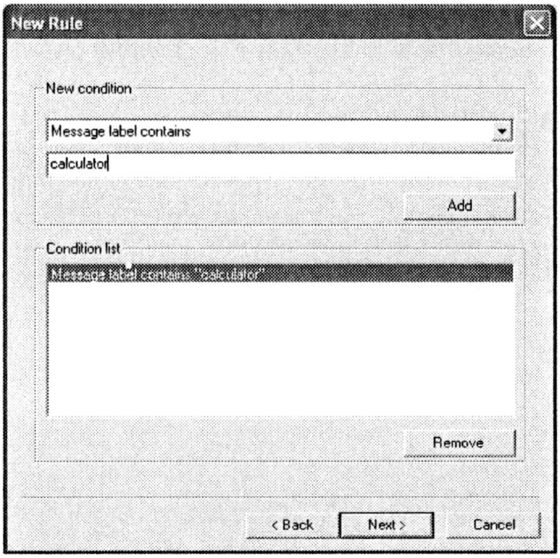

Figure 5-8. Rule conditions

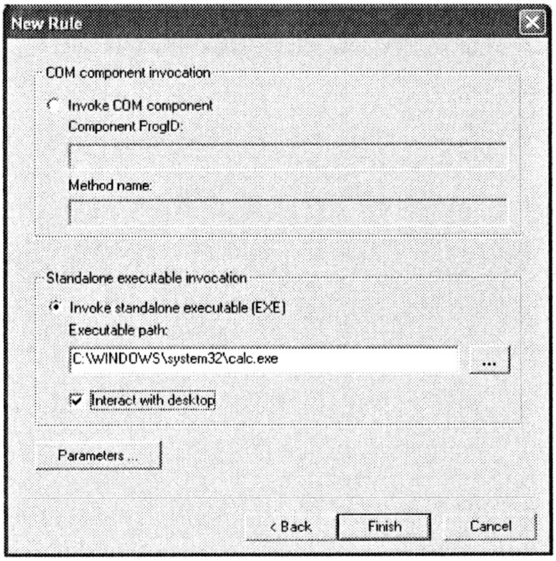

Figure 5-9. Specifying the rule invocation type

8. You can view your new rules by clicking on the Rules entry under
   Message Queuing Triggers.

Create the Trigger

1. Rules need to be attached to triggers in order to work. You can create a trigger either by right-clicking on the Rules entry under Message Queuing Triggers, or by expanding your private queue (exedemoqueue) node, right-clicking Triggers, selecting New, and then selecting Trigger. The latter option saves you the hardship of having to type in a queue name.

2. The queue path name has already been populated, so let's give our trigger the name exeDemoTrigger and leave the processing type as Peeking and not serialized, as shown in Figure 5-10. The Enabled check box will simply turn the trigger on or off.

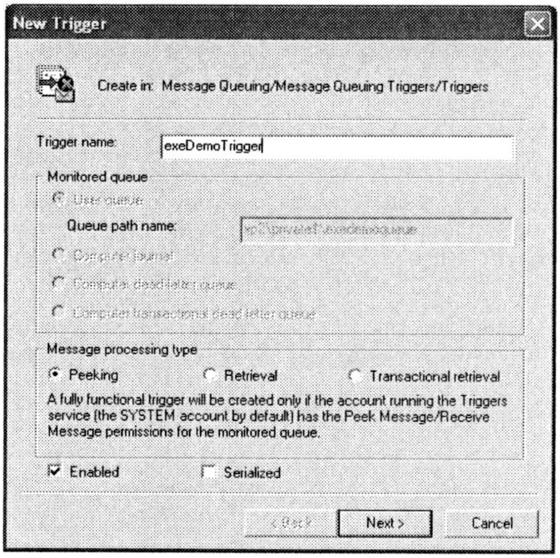

Figure 5-10. Trigger creation—description and type

3. Click the Next button.

Under Windows 2000, you may witness a strange warning message claiming the queue path was not validated. The message asks you to check that the queue exists and that it allows peek access. This message sometimes appears even if the queue was set up correctly and access was okay, so don't be alarmed.

Attach the Rule to the Trigger

Our rule should appear in the list box at the left, as shown in Figure 5-11. You can attach it to the trigger by selecting it and then clicking Attach. Finally, click Finish.

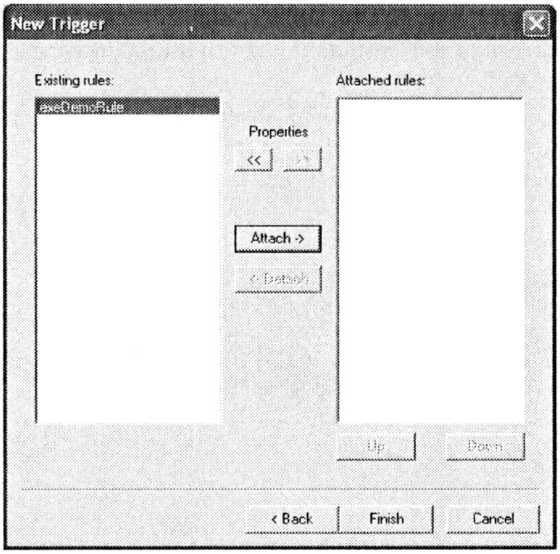

Figure 5-11. Attaching rules to triggers

The left- and right-pointing buttons beneath the Properties label display the rule properties for the highlighted rules on their respective sides. The Up and Down buttons enable you to change the sequence for the rules.

Sending any message to exeDemoQueue with a message label containing the word "calculator" will run up an instance of the calculator application. Send two or three messages and watch those calculators appear. Once you are happy with this, try out the following:

1. Examine the messages on the exeDemoQueue queue. Look at the queue in Computer Management, and you will notice the messages are still waiting to be consumed, due to the peeking access method.

2. Restart the Message Queuing Triggers Service. In Services, under Administrative Tools, locate the Message Queuing Triggers Service and restart it. In addition, watch those calculators appear again.

3. Run the Notepad executable. Create a notepad rule and attach it to a new notepad trigger that is created against our exeDemoQueue queue. Now send some messages with "notepad" in the label, some with "calculator," and some with both; stand back and watch the desktop burst into life!

4. Make the trigger access mode retrieval (MSMQ 3.0 only). Modify the access method of the trigger to retrieval and then restart the Triggers Service; the messages will now all be consumed.

NOTE *Remember that if two rules are attached to one trigger, they will fire one at a time; the Triggers Service will wait for the first one to complete before executing the second one. If rules are attached to different triggers, they will fire independently of one another.*

Triggers and Executables

Before moving on, it's worth repeating that the Triggers Service can run any executable, regardless of whether it's a COM or a .NET application. The development time is nonexistent, and although this is a simple example, it shows how easy this is to configure and invoke. We could be starting a Windows Service, running a backup job, or sending an alert to the user.

Invoking COM Methods

In addition to running an executable, MSMQ triggers enable the user to invoke a COM public method. This is achieved by entering the ProgID of the component, which is in the format PROJECT.CLASSNAME and will be familiar to those of you who have used Visual Basic's CreateObject or ASP's Server.Createobject command. This approach provides several benefits:

- **Independent of COM+:** The component does not have to reside in COM+ (MTS) as a package or a queued component. We can therefore utilize legacy components.

- **MSMQ free:** No MSMQ coding is required in the component, and therefore just about any COM component could be used without a development resource being required to upgrade it. (On Windows 2000, it will be necessary to perform a cleanup of consumed messages. On Windows XP [MSMQ 3.0] we can use the retrieval message processing type.)

- **No user interface required:** The component can remain exactly what it is—a component—and will not need a user interface consuming valuable processor and memory resources to poll for messages, which will be done by the Triggers Service instead.

Parameters

The other piece of information required is the method name and its associated parameters. Parameters must be selected from a drop-down box and consist of the options shown in Table 5-1.

Table 5-1. Trigger Parameters and Their Data Types

TRIGGER PARAMETER	DATA TYPE
Message ID	Variant
Message label	String
Message body	String
Message body	Variant
Message priority	Number
Message arrival time	Date Variant
Message sending time	Date Variant
Message correlation ID	Variant
Message application-specific number	Number
Queue path name	String
Queue format name	String
Response queue format name	String

continued

Table 5-1. Trigger Parameters and Their Data Types (continued)

TRIGGER PARAMETER	DATA TYPE
Administration queue format name	String
Message source computer ID	String
Message lookup ID	Variant
Trigger name	String
Trigger ID	String
String literal	String
Numeric literal	Number

The table shows all the parameters that can be passed into your component. The string literal and numeric literal at the bottom can be used to pass fixed-value parameters into the component. If you need to pass a parameter, such as a database name, that can change on a message-by-message basis, you will have to pass it in the label or body of the message and access it programmatically from within the method call.

NOTE *With the widespread use of XML, it would be nice if we had the ability to apply an XPath expression to the body of the message and pass the result as a parameter. This would address the issue of passing information, such as a database name or customer reference, derived from the body of the message into the method, without having to modify the legacy component to include an XML parser. (This could be a nice feature for MSMQ 4.0.)*

Triggers and .NET

Sending a message in .NET couldn't be any easier; in fact, reading the message at the other end is just as easy. However, using triggers with .NET adds a couple of complexities:

- **COM and .NET:** The Triggers Service is COM-based and therefore not .NET-aware. In order for the service to recognize your component, you have to build a wrapper for your .NET component using a **COM-Callable Wrapper (CCW).**

- **Message format:** By default, .NET sends its messages in UTF-8 encoded XML. When this passes through the Triggers Service, the CCW, and your component, it becomes unreadable and needs converting. You can either convert the incoming data in your method or send the message in a COM-readable format in the first place. Which option you choose depends on the amount of control you have over the code in the message-sending application.

Method Invocation

For this example, let's create a private queue called .\private$\COMdemoqueue, then create a .NET component, wrap it up using a CCW, and build it into a rule. The component will take as parameters the message body, message receive time, message priority, and a string literal for the path name, and append them out to a file called COMTriggerDemo.txt.

.NET Component

Using Visual Studio .NET, we create a Class Library application called COMTrigger and rename the class module to COMTriggerClass. The code for the class is listed next. This component uses an internal method called ConvID, which we explain later, but essentially it converts the message ID into a valid format.

```
using System;
using System.IO;
using System.Messaging;

public class ComTriggerClass
{
    // COM Activated method
    public void COMTriggerMethod(string message, string dateRec,
                                 string priority, byte[] messageID,
                                 string filePath)
    {
        string outputFile = filePath + "COMTriggerDemo.txt";
        TextWriter output;

        string messageIdout = ConvID(messageID);

        // Create output file
        if (!File.Exists(outputFile))
            output = File.CreateText(outputFile);
        else
```

```
        output = File.AppendText(outputFile);

    // Write to output file
    output.WriteLine(String.Format(
        "Message: {0} Received: {1} Priority {2} ID: {3}",
        message, dateRec, priority, messageIdout));
    output.Close();
    }
}
```

In order for the Triggers Service to be able to "see" and find the .NET component, we need to make it COM-friendly by creating a "COM-aware" proxy, and store it in a central location. This is achieved by performing the following tasks:

- Creating a CCW

- Placing the component in the Global Assembly Cache (GAC)

COM-Callable Wrappers (CCWs)

Before the assembly is built, an option can be set that will automatically create the CCW. You'll find this option under the Configuration Properties folder for your project's properties within Visual Studio .NET, and it's called Register for COM Interop. You need to check this property, as shown in Figure 5-12.

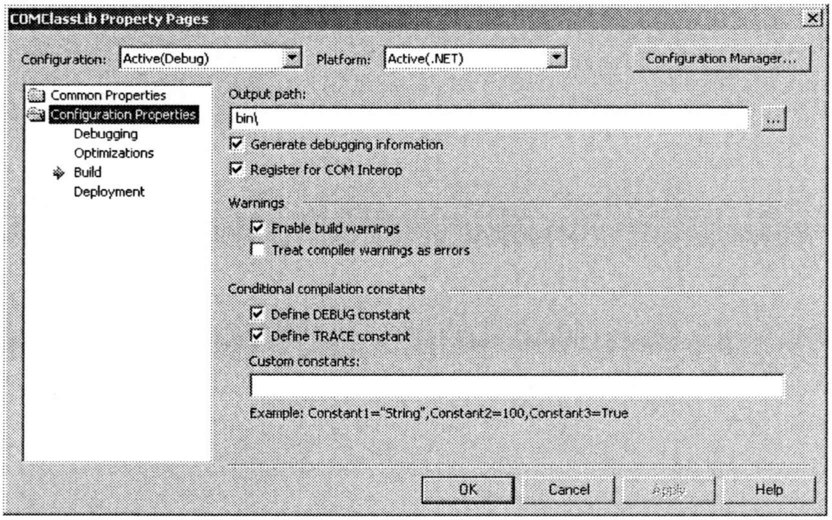

Figure 5-12. Registering an assembly for COM Interop

Adding the Component to the Global Assembly Cache

The Global Assembly Cache (GAC) is essentially a repository for storing shared assemblies. In the .NET world, if you wish to make your assembly available to other applications (including triggers) on the machine, it will have to be stored in the GAC.

Two steps are required for adding the assembly to the GAC. The first is to generate a **strong name** and the second is to use the gacutil tool to insert the assembly in the GAC. Strong names guarantee the uniqueness of your assembly by relying on unique key pairs.

1. Ensure the Register for COM Interop option is selected.

2. Use the .NET command line to generate a strong name key file into your project directory.

    ```
    > Sn -k snKey.snk
    ```

3. Add the following attribute above the topmost Assembly: entry in the AssemblyInfo.cs file. This will bind your key file to your assembly.

    ```
    [Assembly: AssemblyKeyFile("./bin/snKey.snk")]
    ```

4. Build the assembly.

5. Open the .NET command-line prompt, locate your assembly, and use the gacutil tool to place it into the GAC:

    ```
    > gacutil -i COMTrigger.dll
    ```

6. You can view your assembly in the Windows/Assembly directory or by using the gacutil /l command to list all assemblies.

The rule is created as in the previous example. You can use "message label contains 'com'" as a condition. To invoke a COM method, you must now click the Rule Action tab in the Properties dialog box, shown in Figure 5-13. Select the option to Invoke COM component, and enter a component ProgID of COMTrigger.COMTriggerClass and a method of COMTriggerMethod.

 CAUTION   *Take extreme care when adding a* ProgID *to a trigger. The* ProgID *is not checked until runtime, and an incorrect name will fail to do anything except log an almost completely unhelpful entry into the event log. The event log is the first port of call when triggers fail.*

Here's an example of an event log entry upon entering an invalid `ProgID`:

```
The action defined by the rule COMDemoRule with the ID e79db56a-4ad6-41ae-b134-
2fdcf28c749c was not invoked (Error: 0xc00e0e0a). The COM object may not
be registered, or the executable file may not exist in your path. For more
information, see Help and Support Center at http://go.microsoft.com/fwlink/
events.asp.
```

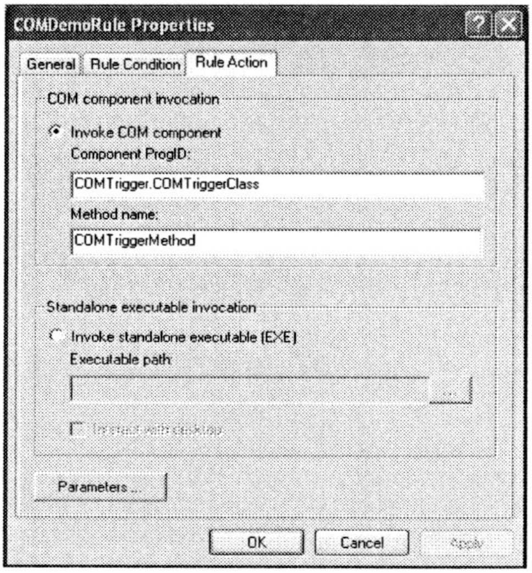

Figure 5-13. Invoking the trigger method

In order to pass parameters to your method, click the Parameters button on the Rule Action tab. The resulting dialog box (shown in Figure 5-14) enables you to add, remove, and re-sequence parameters to your method.

Table 5-2 shows the entries to be added as parameters.

Table 5-2. Sample Parameters for COMDemoQueue

METHOD PARAMETER	MESSAGE ITEM
Message body	Message body as string
Message arrival time	Message arrival time
Priority	Message priority
Message ID	Message Unique ID
File path	String literal "c:\"

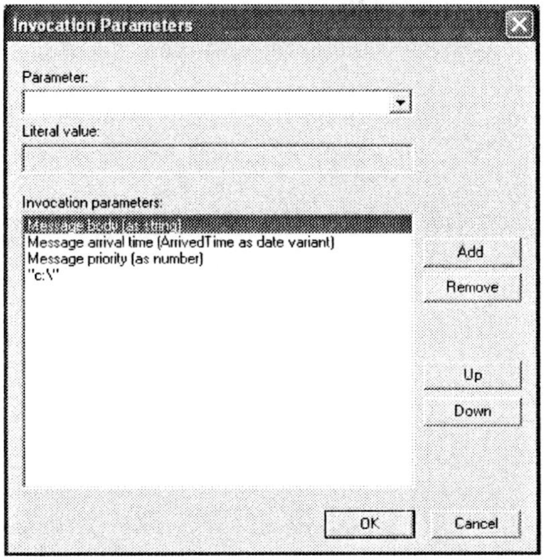

Figure 5-14. Invocation Parameters dialog box

As with the previous example, all that is now needed is to create a trigger against your COMDemoQueue and attach the new rule to it (which we covered in the last demonstration). If you are running Windows XP, use the retrieval message processing method against the trigger to consume the messages directly.

Windows 2000 Message Consumption

For XP users everything is fine and dandy—you just set the message processing type to "retrieve" and your messages are consumed as you use them. What about "consuming" messages on Windows 2000? Your messages can be consumed programmatically by writing a generic method, which receives the Queue path name parameter in addition to the Message ID parameter in your parameter list. Given these two pieces of information, you can read the specified queue until you have a match on the Message ID and then it can be removed.

By creating a rule that uses the COM method invocation, you can attach your method passing the Queue path name and Message ID from the incoming message.

NOTE *An action on a rule will always be performed if the condition list is blank.*

This rule will be added as the last rule on a single trigger. If you created and attached an additional trigger to the queue, you could not guarantee what order the triggers will fire in.

In order to achieve this, you should utilize the following two code samples.

Identifying the Message Method Call

This method is also invoked as an ActiveX method by the trigger and receives as parameters the two pieces of information needed to find and remove the message. The Message ID that is passed into your call must be converted (using an additional method called ConvID), as you receive it as a variant. The queue name is used to open the queue, and you then read the messages until you get a match. If you find a match, you consume the message using the RemoveCurrent() method:

```
// Method to remove message from queue
public void COMTriggerRemove(string queuename, byte[] messageID)
{
    string msgId = ConvID(messageID);
    try
    {
        // Define our queue
        MessageQueue q = new MessageQueue(queuename);
        MessageEnumerator mEnum = q.GetMessageEnumerator();

        // Loop through messages until we find ours, then remove it
        while (mEnum.MoveNext())
        {
            Message message = mEnum.Current;

            if (message.Id == msgId)
            {
                // Message found - remove it
                mEnum.RemoveCurrent();
                break;
            }
        }
    }
    catch {}
}
```

Converting the Message ID Using the ConvID Method

As the Message ID is passed in via COM as a variant, you need to convert it back to its original format. This method takes an array of bytes (which was originally the variant) and converts it into the standard Message ID format as a string. An example of a Message ID is 88c5a70b-6f4e-4ea4-9db0-7e2d9299cc8e\32835.

```
// Method to convert the Message ID to a string
// Example Format: 88c5a70b6f4e4ea49db07e2d9299cc8e\32835
private string ConvID(byte[] msg)
{
    byte[] outguid = new byte[16];
    Array.Copy(msg, outguid, 16);

    Guid oguid = new Guid(outguid);

    // Start at position 16 to get the unique message id
    ulong intdword = BitConverter.ToUInt32(msg, 16);

    // Return the Message Queue ID
    return oguid.ToString() + "\\" + intdword.ToString();
}
```

Triggers and Components

You now have the power to utilize those old components you wrote; the only real restriction is mapping the message properties into the method call parameters. You could call an email-sending component, update a stock transaction database, or put a message on a queue—now there's a thought!

We even have a workaround for the issue of peek-only message access in Windows 2000 (MSMQ 2.0).

Trigger Deployment

We have covered in depth the creation and maintenance of triggers and rules using Computer Manager. But what happens when you want to deploy an application? How do you create triggers without having to send a developer into the cold, air-conditioned server room for 3 hours, and what happens if several machines are running the Triggers Service?

The good news is Microsoft provides a utility for this; the bad news is that it's not very elegant. Tracking down this utility took weeks. I finally found it on a newsgroup posting and then, finally, Microsoft posted them (one for MSMQ 3.0 and one for versions 2.0–1.0) onto the MSMQ web site (http://www.microsoft.com/windows2000/technologies/communications/msmq/default.asp) following many newsgroup questions.

Unfortunately, this utility does not take the form of an assembly or COM component, but is just run from the command line. Welcome to `TrigAdm.exe`.

TrigAdm.exe

The Triggers admin utility allows you to perform the following tasks from the command line on the local computer:

- Create, update, view, and delete triggers.

- Create, update, view, and delete rules.

- Attach or detach a rule to/from a trigger.

- List all triggers and rules on the local computer.

- View and update the MSMQ triggers configuration parameters.

To see a full list of what the utility can do, type the following command:

```
> Trigadm /?
```

Running this command returns a list of the operations that can be performed by the utility. Table 5-3 shows these operations.

Table 5-3. TrigAdmin Operations

REQUEST TYPE	DESCRIPTION
GetConfig	Prints the Triggers Service configuration parameters
UpdateConfig	Updates the Triggers Service configuration parameters
AddTrigger	Adds a new trigger
UpdateTrigger	Updates a trigger's properties
DeleteTrigger	Deletes a trigger
GetTrigger	Displays a trigger's properties
AddRule	Adds a new rule
UpdateRule	Updates a rule
DeleteRule	Deletes a rule
GetRule	Displays a rule's properties

Table 5-3. TrigAdmin Operations (continued)

REQUEST TYPE	DESCRIPTION
AttachRule	Attaches a rule to a trigger
DetachRule	Detaches a rule from a trigger
GetTriggersList	Displays a list of all triggers
GetRulesList	Displays a list of all rules

To execute each command, you add a request argument to it. The following example returns a list of all triggers on the local computer:

```
> Trigadm /request:GetTriggersList
Total number of Triggers is:2
The list of Triggers' IDs is:


TriggerID                             TriggerName       TriggerQueuePath
---------                             -----------       ----------------
8634bace-5f21-4d4b-ba53-6f3c23053354  COMDemoTrigger
xp2\private$\comdemoqueue
9a0ceb91-1e62-4644-a49e-31e87770b818  exeDemoTrigger
xp2\private$\exedemoqueue
```

Creating a trigger is almost as simple, although it will allow you to create a trigger against a queue that does not exist:

```
> Trigadm /request:addtrigger /queue:xp2\private$\UtilQueue
/Name:UtilTrigger
```

The addtrigger request command returns the trigger identifier. Running the GetTriggersList request again shows the newly created trigger:

```
Total number of Triggers is:3
The list of Triggers' IDs is:


TriggerID                             TriggerName       TriggerQueuePath
---------                             -----------       ----------------
8634bace-5f21-4d4b-ba53-6f3c23053354  COMDemoTrigger
xp2\private$\comdemoqueue
9a0ceb91-1e62-4644-a49e-31e87770b818  exeDemoTrigger
xp2\private$\exedemoqueue
9d97b670-9d3b-4781-bd8b-974de4715136  UtilTrigger
xp2\private$\utilqueue
```

To get help on individual commands, add the help argument to the command line:

```
> Trigadm /request:addtrigger /?
```

The only real way to work with this utility in a deployment environment is to write an application that shells out to the command prompt, executes the instruction, and then catches and parses the result. In the previous example the TriggerID is created internally; this piece of information is required when attaching rules to the trigger and updating the trigger itself.

It's not an elegant solution, but it is a solution. How your organization handles it comes down to a business decision in relation to the amount of effort to create the triggers manually against the time to develop the application to be used in the installation process.

NOTE *Let's hope Microsoft creates this functionality as a part of the* System.Messaging *namespace sometime soon.*

Summary

MSMQ answers all those unpredictable elements found in today's disconnected, disparate, and online environments. Triggers add extra value; they are the icing on the MSMQ cake. Being able to attach a method or executable to a queue via a trigger adds a layer of abstraction between the queue and the component.

Although MSMQ triggers make the setup slightly more complex, they provide an easy-to-maintain and flexible disconnected architecture. Having said that, it is still early days for MSMQ triggers, and some of the tools show this. I for one cannot wait to see what is in the next version.

In this chapter, you learned

- How the Triggers Windows Service monitors the message queues, reacting to incoming messages and providing a flexible message queue listening service.

- That triggers are highly configurable; you can add, modify, and delete triggers, conditions, and actions without compilation.

- That from a maintenance and extensibility perspective, you can utilize existing legacy COM components without introducing Message Queuing code and user interfaces.

- How to deploy triggers using the Triggers admin utility (TrigAdm.exe).

CHAPTER 6

MSMQ COM and Win32 API

I<small>N THIS CHAPTER, WE EXPLORE</small> the basic operations in MSMQ using unmanaged C++ to access the COM and Win32 MSMQ APIs. For each API we show you how to create, delete, open, or close a queue, and send or receive a message. We also demonstrate how to receive a message asynchronously using both the COM and Win32 APIs, and how to use the new LookupID property, which Microsoft introduced in MSMQ 3.0 for Windows XP. Finally, you'll learn how to access the COM API from within the managed .NET environment using C#.

MSMQ COM API: mqoa.dll

The MSMQ COM API contains several interfaces based on the IDispatch interface, including IMSMQQueueInfo, IMSMQQueue, IMSMQMessage, and IMSMQEvent. The coclasses exposed in the COM API provide most of the feature set available from the Win32 API, in a form much easier to use in Visual Basic and Visual C++. The ProgIDs for these classes follow the form MSMQ.MSMQ<x>, where <x> is the name of the specific class, such as Queue or Message.

The MSMQ COM API is contained in MQOA.DLL, which Windows installs into the WINNT\System32 directory by default. It contains the classes and the type library, so that is the file you need to reference from within Visual Basic or using the #import directive, as you will see next. MQOA.DLL ships with all versions of Windows NT, version 2 of MQOA.DLL comes with Windows 2000, and version 3 of MQOA.DLL comes with Windows XP.

Using #import in Visual C++

For the COM code samples in this chapter, we have chosen to use the #import directive available in Visual C++. This directive reads a given type library and generates a series of wrapper classes based on the _com_ptr_t template class. By default, these classes are defined within the namespace(s) specified by the type library (in this case, MSMQ) and are named <Interface>Ptr, where <Interface> is the interface to be wrapped (for example, IMSMQQueuePtr and IMSMQMessagePtr). The _com_ptr_t class transparently handles the AddRef(), Release(), and QueryInterface() functions of IUnknown as well as the details of using properties and methods via IDispatch. It can also be used to instantiate the coclass in place of CoCreateInstance(). Instead of returning HRESULTs, these classes normally wrap the HRESULT in a _com_error exception class and throw the exception, so the programmer needs to catch those exceptions.

The code samples in this chapter also take advantage of two other COM support classes in Visual C++: _bstr_t and _variant_t. The samples use these classes in place of BSTR and VARIANT declarations, respectively. They provide easy conversions from standard types to the BSTR type and other types encapsulated by VARIANT.

For each C++ code sample in this chapter, the following line is implied at the top of the file:

```
#import <mqoa.dll>
```

Creating and Deleting Queues

Creating and deleting queues is a simple process using the COM API. Both operations use the IMSMQQueueInfo interface. The IMSMQQueueInfo interface provides methods and properties for managing a single queue, including Create() and Delete(), which we need.

```
void CreateMSMQQueue(_bstr_t QueueName)
{
    MSMQ::IMSMQQueueInfoPtr myQueueInfo("MSMQ.MSMQQueueInfo");
    try {
/* Creating a queue requires setting the Path Name value first*/
        myQueueInfo->PutPathName(QueueName);
        myQueueInfo->Create(&(_variant_t)false, &(_variant_t)true);
    } catch (_com_error Result) {ErrorDlg(Result.Error());};
}
```

After setting the PathName property of IMSMQQueueInfo with the name of the new queue, a successful call to Create() is all that's necessary to create the queue. In this case, MSMQ uses default values for all the unspecified properties. To avoid this, simply set the properties before calling Create().

For more information on path names, refer to Chapter 1.

Create() takes two Boolean parameters: the first to indicate whether the queue is transactional, and the second to indicate if the queue is readable only by the owner. In the previous example, the queue we create is not transactional but is world readable—any user, including the owner, may access it.

Calling Delete() also requires setting the PathName beforehand, but no parameters:

```
void DeleteMSMQQueue(_bstr_t QueueName)
{
   MSMQ::IMSMQQueueInfoPtr myQueueInfo("MSMQ.MSMQQueueInfo");
   try {
/* Deleting a queue requires setting the Path Name value first*/
      myQueueInfo->PutPathName(QueueName);
      myQueueInfo->Delete();
   } catch (_com_error Result) {ErrorDlg(Result.Error());};
};
```

Opening and Closing Queues

Opening and closing queues is also straightforward:

```
void SendMSMQMessage(_bstr_t QueueFormatName, bstr_t Label, _bstr_t Body)
{
   MSMQ::IMSMQQueueInfoPtr  myQueueInfo("MSMQ.MSMQQueueInfo");
   try {
      /* Creating a queue requires setting the PathName or FormatName value first*/
      myQueueInfo->PutFormatName(QueueFormatName);
      /* Open must select send, receive or peek mode*/
      MSMQ::IMSMQQueuePtr myQueue =
         myQueueInfo->Open(MSMQ::MQ_SEND_ACCESS, MSMQ::MQ_DENY_NONE);
      /* The following function sends a message */
      SendSingleMessage(myQueue, Label, Body);
      /* Close the queue */
      myQueue->Close();
   } catch (_com_error Result) {ErrorDlg(Result.Error());};
}
```

Open() requires you to specify the type of access you require (Peek, Read, or Send access), whether queue access will be shared, or whether the calling process requires sole access. Sole access is not available for Peek or Send modes. A successful call to Open() returns an IMSMQQueue interface pointer representing the desired queue.

Close(), like Delete(), has no parameters.

For best performance, you should hold the queue open to send multiple messages rather than open and close the queue repeatedly.

Sending and Receiving Messages

After you create and open a queue, your next step is normally sending messages. Messages in MSMQ are composed of a list of properties. These properties range from simple descriptors like Label to transaction tracking properties like TransactionID and TransactionStatusQueueInfo and other properties related to security, SOAP, timestamps, and so forth.

In the MSMQ COM API, the MSMQ.MSMQMessage coclass encapsulates a message by exposing the IMSMQMessage interface. IMSMQMessage derives from IDispatch, and IMSMQMessage exposes the message properties as IDispatch properties. IMSMQMessage also has one important method: Send(). Send() takes two parameters: an IMSMQQueue interface pointer representing the opened queue where the message will be sent, and an optional IMSMQTransaction interface or one of a set of transaction constants (including MQ_NO_TRANSACTION, which we use here):

```
void SendSingleMessage(MSMQ::IMSMQQueuePtr OpenedQueue,
            _bstr_t Label, _bstr_t Body)
{   /* Exceptions from this function flow up to the caller*/
   MSMQ::IMSMQMessagePtr myMessage("MSMQ.MSMQMessage");

   myMessage->PutLabel(Label);
   myMessage->PutBody(Body);
   /* Send defaults to MQ_NO_TRANSACTION as the second parameter */
   myMessage->Send(OpenedQueue);
};
```

As you can see in the previous two code samples, sending a message is normally a five-step process:

1. Open the destination queue, specifying MQ_SEND_ACCESS.

2. Create an MSMQMessage object and set important properties on it. (Any unspecified property will be set to a default value by Send()—see the MSMQ documentation in MSDN for the defaults.)

3. Call Send(), passing the IMSMQQueue interface from Step 1.

4. Repeat steps 2 and 3 for all the messages you want to send.

5. Close the queue.

It is worth noting that one of the critical message properties available under the MSMQ Win32 API is not available through the IMSMQMessage interface. In the

MSMQ Win32 API, the programmer sending the message uses PROPID_M_BODY_TYPE
to indicate what kind of data they are sending. It is then used by the programmer receiving the message to interpret the message body. When you send or
receive a message with the COM API, this type is automatically set by the API.
In order to set a message type, use the AppSpecific property of IMSMQMessage
(PROPID_M_APPSPECIFIC).

Receiving a message is an even simpler process—you open a queue specifying MQ_RECEIVE_ACCESS and call the Receive() method on the IMSMQQueue interface:

```
void RecvMSMQMessage(_bstr_t QueueName)
{
    MSMQ::IMSMQQueueInfoPtr myQueueInfo("MSMQ.MSMQQueueInfo");
    try {
        myQueueInfo->PutPathName(QueueName);
        MSMQ::IMSMQQueuePtr myQueue =
        myQueueInfo->Open(MSMQ::MQ_RECEIVE_ACCESS, MSMQ::MQ_DENY_NONE);
        MSMQ::IMSMQMessagePtr myMessage = myQueue->Receive(
            &(_variant_t)MSMQ::MQ_NO_TRANSACTION, &(_variant_t) false,
            &(_variant_t) true, &(_variant_t) 1000);
        myQueue->Close();
    } catch (_com_error Result) {ErrorDlg(Result.Error());};
};
```

Receive(), like Send(), takes an IMSMQTransaction interface pointer or one of
a set of constants (including MQ_NO_TRANSACTION to indicate no transaction). The
second, third, and last parameters are Booleans that indicate if the receiver
wants the DestinationQueueInfo, Body, and ConnectorTypeGuid properties, respectively. If you do not need those properties, passing false for those parameters
can speed up the return of the function. The fourth parameter is a timeout value,
which indicates how long the Receive() function should wait for a message to
arrive when there is not already a message in the queue. This value is specified
in milliseconds or the default constant INFINITE.

Once the function returns successfully, you can read the message properties
through the IMSMQMessage interface.

Enumerating Messages in a Queue

MSMQ allows you to "peek" at messages, or retrieve them without removing
them from the queue. This of course is very useful if you want to browse a queue
in use by a program, to debug or monitor it.

IMSMQQueue provides two methods for peeking at messages: PeekCurrent() and
PeekNext(). PeekCurrent() retrieves the first message in the queue and sets up a

cursor internally marking the location of the last message read. PeekNext() reads the next message after the cursor and moves the cursor forward. ReceiveCurrent() retrieves the message at the cursor location and removes it from the queue.

In the following code sample, PeekCurrent() and PeekNext() are used to look for a message with a particular label, then ReceiveCurrent() retrieves that message from the queue:

```
void EnumMSMQQueue(_bstr_t QueueFormatName, _bstr_t TargetLabel)
{
    MSMQ::IMSMQQueueInfoPtr myQueueInfo("MSMQ.MSMQQueueInfo");
    MSMQ::IMSMQQueuePtr myQueue;
    MSMQ::IMSMQMessagePtr myMessage;
    _bstr_t myLabel;

    try {
        myQueueInfo->PutFormatName(QueueFormatName);
        myQueue = myQueueInfo->Open(MSMQ::MQ_PEEK_ACCESS,
            MSMQ::MQ_DENY_NONE);
        myMessage = myQueue->PeekCurrent(&(_variant_t)false,
            &(_variant_t)false, &(_variant_t)1000);
        if (myMessage != NULL)
            myLabel = myMessage->GetLabel();
        /* loop until we find a target label, or run out of messages */
        while ((myLabel != TargetLabel) && (myMessage != NULL))
        {
            myMessage = myQueue->PeekNext(&(_variant_t)false,
                &(_variant_t)true, &(_variant_t)1000);
            myLabel = myMessage->GetLabel();
        };
        /* Process/Display peeked message (not shown)*/
        myQueue->Close();
    } catch (_com_error Result) {ErrorDlg(Result.Error());};
};
```

ReceiveCurrent() uses the same parameters as Receive(). PeekNext() and PeekCurrent() also use the same parameters, except for the transaction interface—PeekNext() and PeekCurrent() cannot be used in a transaction. ReceiveCurrent() will fail if the queue isn't opened with MQ_RECEIVE_ACCESS; PeekNext() and PeekCurrent() will work with either MQ_RECEIVE_ACCESS or MQ_PEEK_ACCESS.

Enumerating with LookupIDs

MSMQ 3.0 features a series of new methods on the IMSMQQueue3 interface that allow you to peek and receive messages based on a unique 64-bit identifier— the lookup identifier, or lookupID—and then to traverse forward and backward through the queue using those lookupIDs. You can also jump directly to the end of a queue and peek or receive the last message. The most common use of lookupIDs is to quickly find a message that was already peeked. The receiving queue sets lookupIDs and they only apply to that queue. LookupID is a property on the IMSMQMessage3 interface.

PeekFirstByLookupID(), PeekLastByLookupID(), ReceiveFirstByLookupID(), and PeekLastByLookupID() do not require a lookupID as a parameter, because they begin at one end of the queue. They also do not use a timeout parameter as the Peek() and Receive() methods from previous versions of MSMQ do. They return immediately if there is no message in the queue.

PeekByLookupID() and ReceiveByLookupID() do require a lookupID as a parameter, and retrieve the message that matches that lookupID. PeekNextByLookupID(), PeekPreviousByLookupID(), ReceiveNextByLookupID(), and ReceivePreviousByLookupID() all take a lookupID as a parameter and retrieve the message adjacent to the message specified. The Receive methods remove the message from the queue after retrieving it and will return an error if the queue was not opened with receive access specified.

PeekLastByLookupID() and PeekPreviousByLookupID(), in the following code sample, are used to traverse the queue backward, looking for a given message label, and then retrieve the matching message using ReceiveByLookupID():

```
void EnumMSMQQueueByID(_bstr_t QueueFormatName, _bstr_t TargetLabel)
{
    MSMQ::IMSMQQueueInfoPtr myQueueInfo("MSMQ.MSMQQueueInfo");
    MSMQ::IMSMQQueue3Ptr myQueue;
    MSMQ::IMSMQMessage3Ptr myMessage;
    _bstr_t myLabel;
    _variant_t myLookupID;

    try {
        myQueueInfo->PutFormatName(QueueFormatName);
        myQueue = myQueueInfo->Open(MSMQ::MQ_PEEK_ACCESS,
            MSMQ::MQ_DENY_NONE);
        myMessage = myQueue->PeekLastByLookupId(
            &(_variant_t) false, &(_variant_t) false,
            &(_variant_t) false);
```

```
        if (myMessage != NULL)
            myLabel = myMessage->GetLabel();
        else
            return;

        while ((myLabel != TargetLabel) && (myMessage != NULL))
        {
            myMessage = myQueue->PeekPreviousByLookupId(
                myMessage->GetLookupId(), &(_variant_t) false,
                &(_variant_t) false, &(_variant_t) false);
            myLabel = myMessage->GetLabel();
        };
    } catch (_com_error Result) {ErrorDlg(Result.Error());};
};
```

Receiving Messages Asynchronously

The MSMQ COM API allows the programmer to have MSMQ notify them when
a message arrives in the queue, rather than calling Receive() to see if a message
is pending. To be notified by MSMQ of a waiting message in a particular queue,
the client must implement the _DMSMQEventEvents interface and then call the
EnableNotification() method of IMSMQQueue. For example:

```
HRESULT AdviseMSMQSource(IMSMQQueuePtr pQueue, bool bPeekMsgs)
{
    HRESULT hr;
    try {
        m_bPeek = bPeekMsgs;
        m_pEvent.CreateInstance("MSMQ.MSMQEvent");
        hr = DispEventAdvise(m_pEvent);
        pQueue->EnableNotification(m_pEvent);
    // cursor value for EnableNotification defaults to
    // MQMSG_FIRST
    } catch (_com_error Result) {hr = Result.Error();};
    return hr;
};
```

The previous function is implemented on an ATL object implementing
IDispEventImpl<>. DispEventAdvise() signs up the object to the connection point

exposed by m_pEvent. A companion function, DispEventUnAdvise(), should be used later to free the connection.

_DMSMQEventEvents has two methods: Arrived() and ArrivedError(). MSMQ calls Arrived() when a message arrives, passing an IMSMQQueue interface pointer and a cursor value. The interface pointer points to the queue that has received the message, and the cursor reflects the value passed to EnableNotification() by the client. ArrivedError() is called in when an error occurs, and has both the IMSMQQueue interface pointer and cursor value, along with an error code in the form of an HRESULT.

EnableNotification() provides only one notification before resetting. In order to receive continuous notifications, the handler of Arrived() needs to call EnableNotification() again. The two most common implementations of Arrived() are to peek messages in the queue or to receive them. If Arrived() only peeks at the message at the current cursor location, then it has to call EnableNotification() with a cursor value of MQMSG_NEXT to advance the cursor through the queue. If Arrived() retrieves the current message, the cursor value for EnableNotification() must be passed as MQMSG_CURRENT or EnableNotification() will return an error. For example, Arrived() could be implemented like so:

```
STDMETHODIMP Arrived(LPDISPATCH Queue, long Cursor)
{
    IMSMQQueuePtr myQueue = Queue;
    IMSMQMessagePtr myMessage = NULL;
    HRESULT hr;
    try {
        if (m_bPeek){
            myMessage = myQueue->PeekCurrent(&(_variant_t)false,
                &(_variant_t)false, &(_variant_t)1000);
            myQueue->EnableNotification(m_pEvent, &(_variant_t)MQMSG_NEXT);
        }
        else {
            myMessage = myQueue->Receive(&(_variant_t)MQ_NO_TRANSACTION,
                &(_variant_t) false, &(_variant_t) true, &(_variant_t) 1000);
            myQueue->EnableNotification(m_pEvent, &(_variant_t)MQMSG_CURRENT);
        }
    } catch (_com_error Result) {hr = Result.Error();};
    return hr;
}
```

m_bPeek is used by the object implementing Arrived() to determine whether to peek messages or receive them.

Using IDispEventImpl

The best way to implement an event sink in ATL is to derive an object from IDispEventImpl, implement Arrived() and ArrivedError(), and declare a sink map, as shown here:

```
class CEventImpl : public IDispEventImpl<0, CEventImpl,
    &DIID__DMSMQEventEvents, &LIBID_MSMQ, /*wMajor = */ 3, /*wMinor = */ 0>
{
    STDMETHODIMP Arrived(LPDISPATCH Queue, long Cursor);
    STDMETHODIMP ArrivedError(LPDISPATCH Queue, long ErrorCode,
        long Cursor);

    BEGIN_SINK_MAP(CEventImpl)
        SINK_ENTRY_EX(0, DIID__DMSMQEventEvents, 0, Arrived)
        SINK_ENTRY_EX(0, DIID__DMSMQEventEvents, 1,
        ArrivedError)
    END_SINK_MAP()
}
```

IDispEventImpl, as a template class, takes the control ID (0, since we are not sinking a control), the name of the inheriting class, the IID (COM interface identifier) of the interface to sink, the type library where that interface definition resides, and the major and minor version of that type library.

If the class is set up automatically by pointing the ATL wizard at mqoa.dll, the following #import line will end up in stdafx.h:

```
#import "c:\winnt\system32\mqoa.dll" raw_interfaces_only, raw_native_types, ⏎
no_namespace, named_guids, auto_search
```

This provides the declarations for DIID__DMSMQEventEvents, LIBID_MSMQ, and the _DMSMQEventEvents interface itself for the ATL class to implement.

Since _DMSMQEventEvents is based on IDispatch, the sink map is declared by BEGIN_SINK_MAP to assign Dispatch IDs to Arrived() and ArrivedError(). MSMQ calls Arrived() and ArrivedError() via IDispatch::Invoke(), so the Dispatch ID assigned to our implementation of _DMSMQEventEvents needs to match the Dispatch ID MSMQ expects for Arrived(). As shown earlier, the Dispatch ID for Arrived() is 0 and for ArrivedError() it is 1.

Using the COM API in C#

The COM API is also accessible from within the managed environment, using any managed language. For this example we use C# in Visual Studio .NET. For MSMQ in a managed environment, the best route is to use the System.MSMQ set of classes in the .NET Framework. In MSMQ 3.0 there are a few features in the COM API that are not exposed in the .NET classes, such as lookupIDs. Programmers can access those features by loading the COM objects in the .NET managed environment, although there are performance drawbacks (which we'll discuss later).

Importing a Type Library in .NET

To access the COM library from within C#, we must do two things. First, we need to create an assembly containing the type library data in mqoa.dll. Second, we need to add that new assembly as a reference in our C# project.

The .NET Framework ships with a command-line tool for converting type libraries to assemblies: tlbimp.exe. It is located in the FrameworkSDK\bin directory (or \Program Files\Microsoft Visual Studio .NET\FrameworkSDK\bin if you installed .NET with Visual Studio .NET). Users of the Visual Studio Command Console will find Tlbimp already in their path. Tlbimp has many options, but the only required parameter is the name of the type library you want to convert into an assembly. So the command

```
Tlbimp c:\winnt\system32\mqoa.dll
```

is all that's required to have Tlbimp produce msmq.dll, an assembly wrapper for mqoa.dll's type library. By default, Tlbimp names the output assembly after the namespace of the type library.

Assembly in hand, we can load our C# project in Visual Studio, and select Add New References from the Project menu. This opens a dialog box that allows us to add class references to our project. The COM tab lets us specify assemblies or COM libraries to convert (although we've found automatic conversion does not always work). After we browse for msmq.dll in this dialog box, the new assembly is loaded and ready for work.

As a final, optional step, we can add a using statement with the namespace of the COM object to our C# file, in this case

```
using MSMQ;
```

to bring the COM classes, interfaces, enumerations, and constants from the type library into the default namespace.

Coding with COM Objects in C#

Once we have finished all the preliminaries, we can jump in and code. In the sample that follows we use PeekFirstByLookupID() and PeekNextByLookupID(), to move forward through the queue until we find a message with a particular label, and then call ReceiveByLookupID() to retrieve that message:

```csharp
private void COMEnumMSMQQueueByID(string QueueName, string TargetLabel)
{
    IMSMQQueueInfo3 myQueueInfo = new MSMQ.MSMQQueueInfoClass();
    IMSMQQueue3 myQueue;
    IMSMQMessage3 myMessage;
    string myLabel = "";

    // MSMQ COM Variant parameters and constants which need conversion
    int mqAccess = (int) MQACCESS.MQ_RECEIVE_ACCESS;
    int mqShare = (int) MQSHARE.MQ_DENY_NONE;
    Object mqFalse = false;
    Object mqNoTransaction = MQTRANSACTION.MQ_NO_TRANSACTION;
    Object mqTrue = true;
    Object mqTimeout = 1000;

    // Use the path name to open the queue
    myQueueInfo.PathName = QueueName;
    myQueue = myQueueInfo.Open(mqAccess, mqShare);

    // Peek the first message
    myMessage = myQueue.PeekFirstByLookupId(ref mqFalse, ref mqFalse,
            ref mqFalse);
    if (myMessage != null)
        myLabel = myMessage.Label;

    // Loop until we find a matching message, or reach the end of the queue
    while ((myLabel != TargetLabel) && (myMessage != null))
    {
        myMessage = myQueue.PeekNextByLookupId(myMessage.LookupId,
            ref mqFalse, ref mqFalse, ref mqFalse);
        myLabel = myMessage.Label;
    };
    // Pull the matching message
    myMessage = myQueue.ReceiveByLookupId(myMessage.LookupId,
        ref mqNoTransaction, ref mqFalse, ref mqTrue, ref mqTimeout);
}
```

Programmers should take special note of the following four lines:

```
Object mqFalse = false;
Object mqNoTransaction = MQTRANSACTION.MQ_NO_TRANSACTION;
Object mqTrue = true;
Object mqTimeout = 1000;
```

These variables are used as parameters to ReceiveByLookupID() where VARIANT types would be used in unmanaged C++. The .NET Framework does not have a VARIANT type but instead uses Object in much the same way, and converts a VARIANT to Object, and vice versa, automatically. The String type automatically converts to BSTR.

Performance Considerations

Each time a COM method is called or a COM property is set from within the .NET managed environment, .NET has to copy the parameter data out of the managed memory pool and into the unmanaged part of the process (in the case of a COM library). Then it invokes the method, reversing the copying process for return values and out parameters. .NET copies (marshals) data referenced by a pointer in the same manner as a static parameter; interface pointers have to have managed stubs created for them, for example. All of this takes time—more time than calling similar native methods (like those in System.Messaging).

For some applications, the time delays will not be important. However, when programmers need optimal performance, they should breach the COM barrier as infrequently as possible. As an example, it is better to group a set of unmanaged operations behind one method call in a customized (unmanaged) function than to call a COM object repeatedly from within managed code.

MSMQ Win32 API: mqrt.dll

The Win32 API for MSMQ contains all of the available functionality of MSMQ in a series of functions, such as MQSendMessage() and MQReceiveMessage(). Some aspects of these functions are familiar to Win32 programmers—they return an HRESULT and use callbacks in a familiar manner. Other aspects are unusual, most notably the use of the PROPVARIANT type instead of VARIANT, and some are merely complicated, such as the MQQUEUEPROPS and MQMSGPROPS structures.

The MSMQ Win32 API is contained in MQRL.DLL, which Windows installs into the WINNT\System32 directory by default. In order to program the Win32 API in C or C++ you will need to include mq.h from the Win32 SDK and link to MQRT.LIB.

PROPVARIANTs

PROPVARIANTs (or PropVariants) are a type used primarily when dealing with the IPropertyStorage COM interface. A sibling of VARIANT, it contains a union of many types, some of which are not declared in VARIANT. Table 6-1 shows some selected types from PROPVARIANT and whether they are found in VARIANT.

Table 6-1. PropVariant Types

TYPE	VALUE	DESCRIPTOR	INCLUDED IN VARIANT?
CHAR	cVal	VT_I1	Yes
UCHAR	bVal	VT_UI1	Yes
SHORT	iVal	VT_I2	Yes
USHORT	uiVal	VT_UI2	Yes
LONG	lVal	VT_I4	Yes
INT	intVal	VT_INT	Yes
ULONG	ulVal	VT_UI4	Yes
UINT	uintVal	VT_UINT	Yes
LARGE_INTEGER	hVal	VT_I8	No
ULARGE_INTEGER	uhVal	VT_UI8	No
FLOAT	fltVal	VT_R4	Yes
DOUBLE	dblVal	VT_R8	Yes
CY	cyVal	VT_CY	Yes
DATE	date	VT_DATE	Yes
BSTR	bstrVal	VT_BSTR	Yes
VARIANT_BOOL	boolVal	VT_BOOL	Yes
SCODE	scode	VT_ERROR	Yes
FILETIME	filetime	VT_FILETIME	No
LPSTR	pszVal	VT_LPSTR	No
LPWSTR	pwszVal	VT_LPWSTR	No
CLSID*	puuid	VT_ CLSID	No
CLIPDATA*	pclipdata	VT_CF	No

Table 6-1. PropVariant Types (continued)

TYPE	VALUE	DESCRIPTOR	INCLUDED IN VARIANT?
BLOB	blob	VT_BLOB	No
IStream*	pStream	VT_STREAM	No
IStorage*	pStorage	VT_STORAGE	No
IUnknown*	punkVal	VT_UNKNOWN	Yes
IDispatch*	pdispVal	VT_DISPATCH	Yes
LPSAFEARRAY	parray	VT_ARRAY | VT_*	No

MSMQ programmers should be aware that PROPVARIANT is different from VARIANT, that the initialization and clearing APIs are different (PropVariantInit() and PropVariantClear()), and that some VARIANT APIs are not duplicated for PROPVARIANT—most notably VariantChangeType().

MQQUEUEPROPS/MQMSGPROPS

The MSMQ Win32 API uses arrays of PROPVARIANT quite extensively to hold data. These arrays are each referenced in an MSMQ-specific structure with an array of property identifiers, an array of error codes, and a value for the size of the arrays. In this chapter, the two property structures we will be dealing with are MQQUEUEPROPS for creating a queue and MQMSGPROPS for sending and receiving messages:

```
typedef struct tagMQMSGPROPS
{
    DWORD           cProp;
    MSGPROPID*      aPropID;
    MQPROPVARIANT*  aPropVar;
    HRESULT*        aStatus;
} MQMSGPROPS;

typedef struct tagMQQUEUEPROPS
{
    DWORD           cProp;
    QUEUEPROPID*    aPropID;
    MQPROPVARIANT*  aPropVar;
    HRESULT*        aStatus;
} MQQUEUEPROPS;
```

aPropID is a pointer to an array of property identifiers (such as PROPID_Q_PATHNAME for queue names or PROPID_M_LABEL for message labels). aPropVar points to an array containing PROPVARIANT, and aStatus points to an array of HRESULT, both with the same number of elements as aPropID. cProp indicates the common number of elements in the three arrays.

For each property ID in the aPropID array, aPropVar holds a corresponding PROPVARIANT at the same index position giving the value of that property. For each property ID and property, aStatus holds an HRESULT for reporting errors regarding that property.

In most cases, the array sizes used in MQMSGPROPS and MQQUEUEPROPS are constant—programmers only have to declare arrays to fit the number of properties they need to use. All of the examples in this chapter use fixed size arrays.

MQFreeMemory

MSMQ allocates memory for four different queue properties (PROPID_Q_INSTANCE, PROPID_Q_LABEL, PROPID_Q_TYPE, and PROPID_Q_PATHNAME) along with any PROPID_QM_* property. MSMQ allocates memory for these properties when the programmer gives MSMQ a PROPVARIANT set to VT_NULL to hold the property. In these cases it is up to that programmer to free the memory by calling MQFreeMemory(), passing the pointer to the allocated data. Neglecting to call MQFreeMemory() will result in memory leaks in your application.

For PROPID_QM_* properties, only the properties that are returned as VT_CLSID, VT_LPWSTR, VT_VECTOR | VT_UI, and VT_VECTOR | VT_LPWSTR need to be freed by MQFreeMemory().

None of the examples in this chapter require MQFreeMemory().

Creating and Deleting Queues

Creating a queue using the MSMQ Win32 API is a multistep process. Deleting a queue is very simple.

To create a queue, we need to call MQCreateQueue() with four parameters: a pointer to a SECURITY_DESCRIPTOR structure (or NULL), a pointer to an MQQUEUEPROPS structure, a pointer to an LPWSTR string buffer, and a pointer to a DWORD indicating the size of that buffer. MQCreateQueue() returns an HRESULT indicating success or error, and if the queue is created will fill the LPWSTR string buffer with the format name of the queue. (For a discussion of format names, see Chapter 1.)

```
void CreateQueue(LPWSTR PathName)
{
    MQQUEUEPROPS    QueueProps;
```

```
    // Needs to be initialized
    QUEUEPROPID      PropID[1];
    // Needs to be initialized
    MQPROPVARIANT    PropVars[1];
    // Does not need to be initialized
    HRESULT          hrStatus[1];
    // 54 is max size of private queue name
    WCHAR            FormatName[256];
    DWORD            FormatNameLen = 256;

    PropID[0] = PROPID_Q_PATHNAME;
    PropVars[0].vt = VT_LPWSTR;
    PropVars[0].pwszVal = PathName;

    QueueProps.cProp = 1;
    QueueProps.aPropID = PropID;
    QueueProps.aPropVar = PropVars;
    QueueProps.aStatus = hrStatus;

    HRESULT hr = MQCreateQueue(NULL /*Security descriptor*/,&QueueProps,
        FormatName, &FormatNameLen);
};
```

In the previous code, we see the first example of triple arrays in action, even though for this call we use arrays of only one element. The arrays use one element because we are setting only one queue property when we create the queue: the only required property, PathName, identified as PROPID_Q_PATHNAME. We set that value as the first element property ID, and then set the PathName we want into value field of the first element in the PROPVARIANT array. At the same time we set the type of the PROPVARIANT to VT_LPWSTR.

Once our arrays are set, we fill in the MQQUEUEPROPS structure, QueueProps, with the number of elements in cProp, and the arrays into the aPropID, aPropVar, and aStatus pointers. If MQCreateQueue() returns an error because of the path name, the first element in the aStatus array will contain an HRESULT specifically referring to that property.

If MQCreateQueue() succeeds in creating the queue, it will return a format name by setting the value into the string buffer passed as the third parameter, and returning the size of the string buffer in the DWORD indicated by the last parameter. The format name identifies a queue in MSMQ and is used to open the queue with MQOpenQueue() and to delete the queue with MQDeleteQueue().

It is possible to pass NULL for the string buffer and set the length to zero. In this case, MQCreateQueue() can still create the queue but will return 0x400E0009, MQ_INFORMATION_FORMATNAME_BUFFER_TOO_SMALL. MQCreateQueue() returns that error code any time the format name buffer is too small.

To delete a queue, just call `MQDeleteQueue()` with the format name:

```
void DeleteQueue(LPWSTR FormatName)
{
    HRESULT hr = MQDeleteQueue(FormatName);
};
```

Opening and Closing Queues

`MQOpenQueue()` provides the `QUEUEHANDLE` necessary to send, receive, or peek messages in MSMQ. To call `MQOpenQueue()` we have to specify a format name for the queue, our access mode (`MQ_PEEK_ACCESS`, `MQ_SEND_ACCESS`, or `MQ_RECEIVE_ACCESS`), and whether we want to deny access to the queue while we are receiving messages (`MQ_DENY_RECEIVE_SHARE` if so, `MQ_DENY_NONE` otherwise). Here, we are requesting send access so we cannot deny use of the queue:

```
QUEUEHANDLE      DestQueue;
HRESULT hr = MQOpenQueue(QueueName, MQ_SEND_ACCESS, MQ_DENY_NONE,
    &DestQueue);
```

Once we have finished using the queue, we can simply pass the `QUEUEHANDLE` back to `MQCloseQueue()`:

```
hr = MQCloseQueue(DestQueue);
```

Sending and Receiving Messages

Sending a message using the MSMQ Win32 API is normally a four-step process:

1. Create the message to send using `MQMSGPROPS`.

2. Open the destination queue with Send access.

3. Call `MQSendMessage()` to send the message.

4. Close the queue.

Creating an `MQMSGPROPS` structure is similar to creating an `MQQUEUEPROPS`. After defining a copy of the structure and the three arrays that comprise its data, you have to set the property identifiers and values of the message properties you are using. In the example that follows, we set PROPID_M_LABEL, PROPID_M_BODY, and PROPID_M_BODY_TYPE—the message label, the body of the message, and a type to indicate to the receiver what to expect in the body. Step 1 of our function yields the following code:

```
void SendMSMQMessage(LPWSTR QueueName, LPWSTR Label, LPWSTR Body)
{
    MQMSGPROPS       Message;
    MSGPROPID        PropID[3];
    MQPROPVARIANT    PropVars[3];
    HRESULT        hrStatus[3];

    PropID[0] = PROPID_M_LABEL;
    PropVariantInit(&PropVars[0]);
    PropVars[0].vt = VT_LPWSTR;
    PropVars[0].pwszVal = Label;

    PropID[1] = PROPID_M_BODY;
    PropVars[1].vt = VT_VECTOR | VT_UI1;
/* Variant type for body is always a string of bytes to MSMQ regardless of what
BODY_TYPE indicates*/
    PropVars[1].caub.pElems = (LPBYTE) Body;
    PropVars[1].caub.cElems =
        (ULONG) sizeof(WCHAR)*wcslen(Body); // length of Body string

    PropID[2] = PROPID_M_BODY_TYPE;
    PropVars[2].vt = VT_UI4;
    PropVars[2].ulVal = VT_LPWSTR;

    Message.cProp = 3;
    Message.aPropID = PropID;
    Message.aPropVar = PropVars;
    Message.aStatus = hrStatus;
```

Note that the PROPVARIANT holding the body data (for PROPID_M_BODY) carries a type of VT_VECTOR | VT_UI1 while we are indicating to the recipient (through PROPID_M_BODY_TYPE) that we are sending a string. This is not quite a contradiction; MSMQ always treats the data as an array of bytes, even when the data means something else to the sender and receiver. The property descriptor for PROPID_M_BODY is always VT_VECTOR | VT_UI1, and the property descriptor for PROPID_M_BODY_TYPE is always VT_UI4. The receiver will access the body as an array of bytes and can cast it back to the "real" data type. The sender is limited to a subset of PROPVARIANT types for PROPID_M_BODY_TYPE: VT_I1, VT_12, VT_I4, VT_R4, VT_R8, VT_CY, VT_DATE, VT_BSTR, VT_DISPATCH, VT_BOOL, VT_UNKNOWN, VT_UI1, VT_UI2,

`VT_UI4`, `VT_LPSTR`, `VT_LPWSTR`, `VT_STREAMED_OBJECT`, `VT_STORED_OBJECT`, and `VT_ARRAY |` `VT_UI1`. A sender can also indicate `VT_EMPTY`.

Once we have created the message structure, the last three steps go quickly:

```
QUEUEHANDLE DestQueue;
HRESULT hr = MQOpenQueue(QueueName, MQ_SEND_ACCESS,
        MQ_DENY_NONE, &DestQueue);
hr = MQSendMessage(DestQueue,&Message,MQ_NO_TRANSACTION);
hr = MQCloseQueue(DestQueue);
};
```

`MQSendMessage()` has only three parameters: the destination queue specified by a `QUEUEHANDLE`, the message itself in an `MQMSGPROPS`, and an `ITransaction` interface pointer or one of a few transaction constants, such as `MQ_NO_TRANSACTION`.

If you wanted to specify more message properties (such as `PROPID_M_RESP_QUEUE` to indicate a queue for response messages), you could just declare larger arrays and set the properties before calling `MQSendMessage()`.

Receiving a message is a more complicated process. `MQReceiveMessage()` requires you to fill out an `MQMSGPROPS` structure to indicate which message properties you want to retrieve. Retrieving a message body requires knowing the size of the incoming message body in advance (so you can allocate memory to hold it). For this reason, you can try to receive the message in order to retrieve the body size (and check the body type, as a precaution) before retrieving the message. In this case retrieving a message is a multistep process:

1. Get a handle to the queue containing the message you want to retrieve.

2. Create a message structure for retrieval, specifying `PROPID_M_BODY`, `PROPID_M_BODY_SIZE`, `PROPID_M_LABEL`, and `PROPID_M_LABEL_LEN`.

3. Call `MQReceiveMessage()`.

4. Check for `MQ_ERROR_BUFFER_OVERFLOW` and reset the memory buffer for `PROPID_M_BODY` and set `PROPID_M_BODY_SIZE`.

5. Call `MQReceiveMessage()` with the new size to remove the message from the queue.

6. Process the message.

For step 2, we create the message for retrieval, as well as the appropriate arrays large enough to hold four properties. Then we specify the `PROPID_M_BODY`, `PROPID_M_LABEL`, `PROPID_M_LABEL_LEN`, and `PROPID_M_BODY_SIZE` properties for retrieval:

```
void ReceiveSingleMessage(QUEUEHANDLE hSrcQueue)
{
    MQMSGPROPS        Message;
    int               numprops = 4;
    MSGPROPID         PropID[4];
    MQPROPVARIANT     PropVars[4];
    HRESULT           hrStatus[4];
    DWORD             BodySize = 0;

    // Begin initialization of message structure
    for (int i = 0; i<numprops; i++)
    PropVariantInit(&PropVars[i]);

    WCHAR LabelBuffer[MQ_MAX_MSG_LABEL_LEN];
    PropID[0] = PROPID_M_LABEL;
    PropVars[0].vt = VT_LPWSTR;
    PropVars[0].pwszVal = LabelBuffer;

    PropID[1] = PROPID_M_LABEL_LEN;
    PropVars[1].vt = VT_UI4;
    PropVars[1].ulVal = MQ_MAX_MSG_LABEL_LEN;
```

Because we are retrieving the label, we have to supply the maximum label length we are prepared to allow. MSMQ provides a predefined constant for this, MQ_MAX_MSG_LABEL_LEN. Allocating this maximum (250 characters, currently) is simpler than retrieving the label size along with the body size and type. We do not follow the same policy with body size because the maximum body size is 4 MB, a significant amount to allocate for each retrieved message.

```
    LPWSTR BodyBuffer = (LPWSTR) malloc(BodySize);
    PropID[2] = PROPID_M_BODY;
    PropVars[2].vt = VT_VECTOR | VT_UI1;
    PropVars[2].caub.pElems = (UCHAR*)BodyBuffer;
    PropVars[2].caub.cElems = BodySize;

    PropID[3] = PROPID_M_BODY_SIZE;
    PropVars[3].vt = VT_UI4;
    PropVars[3].ulVal = BodySize;

    Message.cProp = numprops;
    Message.aPropID = PropID;
    Message.aPropVar = PropVars;
    Message.aStatus = hrStatus;
```

After defining PROPID_M_LABEL_LEN, we finish by defining PROPID_M_BODY. MSMQ expects a PROPVARIANT of type VT_VECTOR | VT_UI1 (remember, regardless of the contents MSMQ treats message bodies as arrays of unsigned bytes). To set the array fields in the PROPVARIANT we set the array pointer to a buffer we created with the body size we retrieved by peeking at the message.

For step 3, we make an attempt to retrieve the message. If the body size we've set is large enough for the message, MQReceiveMessage will return it immediately and remove it from the queue. If the body size is not large enough, the buffer will overflow, but MQReceiveMessage will return all the other message properties and leave the message intact:

```
// Try to receive the message
HRESULT hr = MQReceiveMessage(hSrcQueue, 1000, MQ_ACTION_RECEIVE,
    &Message, NULL, NULL, NULL, MQ_NO_TRANSACTION);
```

In this example, we put steps 4 and 5 in a loop. This code will keep attempting to resize the message structure and retrieve a message as long as MQ_ERROR_BUFFER_OVERFLOW is returned. If the message we didn't receive in step 3 is retrieved before we execute step 5, then we may not get the next message when we call MQReceiveMessage again. Putting steps 4 and 5 in a loop handles this possibility by continuing to try and retrieve a message as long as the body size mismatch indicated by MQ_ERROR_BUFFER_OVERFLOW is the only problem:

```
// If the message is too large, this is the error
while (MQ_ERROR_BUFFER_OVERFLOW == hr)
{
    // Free the body and resize to fit the message
    free(BodyBuffer);
    BodySize = Message.aPropVar[3].ulVal;
    BodyBuffer = (LPWSTR) malloc(BodySize);
    PropVars[2].caub.pElems = (UCHAR*)BodyBuffer;
    PropVars[2].caub.cElems = BodySize;
    PropVars[3].ulVal = BodySize;

    // Try to receive again
    hr = MQReceiveMessage(hSrcQueue, 1000, MQ_ACTION_RECEIVE, &Message,
        NULL, NULL, NULL, MQ_NO_TRANSACTION);
}
```

Once we've retrieved a message, we can process it—but not without freeing the memory we've allocated for the message body:

```
    /* Message processing goes here */
    free(BodyBuffer);
};
```

Enumerating Messages in a Queue

In the previous section you saw that MQReceiveMessage() can be used to "peek" at a message—retrieve it without removing it from the queue. MQReceiveMessage() has two peek modes: MQ_ACTION_PEEK_CURRENT and MQ_ACTION_PEEK_NEXT. While you can use MQ_ACTION_PEEK_CURRENT to look at the front of the queue, moving through the queue requires a cursor (of type HANDLE). A cursor is normal database terminology for a position in a row—or in this case a queue. You create the cursor with MQCreateCursor() and pass it as a parameter to MQReceiveMessage() when you want to refer to the cursor's current position or move it forward. Using a cursor allows you to traverse a queue, peeking at each message as you go. You can also use MQReceiveMessage() to retrieve the message at the current cursor location. Once you have finished with the cursor, you use MQCloseCursor() to release it.

The code sample in this section peeks at messages until we find a message matching a given label, or until we reach the end of the queue. If we do find a matching label, we use MQReceiveMessage() to retrieve the message. We start by opening the queue and getting a cursor for that queue:

```
void EnumerateMSMQQueue(LPWSTR QueueName, LPWSTR Label)
{
    QUEUEHANDLE      SrcQueue;
    HRESULT hr = MQOpenQueue(QueueName, MQ_RECEIVE_ACCESS,
          MQ_DENY_RECEIVE_SHARE, &SrcQueue);

    HANDLE Cursor;
    hr = MQCreateCursor(SrcQueue, &Cursor);
```

After we have a cursor, we can peek at the first message in the queue, retrieving the label along with the body size and body type. We request body size in case we decide to retrieve the message, and we request body type as an opportunity to double-check that the message is in a format we expect:

```
    MQMSGPROPS       peekMessage;
    int              numprops = 4;
    MSGPROPID        peekPropID[4];
    MQPROPVARIANT    peekPropVars[4];
    HRESULT          peekStatus[4];
```

```
for (int i = 0; i<numprops; i++)
    PropVariantInit(&peekPropVars[i]);

peekPropID[1] = PROPID_M_BODY_TYPE;
peekPropVars[1].vt = VT_UI4;

peekPropID[0] = PROPID_M_BODY_SIZE;
peekPropVars[0].vt = VT_UI4;

WCHAR LabelBuffer[MQ_MAX_MSG_LABEL_LEN];
peekPropID[2] = PROPID_M_LABEL;
peekPropVars[2].vt = VT_LPWSTR;
peekPropVars[2].pwszVal = LabelBuffer;

peekPropID[3] = PROPID_M_LABEL_LEN;
peekPropVars[3].vt = VT_UI4;
peekPropVars[3].ulVal = MQ_MAX_MSG_LABEL_LEN;

peekMessage.cProp = numprops;
peekMessage.aPropID = peekPropID;
peekMessage.aPropVar = peekPropVars;
peekMessage.aStatus = peekStatus;

hr = MQReceiveMessage(SrcQueue, 1000, MQ_ACTION_PEEK_CURRENT,
    &peekMessage, NULL, NULL, Cursor, MQ_NO_TRANSACTION);
```

We have to initialize the cursor before we can use MQ_ACTION_PEEK_NEXT by using it with MQ_ACTION_PEEK_CURRENT. MQReceiveMessage() takes a cursor as an optional seventh parameter, so we pass the cursor from MQCreateCursor() instead of NULL.

Next we compare the message label with the search label, and use MQ_ACTION_PEEK_NEXT if the label does not match. That moves the cursor to the next most recent message, until we reach the end of the queue:

```
while ((0 != wcscmp(peekMessage.aPropVar[2].pwszVal, Label))
    && (SUCCEEDED(hr)))
{
    peekPropVars[3].ulVal = MQ_MAX_MSG_LABEL_LEN;

    hr = MQReceiveMessage(SrcQueue, 1000,
    MQ_ACTION_PEEK_NEXT, &peekMessage, NULL, NULL,
    Cursor, MQ_NO_TRANSACTION);
}
```

Once we have exited the while loop, we check and see if it's time to close the queue and the cursor, or retrieve the message at the cursor location:

```
ULONG BodySize, BodyType = 0;

// 0xC00E001B indicates no more messages
if SUCCEEDED(hr)
{
    BodyType = peekMessage.aPropVar[1].ulVal;
    BodySize = peekMessage.aPropVar[0].ulVal;
}
else
{
    hr = MQCloseCursor(Cursor);
    hr = MQCloseQueue(SrcQueue);
    return;
};

if (BodyType != VT_LPWSTR)
{
    hr = MQCloseCursor(Cursor);
    hr = MQCloseQueue(SrcQueue);
    return;
};
```

If we have made it this far, there is a matching message at the current cursor location, so for the final part of the example we create an MQMSGPROPS and call MQReceiveMessage(), specifying MQ_ACTION_RECEIVE and the cursor that indicates the last message we peeked:

```
MQMSGPROPS          Message;
numprops = 3;
MSGPROPID           PropID[3];
MQPROPVARIANT       PropVars[3];
HRESULT             hrStatus[3];

for (int i = 0; i<numprops; i++)
    PropVariantInit(&PropVars[i]);

PropID[0] = PROPID_M_LABEL;
PropVars[0].vt = VT_LPWSTR;
PropVars[0].pwszVal = LabelBuffer;
```

```
          PropID[1] = PROPID_M_LABEL_LEN;
          PropVars[1].vt = VT_UI4;
          PropVars[1].ulVal = MQ_MAX_MSG_LABEL_LEN;

          LPWSTR BodyBuffer = (LPWSTR) malloc(BodySize);
          PropID[2] = PROPID_M_BODY;
          PropVars[2].vt = VT_VECTOR | VT_UI1;
          PropVars[2].caub.pElems = (UCHAR*)BodyBuffer;
          PropVars[2].caub.cElems = BodySize;

          Message.cProp = numprops;
          Message.aPropID = PropID;
          Message.aPropVar = PropVars;
          Message.aStatus = hrStatus;

          hr = MQReceiveMessage(SrcQueue, 1000, MQ_ACTION_RECEIVE,
              &Message, NULL, NULL, Cursor, MQ_NO_TRANSACTION);

          hr = MQCloseCursor(Cursor);

          hr = MQCloseQueue(SrcQueue);

          /* Message processing goes here */
          free(BodyBuffer);
};
```

In this example, we close the cursor as soon as we find one matching message. MQ_ACTION_RECEIVE moves the cursor forward one position (to the next message or to the end of the queue), so if we continued peeking messages we would have to start with an MQ_ACTION_PEEK_CURRENT call instead of MQ_ACTION_PEEK_NEXT.

In the time that elapses between peeking the message and trying to receive the message, it is possible for the message we seek to be retrieved by another application. This will result in MQ_ERROR_BUFFER_OVERFLOW if the new message at the current cursor location is larger than the message we peeked; otherwise MQReceiveMessage will return the wrong message. You can safeguard against this by making sure that only one application is retrieving messages from the queue, or use lookupIDs in MSMQ 3.0.

Enumerating with LookupID

MSMQ 3.0 provides a new function for peeking or retrieving messages, MQReceiveMessageByLookupId(). A lookupID, as we explained earlier, is a unique number assigned to each message as it enters the queue. MQReceiveMessageByLookupId()

allows programmers to peek or retrieve messages identified by the lookupID; messages immediately before or after the identified message; or messages at either end of the queue without specifying a lookupID. MSMQ exposes the lookupID of a message as the PROPID_M_LOOKUPID property on that message.

MQReceiveMessageByLookupId() is nearly identical to MQReceiveMessage(). Instead of an optional cursor parameter, MQReceiveMessageByLookupId() has an optional LookupID parameter; instead of three actions (e.g., MQ_ACTION_PEEK_NEXT), there are ten actions. Those ten actions consist of five peek actions and five receive actions: peek or receive the first or last message in the queue, and peek or receive the message at the given lookupID or the one immediately before and after that message.

Needless to say, this new function allows a lot more flexibility in traversing a queue than MQReceiveMessage() allows. In the code sample for this section, we are simply going to use MQ_LOOKUP_PEEK_LAST, MQ_LOOKUP_PEEK_PREV, and MQ_LOOKUP_RECEIVE_CURRENT to start at the end of the queue, with the most recently received messages, and traverse the queue backward, looking for a given message label. If we find the right message label, we will call MQReceiveMessageByLookupId() with the lookupID of the message we found, and retrieve it.

To start, after opening the queue we create a message designed for peeking, adding PROPID_M_LOOKUPID to the properties we normally peek:

```
void EnumMSMQQueueByID(LPWSTR QueueName, LPWSTR Label)
{
    QUEUEHANDLE      SrcQueue;
    HRESULT hr = MQOpenQueue(QueueName, MQ_RECEIVE_ACCESS,
        MQ_DENY_RECEIVE_SHARE, &SrcQueue);

    MQMSGPROPS       peekMessage;
    int              numprops = 5;
    MSGPROPID        peekPropID[5];
    MQPROPVARIANT    peekPropVars[5];
    HRESULT          peekStatus[5];

    for (int i = 0; i<numprops; i++)
        PropVariantInit(&peekPropVars[i]);

    peekPropID[1] = PROPID_M_BODY_TYPE;
    peekPropVars[1].vt = VT_UI4;

    peekPropID[0] = PROPID_M_BODY_SIZE;
    peekPropVars[0].vt = VT_UI4;
```

```
WCHAR LabelBuffer[MQ_MAX_MSG_LABEL_LEN];
peekPropID[2] = PROPID_M_LABEL;
peekPropVars[2].vt = VT_LPWSTR;
peekPropVars[2].pwszVal = LabelBuffer;

peekPropID[3] = PROPID_M_LABEL_LEN;
peekPropVars[3].vt = VT_UI4;
peekPropVars[3].ulVal = MQ_MAX_MSG_LABEL_LEN;

peekPropID[4] = PROPID_M_LOOKUPID;
peekPropVars[4].vt = VT_UI8;

peekMessage.cProp = numprops;
peekMessage.aPropID = peekPropID;
peekMessage.aPropVar = peekPropVars;
peekMessage.aStatus = peekStatus;
```

Next, we peek at the last message in the queue, passing "0" as the lookupID and specifying MQ_LOOKUP_PEEK_LAST as the peek action. Then we compare the label, and if it doesn't match we call MQReceiveMessageByLookupId() again with the lookupID of the last message, and MQ_LOOKUP_PEEK_PREV to peek the message immediately before (that is to say, older than) the last message we peeked:

```
hr = MQReceiveMessageByLookupId(SrcQueue, 0, MQ_LOOKUP_PEEK_LAST,
    &peekMessage, NULL, NULL, MQ_NO_TRANSACTION);

while ((0 != wcscmp(peekMessage.aPropVar[2].pwszVal, Label))
    && (SUCCEEDED(hr)))
{
    peekPropVars[3].ulVal = MQ_MAX_MSG_LABEL_LEN;

    hr = MQReceiveMessageByLookupId(SrcQueue,
        peekMessage.aPropVar[4].uhVal.QuadPart,
        MQ_LOOKUP_PEEK_PREV, &peekMessage, NULL,
        NULL, MQ_NO_TRANSACTION);
};
```

After the while loop, we check to make sure there were no errors (such as reaching the end of the queue, or finding a message with the wrong body type), and if there are no errors, we set up a new MQMSGPROPS message structure to retrieve the body. A final call to MQReceiveMessageByLookupId() with MQ_LOOKUP_RECEIVE_CURRENT and the lookupID of the message we found retrieves the message. After closing the queue, we are free to process the message:

```
ULONG BodySize, BodyType = 0;
ULONGLONG LookupID = 0;

if SUCCEEDED(hr)
{
    BodyType = peekMessage.aPropVar[1].ulVal;
    BodySize = peekMessage.aPropVar[0].ulVal;
    LookupID = peekMessage.aPropVar[4].uhVal.QuadPart;
}
else
{
    hr = MQCloseQueue(SrcQueue);
    return;
};

if (BodyType != VT_LPWSTR)
{
    hr = MQCloseQueue(SrcQueue);
    return;
};

MQMSGPROPS        Message;
numprops = 3;
MSGPROPID         PropID[3];
MQPROPVARIANT     PropVars[3];
HRESULT           hrStatus[3];

for (int i = 0; i<numprops; i++)
    PropVariantInit(&PropVars[i]);

PropID[0] = PROPID_M_LABEL;
PropVars[0].vt = VT_LPWSTR;
PropVars[0].pwszVal = LabelBuffer;

PropID[1] = PROPID_M_LABEL_LEN;
PropVars[1].vt = VT_UI4;
PropVars[1].ulVal = MQ_MAX_MSG_LABEL_LEN;

LPWSTR BodyBuffer = (LPWSTR) malloc(BodySize);
PropID[2] = PROPID_M_BODY;
PropVars[2].vt = VT_VECTOR | VT_UI1;
PropVars[2].caub.pElems = (UCHAR*)BodyBuffer;
PropVars[2].caub.cElems = BodySize;
```

```
    Message.cProp = numprops;
    Message.aPropID = PropID;
    Message.aPropVar = PropVars;
    Message.aStatus = hrStatus;

    hr = MQReceiveMessageByLookupId(SrcQueue,
        peekMessage.aPropVar[4].uhVal.QuadPart, MQ_LOOKUP_RECEIVE_CURRENT,
        &Message, NULL, NULL, MQ_NO_TRANSACTION);

    hr = MQCloseQueue(SrcQueue);

    /* Message processing goes here */
    free(BodyBuffer);
};
```

Receiving Messages Asynchronously

MQReceiveMessage() has three different modes for receiving messages asynchronously: a callback function, a Win32 Event, or a completion port. Let's now demonstrate the callback function, the easiest way to receive messages asynchronously. When you specify a callback function, MQReceiveMessage() calls that function if a message enters the queue before the given timeout period elapses (or if a message is already waiting).

In the code sample for this section, we break the "peek, then receive" cycle into two pieces: we call MQReceiveMessage() with the properties we want to peek, and then our callback function examines those properties and retrieves the message if the body type matches.

We start with a forward declaration of our callback, and then the calling function takes an open queue and creates an MQMSGPROPS with the properties for body type, body size, label, and label length:

```
void CALLBACK MessageCallback(HRESULT hr, QUEUEHANDLE hSource,
    DWORD dwTimeout, DWORD dwAction, MQMSGPROPS* pMessageProps,
    LPOVERLAPPED lpOverlapped, HANDLE hCursor);

void CallMSMQAsync(QUEUEHANDLE hSrcQueue)
{
    MQMSGPROPS*      pPeekMessage = (MQMSGPROPS*) malloc(sizeof(MQMSGPROPS));
    int              numprops = 4;
    MSGPROPID*       pPeekPropID = new MSGPROPID[4];
    MQPROPVARIANT*   pPeekPropVars = new MQPROPVARIANT[4];
    HRESULT*         pPeekStatus = new HRESULT[4];
```

```
for (int i = 0; i<numprops; i++)
    PropVariantInit(&pPeekPropVars[i]);

pPeekPropID[1] = PROPID_M_BODY_TYPE;
pPeekPropVars[1].vt = VT_UI4;

pPeekPropID[0] = PROPID_M_BODY_SIZE;
pPeekPropVars[0].vt = VT_UI4;

WCHAR LabelBuffer[MQ_MAX_MSG_LABEL_LEN];
pPeekPropID[2] = PROPID_M_LABEL;
pPeekPropVars[2].vt = VT_LPWSTR;
pPeekPropVars[2].pwszVal = LabelBuffer;

pPeekPropID[3] = PROPID_M_LABEL_LEN;
pPeekPropVars[3].vt = VT_UI4;
pPeekPropVars[3].ulVal = MQ_MAX_MSG_LABEL_LEN;

pPeekMessage->cProp = numprops;
pPeekMessage->aPropID = pPeekPropID;
pPeekMessage->aPropVar = pPeekPropVars;
pPeekMessage->aStatus = pPeekStatus;
```

In this function, rather than declaring the message on the stack, we use malloc() to place the MQMSGPROPS structure and the MQPROPID, MQPROPVARIANT, and HRESULT arrays on the heap. This is because MQReceiveMessage(), if successful, will pass the structure to the callback function after the calling function has exited. It will then be up to the callback function to remove the data from the heap.

Next we call MQReceiveMessage(), and deallocate the peek message if that call fails:

```
HRESULT hr = MQReceiveMessage(hSrcQueue, 3000, MQ_ACTION_PEEK_CURRENT,
    pPeekMessage, NULL, &MessageCallback, NULL, MQ_NO_TRANSACTION);

if (FAILED(hr))
{
    delete [] pPeekPropID;
    delete [] pPeekPropVars;
    delete [] pPeekStatus;
    free(pPeekMessage);

    // No further use for this queue
    MQCloseQueue(hSrcQueue);
};
```

In this call to MQReceiveMessage(), we set a timeout of 30 seconds, ask for a peek of the current message, and pass our message structure and the address to our callback function.

If a message exists in the queue, or arrives in the next 30 seconds, we can expect a call to our callback function. The callback function receives an HRESULT indicating the error status of the call, along with most of the parameters originally passed to MQReceiveMessage(). In our callback function, we make use of the handle indicating where the message resides and the MQMSGPROPS now filled out with properties from the first message in the queue. Our first step is to retrieve the body properties and deallocate the memory allocated by the calling function. If the MQReceiveMessage() function passes an error, or the message body type is not what we expect, we close the queue and return:

```
void CALLBACK MessageCallback(HRESULT hr, QUEUEHANDLE hSource,
    DWORD dwTimeout, DWORD dwAction, MQMSGPROPS* pMessageProps,
    LPOVERLAPPED lpOverlapped, HANDLE hCursor)
{
    ULONG BodySize, BodyType = 0;

    BodyType = pMessageProps->aPropVar[1].ulVal;
    BodySize = pMessageProps->aPropVar[0].ulVal;

    delete [] pMessageProps->aPropID;
    delete [] pMessageProps->aPropVar;
    delete [] pMessageProps->aStatus;
    free(pMessageProps);

    if ((FAILED(hr) || (BodyType != VT_LPWSTR))
    {
        MQCloseQueue(hSource);
        return;   // error handling would go here
    };
```

Once we have retrieved the properties and confirmed they are to our liking, we are free to create a message structure to retrieve the message body, and make a synchronous call to retrieve the message:

```
MQMSGPROPS       Message;
int              numprops = 3;
MSGPROPID        PropID[3];
MQPROPVARIANT    PropVars[3];
HRESULT          hrStatus[3];
```

```
for (int i = 0; i<numprops; i++)
    PropVariantInit(&PropVars[i]);

WCHAR LabelBuffer[MQ_MAX_MSG_LABEL_LEN];
PropID[0] = PROPID_M_LABEL;
PropVars[0].vt = VT_LPWSTR;
PropVars[0].pwszVal = LabelBuffer;

PropID[1] = PROPID_M_LABEL_LEN;
PropVars[1].vt = VT_UI4;
PropVars[1].ulVal = MQ_MAX_MSG_LABEL_LEN;

LPWSTR BodyBuffer = (LPWSTR) malloc(BodySize);
PropID[2] = PROPID_M_BODY;
PropVars[2].vt = VT_VECTOR | VT_UI1;
PropVars[2].caub.pElems = (UCHAR*)BodyBuffer;
PropVars[2].caub.cElems = BodySize;

Message.cProp = numprops;
Message.aPropID = PropID;
Message.aPropVar = PropVars;
Message.aStatus = hrStatus;

hr = MQReceiveMessage(hSource, 1000, MQ_ACTION_RECEIVE, &Message,
    NULL, NULL, NULL, MQ_NO_TRANSACTION);

/* Message processing goes here */
free(BodyBuffer);
```

Before closing the queue and ending the function, we have the option of calling our first function again to retrieve the next message asynchronously (similar to the way we called EnableNotification() in the COM asynchronous processing). Since our original function takes a handle to an opened queue, we can pass the handle MSMQ gave us:

```
/* Reset Async */
CallMSMQAsync(hSource);
};
```

Calling the CallMSMQAsync() function again will have the effect of making this process loop until all the messages are cleared from the queue and the timeout expires, or until an error is encountered. If CallMSMQAsync() fails, it will call MQCloseQueue for us, cleaning up the open queue handle.

Summary

In this chapter, we've explored how to use the MSMQ COM API with unmanaged C++ and from a managed application using C#. We've also seen how to use the MSMQ Win32 API from unmanaged C++. With both APIs we've learned to create, delete, open, and close queues; enumerate a queue; send a message synchronously; and receive messages synchronously and asynchronously. These operations provide a starting place for building MSMQ applications and exploring the full functionality of the COM and Win32 APIs.

CHAPTER 7

MSMQ 3.0

SO FAR IN THIS BOOK, WE'VE BEEN CONCENTRATING on the core MSMQ functionality available in MSMQ 2.0, as it's still going to be some time before installations of Windows Server 2003 are rolled out in live environments. However, MSMQ 3.0 introduces several major new features that were designed to expand the application developer's set of tools, and we'll look in detail at these new features in this chapter. The key enhancements are found in the following new areas:

- *Internet Messaging*, which provides support for sending and retrieving messages through Hypertext Transfer Protocol (HTTP)

- *The Programmable Management COM interface*, which provides several classes for managing queues and computers programmatically

- *Queue Aliases*, which are Active Directory objects used to reference queues by means of an alias

- *Multiple-Destination Messaging*, which allows you to send messages to multiple destinations using distribution lists, multicast addresses, and multiple-element format names

MSMQ 3.0 also integrates MSMQ Triggers as a part of the setup process (we looked at triggers in Chapter 5), and allows you to retrieve a specific message efficiently based on its lookup identifier, or lookupID (which we studied in Chapter 6).

This new version is available for

- Windows 2003 Server

- Windows XP Professional

NOTE *The* System.Messaging *namespace of the .NET Framework was designed for MSMQ 2.0. The majority of features introduced by MSMQ 3.0 aren't supported by* System.Messaging; *that's why the examples shown through this chapter are coded in Visual Basic 6.0 using the Message Queuing COM Component. In spite of that, the topics that have .NET compatibility are expressly detailed throughout the chapter.*

Installation Guideline

MSMQ 2.0 and 3.0 have the same architecture and use the same Active Directory model. However, MSMQ 3.0 client can access Active Directory directly, whereas MSMQ 2.0 clients must talk to an MSMQ Active Directory server that uses the same interface as an old MSMQ 1.0 Directory Service (DS) server.

The installation of MSMQ 3.0 differs from that of MSMQ 2.0, and the new features must be explicitly requested in order to be installed. Let's examine this installation process using Windows 2003 Server.

Setup Features

In order to start the MSMQ setup process, you have to launch Add/Remove Programs from Control Panel, and then select Add/Remove Windows Components.

The MSMQ 3.0 setup process allows us to specify the following subcomponents (Figure 7-1):

- **Active Directory Integration:** Provides integration with Active Directory whenever the computer belongs to a domain

- **Common:** Provides basic functionality for local messaging services

- **Downlevel Client Support:** Installs the Message Queuing Directory Service on a domain controller

- **MSMQ HTTP Support:** Enables the sending and receiving of messages over HTTP

- **Routing Support:** Provides store-and-forward messaging, as well as efficient routing services

- **Triggers:** Associates the incoming messages of a queue with a method in a COM component or a stand-alone executable program

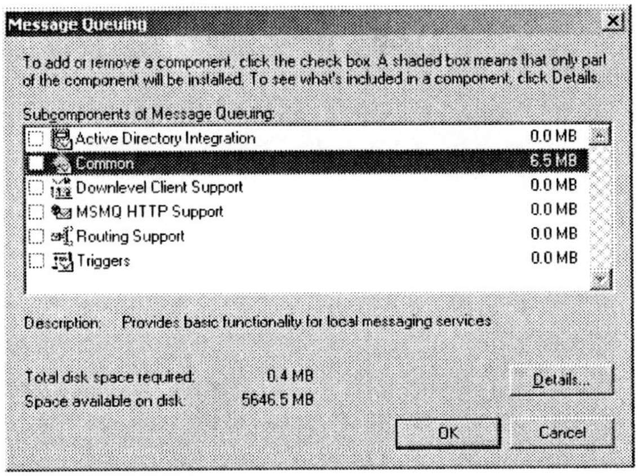

Figure 7-1. First window of the Setup wizard running in a Windows 2003 Server

Setup Considerations

In this section, we discuss factors you should bear in mind when you install some of these features.

Common

The Common item from the previous list is required for installing MSMQ, and is checked by default. This is the only dialog box that enables the Details button, as shown in Figure 7-2.

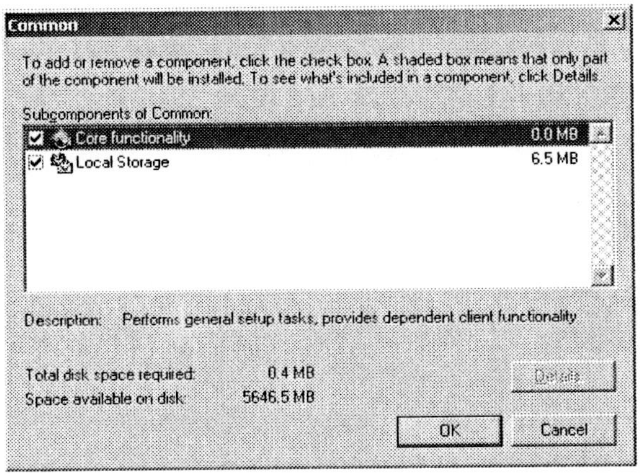

Figure 7-2. The Common dialog box

The subcomponents of Common include

- **Core functionality:** Installs the local queue manager, providing dependent client functionalities. This is a prerequisite for installing MSMQ.

- **Local Storage:** Stores messages locally, and is able to send and receive messages, even if it is not connected to a network. This optional feature provides independent client functionality. Without this feature, MSMQ is installed as a "dependent client."

Downlevel Client Support

To install an MSMQ Server, you have to select Downlevel Client Support. This option is only available on domain controllers. As the name implies, it is required only if you need to support MSMQ 1.0/2.0 clients. If you have only MSMQ 3.0 clients in your domain, you don't have to select this option. Note that selecting this option causes an additional service to run on your server.

MSMQ HTTP Support

To provide MSMQ HTTP support, the setup process automatically installs Internet Information Services (IIS), if necessary, and installs the Internet Services Application Programming Interface (ISAPI) extension required by the Message Queuing service.

Routing Support

Routing Support cannot be installed in Workgroup mode.

Direct Messaging

Although direct format names have existed since MSMQ 1.0, direct messaging is a convenient way of using format names without explicitly opening a queue.

Applications can use direct messaging at any time, but they should use it when messages have to be sent to the destination queue *in one hop*, or when applications must set a queue for sending or receiving messages that don't belong to the same enterprise. Direct messaging applies when routing, authentication, and encryption are not needed.

Internet Messaging and one-to-many messaging use direct messaging to communicate.

To locate the queues (except from local public queues), direct messaging uses application information instead of querying the Directory Service, and therefore applications have to provide direct format names.

TIP *Although the* System.Messaging *namespace of the .NET Framework already had this functionality, it is now supported by the Message Queue COM Component.*

This functionality is implemented by the MSMQDestination class, which represents one or more queues. An instance of this class can be used to send messages or to specify response queues. We can explicitly Open() or Close() an MSMQDestination object, or this can be performed automatically by the MSMQMessage when it calls the Send() method.

This code snippet shows how to send a message using direct messaging and specifying a direct format name:

```
Dim destQueue As MSMQ.MSMQDestination
Dim msg as MSMQ.MSMQMessage

Set destQueue = new MSMQ.MSMQDestination
Set msg = new MSMQ.MSMQMessage

destQueue.FormatName = "DIRECT=OS:vemn\anyQueue"
msg.Body = "Something to send"
msg.Send destQueue
```

You can also specify a response queue using direct messaging and a direct format name:

```
Dim destQueue As MSMQ.MSMQDestination
Dim respQueue As MSMQ.MSMQDestination
Dim msg as MSMQ.MSMQMessage

Set destQueue = new MSMQ.MSMQDestination
Set respQueue = new MSMQ.MSMQDestination
Set msg = new MSMQ.MSMQMessage

destQueue.FormatName = "DIRECT=OS:vemn\anyQueue"
respQueue.FormatName = "DIRECT=OS:vemn2003\PRIVATE$\respQueue"
Set msg.ResponseDestination = respQueue
msg.Body = "Something to send"
msg.Send destQueue
```

Internet Messaging

One of the most important new features of Microsoft Message Queue 3.0 version is the ability to send messages over the Internet. Message Queuing 3.0 provides support for sending and retrieving messages through HTTP. This support includes

- Referencing queues by URLs

- Sending and reading SOAP-formatted messages

- Authenticating messages sent over HTTPS

MSMQ 3.0 allows you to specify HTTP as the delivery protocol for the messages. Of course, the proprietary TCP-based MSMQ protocol is still supported. Sending applications can also specify the use of HTTPS for secured communication. HTTPS is the protocol name used to ensure the HTTP transport through a **Secure Sockets Layer (SSL)** connection.

Internet Messaging also provides improvements in communication between organizations. Thanks to this technology, organizations can connect to the internal message-based systems of other organizations, easily incorporating all the benefits of Messaging Queuing. With Internet Messaging there is no need to create a proxy web service to receive HTTP messages and convert them to MSMQ messages within the organization or to use Microsoft Windows HTTP Services (WinHTTP) to send them. All this functionality is supplied by Internet Messaging.

By default, Message Queuing is implemented over TCP on port 1081 for performance reasons. If you have to receive messages from a computer that belongs to another enterprise, on another network, you will have to configure your firewall to accept traffic on port 1081. As MSMQ 3.0 supports HTTP messaging through port 80, which is usually open on **firewalls** to permit HTTP traffic, no special configuration is needed, so security is not compromised.

Referencing Queues by URL

Direct format names are used to open and send HTTP messages. They are included in a URL that references a remote queue:

```
DIRECT=HTTP://www.apress.com/msmq/anyQueue
```

- `www.apress.com:` The site

- `msmq:` The IIS default virtual directory

- `anyQueue:` The queue name

To reference a machine, you can use an IP address, a complete DNS name, or just the name of the computer within the enterprise.

Table 7-1 contains examples of direct format names used to send HTTP messages.

Table 7-1. Examples of Direct Format Names

DIRECT FORMAT NAMES	PURPOSE
DIRECT=HTTP://vemn2003/msmq/anyQueue	For single computer of your enterprise
DIRECT=HTTP://200.128.7.6/msmq/anyQueue	Using TCP/IP address
DIRECT=HTTP://www.apress.com/msmq/anyQueue	Over the Internet
DIRECT=HTTPS://www.apress.com/msmq/anyQueue	Using SSL

Although you can reference a queue using a direct format name in order to read HTTP messages, remote reading is implemented using Remote Procedure Call (RPC), not over HTTP. *It is highly recommended that you retrieve messages only from local queues.*

TIP   *Queues can be referenced by URL from the* System.Messaging *.NET Framework namespace.*

Using SOAP Messages

The HTTP messages are sent in a Simple Object Access Protocol (SOAP) format. SOAP is a lightweight XML-based protocol for exchanging information in a decentralized, distributed environment. SOAP provides an open protocol for application-to-application communication, supported by all vendors. A SOAP message, similar to a web service request, is based on XML and contains the following parts:

- **Envelope:** The top-level container representing the message, containing both header and body.

- **Header:** A generic container for the message's properties. It is also used to add meta-information to a SOAP message, such as routing or proprietary application support. SOAP defines attributes to indicate who should deal with a feature and whether understanding is optional or mandatory.

- **Body:** A container for mandatory information intended for the end message receiver.

Let's see an example of a SOAP-formatted MSMQ Message within an HTTP packet:

```
POST //LocalHost HTTP/1.1
Host: vemn2003
Content-Type: multipart/related;
boundary="MSMQ - SOAP boundary, 19264"; type=text/xml
Content-Length: 1144
SOAPAction: "MSMQMessage"
Proxy-Accept: NonInteractiveClient

--MSMQ - SOAP boundary, 19264
Content-Type: text/xml; charset=UTF-8
Content-Length: 852
```

This is the XML Envelope section containing the header and the body:

```
<se:Envelope xmlns:se="http://schemas.xmlsoap.org/soap/envelope/"
            xmlns="http://schemas.xmlsoap.org/srmp/">
   <se:Header>
      <path xmlns="http://schemas.xmlsoap.org/rp/"
            se:mustUnderstand="1">
         <action>MSMQ:Customer_GetByCountry</action>
         <to>MSMQ:DIRECT=OS:vemn2003\private$\ado</to>
         <rev>
            <via>HTTP://localhost/msmq/PRIVATE$/Response</via>
         </rev>
         <id>uuid:4243@ef252fe2-65a9-49a2-8529-fe8318db49f0</id>
      </path>
      <properties se:mustUnderstand="1">
         <expiresAt>20380119T031407</expiresAt>
         <sentAt>20020730T150105</sentAt>
      </properties>
      <Msmq xmlns="msmq.namespace.xml">
         <Class>0</Class>
         <Priority>3</Priority>
         <Correlation>AAAAAAAAAAAAAAAAAAAAAAAAAAAA=</Correlation>
         <App>0</App>
         <BodyType>8</BodyType>
         <HashAlgorithm>32772</HashAlgorithm>
```

```
            <SourceQmGuid>ef252fe2-65a9-49a2-8529-fe8318db49f0
            </SourceQmGuid>
            <TTrq>20020730T150115</TTrq>
        </Msmq>
    </se:Header>
    <se:Body></se:Body>
</se:Envelope>
```

The body of the message looks like this:

```
--MSMQ - SOAP boundary, 19264
Content-Type: application/octet-stream
Content-Length: 18
Content-Id: body@ef252fe2-65a9-49a2-8529-fe8318db49f0


S p a i n --MSMQ - SOAP boundary, 19264-
```

Message Queuing uses SRMP, WS-Routing, and the MSMQ Namespace (see the next section) to format the packets in messages, which are sent over HTTP/ HTTPS or to a multicast address. Keep in mind that you are passing sensitive data in these messages, and you are compromising your application's security. If these messages need to be secure, you can use the HTTPS protocol, which includes SSL encryption.

SRMP, the WS-Routing Protocol, and the MSMQ Namespace

The `<Envelope>` element links to the `xmlns=http://schemas.xmlsoap.org/srmp/` namespace, which points to an SRMP specification. **SOAP Reliable Messaging Protocol (SRMP)** is an open extension of the **Web Services Routing Protocol (WS-Routing)**. WS-Routing is a simple SOAP-based protocol for routing SOAP messages in an asynchronous manner, through one or more SOAP routers. With WS-Routing, the entire message path for a SOAP message (as well as its return path) can be described directly within the SOAP envelope. It supports one-way messaging, two-way messaging such as request/response and peer-to-peer conversations, long-running dialog boxes, and dynamic routing.

The SOAP-based protocols also provide the following features:

- Express messages

- End-to-end reliable messages

- End-to-end authentication

- Notifications of message delivery

- Message authentication and digital signatures.

Let's study the SOAP message format of our HTTP message example:

```
<path xmlns="http://schemas.xmlsoap.org/rp/" se:mustUnderstand="1">
   <action>MSMQ:Customer_GetByCountry</action>
   <to>MSMQ:DIRECT=OS:vemn2003\private$\ado</to>
   <rev>
      <via>HTTP://localhost/msmq/PRIVATE$/Response</via>
   </rev>
   <id>uuid:4243@ef252fe2-65a9-49a2-8529-fe8318db49f0</id>
</path>
```

The `<path>` element is defined by the WS-Routing protocol (in the `"http://schemas.xmlsoap.org/rp/"` namespace), and has the following child elements:

- **`<action>`:** Maps to the `Label` property of the message.

- **`<to>`:** Specifies the ultimate destination of the queue. It contains a direct format name.

- **`<rev>`:** Indicates the response queue. It too contains a direct format name.

- **`<id>`:** Contains a unique MSMQ-generated message identifier.

The `<properties>` element is defined by the SRMP protocol:

```
<properties se:mustUnderstand="1">
   <expiresAt>20380119T031407</expiresAt>
   <sentAt>20020730T150105</sentAt>
</properties>
```

It has two child elements:

- **`<sentAt>`:** Specifies the absolute Universal Time Coordinates (UTC), the date and time when the message was transmitted. It is formatted as *yyyymmddTseconds*.

- **`<expiresAt>`:** Specifies the expiration date and time of the message in the format *yyyymmddTseconds*.

The <msmq> section is defined by the MSMQ namespace:

```
<Msmq xmlns="msmq.namespace.xml">
    <Class>0</Class>
    <Priority>3</Priority>
    <Correlation>AAAAAAAAAAAAAAAAAAAAAAAAAAAA=</Correlation>
    <App>0</App>
    <BodyType>8</BodyType>
    <HashAlgorithm>32772</HashAlgorithm>
    <SourceQmGuid>ef252fe2-65a9-49a2-8529-fe8318db49f0</SourceQmGuid>
    <TTrq>20020730T150115</TTrq>
</Msmq>
```

Its child elements are

- **<class>:** Specifies whether this is a normal message, an acknowledgment, or a report message

- **<priority>:** Maps to the Priority property of the MSMQ message

- **<Correlation>:** Contains the Correlation ID of the message

- **<App>:** The AppSpecific property

- **<BodyType>:** Specifies the type of data contained in the body

- **<HashAlgorithm>:** Indicates the hashing algorithm used to authenticate the message

- **<SourceQmGuid>:** Contains the GUID of the machine that created the message

- **<TTrq>:** Specifies the time-to-be-received timer in the format *yyyymmddTseconds*

When authentication is requested for an HTTP message or multicast message, Message Queuing automatically signs it with an **XML Digital Signature**, adding the following section to the SOAP header:

```
<Signature xmlns="http://www.w3.org/2000/02/xmldsig#">
    <SignedInfo>
        <SignatureMethod
                Algorithm="http://www.w3.org/2000/02/xmldsig#dsa" />
```

```
    <Reference URI="cid:body@f6a3323c-7c7b-4a5f-b0ed-b3f63a200893">
        <DigestMethod
            Algorithm="http://www.w3.org/2000/02/xmldsig#sha1" />
        <DigestValue>KJUys3j23iSJja34SJSsjKJSUjk=</DigestValue>
    </Reference>
</SignedInfo>
<SignatureValue>
    KsdLSKDLlk+asl93kal/asldKDISMVV9402CCaksDiq1OmaDThhaH2300kjspk
    67C/abfDrvew34f56yh7kdC2==
</SignatureValue>
</Signature>
```

MSMQMessage SOAP Properties

There is a set of new properties for the `MSMQMessage` class dealing with the SOAP message format:

- **`CompoundMessage`:** An array of bytes that represents the entire content of an HTTP message, including the SOAP envelope and the SOAP attachments associated with it

- **`SOAPBody`:** A variant containing a string of UTF-8 characters that represent XML body elements to be included in the SOAP envelope of the HTTP message

- **`SOAPEnvelope`:** A variant containing a string of Unicode characters representing the SOAP envelope of the HTTP message

- **`SOAPHeader`:** A variant containing a string of Unicode characters representing the XML header elements to be included in the SOAP envelope

Although all these properties are available for working with the Message SOAP format, you don't have to deal with them. You only need to set the traditional properties of the message, such as `Label`, `Body`, `ResponseDestination`, `CorrelationID`, and `MaxTimeToReceive`, and MSMQ will generate the required SOAP format. Similarly, when you receive a message sent via HTTP, you only have to read the traditional properties, so you treat it as a normal message.

MSMQ HTTP Support Implementation

Now, let's see how Windows 2003 Server implements this MSMQ HTTP support. During the HTTP support setup process, it creates an **Internet Information Services application** and a **COM+ application**. MSMQ creates a default IIS application called MSMQ, which will respond to the POST requests. Although it is not necessary, you can also create your own IIS virtual directory, as shown in Figure 7-3.

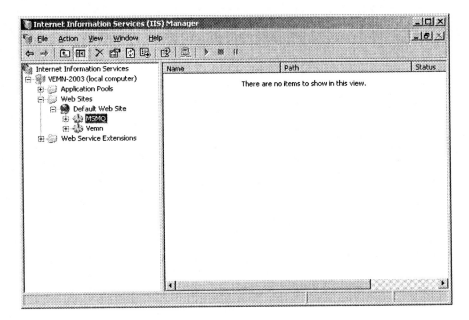

Figure 7-3. The MSMQ IIS virtual directory

This IIS application maps to an ISAPI extension—all the POSTs made to the application are mapped to the C:\Windows\System32\MQISE.DLL ISAPI executable. This ISAPI extension parses the SOAP messages, creates a new MSMQ message, maps the properties, and routes the message to the local queue defined in the direct format name. Figure 7-4 shows the Application Configuration dialog box, which you open by left-clicking the virtual directory, selecting Properties, and clicking the Configuration button.

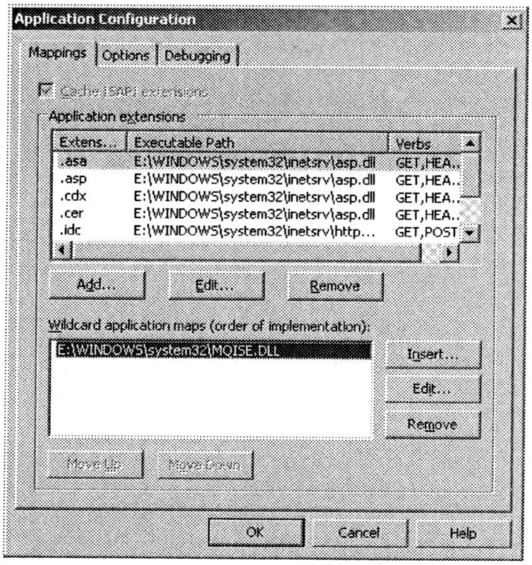

Figure 7-4. IIS window console showing the ISAPI mappings

You can restrict access to the queue to specific users by changing the permissions of the virtual directory in the IIS snap-in.

NOTE   *Remember to check that both Message Queuing and the IIS service are started in order to receive MSMQ HTTP messages.*

The installer also creates a COM+ application, which contains a Web Application Manager object. Internally, IIS coordinates isolate applications through an object known as the **Web Application Manager**. This object includes a public interface called IWAMAdmin that can be used to create programs to administer web applications. When you run a web application inside an isolated process, IIS uses Component Services to coordinate concurrent access to resources and to pass context information between COM components. Figure 7-5 shows the COM+ application created for our IIS virtual directory.

NOTE   *If you have to send an HTTP message and your application is located behind a firewall, you have to configure the proxy settings using the WinHTTP proxy configuration tool called* ProxyCfg.exe.

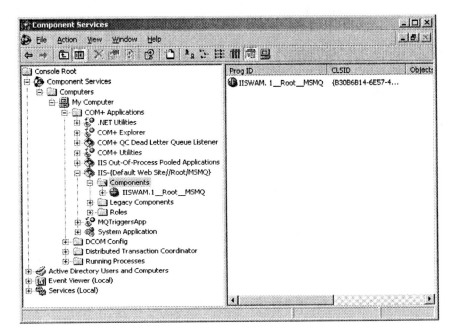

Figure 7-5. COM+ application created for the IIS virtual directory

A Scalable MSMQ Application over the Internet

In this section, we look in depth at an example that demonstrates how HTTP
Message Queuing and direct messaging work. This example consists of a queued
messaging application that works over the Internet; the application will send
and receive SOAP messages over HTTP.

Because this example uses direct messaging, it does not need the Directory
Service; indeed, you can easily convert it to work in a Workgroup installation.
The model we'll implement will allow the application to scale easily; you just run
more instances from the server app listening to the same request queue.

This example consists of two Visual Basic projects:

- Client.vbp (the **client** application)

- Server.vbp (the **server** application)

The application will use two private queues called RequestQueue and ResponseQueue; you also need to create the following stored procedure in the Northwind database in SQL Server:

```
CREATE PROCEDURE Customers_GetByCountry @Country varchar(20)
AS
SELECT CustomerID, CompanyName, ContactName, ContactTitle, Address,
        City, Country, Phone, Fax
FROM Customers
WHERE Country = @Country
```

The Application Architecture

The basic structure of the application is a fairly simple client/server model, as shown in Figure 7-6.

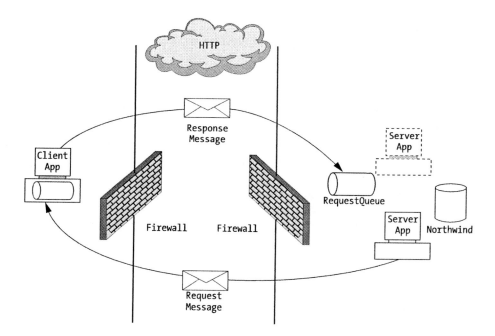

Figure 7-6. The scalable MSMQ application architecture

The example consists of two applications: a server application called Server.exe that tracks received messages in a private queue called RequestQueue, and a client application called Client.exe that will send a request to the server application over the Internet. The client application will receive the message responses in a private queue named ResponseQueue.

The client application will send a country name for the server to query in the Northwind database. In response, the server returns a set of customers living in that country, as an XML document.

The Benefits of This Model

This model has a number of advantages:

- The server manages the RequestQueue. If we open many instances of the server, we can balance the load between them, providing scalability and fault tolerance.

- The server can service many clients, because the request message carries the information about the response queue.

- The server application correlates the response messages, allowing several client applications to share the same response queue. As this model can be perfectly used within an enterprise, it could be applied to web-based applications where several user sessions are running at the same time, sending and receiving messages in the same response queue.

Coding the Example

This example is coded in Visual Basic 6.0 and uses the Message Queuing COM component.

A Common Shared Module

There are some functions that both the Server.exe and Client.exe projects need for dealing with the MSMQ objects; we'll store these in a module called MessageQueue.bas.

First we'll define a useful enum that identifies the mode to open the queue in:

```
Option Explicit

'Indicates the open mode for the Queue
Public Enum msmqOpenMode
    msmqPeek = MQ_PEEK_ACCESS
    msmqSend = MQ_SEND_ACCESS
    msmqReceive = MQ_RECEIVE_ACCESS
End Enum
```

The MSMQ_OpenLocalQueue() function opens a local queue called oQueue. It receives four parameters: an MSMQQueue object that holds a reference to the queue to open, the queue name, a Boolean bPrivate that indicates whether it is a private queue, and the access mode (Peek, Send, or Receive) to open the queue in:

```
Public Function MSMQ_OpenLocalQueue(
                    ByRef oQueue As MSMQ.MSMQQueue, _
                    ByVal sQueueName As String, _
                    ByVal bPrivate As Boolean, _
                    ByVal iOpenMode As msmqOpenMode) As Boolean

    On Error GoTo ErrorHandler

    Dim oInfo As MSMQ.MSMQQueueInfo
```

The MSMQQueueInfo object provides methods for creating, opening, modifying, and deleting a single queue. Here we set the FormatName property of the queue to avoid depending on the Directory Service. Note that this FormatName syntax will open the queue on the local machine using TCP/IP:

```
    Set oInfo = New MSMQ.MSMQQueueInfo

    ' Set the FormatName property to locate the queue
    If bPrivate Then
        oInfo.FormatName = "DIRECT=OS:.\Private$\" & sQueueName
    Else
        oInfo.FormatName = "DIRECT=OS:.\" & sQueueName
    End If
```

The Open() method of the MSMQQueueInfo object opens the queue and returns an MSMQQueue object that represents it:

```
Set oQueue = oInfo.Open(iOpenMode, MQ_DENY_NONE)

MSMQ_OpenLocalQueue = True

GoOut:
    Set oInfo = Nothing
    Exit Function

ErrorHandler:
    MSMQ_OpenLocalQueue = False
    Resume GoOut

End Function
```

The MSMQ_Listen() function starts event notifications so that the messages in the queue can be read *asynchronously*. Once this method is called, the class can asynchronously retrieve messages from the queue to a user-defined event handler:

```
Sub MSMQ_Listen(oQueue As MSMQ.MSMQQueue, oEvent As MSMQ.MSMQEvent)

    Call oQueue.EnableNotification(oEvent)
End Sub
```

The MSMQ_ID() function converts the ID of a message into a string format, which we need to do in order to correlate a response to the original message. MSMQ assigns messages an ID in the form of a 20-byte array. We will convert this to a string in the format "{7865B5232-CA71-11A2-907C-00400524FE0C}/5421564":

```
Function MSMQ_ID(ByVal ID As Variant) As String

    On Error GoTo ErrorHandler

    Dim aID(25) As String
    Dim i As Integer

    For i = LBound(ID) To UBound(ID)
        aID(i) = ""
        If Len(Hex(ID(i))) = 1 Then aID(i) = "0"
        aID(i) = aID(i) & Hex(ID(i))
```

```
      Next
      ' Create a string representation of the Message ID
      MSMQ_ID = "{" & aID(3) & aID(2) & aID(1) & aID(0) & "-" & _
                aID(5) & aID(4) & "-" & aID(7) & aID(6) & "-" & _
                aID(8) & aID(9) & "-" & aID(10) & aID(11) & aID(12) & _
                aID(13) & aID(14) & aID(15) & "}\" & Str(ID(16) + _
                256 * ID(17) + 65535 * ID(18) + 16777216 * ID(19))

  GoOut:
      Exit Function


  ErrorHandler:
      MSMQ_ID = ""
      Resume GoOut


  End Function
```

The MSMQ_FindMessage() function looks up a message in a queue based on its CorrelationID, returning an MSMQMessage object. We can read all the messages stored in a queue from the first to the last one, using a cursor:

```
  Function MSMQ_FindMessage(oQueue As MSMQ.MSMQQueue, _
                            ByVal sCorrelationID As String) _
                                        As MSMQ.MSMQMessage


      '### Look up a message in a queue based on its CorrelationID


      On Error GoTo ErrorHandler


      Dim oMsg As MSMQ.MSMQMessage
      Dim oMsgHeader As MSMQ.MSMQMessage
      Dim bFound As Boolean


      bFound = False
```

The Reset() method of the Queue object returns the cursor to its initial position, so we call this before we start to iterate through the messages:

```
  oQueue.Reset
```

The PeekCurrent() method reads the message at its current cursor position, but does not remove the message from the queue. This could potentially be a slow business, so fortunately it has some parameters to speed up this task. The first parameter decides whether the ResponseDestination or the ResponseQueueInfo property of the message has to be updated when it is read; the second specifies whether or not the message body has to be retrieved. The last parameter specifies the ReceiveTimeOut in milliseconds, which is the time Message Queuing will wait for a message to arrive if the queue is empty. We set this parameter to 15 milliseconds:

```
Set oMsgHeader = oQueue.PeekCurrent(False, False, 15)


If oMsgHeader Is Nothing Then GoTo GoOut
```

Next we compare the current message CorrelationID with the variable received in the function:

```
bFound = (MSMQ_ID(oMsgHeader.CorrelationId) = sCorrelationID)
```

Then we loop while the message is not found, reading each message in the queue with the PeekNext() method. This method moves the cursor to the next message to read it. If the cursor reaches the bottom of the queue it returns Nothing:

```
Do While Not bFound
    'Peek the next Message
    Set oMsgHeader = oQueue.PeekNext(False, False, 15)

    'If there is no message, Go Out !
    If oMsgHeader Is Nothing Then GoTo GoOut

    'Check the provided CorrelationID with the current message
    bFound = (MSMQ_ID(oMsgHeader.CorrelationId) = sCorrelationID)
Loop
```

Finally, if the message is found, we read and remove it from the queue, returning it from the function. Each time we retrieve a message using the ReceiveCurrent() method, we have to specify whether it should be done within the context of a transaction. The other three parameters are the same as for the PeekCurrent() method:

```
If bFound Then
    'Receive the found message erasing it from the queue
    Set MSMQ_FindMessage = oQueue.ReceiveCurrent( _
                                MQ_NO_TRANSACTION, False, True, 15)
Else
    Set MSMQ_FindMessage = Nothing
End If
```

```
GoOut:
    Set oMsgHeader = Nothing
    Exit Function

ErrorHandler:
    Resume GoOut

End Function
```

We now come to the last function of this module. MSMQ_LogSOAP() saves the SOAP-formatted message in a text file. Although this functionality wouldn't be required for a production application, it is useful for understanding how MSMQ creates the SOAP messages:

```
Function MSMQ_LogSoap(oMsg As MSMQ.MSMQMessage)

    Dim s As String
    Dim v As Variant
    Dim i As Integer
    Dim Nral As Integer

    On Error Resume Next
```

The CompoundMessage is an array of bytes that represents the entire HTTP message. We loop through it to retrieve the message into a string:

```
v = oMsg.CompoundMessage

For i = LBound(v) To UBound(v)
    s = s & Chr(v(i))
Next

Nral = FreeFile
Open App.Path & "\SOAP.LOG" For Append Shared As #Nral

Print #Nral, "************** CompoundMessage *****************"
Print #Nral, s
Print #Nral, "****************** Envelope ********************"
```

The SoapEnvelope property is a string of Unicode characters containing the SOAP envelope:

```
Print #Nral, oMsg.SoapEnvelope
Print #Nral, "***********************************************"
```

```
    Print #Nral, "*************************************************"

    Close #Nral

End Function
```

The Server Application

Our Server.exe application listens to the messages that arrive in the local private queue called RequestQueue. Once a message has arrived, it executes a stored procedure called Customers_GetByCountry in the Northwind database. Then it sends a response message to the client application containing the result in XML format.

The application has a simple user interface, so the user can see what's going on (Figure 7-7).

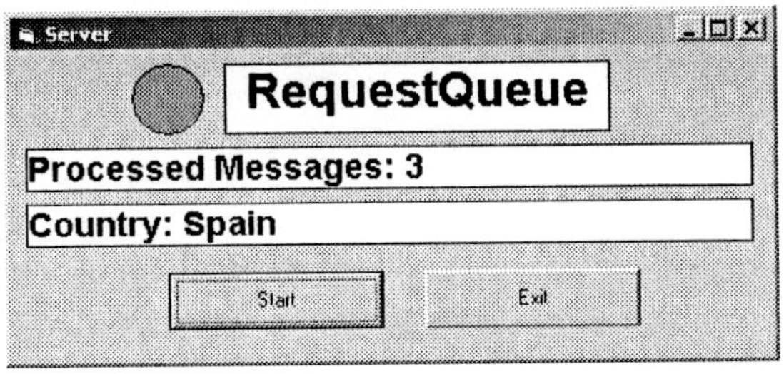

Figure 7-7. The server application's user interface

The Start button opens the local queue and begins to listen for the messages. The green circle indicates the status of the queue (in this case, that it's open). Each request is shown in the Country label.

Server Dependencies

The server application requires the following dependencies, so add references to these type libraries:

- Microsoft XML, version 3.0

- Microsoft ActiveX Data Objects 2.7 Library

- Microsoft Message Queue 3.0 Object Library

The Messaging Class

Most of the work in our server application will be performed by a user-defined class called Messaging. It has three methods:

- OpenLocalQueue()

- Response()

- AlertNextMessage()

It raises an event called Arrived to alert the application that a message has arrived asynchronously.

The code for the class starts by declaring some private variables to hold the LocalQueue, CorrelationID, and ResponseDestination of the arrived message, as well as the MSMQEvent. We declare the oEvent object with the WithEvents keyword. This specifies that oEvent is an instance of a class that can raise events. MSMQ will raise an event when a message arrives to a queue, so we have to define an event handler to react to this:

```
Option Explicit

Private oQueueLocal As MSMQ.MSMQQueue
Private oResponseDestination As MSMQ.MSMQDestination
Private vCorrelationID As Variant
Private WithEvents oEvent As MSMQ.MSMQEvent
```

This is the declaration of the Arrived event that will be raised when a message arrives in the queue:

```
Public Event Arrived(ByVal sLabel As String, ByRef vBody As Variant)
```

When the class is initialized, we set the oQueueLocal (Local Queue object) and the oEvent (Event) object:

```
Private Sub Class_Initialize()
    Set oQueueLocal = New MSMQ.MSMQQueue
    Set oEvent = New MSMQ.MSMQEvent
End Sub
```

The OpenLocalQueue() public method opens the queue to receive the requests. First we create an instance of the MSMQQueue class if the oQueueLocal object isn't already set:

```
Public Function OpenLocalQueue(ByVal sQueueName As String, _
                               ByVal bPrivate As Boolean) As Boolean

    On Error GoTo ErrorHandler

    'Instantiate the Queue object
    If Not oQueueLocal Is Nothing Then
        Set oQueueLocal = New MSMQ.MSMQQueue
    End If
```

Next we pass this object into the MSMQ_OpenLocalQueue() function of the shared module we discussed earlier:

```
    OpenLocalQueue = MSMQ_OpenLocalQueue(oQueueLocal, sQueueName, _
                                         bPrivate, msmqReceive, True)

GoOut:
    Exit Function

ErrorHandler:
    OpenLocalQueue = False
    Resume GoOut

End Function
```

The AlertNextMessage() function enables the event handler. Although there could be many messages in a queue, each time you receive an event alerting the arrived message, MSMQ stops raising events and the event handler remains disabled. This allows you to process the message without losing further events. Once we finish the process, we can enable the event handler again to attend to the next message in the queue:

```
Public Function AlertNextMessage()

    Call MSMQ_Listen(oQueueLocal, oEvent)

End Function
```

This is the MSMQEvent event handler, which is called when messages arrive in the queue:

```
Private Sub oEvent_Arrived(ByVal Queue As Object, ByVal Cursor As Long)

    On Error GoTo ErrorHandler
```

```
Dim oRespInfo As MSMQ.MSMQQueueInfo
Dim oMsgReceived As MSMQ.MSMQMessage
```

We start by reading and removing the message from the current position in the queue and logging the SOAP message:

```
Set oMsgReceived = oQueueLocal.Receive

'Log the Message SOAP format
Call MSMQ_LogSoap(oMsgReceived)
```

Next we store the message ID and ResponseDestination of the message. Here are the CorrelationID and DestinationQueue of the response message for this request:

```
vCorrelationID = oMsgReceived.ID

'Get the Response Queue
Set oResponseDestination = oMsgReceived.ResponseDestination
```

Finally, we bubble up the event to the event handler for the class:

```
RaiseEvent Arrived(oMsgReceived.Label, oMsgReceived.Body)

GoOut:
    Set oMsgReceived = Nothing
    Set oRespInfo = Nothing
    Exit Sub


ErrorHandler:
    Resume GoOut


End Sub
```

Next comes the function that sends the response message:

```
Public Function Response(ByVal sLabel As String, _
                         ByVal vBody As Variant) As Boolean

    On Error GoTo ErrorHandler

    Dim oMsg As MSMQ.MSMQMessage
```

We start by creating a message and setting its properties. We have to set the CorrelationID property to the ID of the requested message:

```
Set oMsg = New MSMQ.MSMQMessage
oMsg.Label = sLabel
oMsg.Body = vBody
oMsg.CorrelationId = vCorrelationID
```

Finally, we send the message to the queue indicated by the ResponseDestination specified in the request message, using the direct messaging technique:

```
oMsg.Send DestinationQueue:=oResponseDestination

Response = True

GoOut:
    Set oMsg = Nothing
    Exit Function

ErrorHandler:
    Response = False
    Resume GoOut


End Function
```

When the class is terminated, we must close the local queue; we also set the class variables to Nothing:

```
Private Sub Class_Terminate()

    On Error Resume Next

    oQueueLocal.Close
    Set oQueueLocal = Nothing
    Set oEvent = Nothing
    Set oResponseDestination = Nothing

End Sub
```

The Server Form

Now let's look at the code behind the user interface for our server application.

First we declare a variable to hold the Messaging object that deals with the RequestQueue queue, listening to the request messages and responding to them. It processes the messages **asynchronously**. This variable is set when the form loads:

```
Dim WithEvents oMessaging As Messaging
Dim lMessages As Long

Private Sub Form_Load()

    Set oMessaging = New Messaging

End Sub
```

The server starts to listen for requests when the Start button is clicked. In the click event handler for this button, we use the oMessaging object to open the local private queue named XmlQueue. If the queue is open, we can enable the event handler calling the AlertNextMessage() method:

```
Private Sub btnStart_Click()

    'Open the local queue
    If oMessaging.OpenLocalQueue("XmlQueue", True) Then
        shpXML.BackColor = vbGreen
        'Listen for the first message arrival
        oMessaging.AlertNextMessage
    End If

End Sub
```

When a message arrives in the queue, the Arrived event will be raised in our Messaging object. In the handler for this event, we need to process the newly arrived message:

```
Private Sub oMessaging_Arrived(ByVal sLabel As String, _
                              vBody As Variant, ByVal lTag As Long)
    Dim oRs As ADODB.Recordset
    Dim oXML As MSXML2.DOMDocument40
    Set oXML = New MSXML2.DOMDocument40
```

First we display some activity information (the number of messages processed and the country for which customers were requested):

```
lMessages = lMessages + 1
lblMessages.Caption = "Processed Messages: " & CStr(lMessages)
lblCountry.Caption = "Country: " & CStr(vBody)
Me.Refresh
```

We process the request by retrieving an ADO recordset containing all the customers from the specified country and saving this recordset into an XML document:

```
Set oRs = Customers_GetByCountry(vBody)

'Save the recordset in XML format:
oRs.save oXML, adPersistXML
```

Once we have the XML DOM document, we can send it as the body of the response message. Finally, we need to call the AlertNextMessage() method of our Messaging object to carry on listening for the next message:

```
oMessaging.Response "Customers_ByCountry", oXML
oMessaging.AlertNextMessage

Set oRs = Nothing
Set oXML = Nothing

End Sub
```

The Customers_GetByCountry() function simply calls a stored procedure in the Northwind database and returns a disconnected recordset:

```
Private Function Customers_GetByCountry(ByVal sCountry As String) _
                                                As ADODB.Recordset

    On Error GoTo ErrorHandler

    Dim oConn As ADODB.Connection
    Dim oCmd As ADODB.Command
    Dim oRs As ADODB.Recordset
    Dim oParam As ADODB.Parameter
    Set oConn = New ADODB.Connection
    Set oCmd = New ADODB.Command
```

```
            Set oRs = New ADODB.Recordset

            oConn.ConnectionTimeout = 2
            'Open the connection using a ConnectionString
            'stored in an UDL file
            oConn.Open "File Name=" & App.Path & "\Northwind.udl"

            'Set the recordset properties
            oRs.CursorLocation = adUseClient
            oRs.LockType = adLockBatchOptimistic
            oRs.CursorType = adOpenStatic

            'Set the Command properties
            Set oCmd.ActiveConnection = oConn
            oCmd.CommandTimeout = 2
            oCmd.CommandType = adCmdStoredProc
            oCmd.CommandText = "Customers_GetByCountry"
            Set oParam = oCmd.CreateParameter("@Country", adVarChar, _
                                            adParamInput, 12, sCountry)
            oCmd.Parameters.Append oParam

            'Open the recordset based in the oCmd command object
            oRs.Open oCmd

            'Detach the recordset from the connection
            Set oRs.ActiveConnection = Nothing
            Set Customers_GetByCountry = oRs

GoOut:
    oCmd.Cancel
    oConn.Close
    Set oConn = Nothing
    Set oCmd = Nothing
    Set oParam = Nothing
    Exit Function

ErrorHandler:
    Set Customers_GetByCountry = Nothing
    Resume GoOut
End Function
```

Finally, when the form is closed, we set the objects to nothing:

```
Private Sub Form_Unload(Cancel As Integer)

    Set oXMLMessaging = Nothing
    Set oADOMessaging = Nothing

End Sub
```

The Client Application

The client application allows the user to send a message to the server to request all the customers from a particular country. The user can enter the country name in the text box labeled Country and send the request by clicking the Request button. When the user clicks the Response button, the application looks up the response in the local private ResponseQueue queue and displays the result in the grid, as shown in Figure 7-8. The green circle indicates the open status of the ResponseQueue queue.

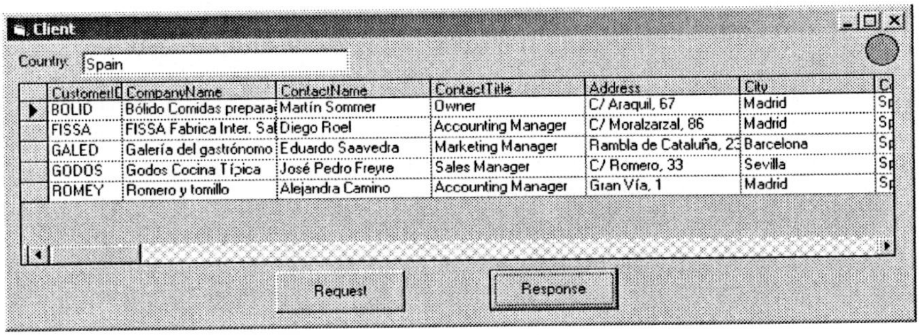

Figure 7-8. The client application's user interface

The client application requires the following dependencies:

- Microsoft XML, version 3.0

- Microsoft ActiveX Data Objects 2.6 Library or later

- Microsoft DataGrid Control 6.0 (OLEDB)

- Microsoft Message Queue 3.0 Object Library

Messaging Class

Again, we'll write most of the actual MSMQ-related code in a user-defined class called `Messaging`. This class has three methods:

- `OpenLocalQueue()`

- `Response()`

- `Request()`

When the class is loaded, we initialize the local queue object:

```
Option Explicit

Private oQueueLocal As MSMQ.MSMQQueue

Private Sub Class_Initialize()

    Set oQueueLocal = CreateObject("MSMQ.MSMQQueue")

End Sub
```

The `OpenLocalQueue()` function is the same as the `OpenLocalQueue()` function of the server's `Messaging` class, except for one difference: in the client application, the `oQueueLocal` will manage the response queue:

```
Public Function OpenLocalQueue(ByVal sQueueName As String, _
                               ByVal bPrivate As Boolean) As Boolean
...
End Function
```

The `Response()` function will look up the response messages based on their `CorrelationID`, which allows the message to be linked to the original request. An optional parameter allows the process to wait for any arriving message:

```
Public Function Response(ByVal sID As String, _
                         Optional ByVal iTimeOut As Integer = 0) _
                                                        As Variant

    On Error GoTo ErrorHandler

    Dim oMsg As MSMQ.MSMQMessage
```

Here we use the MSMQ_FindMessage() coded in the shared MessageQueue.bas module to find the message based on its CorrelationID:

```
Set oMsg = MSMQ_FindMessage(oQueueLocal, sID)

'Check for the found message
If Not oMsg Is Nothing Then
    If IsObject(oMsg.Body) Then
        'Log the Message
        Call MSMQ_LogSoap(oMsg)
        Set Response = oMsg.Body
    Else
        Response = oMsg.Body
    End If
Else
    Response = Null
End If

GoOut:
    Set oMsg = Nothing
    Exit Function

ErrorHandler:
    Response = Null
    Resume GoOut

End Function
```

The Request() function is almost the same as the Response() method of the server's Messaging class, except for the last parameter, sReponseDestination. This contains a direct format name specifying the queue to address the response to:

```
Public Function Request(ByVal sDestination As String, _
                        ByVal sLabel As String, vBody As Variant, _
                        Optional ByVal sResponseDestination As String) _
                                                            As String

    '### Send the Request message

    On Error GoTo ErrorHandler

    Dim oMsg As MSMQ.MSMQMessage
    Dim oResponseDestination As MSMQ.MSMQDestination
    Dim oDestination As MSMQ.MSMQDestination
```

```
    'Create a new Message
    Set oMsg = New MSMQ.MSMQMessage

    'Set the Destination queue
    Set oDestination = New MSMQ.MSMQDestination
    oDestination.FormatName = sDestination

    'Set the message properties
    oMsg.Label = sLabel
    oMsg.Body = vBody

    'Set the Response queue
    If Len(sResponseDestination) > 0 Then
        Set oResponseDestination = New MSMQ.MSMQDestination
        oResponseDestination.FormatName = sResponseDestination
        Set oMsg.ResponseDestination = oResponseDestination
    End If

    'Send the message in a hop
    oMsg.Send DestinationQueue:=oDestination

    'Return the ID of the sent message
    Request = MSMQ_ID(oMsg.ID)

GoOut:
    Set oMsg = Nothing
    Set oResponseDestination = Nothing
    Set oDestination = Nothing
    Exit Function


ErrorHandler:
    Request = ""
    Resume GoOut


End Function
```

When the class is terminated, we have to close the local queue:

```
Private Sub Class_Terminate()

    On Error Resume Next
    oQueueLocal.Close
    Set oQueueLocal = Nothing

End Sub
```

The Client Form

Now let's look at code behind the user interface for the client.

First we declare a few form-level variables. There's a variable named oMessaging to hold the Messaging object that will deal with the response queue. We also need a variable called sCorrelationID to hold the CorrelationID in order to correlate the responses. Finally, there are two string variables to store the direct format names of the request and response queues:

```
Option Explicit

Dim oMessaging As New Messaging
Dim sSendFormatName As String
Dim sResponseFormatName As String
Dim sCorrelationID As String
```

When the form loads, we set the direct format names of the destination and response queues, and open the response queue to find the messages:

```
Private Sub Form_Load()

    Set oMessaging = New Messaging

    'Specifies the direct format name for the queues
    sSendFormatName = "DIRECT=HTTP://localhost/msmq/Private$/RequestQueue"
    sResponseFormatName = "DIRECT=HTTP://localhost/msmq/" & _
                          "Private$/ResponseQueue"

    'Open the local response queue
    If oMessaging.OpenLocalQueue("ResponseQueue", True) Then
        shpResponse.BackColor = vbGreen
    End If

End Sub
```

When the Request button is clicked, we send the request to the server, passing a country name and storing the CorrelationID of the message:

```
Private Sub btnRequest_Click()

    Dim sCountry As String

    sCountry = txtCountry.Text
```

```
'Send the request
sCorrelationID = oMessaging.Request(sSendFormatName, _
                                    "Customer_GetByCountry", _
                                    sCountry, sResponseFormatName)

End Sub
```

When the Response button is clicked, we look up the response messages:

```
Private Sub btnResponse_Click()

    Dim oRs As ADODB.Recordset
    Dim oXML As MSXML2.DOMDocument30
    Dim vXML As Variant

    'Look for the response based on the CorrelationID
    Set vXML = oMessaging.Response(sCorrelationID)

    'If there is a response
    If Not vXML Is Nothing Then
        Set oRs = New ADODB.Recordset
        'Open a recordset based in the xml
        oRs.Open vXML
        'Show it in the grid
        Set dbgCustomers.DataSource = oRs
    Else
        MsgBox "There is no Response", vbExclamation
    End If

End Sub
```

Finally, when the form is closed, we need to release the Messaging object:

```
Private Sub Form_Unload(Cancel As Integer)

    Set oMessaging = Nothing

End Sub
```

As you can see, there are many situations where we cannot gain access to a Directory Service to locate queues. One of them is the MSMQ Workgroup mode setup; another one might be when we need to send messages to queues that are outside the MSMQ Enterprise environment. This example combines the benefits of the MSMQDestination class that sends messages without querying the Directory

Service and the new protocol that allows us to send messages in SOAP format. Because MSMQ 3.0 supports HTTP messaging through port 80, which is usually open on firewalls to permit HTTP traffic, no special configuration is needed that may compromise security. The example also shows a scalable model of application that can be easily applied using MSMQ.

Programmable Management COM Interface

Programmable management and information is available through the Admin API downloadable package for MSMQ 1.0/2.0, but only through the C APIs interface.

Message Queuing 3.0 incorporates queue and computer administration functionality that can be used to administer Message Queuing programmatically through the COM interface. This management functionality and information will help you to develop monitoring systems and analysis tools to build a strong message-based distributed environment. This functionality is very useful in a distributed application to track its health in order to identify and prevent issues that could slow down the whole system.

There are many uses for this management functionality. For example, you can provide intelligence to your client applications, enabling them to select from queues that offer the same service as the one that has fewer messages hosted. You can enhance your distributed application by adding client load balancing.

Summing up, MSMQ 3.0 introduces a set of management APIs and COM object models. Among other things, you can do the following:

- Monitor and control the MSMQ service's state

- Obtain messaging statistics

- Pause/resume an MSMQ queue

- Administer properties of outgoing queues

The following sections will look at the new management classes provided by MSMQ 3.0.

Application Management

The MSMQApplication class can be used to obtain information about the Message Queuing service that is running on an MSMQ machine. This class was launched with MSMQ 2.0, but MSMQ 3.0 adds new properties and methods that we will study in this section.

Connecting and Disconnecting Computers

The Connect() method of the MSMQApplication object connects the computer to the network and to the Directory Service server; the Disconnect() method does exactly the opposite. This action prevents MSMQ from sending or receiving messages; all the other network services, including Active Directory, work normally. By default, the Disconnect() method applies to the local computer. To disconnect a remote computer, set the MSMQApplication.Machine property to the name of the remote computer before calling Disconnect.

The following code fragment toggles the connection of a remote machine:

```
Dim oApp As MSMQ.MSMQApplication
Set oApp = New MSMQ.MSMQApplication

oApp.Machine = "vemn-2000"

If Not oApp.IsConnected Then
    oApp.Disconnect
Else
    oApp.Connect
End If
```

The IsConnected property returns False if the computer has been disconnected from the network.

Cleaning Up Empty Message Files

MSMQ message files are memory-mapped files that consume virtual memory. While Message Queuing is working, it automatically compresses memory used by messages based on its default six-hour cleanup interval.

The Tidy() method's purpose is to compress messages and handle situations when there are many message files (4 MB each) with only a few small messages in each file, regardless of the automatic cleanup Message Queuing's interval:

```
Dim oApp As MSMQ.MSMQApplication
Set oApp = New MSMQ.MSMQApplication

oApp.Tidy
```

As well as calling the Tidy() method to clean up the empty files immediately, you can change the MessageCleanUpInterval value in the Registry.

Obtaining Information About a Computer

The MSMQApplication class has a number of properties that allow you to obtain information about the MSMQ setup of a computer:

- **ActiveQueues:** Returns the format names of the active queues in the computer. The active queues in a computer include queues that contain messages or are currently opened by applications, and outgoing queues that contain messages to be sent.

- **PrivateQueues:** Returns a list of the path names of all the private queues registered on the computer.

- **BytesInAllQueues:** Returns the number of bytes of the messages currently stored in all the queues of the computer.

- **DirectoryServiceServer:** Indicates the name of the Directory Service server, if the MSMQ 3.0 client is installed in a Windows NT 4.0 environment, and contains the relevant Primary Enterprise Controller (PEC), Primary Site Controller (PSC), or Backup Site Controller (BSC). However, if the MSMQ 3.0 client connects to Active Directory directly, this property is meaningless.

Let's query the active queues of the local computer:

```
Dim oApp As MSMQ.MSMQApplication
Dim i As Long

Set oApp = New MSMQ.MSMQApplication

Debug.Print "The Active Queues of the " & oApp.Machine & " are: "

For i = 0 To UBound(oApp.ActiveQueues)
    Debug.Print oApp.ActiveQueues(i)
Next

Debug.Print "Bytes in all Queues: " & oApp.BytesInAllQueues
```

The result is

```
The Active Queues of the vemn-2003 are:
DIRECT=OS:vemn-2003\private$\anyqueue
DIRECT=OS:vemn-2003\otherqueue
Bytes in all Queues: 56230
```

If we want to obtain information about another computer, we have to set the MSMQApplication.Machine property before getting the properties' values.

Queue Management

The MSMQManagement class has properties for both *destination* and *outgoing queues*, and provides administrative information about a queue:

- **BytesInQueue:** Returns the number of bytes in the queue.

- **MessageCount:** Indicates how many messages are stored in the queue.

- **ForeignStatus:** Indicates whether the destination queue is a foreign queue or the outgoing queue is associated with a foreign queue. A foreign queue is a queue that resides on another computer that is running a messaging service other than Microsoft Message Queuing.

- **FormatName:** Contains the format name of the queue.

- **IsLocal:** Specifies whether the queue is located in the local computer or in a remote one.

- **Machine:** Indicates the name of the computer that holds the queue.

- **QueueType:** Indicates whether it is a public, private, journal, dead-letter, connector, or multicast outgoing queue.

- **TransactionalStatus:** Indicates whether the destination queue is transactional or nontransactional, or if the outgoing queue is associated with a transactional or nontransactional queue.

The following example explains the Lighter Queue Factory that enables you to select a receiver queue depending on the number of messages it contains. This provides **client-side load balancing** for applications that render the same service on different queues from different sites of your MSMQ Enterprise:

```
Function LighterQueue(sServiceTypeGUID As String) As MSMQ.MSMQQueue

    On Error GoTo ErrorHandler
```

The LighterQueue() function returns the queue containing the lowest number of messages from a group of queues that provide the same service. Queues that render the same service can be grouped by the ServiceTypeGUID property.

The ServiceTypeGUID is an application-generated GUID and can either be assigned to the queue the moment it is created or changed later.

```
Dim oQuery As MSMQ.MSMQQuery
Dim oInfos As MSMQ.MSMQQueueInfos
Dim oInfo As MSMQ.MSMQQueueInfo
Dim oMgmt As MSMQ.MSMQManagement
Dim oQueue As MSMQ.MSMQQueue
```

We need to use some MSMQ classes to find the queues that belong to the same ServiceTypeGUID.

The MSMQQuery class looks up queues in the Directory Service. It returns an MSMQQueueInfos collection of MSMQQueueInfo objects that contain information about the queues found:

```
Dim oMinInfo As MSMQ.MSMQQueueInfo
Dim lMin As Long
```

The oMinInfo object will contain the MSMQQueueInfo object of the queue that has the fewest messages; lMin is used to store the current minimum number of messages in an individual queue as we iterate through the queues:

```
lMin = 2147483647
Set oQuery = New MSMQ.MSMQQuery
Set oMgmt = New MSMQ.MSMQManagement
Set oQueue = Nothing
```

The LookupQueue() method of the MSMQQuery class returns the MSMQQueueInfos collection based on the ServiceTypeGUID. The Reset() method locates the cursor at the BOF position of the collection, and the Next() method retrieves the following element and moves the cursor one step forward:

```
Set oInfos = oQuery.LookupQueue(ServiceTypeGuid:=sServiceTypeGUID)
oInfos.Reset
Set oInfo = oInfos.Next
```

Then we traverse all the collection looking for the lighter queue. The oMgmt object, which is an instance of the MSMQManagement class, obtains the information from the current queue referenced by the oInfo object using the format name:

```
While Not oInfo Is Nothing
    oMgmt.Init FormatName:=oInfo.FormatName
```

If the current queue has fewer messages than 1Min, then we set oMinInfo to point to this queue and update 1Min to contain the number of messages in it:

```
If oMgmt.MessageCount < lMin Then
    Set oMinInfo = oInfo
    lMin = oMgmt.MessageCount
End If
Set oInfo = oInfos.Next
Set oMgmt = New MSMQ.MSMQManagement
Wend
```

If we find a valid queue, we Open() it for send access (MQ_SEND_ACCESS), and full share (MQ_DENY_NONE):

```
If Not oMinInfo Is Nothing Then
    Set oQueue = oMinInfo.Open(MQ_SEND_ACCESS, MQ_DENY_NONE)
End If
```

Finally, we return the opened queue and destroy the objects:

```
GoOut:
    Set LighterQueue = oQueue
    Set oQuery = Nothing
    Set oInfos = Nothing
    Set oInfo = Nothing
    Set oMgmt = Nothing
    Set oMinInfo = Nothing
    Exit Function


ErrorHandler:
    Resume GoOut


End Function
```

The following code section shows how to send a message using the LighterQueue() function:

```
Dim o As MSMQ.MSMQQueue
Dim msg As New MSMQMessage

Set oQueue = LighterQueue("{9844FD65-8DF6-4e8e-9ADC-53F858346093}")
If Not oQueue Is Nothing Then
    msg.Label = "Caption"
    msg.Body = "Data to send"
```

```
    msg.Send oQueue
End If
```

Remember to set a GUID to the ServiceTypeGUID for the queues that render the same service. The administrative tool provides a textbox called Type ID in the Properties dialog box of the public queue to achieve this, as shown in Figure 7-9.

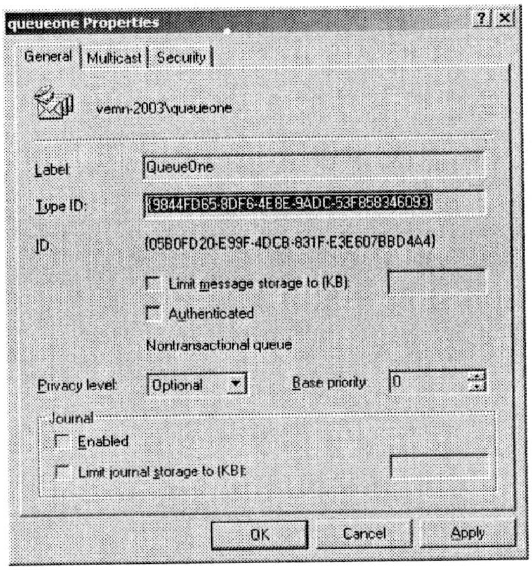

Figure 7-9. The Properties window of a public queue

Exactly-Once-Delivery Information

Since version 1.0, Message Queuing uses the **Exactly-Once-Delivery (EOD)** protocol to send more than one message within a transactional context. The EOD protocol guarantees that

- Only one copy of each message will arrive at the queue, avoiding duplication.

- The messages will arrive in the order in which they were sent.

The destination queue manager can discard duplicate and out-of-order messages, because additional information is attached to each transactional message.

MSMQ 3.0 provides EOD information through its COM interface only for transactional messages sent from a computer to a destination queue.

Destination Queue Management

The MSMQQueueManagement class is used to obtain the state of a destination queue.

Obtaining EOD Information

Only transactional messages are delivered with an EOD guarantee. The local queue manager of the receiver queue maintains EOD information containing data about each computer that has sent transactional messages to a queue. The EodGetReceiveInfo() method returns an MSMQCollection, which contains the following elements:

- **QueueFormatName:** The format name of the destination queue used to send the transactional message

- **SenderID:** The GUID of the queue manager that sent the transactional message

- **LastAccessTime:** The last time the sender queue manager accessed the queue

- **SeqID:** The sequence identifier of the last transactional message sent to the queue

- **SeqNo:** The sequence number of the last transactional message sent to the queue

- **RejectCount:** The number of times the last message was rejected before being accepted by the receiving queue manager

We'll show the EodGetReceiveInfo() method in action with a code snippet that lists the number of messages sent by each machine to a transactional queue.

As the EodGetReceiveInfo() method returns an array of variants, we will hold it in a variable called aInfo(), which we declare as a variant array:

```
Dim aInfo() As Variant
Dim oMgmt As MSMQ.MSMQManagement
Dim oQMgmt As MSMQ.MSMQQueueManagement
```

To obtain an instance of the MSMQQueueManagement class, we need to call the Init() method of the MSMQManagement class, and then set our MSMQQueueManagement instance to the initialized MSMQManagement object. What we are doing here is performing an implicit cast, which isn't such a common technique in Visual Basic because of its object-oriented limitations:

```
Set oMgmt = New MSMQ.MSMQManagement

oMgmt.Init "vemn-2003", "vemn-2003\anyTransactionalQueue"
Set oQMgmt = oMgmt

aInfo() = oQMgmt.EodGetReceiveInfo()
For i = 0 To UBound(aInfo)
    Debug.Print "The computer " & aInfo(i)("SenderID") & _
                " has sent " & aInfo(i)("SeqNO") & " messages"
Next
```

Obtaining Administrative Information

We can obtain administrative information from a journal queue associated with a destination queue, getting the values from the following properties of the MSMQQueueManagement class:

- BytesInJournal: Returns the number of bytes stored in a journal queue

- JournalMessageCount: Returns the number of messages stored in a journal queue

For example, you can use these properties to centralize the information about the activity performed by your server applications, obtaining the number of messages and bytes processed from your receiving applications and showing them in a centralized monitor.

Outgoing Queue Management

Outgoing queues are system-generated queues created on an independent client. They temporarily keep the messages that cannot be sent until the computer reestablishes the connection to the network. The MSMQOutgoingQueueManagement class provides management functionalities for the outgoing queues.

Obtaining EOD Information

As you have seen, only transactional messages are delivered with an EOD guarantee. We can obtain EOD information about the messages in an outgoing queue that have not been sent yet. The EodGetSendInfo() method returns an MSMQCollection, which contains the following elements:

- **EodLastAckCount:** Specifies the number of times that the last acknowledgment was received

- **EodLastAckTime:** Contains the time when the last acknowledgment was received

- **EodNoAckCount:** Indicates the number of sent messages for which an acknowledgment has not yet been received

- **EodNoReadCount:** Indicates the number of messages sent that are waiting in the destination queue for a receiving application to read them

- **EodResendCount:** Indicates how many times the last message was sent

- **EodResendInterval:** Specifies the interval in seconds between the retransmission of messages

- **EodResendTime:** Specifies the time when the next messages will be re-sent

The next four elements contain an inner collection with the message's sequence identifier (SeqID), the message's sequence number (SeqNo), and the sequence number of the previous message (PrevNo):

- **EodFirstNonAck:** Contains sequence information about the first transactional message for which an acknowledgment has not yet been received

- **EodLastAck:** Contains sequence information about the first transactional message for which an acknowledgment has already been received

- **EodLastNonAck:** Contains sequence information about the last transactional message for which an acknowledgment has not yet been received

- **EodNextSeq:** Contains sequence information about the next message waiting to be sent

The following function returns the number of messages that were sent but have not been processed yet. If something goes wrong, it returns –1. The parameter is the path name of the outgoing queue, which is equivalent to the path name of the corresponding receiving queue:

```
Function NumberOfUnProcessedMessages(sPathName As String) As Long

On Error GoTo ErrorHandler

    Dim oColl As MSMQCollection
    Dim oMgmt As MSMQ.MSMQManagement
    Dim oOutQMgmt As MSMQ.MSMQOutgoingQueueManagement
```

To obtain an instance of the MSMQOutgoingQueueManagement class, we have to call the Init() method of the MSMQManagement class, just as we did for the MSMQQueueManagement class:

```
    Set oMgmt = New MSMQ.MSMQManagement

    oMgmt.Init sPathName

    Set oOutQMgmt = oMgmt
    Set oColl = oOutQMgmt.EodGetSendInfo()

    NumberOfUnProcessedMessages = oColl("EodNoReadCount")

GoOut:
    Set oColl = Nothing
    Set oMgt = Nothing
    Set oOutQMgmt = Nothing
    Exit Function

ErrorHandler:
    NumberOfUnProcessedMessages = -1
    GoTo GoOut

End Function
```

Pausing and Resuming the Queue

Sometimes you need to control the transmission of messages out of the outgoing queue. The MSMQOutgoingQueueManagement class provides three methods for this purpose:

- Pause(): Stops sending outgoing messages to the destination queue

- Resume(): Restarts sending outgoing messages to the destination queue

- EodResend(): Sends only the pending transaction sequence that the pause method interrupted

Queue Aliases

MSMQ uses Active Directory to create a **queue alias**. A queue alias is an Active Directory object of the MSMQ-Custom-Recipient class that allows you to reference a queue using a user-friendly name. Here are the benefits of using queue aliases:

- Queue aliases are useful for referencing queues that are not stored in Active Directory, such as private queues or URL-named queues, allowing them to be part of a distribution list.

- A queue alias acts as constant reference to a queue, allowing the message-based application to change the queue's location without affecting other applications.

- When a queue alias is deleted from Active Directory, it is automatically removed from all the distribution lists to which it belongs.

To reference a queue, you have to store a format name or a direct format name in a queue alias object.

Let's create a queue alias for our Internet RequestQueue queue. The messages from this queue were processed by the server application of the scalable message-based Application over Internet example earlier in this chapter. As the Server application works in conjunction with the Northwind database, we will give the queue the alias Northwind.

First, open the Active Directory Users and Computers MMC snap-in, shown in Figure 7-10.

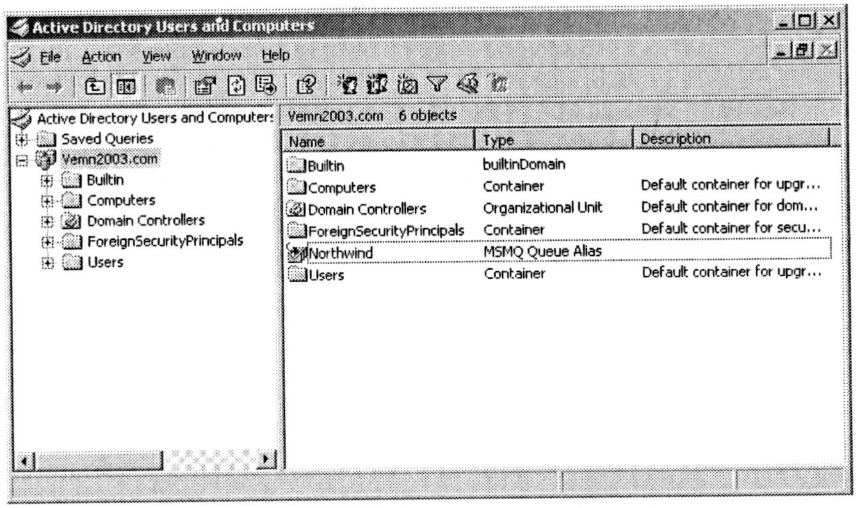

Figure 7-10. Active Directory Users and Computers MMC snap-in

Select the domain node in the console tree (Vemn2003.com in our screen-shot). Then select Action ➤ New ➤ MSMQ Queue Alias. Enter the Queue alias name and the Format name in the resulting dialog box, shown in Figure 7-11.

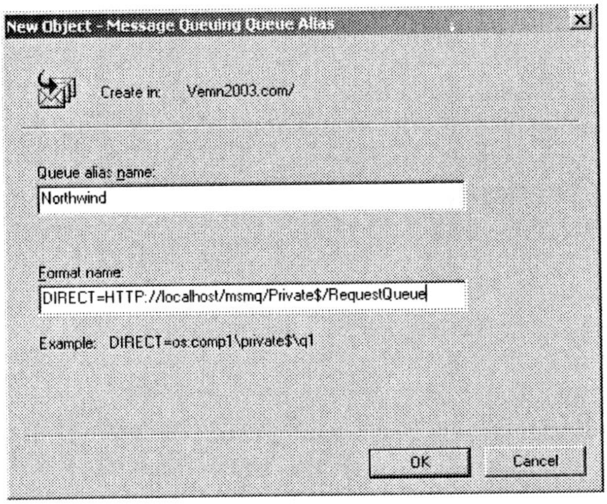

Figure 7-11. Creating an MSMQ alias

TIP *You can also create queue aliases programmatically using the Active DS Type Library or the* System.DirectoryServices *managed code API.*

Now you can change the format name to send the message. MSMQ uses the **Lightweight Directory Access Protocol (LDAP)** for querying Active Directory to obtain the queue alias. Taking advantage of direct messaging, you can reference the queue through an LDAP format name instead of using a URL direct format name, as shown here:

```
LDAP://LdapServerName/CN=Northwind,OU=Domain Controllers,DC=DomainName,⤦
DC=CompanyName,DC=COM
```

Multiple-Destination Messaging

In some scenarios, you may need to send the same message to several destinations. It probably won't be too much hard work for the sending application to send a few copies of the same message; however, there will be a loss of performance if the quantity increases. There is another point in this situation—as you saw earlier, each message sent by MSMQ will have its own ID, and this could be a design issue for an app that sends several copies of a message.

If you need to send the same message to several applications, you don't have to send it several times. MSMQ 3.0 allows you to send a single message to multiple destinations. Message Queuing provides three mechanisms to send messages to multiple destinations:

- Multiple-element format names

- Distribution lists

- Multicast addresses

When an application sends a single message to multiple destination queues using multiple-element format names and distribution lists, the local queue manager duplicates the message, assigning them the same ID, and sends a copy to the specified destinations. In the case of using a multicast, only one message is sent to the multicast address.

Similarly, an application can send a request message, which specifies multiple response queues.

NOTE *Message Queuing uses direct messaging to send messages to multiple destinations.*

Multiple-Element Format Names

As you've seen, MSMQ uses format names to locate queues within an organization; direct format names are used to send messages directly to a queue within an organization, to computers across the Internet, or to read and send messages in Domain and Workgroup modes. We can combine both in a string to create a **private multiple-element format name**. Multiple-element format names are useful for sending messages to multiple destinations. When MSMQ detects one, the local queue manager duplicates the message and sends a copy to each destination.

Sending applications can specify sets of response queues to spread the response into several queues.

A multiple-element format name is dynamically constructed and contains several format names separated by commas. First, this multiple-element format name contains information about the two queues' IDs:

```
PRIVATE=A1235F02-9863-47ba-A004-B5F9F0203390\00000a3d,
PUBLIC=6552002F-175F-4764-80EB-F9A919D9D0B5
```

The following specifies three queues combining TCP/IP addresses and computer names:

```
DIRECT=OS:vemn\anyQueue, DIRECT=TCP:192.168.0.200\PRIVATE$\otherQueue,
DIRECT=TCP:192.168.0.207\anotherQueue
```

This one links to queues published on the Internet:

```
DIRECT=HTTP://www.vemn.com.ar/msmq/anyQueue,
DIRECT=HTTP://www.apress.com/msmq/otherQueue
```

As with single messages, full security support, authentication, authorization, and encryption are available to multiple destination messaging.

Distribution Lists

Distribution lists aren't application-generated addresses like multiple-element format names, but instead are public sets of destinations stored in Active Directory. They can contain references to

- Public queues

- Queue aliases

- Other distribution lists

Distribution lists support transactions, authentication, and encryption. There are two ways you can administer distribution lists:

- Programmatically using the Active DS Type Library

- The Active Directory Users and Computers MMC snap-in

We will use the second option to demonstrate how to create a distribution list. Begin by opening the Active Directory Users and Computers MMC snap-in, shown in Figure 7-12.

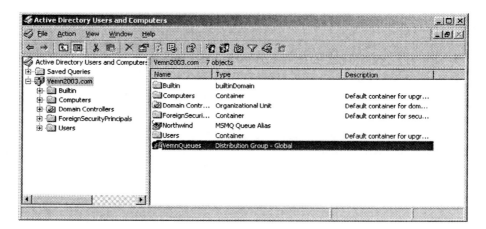

Figure 7-12. Active Directory Users and Computers MMC snap-in

A distribution list is created as a **group**. Select the domain node in the console tree (Vemn2003.com on our system). Then select Action ➤ New ➤ Group.

Enter the Group name and then Distribution under the Group Type, as shown in Figure 7-13.

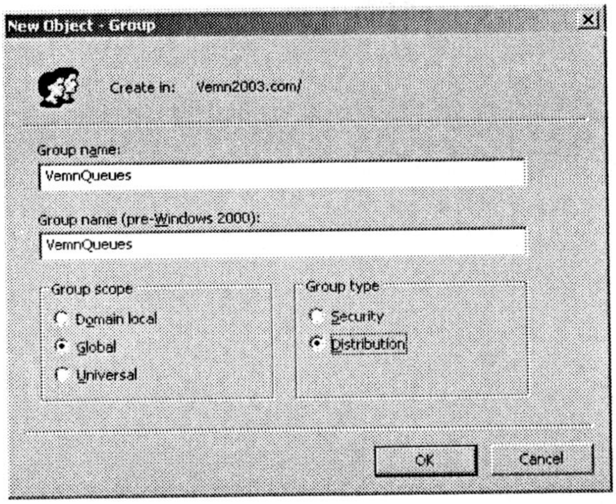

Figure 7-13. Creating a distribution list

Then, in the Members page of the Properties window of the distribution group, we can add the members, as shown in Figure 7-14.

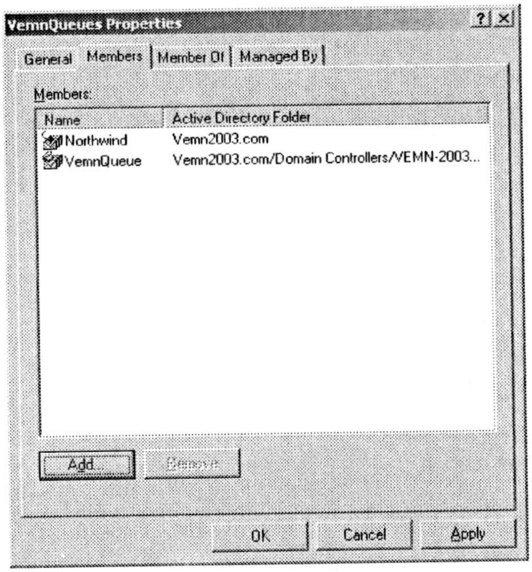

Figure 7-14. Adding members to the distribution list

This opens the Select Users, Contacts, Computers, or Groups dialog box. The Advanced button in this dialog box will help you to find the objects. Remember that you can select public queues, queue aliases, or other distribution lists.

In our case, let's add the Northwind queue alias previously created and a public queue called VemnQueue, as shown in Figure 7-15.

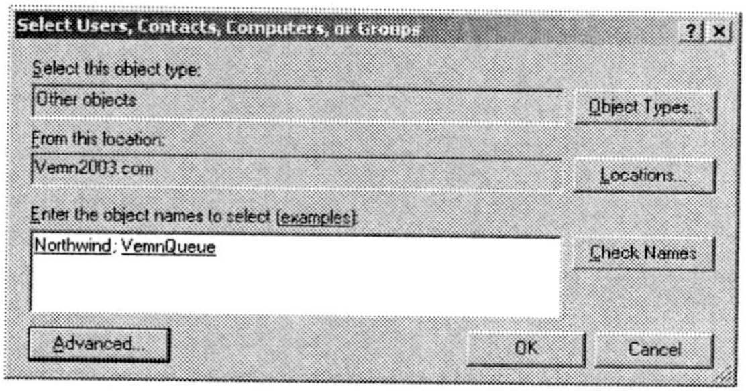

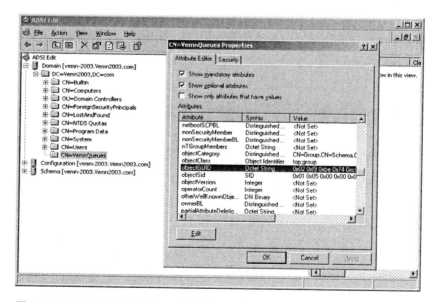

Figure 7-15. Selecting objects to add to the distribution list

To reference a distribution list, we have to use a **distribution list format name**, which contains the GUID for the list:

```
DL=1452002F-165F-4764-40EB-F9AFACD9D0B5
```

We can find the GUID in the objectGUID attribute of the distribution list group using the ADSIEdit.msc MMC snap-in tool provided with Windows 2003 Server. You can install it by running the SUPPORT\TOOLS\SUPTOOLS.MSI on the setup CD. Figure 7-16 shows this program in action.

Figure 7-16. The ADSIEdit.msc MMC snap-in tool provided with Windows 2003 Server

TIP *Distribution lists can be accessed and created from the* System.Messaging *.NET framework namespace.*

Multicast Addresses

MSMQ 3.0 provides a mechanism for sending messages through IP multicasting, using the **Pragmatic General Multicast (PGM)** protocol. PGM is a multicast protocol based on sequenced packets and a sliding transmission window that supplies basic reliability to multicast applications. This new protocol was designed to enable reliable distribution of multicast information to potentially millions of users over intranets, extranets, and the Internet. PGM is recommended for real-time push applications involving relatively small information transfers.

The sending application sends only one copy of a message to a multicast address, which propagates it to a large number of applications. This method was designed to deliver the same message to a huge number of receiving applications.

Nontransactional queues are associated with a multicast address using the administrative tool or setting the MSMQQueueInfo.MulticastAddress programmatically. Figure 7-17 shows the Multicast page of the queue's Properties window opened by the administrative tool.

![Queue's Properties window showing the Multicast tab. Tabs: General, Multicast, Security. Text reads: "A multicast address and port in the following format can be associated with this queue: <address>:<port>". Example: 234.1.1.1:8001. "Multicast address can range from 224.0.0.0 to 239.255.255.255". Multicast address field contains: 235.1.1.1:8001. Buttons: OK, Cancel, Apply.]

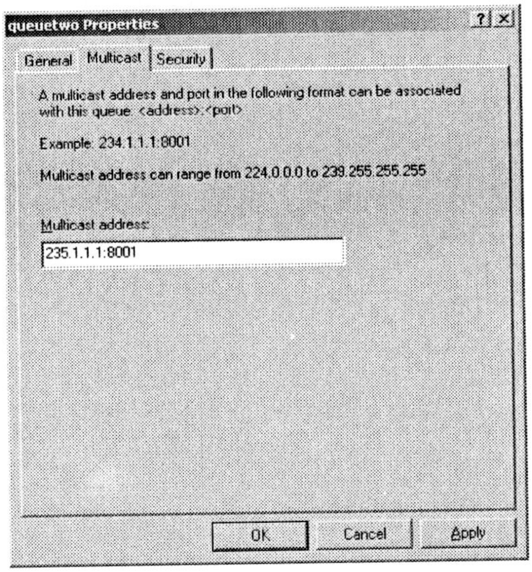

Figure 7-17. Queue's Properties window showing the Multicast option

Since multicast messaging uses direct messaging, we don't have to change our programming model. We just have to specify a multicast address format name to send a real-time multicast message. IP multicast addresses contain a TCP/IP address and a port number, and have to be in the class D range (from 224.0.0.0 to 239.255.255.255).

The following is an example of a multicast address format name:

```
MULTICAST=235.1.1.1:8001
```

Messages cannot be sent to a multicast address within a transaction, nor can they be encrypted by Message Queuing.

TIP   *Multicast addresses can be referenced from the* System.Messaging *.NET framework namespace, but not created.*

Summary

With the introduction of direct messaging, the new version of Message Queuing 3.0 provides new technologies that enlarge the spectrum of communication between message-based applications:

- **Internet Messaging:** Provides support for sending HTTP messages over the Internet

- **Queue aliases:** Allow you to reference queues with an alias instead of the format name or direct format name

- **Multiple-destination messaging:** Extends the regular MSMQ programming model from one-to-one to one-to-many

MSMQ 3.0 also brings several improvements in the following areas:

- Exactly-Once-Delivery information

- Programmable management

- The ability to retrieve a specific message

- Larger message size

Although these features aren't currently supported by the System.Messaging .NET namespace, it's likely that all the new technologies and improvements introduced in Message Queuing 3.0 will be promptly incorporated into the .NET Framework.

MSMQ on Pocket PC

MOBILE DEVICES ARE INCREASINGLY being used by companies to distribute enterprise information to their workforce on computers that have a compact form factor. Personal digital assistants (PDAs) originally used for contact lists and appointments are becoming mobile work centers and information repositories for knowledge workers on the go. These devices often need to communicate with corporate databases and applications, but they suffer the same problems of their mainframe ancestors: slow, unreliable connections and the disadvantage of being disconnected from the corporate network for periods of time. Message Queuing is a technology that will allow these mobile devices, and the applications that run on them, to integrate into the enterprise.

In this chapter we will look at what it takes to create MSMQ applications for the Pocket PC. In particular, we'll focus on the following:

- Understanding the features and limitations of MSMQ on the Pocket PC

- Installing and configuring the Pocket PC version of MSMQ

- Developing Pocket PC MSMQ applications in C++, Microsoft eMbedded Visual Basic (eVB), and C# through the .NET Compact Framework (CF)

- Administering Pocket PC queues using the MSMQ administration APIs

- Troubleshooting Pocket PC messaging problems

Aren't Windows CE and the Pocket PC the Same?

Many software developers are often confused by the variety of terminology that surrounds Microsoft's embedded operating systems. The misconception that is heard most often is that Windows CE and the Pocket PC are one and the same. The confusion stems from the fact that you can use the same tools to write applications for both the Pocket PC and Windows CE embedded devices. Knowing the similarities and differences between developing for a Windows CE platform versus a Pocket PC device will help you better scope your application development.

Windows CE is Microsoft's small-sized operating system for handheld and embedded devices. Built from the ground up to be componentized, Windows CE was first targeted at supplying an operating system for a new set of computers called *handheld PCs*. These devices were solid-state, instant-on, battery-operated computers used to complement a personal computer with appointments, contacts, and other information a person may want in a portable format. The Windows CE operating system has since grown to support not only newer versions of handheld and palm-sized PC devices but also set-top boxes, web-pads, Windows-based terminals, barcode readers, media-playing devices, Smart Displays, and a whole host of other embedded systems.

The Pocket PC is a targeted device aimed at the PDA market. While it has as its core the Windows CE operating system, the Pocket PC (including the Pocket PC 2002 and Pocket PC 2002 Phone Edition) features specialized applications, APIs, and a custom shell that are not found on devices based solely on Windows CE. Most Pocket PC devices on the market today are based on the 3.0 version of the Windows CE operating system.

Windows CE has evolved into its fourth incarnation: Windows CE .NET (also known as Windows CE 4.*x*). Microsoft has recently developed Pocket PC 2003 Second Edition, which is based on Windows CE .NET 4.2. This release includes enhanced MSMQ features such as MSMQ SOAP-formatted messaging over HTTP.

Although this chapter deals mostly with Pocket PC development, all of the sample code will work equally as well on Windows CE–embedded devices that include the MSMQ components.

Pocket PC MSMQ Features and Limitations

The Windows CE operating system is based on a subset of the Win32 API. In keeping with the tradition of most Windows CE software, MSMQ supports only a minimal amount of functionality compared to the MSMQ feature set found on desktop versions of Windows.

MSMQ on Windows CE supports an independent client model only. This model allows a Windows CE device using MSMQ to run without a connection to an MSMQ server or domain controller. This disconnected model is advantageous in wireless deployments of Pocket PC–based applications where continuous connectivity to the corporate network is not technically feasible or is cost prohibitive. MSMQ on CE can actually work in a peer-to-peer configuration, much like the MSMQ workgroup mode found on Windows 2000 and XP. Messages are stored locally on a CE device until they are forwarded to a desktop or server system or to another CE device. Routing of messages through an intermediate server allows one CE device to send messages to another CE device without the need for both devices to be on the network at the same time.

The following is a short summary of the features and limitations of the CE version of MSMQ.

Message Delivery

CE MSMQ supports both express and recoverable messages. Express messages are kept only in the temporary memory and are delivered faster than their recoverable counterparts, which are always written out to files. It may seem that recoverable messages will be necessary for storing messages while the CE device is turned off; however, Pocket PC devices are always running. The RAM file system of a Pocket PC is battery backed, and when the power to the Pocket PC is turned "off," the device is actually only placed in a suspended mode. The only advantage of using recoverable MSMQ messages in CE is when there is a fear that the battery backup may fail or there is no battery backup of the RAM file system when the device is turned off (which is the case with many embedded CE devices). Where battery failure and corruption of the RAM file system is a concern, the MSMQ message store files can be configured to reside on a persistent storage medium on the device, such as CompactFlash.

Public queues are registered with a Directory Service, and the desktop version of MSMQ has APIs to perform simple queries against them. However, the CE version of MSMQ does not support any public queue searching. A CE device can access a public queue in one of two ways. First, if the server on which the public queue resides is preconfigured on the CE device, either by hard-coding the queue path name or by reading the path from a Registry setting, the MSMQ application on that device can address the queue directly. The second way to send messages to a public queue is to use an intermediate server as a routing server. The routing server is identified on the device using the OutFRS Registry value. All messages sent from the device are directed to the routing server, which in turns forwards the message to the final destination public queue.

Transactions

The CE version of MSMQ has very limited support for transactions. CE does not have the ability to communicate with the Distributed Transaction Coordinator (DTC) and therefore cannot participate in a distributed transaction involving Message Queuing. MSMQ on CE can, however, provide a single-message transaction. A single-message transaction guarantees the sender of a message that only a single delivery of the message will occur. The single-message transaction also ensures that all the sender's messages arrive in order at the receiver. Message ordering is not guaranteed if no transaction support is requested by the sender. Despite what the Microsoft documentation states, transactional local queues are supported on CE. As you'll see later in this chapter, you can create local receive queues on your device that can participate in single transaction messages using the MQ_SINGLE_MESSAGE flag.

Journaling

MSMQ on CE supports message journals. A journal tracks messages as they are sent or received. The purpose of message journaling is to provide a mechanism for failure recovery or to audit the dispatching of messages in and out of MSMQ.

MSMQ maintains two system queues for sending applications: a journal queue and a dead-letter queue. By default, sent messages are not tracked by MSMQ. Once a message is sent by an application, there is no way for the application to check its status within the outbound queue. When an application requests journaling for a message, MSMQ will place a copy of the message into its system journal for tracking purposes. An application can also request that the message be sent to the system dead-letter queue if the message becomes undeliverable. Both journaling and dead-letter tracking can be assigned to any individual message sent by an application.

For queues that receive messages, a journal queue can be created. Messages are copied to the queue journal as they are removed by the receiving application. On CE, the journal queue must be created when the local receive queue is created. Unlike on the desktop, CE MSMQ does not allow a journal queue to be created for an existing queue.

Network Tracking

The CE version of MSMQ supports instant reconnection detection, aptly called network tracking. Network tracking allows MSMQ to immediately retry delivery of messages whenever a connection to the network is established when a network card is inserted into the device or a dial-up connection is made. MSMQ will attempt to flush its undelivered messages on a network when a connection is made. Control of network tracking as well as the retry schedule for MSMQ message sending is completely controlled by Registry settings, and can be configured and tuned for a particular application.

Implementation Scenarios

There are numerous situations where MSMQ-based messaging would be very beneficial to a Pocket PC–based application. MSMQ allows Pocket PCs to integrate into the corporate enterprise by providing the technology needed to communicate in a mobile environment without necessarily resorting to using a disconnected database architecture.

Mobile Data Collection Scenario

Pocket PCs excel at supporting mobile data collection applications. The small form factor, battery life, pen interface, and instant-on capabilities enable these devices to operate in places where laptop computers would prove too cumbersome. However, the purpose of data collection is to gather information and feed that data to a central location, such as a database, for processing. Message Queuing on a Pocket PC allows the data collection application to format information datasets as messages that are queued. The messages remain in the queue on the Pocket PC until the device reconnects to headquarters and sends the messages to the data processing system. The receiving queue on the corporate server handles all the incoming messages from multiple devices (or other computer systems) and performs the necessary processing steps, such as inserting the records into a database. The Pocket PC application is relieved of having to execute local database functions and perform complex database synchronization operations.

Mobile Notification Scenario

MSMQ can be used on a Pocket PC to support applications that need to receive notifications. These devices can be outfitted with wireless network cards that connect the devices to a local area network (LAN). A warehouse distribution center may provide their employees with CE devices that display pick orders that have to be collected for shipment to customers. MSMQ can be used by the warehouse allotment server to send pick order messages to the CE devices for fulfillment. The employees can in turn use their application to send a message back to the server acknowledging the picking of the order for shipment, or a problem message such as "out of stock." MSMQ is helpful in this scenario because sometimes the devices may experience network dead spots in the warehouse where communication may be offline for short periods of time. Message Queuing at the device and server allow smooth operation of the messaging between these systems without either side of the application having to worry about network failures.

MSMQ Installation on Pocket PCs

Microsoft Message Queuing is not an inherent part of the Pocket PC operating system. Pocket PCs that are shipping today do not include MSMQ as part of the system ROM. The binary files that make up MSMQ are included with the Pocket PC SDK that ships with eMbedded Visual Tools (http://msdn.microsoft.com/mobility/downloads/). The Pocket PC SDK includes all the header and library files that comprise a Pocket PC device, as well as the source for sample applications; help files; a device emulator (for those developers who do not have a Pocket PC to develop with) that runs on Windows NT, Windows 2000, or Windows XP; and the binary files that make up the Pocket PC MSMQ runtime engine.

The CE MSMQ runtime comprises the following files: the MSMQ engine (MSMQD.DLL), the MSMQ API runtime (MSMQRT.DLL), the MSMQ administrator and configuration tool (MSMQADM.EXE), a visual front-end to the configuration tool (VISADM.EXE), and the NetBIOS network registration engine (NETREGD.DLL), which registers the name of the Pocket PC device with the Windows Internet Naming Service. Each Pocket PC device name must be unique on the network if these devices are expected to receive MSMQ messages.

The MSMQ engine is implemented as a device driver on CE. CE devices do not have the notion of a service, an application that runs in the background even when no one is logged into the system. MSMQ needs to be a service because it must transmit and receive MSMQ messages even if there is no application that uses MSMQ running. To get around the limitation of not having services on CE, the developers of MSMQ implemented the engine as a driver. The MSMQ driver loads when CE is first booted and remains running for the life of the CE session. Drivers on CE are implemented as user-mode DLLs that run under the Device.exe process. Because it's a driver, MSMQ does not occupy one of the valuable 32 process slots allotted by the CE operating system.

You have several options from which to choose when installing MSMQ on a Pocket PC. One method involves copying the files to your device and using the Visadm utility to configure MSMQ. First, use your Pocket PC's ActiveSync connection to explore the files on your device. Copy the MSMQ DLLs and MSMQADM.EXE to your Pocket PC's \Windows directory. Copy all other files to the \Windows\Programs\ MSMQ directory. Run the Visadm.exe utility on your Pocket PC, select Install from the Shortcuts menu, and then choose Register. Visadm.exe places the keys and values needed by MSMQ in the Registry when you press the Install shortcut. The Register shortcut creates a unique system GUID for the device that is used by MSMQ when addressing messages. After configuration of MSMQ is complete, you must reboot the Pocket PC. The reboot forces the Device.exe process to load the MSMQ and NETREG drivers and become active. You can determine if MSMQ is started on your Pocket PC either by looking for the \Temp\MSMQ directory that is automatically created when MSMQ starts, or by using the Remote Process Viewer from eMbedded Visual Tools to look at the Device.exe process to see if the MSMQD.DLL and NETREGD.DLL files are loaded.

Another means by which MSMQ can be installed is to use the MSMQADM.EXE utility. This utility is a command-line process. Since there is no command-line processor on the Pocket PC, your installation application must create the administrative command lines and launch MSMQADM.EXE as a process with those commands.

Ideally, if you are building a CE application that makes use of MSMQ, you should include the MSMQ files in your application's installation CAB file. The CAB file can describe the files needed for MSMQ installation, their destination directories, and the necessary Registry settings. Using CAB files allows ActiveSync to participate in the installation process to keep track of installed programs and to allow the user to remove MSMQ using ActiveSync's Add/Remove Programs feature. The only tricky step in installing MSMQ in a CAB file is the configuration of the device's system GUID setting. A custom setup DLL that generates a unique GUID Registry setting for the device will do the trick. The CAB files supplied with this book include all the source code for the CAB INF file and for the setup DLL that can be incorporated into your custom Pocket PC application install.

Configuring MSMQ on Pocket PC

MSMQ on Pocket PC is completely controlled though the Registry. There is a core set of Registry keys required for it to operate and an extended set of keys and values that are used to fine-tune the messaging runtime behavior. The CE Remote Registry Editor that comes with the eMbedded Visual Tools makes it easy to modify the Pocket PC's Registry.

At the minimum, the MSMQ engine and the NETREGD driver need to be installed as drivers. The NETREGD driver can be omitted in devices that have static IP addresses or in corporate networks that have DNS servers with reverse IP address lookup. (For example, a given IP address can be used to look up a host name using Winsock's gethostbyaddr function.)

The following key and values need to be placed in the Registry to enable Device.exe to load the MSMQ drivers. These Registry entries are fixed and should not be changed to other values. The settings are created by the MSMQADM.EXE program or can be set by a Pocket PC installation program (example CAB files are supplied with this book). You can also modify the Registry of your Pocket PC using the remote Registry editor tool supplied as part of the eMbedded Visual Tools from Microsoft.

```
[HKEY_LOCAL_MACHINE\Drivers\BuiltIn\MSMQD]
    "Dll"="MSMQD.DLL"
    "Entry"="MSMQInitialize"
    "Keep"=DWORD:1
    "Order"=DWORD:9

[HKEY_LOCAL_MACHINE\Drivers\BuiltIn\NETREGD]
    "Dll"="NETREGD.DLL"
    "Entry"= "NETREGDInitialize"
    "Keep"=DWORD:1
    "Order"=DWORD:8
```

To configure MSMQ's base operation, the following keys and values are needed in the Registry:

```
[HKEY_LOCAL_MACHINE\Software\Microsoft\MSMQ\SimpleClient]
  "BaseDir"="\TEMP\MSMQ"
  "CEStartAtBoot"=DWORD:1
  "DefaultQuota"=DWORD:300
  "PingPort"=DWORD:0x00000DC7
  "Port"=DWORD:0x00000709
  "QueueManagerGUID"=HEX:...
  "CETrackNetwork"="Yes"


[HKEY_LOCAL_MACHINE\Software\Microsoft\NETREG]
  "EmulateNB"=DWORD:1
  "TrackNetwork"=DWORD:1
  "Cycle"=DWORD:1000
```

Additional MSMQ Configuration Values

There are a few notable keys worth mentioning here. All of the following values are under [HKEY_LOCAL_MACHINE\Software\Microsoft\MSMQ\SimpleClient].

CETrackNetwork

This string value can be Yes or No. If set to Yes, MSMQ will immediately try to send outgoing messages when the Pocket PC gets a valid network connection through either a PC Card insertion or dial-up networking. If this value is No, MSMQ will follow a set retry schedule without any regard to the state of the network connection. If you are using MSMQ with a Pocket PC that is only occasionally connected, it is important that this Registry value be set to Yes to ensure that MSMQ will offload outgoing messages to the network as soon as it is available. If the value is No, the chances of being connected to the network when the MSMQ retry timer expires are slim. Outgoing messages in this situation will almost always end up being undeliverable.

QueueManagerGUID

This binary Registry value is a GUID value that must be unique to the Pocket PC device. The GUID is used for session management between the Pocket PC and Windows NT or 2000 computers.

OutFRSQueue

This Registry string is a direct format name that designates a Falcon Routing Server queue. The purpose of the `OutFRS` queue is to act as an MSMQ intermediary holding queue. A routing server makes it possible for one Pocket PC device to send messages to another Pocket PC device without the need for both those devices to be connected to the network at the same time. The routing server holds the messages from the first device until the second device comes online to receive the messages.

LanRetrySchedule

This `DWORD` Registry value is used to control the network-tracking functionality of MSMQ. If the value is non-zero, messages will only be sent if there is a network connection (that is, either a network card is inserted or a dial-up connection is made). The value indicates the number of seconds LAN checking will be done. A value of zero means network checking is not done and the `RetrySchedule` will be followed.

RetrySchedule

This binary Registry value is an array of little-endian short (16-bit) numbers that define a schedule of retry timeouts. Each 16-bit value indicates the number of seconds to wait between trying to send messages. The last value is repeated indefinitely. The default schedule for MSMQ is 300, 300, 600, 600, 900. If a message is sent at 3:00 and failed, this schedule would retry to send the message at 3:05 (3:00 + 300 seconds), 3:10 (3:00 + 300s + 300s), 3:20 (3:00 + 300s + 300s + 600s), 3:30 (3:00 + 300s + 300s + 600s + 600s), 3:45 (3:00 + 300s + 300s + 600s + 900s), and every 15 minutes after that.

MSMQ Administration Tools

MSMQ for the Pocket PC provides two simple tools to help you set up and administer queues on your CE device: `MSMQADM.EXE` and `VISADM.EXE`. `MSMQADM.EXE` performs the bulk of the work and has several nice debugging and queue listing features. Unfortunately, this utility has a command-line user interface that can only run on the Pocket PC when launched by another process. As a workaround, Microsoft created `VISADM.EXE`, which is a Windows GUI application that can drive the `MSMQADM.EXE` program.

`VISADM.EXE` (see Figure 8-1) supports a set of shortcut buttons to some of the most frequently used MSMQ administration commands. Install and Register create all the Registry entries necessary for MSMQ to operate. Start and Stop respectively start and stop the MSMQ service. Status and Verify can be used to check the operation of MSMQ and to get a listing of MSMQ configuration settings. Log displays the contents of the MSMQ error log file. Uninstall erases the Registry entries for MSMQ. Install and Uninstall will do nothing to the actual MSMQ files and DLLs themselves; placing and removing those files must be done by hand. Additionally, removing MSMQMD.DLL and NETREGD.DLL requires either stopping the MSMQ service or restarting your Pocket PC after clicking Uninstall. These files are loaded by Device.exe and must be unloaded from that process before they can be removed from the device.

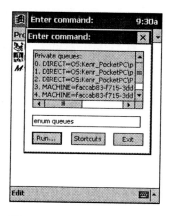

Figure 8-1. Microsoft's minimal VISADM.EXE *application for configuring MSMQ on a Pocket PC*

As Figure 8-1 shows, VISADM.EXE offers a text box where you can type MSMQADM.EXE commands; these are executed when you click the Run button. Some of the more useful commands available are enum queues and enum messages <n>. The enum queues command lists all the queues that are local to the device. The enum messages <n> command lists all the messages in a particular queue. Each queue displayed by enum queues has a number preceding its name. Use this number when running the enum messages <n> command. Note that you can only use enum messages <n> for queues created on the device. Even though enum queues lists both inbound and outbound queues, only messages within inbound queues can be displayed.

Microsoft left much to be desired in the installation and tools provided to make MSMQ operate on a Pocket PC. These tools were designed for embedded systems that had attached keyboards. Fortunately, the samples for this chapter include

- An MSMQ COM object that allows eVB developers to send and receive MSMQ messages

- A fully functional MSMQ admin program, written in C++, for managing local private queues on your Pocket PC

- A CAB file that can install and remove MSMQ, the MSMQ COM object, the admin program, and the sample programs

- The full source to all of these items

Programming MSMQ on the Pocket PC

You have several options when it comes to developing your first MSMQ application for the Pocket PC. You have a variety of languages and tools to choose from, and each has its distinct advantages and drawbacks. The classic toolset for Pocket PC development is eMbedded Visual Tools (eVT). These tools are modeled on the Visual Studio 6.0 and Visual Basic 6.0 development environments. Included in eVT 3.0 are eMbedded Visual C++ (eVC) for C++ development and eVB for VB development, as well as several device SDKs. The SDKs are essential for targeting applications for a particular device. Recall that CE is a modular operating system that can run on many kinds of embedded devices with varying capabilities. To differentiate between the programming interfaces available on one type of device versus another, eVT uses device SDKs. Each SDK indicates to eVT the API sets available on the particular device. eVT ships with SDKs for several types of retail devices (of which only the Pocket PC SDK is still applicable; the Handheld PC SDK and Palm-sized PC SDK are for devices that are no longer on the market). Microsoft provides downloadable versions of the newer SDKs for the Pocket PC and SmartPhone platforms (http://msdn.microsoft.com/mobility/).

The other development alternative for the Pocket PC is Visual Studio .NET 2003, with its integrated support for the .NET Compact Framework. The .NET CF is a slimmed-down version of the .NET Framework found on desktop systems and is designed for developing C# and VB.NET applications for embedded devices. The .NET CF is a managed code environment on Pocket PCs and other CE devices with support for many of the same framework elements found on the desktop, including Windows Forms, ADO.NET access to SQLCE, and Web Service–calling functionality, as well as the base framework elements for objects and interoperability with unmanaged code. Unfortunately, because of size constraints placed on the .NET CF team at Microsoft, the .NET CF does not have APIs for all the facilities found on the desktop, such as GDI+, serialization, Remoting, and—alas—MSMQ. Later in the chapter we'll discuss how you can take advantage of MSMQ in your managed code device applications.

Table 8-1 shows you which of the various development tools can be used on a particular device.

Table 8-1. Tools Supported on Various Mobile Devices

	POCKET PC	POCKET PC 2002	SMARTPHONE	POCKET PC 2003	SMARTPHONE 2003
eVC	X	X	X	X(eVC 4.2)	X(eVC 4.2)
eVB	X	X			
C#	X	X	X (CF 1.0)	X (CF 1.0 SP2)	X (CF 1.0 SP2)
VB.NET	X	X	X (CF 1.0)	X (CF 1.0 SP2)	X(CF 1.0 SP2)

eMbedded Visual Basic Is Not Visual Basic

Visual Basic for CE is a subset of the Visual Basic 6.0 environment available on the desktop. In fact, Visual Basic for CE is really only the VBScript engine ported to CE with the addition of VB forms. Since CE only supports VBScript, all VB applications developed for Pocket PCs are always interpreted. There is no support for COM objects developed in eVB and all object types are VARIANTs. Pocket PC eVB applications can call COM and ActiveX controls objects with a default IDispatch interface and can support handling events fired by those objects. This is similar in nature to late binding objects in VB 6.0. There is no support for early binding to COM objects in eVB. Type checking and IntelliSense are supported in the development environment, but all type information is stripped during compilation. Constants and enumerations contained within the type library of a COM object are not supported, even though the IntelliSense of the eVB IDE makes it seem as if it is.

To access the functionality of MSMQ on a Pocket PC from an eVB application, the source code to a COM object for the Pocket PC that supports the same interface and objects that are found on a desktop system is provided with this book. The interfaces match the desktop MSMQ version 1.0 implementation. Much of the MSMQ functionality that was introduced in version 2.0 relies on capabilities not found on the Pocket PC version of MSMQ.

Microsoft has made it clear that eVB will not be supported in future versions of the Pocket PC, and is impressing on developers that the .NET Compact Framework is the toolset of choice for VB developers creating applications on the Pocket PC. Additionally, eVT 4.x will contain only the C++ IDE for unmanaged code development.

Getting Started

In this section, we'll take a look at what you need to get started with your first MSMQ application on the Pocket PC.

Pocket PC Device

There are several manufacturers of Pocket PC devices. You can find a list of devices and suppliers at `www.microsoft.com/windowsmobile/buyersguide/helpmechoose/default.mspx`.

NOTE *What about the Pocket PC emulator? Unfortunately, Microsoft did not supply the DLLs and EXEs necessary for MSMQ to operate on the emulator.*

eMbedded Visual Tools

Developing VB applications for the Pocket PC requires the eVT development suite from Microsoft. This toolset is free from Microsoft and can be accessed at `http://msdn.microsoft.com/mobility/downloads/`. eVT supports development of applications in C++ and VB, and can target Pocket PC as well as older Palm-sized PC and Handheld PC Professional devices; however, only the Pocket PC can support MSMQ applications at this time.

TIP *The Pocket PC 2002 SDK does not include the MSMQ header file* `MQ.H` *in the* `\Program Files\CE Tools\wce300\Pocket PC 2002\ include` *directory. Copy the* `MQ.H` *file from the Pocket PC SDK installation.*

Visual Studio .NET 2003

You will need VS.NET 2003, which has the integrated .NET Compact Framework tools, to try any of the managed code examples in this chapter.

Windows NT, 2000, or XP

Pocket PC application development is performed on your desktop. The application is downloaded to the device and remote debugging is performed using eVT. A serial, USB, or Ethernet connection through ActiveSync (available with your Pocket PC) is the tether between the workstation and the Pocket PC, and is essential for debugging your application when it is running on the device.

Binaries and Source Code for Pocket PC MSMQ

The sample code for this chapter includes a CAB file for installing the MSMQ binaries and the sample programs. Instructions for installing the MSMQ binaries on your device are included in the readme file. All the source code for the samples, as well as the MSMQ COM object, is included. Note the location of the Typelib subdirectory. This directory contains the type library file and MsmqInc.bas file needed for programming your eVB MSMQ application.

Network Connection

To fully experience how MSMQ operates on a Pocket PC, you will need to have a TCP/IP network configured that allows your device to communicate with your desktop system or MSMQ server. The IP tunneling feature of ActiveSync is not sufficient for the flow of MSMQ messages between desktop and device to occur. You can execute many of the samples in this chapter by sending and reading messages for queues that solely reside on the device, but the real excitement happens when you send that first message from your Pocket PC to another computer.

Tool Choice: eMbedded Visual C++

Developing an MSMQ application in C++ for the Pocket PC is very similar to developing on the desktop. The C API for MSMQ for the Pocket PC is the same as the desktop MSMQ version 1.0 API with a few limitations in functionality.

The CE version of MSMQ does not allow the use of public queues, which require access to ActiveDirectory and multimessage transactions. Table 8-2 lists the differences between the CE implementation of MSMQ and the desktop version. Note that this information is available in the Pocket PC SDK documentation; however, there are some omissions and incorrect statements about the Pocket PC MSMQ capabilities in that documentation. Those mistakes are outlined in *italics*.

Table 8.2. MSMQ Pocket PC SDK Clarifications and Corrections

FUNCTION	COMMENTS
MQCreateQueue	Can create only local private queues. *Local private queues that support single transactional messages can be created by using the* PROPID_Q_TRANSACTION *attribute.*
MQOpenQueue	Can only open queues through the PRIVATE DIRECT format name. Never fails opening outgoing queue if format name is correct and disk space is sufficient. *Outgoing queues that are transactional must have* ;XACTONLY *appended to the queue format name.*
MQSendMessage	Not all properties supported. Single-transaction messages supported *only if queue opened with* ;XACTONLY.
MQReceiveMessage	The pTransaction parameter is not supported and should be set to NULL. *This parameter is of no consequence for local queues that are transactional as only single message transactions are supported.* Encryption properties are not supported.
MQGetMachineProperties	Only local queues supported. Not all properties supported.
MQSetMachineProperties	Only local queues supported. Not all properties supported.
MQCreateCursor	Fully supported.
MQCloseCursor	Fully supported.
MQCloseQueue	Fully supported.
MQDeleteQueue	Can delete only local queue using direct format name.
MQPathNameToFormatName	Returns the private direct format name.
MQHandleToFormatName	Returns direct format name.
MQGetMachineProperties	Can only be called for local machine. The only property supported is PROPID_QM_MACHINE_ID.
MQMgmtGetInfo	*Not documented. Can get information about MSMQ installation and the list of local queues on the device.*
MQMgmtAction	*Not documented. Can start or stop the MSMQ service. Can purge the messages in a queue.*

An alternative to using the MSMQ C API is to try the MSMQ COM component that eVB uses to communicate with MSMQ. The COM component mimics the COM object for MSMQ found on the desktop and supplies an easier interface to the Pocket PC MSMQ facilities. If you are comfortable with using COM interfaces and the ATL library in C++, this may be a better option for your project. In fact, some of the C++ sample code in this chapter and the C++ MSMQ Admin program use that object exclusively.

Tool Choice: eMbedded Visual Basic

eVB has been used extensively by Pocket PC developers for many successful application deployments. However, the eVB runtime environment suffered from the fact that eVB is not compiled Visual Basic but rather embedded VBScript. As a result, there are many cases in which eVB developers ran into a roadblock in their project because of the limited functionality of the runtime. Also, with the introduction of Pocket PC 2003, Microsoft will no longer support the eVB environment. A big part of that decision is based on the recent release of the .NET CF with Visual Studio .NET 2003 and the positioning of that product as the heir apparent to eVB.

eVB still has its place in Pocket PC development, though, as the .NET CF does not support all programming APIs, including MSMQ. There is also a base of existing applications written in eVB that may benefit from MSMQ features. As such, this chapter will cover eVB in addition to C++ and C#/VB.NET managed code development for MSMQ.

Because eVB can't use the MSMQ C API directly, a COM object written in C++ is required to provide an object model for MSMQ for eVB to program against. This COM object, and all of its associated source code, is in the source code directory for this chapter. The compiled DLL for the COM object is also installed by the CAB file that installs the MSMQ binaries on your device.

You must complete a few setup steps before you begin using the COM object in the eVB environment. First, start eVB, select the CE for Pocket PC project, and click OK. Although it is not required for developing your application, IntelliSense makes writing your VB application much easier. The pop-up reference to a COM object's functions and the typing-completion features make writing MSMQ applications simpler. To enable this support in your application, select Project ➤ References from the eVB menu bar. A list of available objects that can be referenced in your application appears. You will need to add the MSMQ component to this list by clicking the Browse button. Find the MsmqCOM.tlb file located under the Typelib directory of the source code, as shown in Figure 8-2.

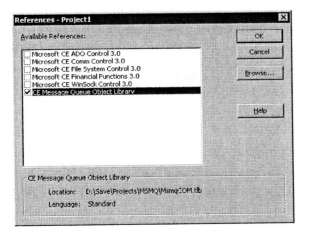

Figure 8-2. Adding the MsmqCOM type library to an eVB project

Select the check box next to CE Message Queue Object Library and click OK. You will now have IntelliSense functionality for the MSMQ objects in the eVB IDE. The eVB environment will remember the location of this type library file. Enabling IntelliSense for another MSMQ application will be as simple as selecting the CE MSMQ reference.

While enabling a reference to the MSMQ objects helps with programming MSMQ applications, eVB will not include the constants and enumerations that are in the type library as part of your application. An additional file called MsmqInc.bas (also found in the Typelib directory) is an eVB module that you should add to your project. This module contains MSMQ constants used by the MSMQ COM objects that will work in the eMbedded Visual Basic environment. To add this module, select Project ➤ Add File and find the MsmqInc.bas file.

Tool Choice: Visual Studio .NET 2003

The clear choice that Microsoft wants you to make for your future device development is VS.NET and the .NET CF. This option affords you the choice of selecting either C# or VB.NET as your programming language, and, unlike eVB, the Common Language Runtime (CLR) that executes on your device is a fully .NET-compliant runtime. The MSIL code created for the .NET CF is exactly the same as that executed on the desktop. You are also able to include in one VS.NET solution your device source code as well as your other projects.

When developing for the .NET CF, you must keep in mind a few caveats. First, the .NET CF is a subset of the full .NET Framework. As such, not all assemblies are available on the device. Most notably absent are System.Messaging (MSMQ support on CE) and object serialization. The absence of System.Messaging is not that troublesome; just as we need a COM object for eVB, we merely need a managed code wrapper for CE MSMQ. In fact, the source code of this chapter provides such a wrapper. However, what limits the usefulness of the wrapper is the omission of object serialization from the .NET CE.

Serialization is the mechanism by which .NET objects can be persisted to a binary or XML format and regenerated from that format. It is that precise operation that System.Messaging uses to stream any managed object, be it a simple data type or a complex class structure, into and out of an MSMQ message. The sample managed code wrapper ties in with some extensions to the CE MSMQ COM object to send simple string messages only. The purpose of the sample is to provide a starting point for you to create the necessary C functions and managed wrapper code for your specific application. Take heart, though, because the rumor from Microsoft is that MSMQ functionality within the .NET CF is high on next version's feature list.

Hello MSMQ World

Your project is now ready for some messaging! To start out, we'll develop a very simple "Hello World" application (Figure 8-3) that will show the basics of working with MSMQ for the Pocket PC using the various development tools we've mentioned: eVC, eVB, and VS.NET with the .NET CF. We will expand the samples to use some of the more advanced MSMQ features, such as journaling and setting some of the optional attributes of a message like time-to-live and acknowledgements, so that you can see how the operation of MSMQ is affected.

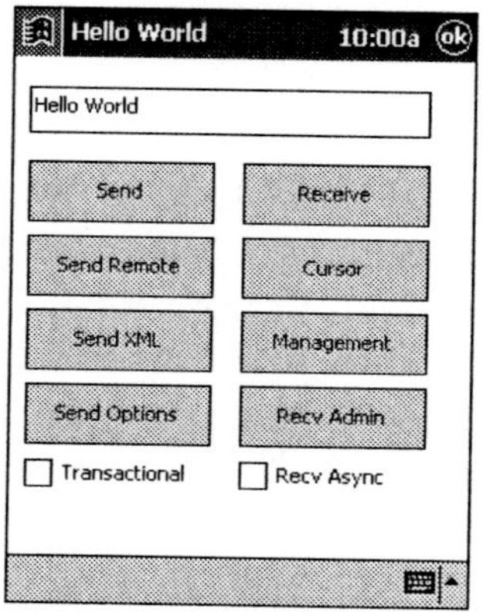

Figure 8-3. The eVB MSMQ Hello World sample application

The source code for the samples is drawn from several areas. Rather than have the exact same Hello World application in three languages, you can choose the tool/language that is right for your application and investigate the appropriate sample source code. But first, a short primer on the samples:

MSMQ COM Object: Look at the source code of this sample for in-depth coverage of the MSMQ C API. The source code for this sample touches on every aspect of using MSMQ on the Pocket PC in a COM component developed in eVC.

MSMQ Admin Program: This sample expands on the MSMQ COM Object code by providing a queue administration program. The admin program is written in C++ and MFC, and uses the MSMQ COM interfaces to drive its functionality. Creating, purging, and deleting queues; sending messages; peeking at messages in local queues; and viewing the properties of queues and messages are all covered by this sample application. Additionally, this application provides you with a better utility for managing queues on Pocket PCs than Microsoft does.

Hello World: This sample is written in eVB and shows how to program MSMQ in that environment. The sample relies on the MSMQ COM Object to operate, and demonstrates how simple it is to get MSMQ functioning on a Pocket PC. The nature of eVB allows you to play with changing message parameters quickly and checking the effect of those properties on your messaging application.

MSMQ_CF: This sample targets the .NET CF and consists of a solution with two projects. This first project is a wrapper class library that provides some basic queue management operations (create, open, purge, close, delete) and the ability to send simple text-only messages. The wrapper class relies on some DLL functions in the MSMQ COM Object to provide an interface between the managed world of the .NET CF and the unmanaged world of the MSMQ C API. The second part of the sample is a simple CF Forms application that drives the wrapper class functions. Use this sample as the starting point for your managed code MSMQ application with the understanding that formatting the contents of your messages will be your biggest obstacle in this programming environment.

Sending Messages

The easiest starting point for working with MSMQ on the Pocket PC is to create a local queue on the device itself and send a message to it. We'll look at this from three approaches: using. eVC, using eVB, and using the .NET CF.

eMbedded Visual C++

The first step is to create the queue on the device. If you are using eVC and the C++ language, you can use the standard MSMQ API functions, just as you would on the desktop. However, because that has already been covered in Chapter 6, we'll look at using COM interfaces to accomplish the same thing. The following code sample shows you how to create a new receiving queue on the device:

```
#include <atlbase.h>
#include "..\\MsmqCOM\\MsmqCOM.h"

HRESULT CreateQueue()
{
    HRESULT hr;
    CComPtr<IMSMQQueueInfo> spQueueInfo;
    CComBSTR bstrQueueName(OLESTR(".\\private$\\HelloWorld"));

    // Create a queueInfo object
    hr = spQueueInfo.CoCreateInstance(CLSID_MSMQQueueInfo);
    if (FAILED(hr))
        return hr;

    // Initialize with path name and journal info
    hr = spQueueInfo->put_PathName(bstrQueueName);
    if (FAILED(hr))
        return hr;

    // Create the queue
    hr = spQueueInfo->Create(VARIANT_FALSE, VARIANT_FALSE);
    if (FAILED(hr))
        return hr;

    return hr;
}
```

The steps involved are quite straightforward. First, an instance of the MSMQQueueInfo object is created with a smart pointer to the IMSMQQueueInfo interface. The PathName property of the queue to create is set and the queue is then created with no journaling and no world-readable flag.

The advantage of using the COM interfaces, even in a C++ program, is evident from the simplicity of this code. The process of establishing the MSMQ properties of a queue or a message with the raw MSMQ C API is difficult and error-prone. Leveraging the Pocket PC MsmqCOM object in your application can ease that burden with the trade-off of a larger application footprint.

eMbedded Visual Basic

The HelloWorld eVB sample performs the same operation of creating a local queue, but also opens the queue to send a simple message:

```
Option Explicit

Private Sub Send_Click()

    Dim qinfo As MSMQQueueInfo
    Dim q As MSMQQueue
    Dim m As MSMQMessage

    ' Create objects
    Set qinfo = CreateObject("CE_MSMQ.MSMQQueueInfo")
    Set m = CreateObject("CE_MSMQ.MSMQMessage")

    ' Create and open local queue for sending
    qinfo.PathName = ".\private$\HelloWorld"
    qinfo.Create
    Set q = qinfo.Open(MQ_SEND_ACCESS, MQ_DENY_NONE)

    ' Send message
    m.Label = Text1.Text
    m.Body = Text1.Text
    m.Send q

    ' Close queue
    q.Close

End Sub
```

Let's examine this code one section at a time. First, the MSMQ objects that are going to be used are declared using the `Dim` statements. This serves two purposes: one is to enable IntelliSense, and the other is to satisfy the eVB compiler because the `Option Explicit` statement is present. The eVB environment does not support the `New` keyword, so each object must be created using the `CreateObject()` function. The ProgID of the MSMQ COM objects is `CE_MSMQ.objectname`. In this example, we create `MSMQQueueInfo` and `MSMQMessage` objects.

The `MSMQQueueInfo` object will always be the first object created in any MSMQ application. This object is used as a reference object to any queue—local or remote—with which the application wishes to interact. The `MSMQQueueInfo` object can create new queues, delete queues, set or get the properties of a queue, and open queue instances. As in the C++ example, this code creates a local private queue named HelloWorld:

```
' Create a local queue
qinfo.PathName = ".\private$\HelloWorld"
qinfo.Create
```

The PathName property of the MSMQQueueInfo object identifies the queue using a naming convention similar to a directory path. The period indicates the local computer (this Pocket PC). Only local private queues can be created on Pocket PCs. The Create function actually creates the queue on the Pocket PC. If the queue already exists, this function will return successfully and reference the existing queue (unlike the desktop version, which will return an "already exists" error).

The next line of code opens the queue:

```
' Open the queue for sending
Set q = qinfo.Open(MQ_SEND_ACCESS, MQ_DENY_NONE)
```

The Open method of the MSMQQueueInfo object opens the queue identified by the PathName property and returns an MSMQQueue object. The MSMQQueue object is an open instance of the queue, whereas the MSMQQueueInfo object just represents the queue. There can be multiple MSMQQueue objects opened from a single MSMQQueueInfo object. The Open method takes two parameters: an access type and a deny type. A queue can be opened for send access (MQ_SEND_ACCESS), receive access (MQ_RECEIVE_ACCESS), or peek access (MQ_PEEK_ACCESS). Exclusive access to a queue opened for receive or peek access is controlled by the second parameter. We'll cover receiving messages in more detail in the next section. For queues opened for send access, only MQ_DENY_NONE is allowed.

The next few lines of code set some of the parameters of the message:

```
' Send message
m.Label = Text1.Text
m.Body = Text1.Text
m.Send q
```

The MSMQMessage object has many parameters that you can set that affect the contents and handling of the message. The contents of the message are sent in the Body property. This property is a variant data type, and can accept any supported VB type. The contents of the body as well as the type information are sent in the MSMQ message. Objects that support the IPersist interface can be sent as well. The only caveat is when you're sending messages from a Pocket PC to a desktop computer: You must be sure that the object that is persisted on your Pocket PC for the message has a desktop counterpart with the same GUID information. Another limitation of the Pocket PC MSMQ COM object is that an array of data types is not supported. In the VBScript world of eVB, arrays are actually arrays of variants. MSMQ on the desktop can only support an array of bytes, so it is not possible to send a message that contains an array of variants to a desktop MSMQ queue, nor is it possible to send an array of bytes from a desktop system to a Pocket PC.

The Body and the Label of the message are set to the same value, the text in the text box. The Send method sends the MSMQ message to the queue specified. The method call seems backward, but the original Microsoft designers of this interface wanted the MSMQMessage object to have the Send method rather than the MSMQQueue object. The sending of the message will almost always succeed. However, the success of this function does not mean the message was delivered to its final destination. Unless there is a problem with the queue or the message, the Send method will always return successfully, because the whole purpose of MSMQ is to allow applications to send a message without worrying about connection problems. If it is important that a sending application needs to know if a message was successfully received and processed, MSMQ supplies some acknowledgment facilities. We'll see some examples of that later.

The last line closes the queue. Even though the queue is closed from the application's perspective, MSMQ will still be working in the background, delivering unsent messages and receiving and storing messages from other computers. All of the objects used in the function are automatically deleted when the function returns and the object variables go out of scope.

Run the program and click the Send button and you will see nothing happen. Actually, a single message will be deposited into the local queue called HelloWorld. To see the message, use the MSMQ Admin program to view all the local queues on the device. You should see the HelloWorld queue in the tree and a list of messages in the queue, one for every time you click the Send button, as shown in Figure 8-4.

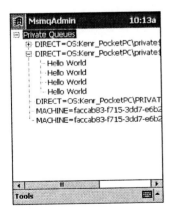

Figure 8-4. Hello World MSMQ messages in the receiving queue on the Pocket PC device

.NET Compact Framework

The key to making MSMQ operate in the managed environment of the .NET Compact Framework is creating a set of DLL functions in unmanaged C++ that wrap the MSMQ C API. The raw C API to MSMQ uses structures that are too complex for the minimal managed-to-unmanaged code interoperability constructs provided by the .NET CF. Coupled with the lack of support for serialization, creating a complete System.Messaging clone for the Pocket PC is a daunting task. Instead of waiting for Microsoft to implement System.Messaging in some future version of the .NET CF, you can create your own wrapper class to the specific MSMQ DLL functions that you need. That is the purpose of this example. The complete VS.NET solution and source code can be found in the MSMQ_CF directory for this chapter.

Limiting the message body content for your application eases your development work. For this example, we'll look at what it takes to send simple string messages in MSMQ from managed code.

Prior to developing your managed code, you will need to define and implement your unmanaged DLL MSMQ API. The following example maps to some additional exported C functions in MsmqCOM.dll:

```
// Internal class wrapper for calling unmanaged MSMQ
// functions

internal class MsmqCOM
{
    [DllImport("MsmqCOM.dll")]
    public static extern int MsmqCOM_CreateQueue(string path);

    [DllImport("MsmqCOM.dll")]
    public static extern int MsmqCOM_PurgeQueue(string path);

    [DllImport("MsmqCOM.dll")]
    public static extern int MsmqCOM_DeleteQueue(string path);

    [DllImport("MsmqCOM.dll")]
    public static extern IntPtr MsmqCOM_OpenQueue(string path,
                                                  int access);

    [DllImport("MsmqCOM.dll")]
    public static extern int MsmqCOM_CloseQueue(IntPtr hQueueHandle);
```

```
[DllImport("MsmqCOM.dll")]
public static extern int MsmqCOM_Send(IntPtr hQueueHandle,
                                      string label,
                                      string body);
}
```

While these unmanaged functions rely on some of the MSMQ COM interfaces internally, you can choose to develop against the raw MSMQ C API itself. These functions supply the basic functions of creating and opening a queue, along with the ability to send a simple text-only message. Upon this rudimentary foundation, it becomes easy to craft the managed code class library that your managed code MSMQ application can take advantage of.

The C# MessageQueue class here mimics to some extent its counterpart in System.Messaging found in the .NET Framework. This is the complete code listing for the class:

```
using System;
using System.Runtime.InteropServices;

namespace MsmqCE
{
    // CE Compact Framework MessageQueue class
    public class MessageQueue
    {
        // Queue access flags
        public const int MQ_RECEIVE_ACCESS = 1;
        public const int MQ_SEND_ACCESS    = 2;
        public const int MQ_PEEK_ACCESS    = 32;

        // Private fields
        private string path;
        private IntPtr ptrMsmqObjRef;

        // Creates a new local queue on the device and opens it with
        // receive access. Returns message queue object.
        public static MessageQueue Create(string path)
        {
            // Create and open with recv access
            return MessageQueue.Create(path, MQ_RECEIVE_ACCESS);
        }
```

```
// Creates a new local queue on the device and opens it with
// given access. Returns message queue object.
public static MessageQueue Create(string path, int access)
{
    int result;

    // Create queue
    result = MsmqCOM.MsmqCOM_CreateQueue(path);
    if (result == 0)
    {
        // Open the queue
        return new MessageQueue(path, access);
    }
    else
    {
        // Failed
        return null;
    }
}

// Delete the given local queue
public static void Delete(string path)
{
    MsmqCOM.MsmqCOM_DeleteQueue(path);
}

// Purge the given local queue of all messages
public static void Purge(string path)
{
    MsmqCOM.MsmqCOM_PurgeQueue(path);
}

// MessageQueue constructors
public MessageQueue(string path)
{
    // Set path
    this.path = path;

    // Open the queue with recv access
    this.ptrMsmqObjRef = MsmqCOM.MsmqCOM_OpenQueue(path,
                                      MQ_RECEIVE_ACCESS);
}
```

```csharp
        public MessageQueue(string path, int access)
        {
            // Set path
            this.path = path;

            // Open the queue with given access
            this.ptrMsmqObjRef = MsmqCOM.MsmqCOM_OpenQueue(path,
                                                           access);

        }

        // MessageQueue properties
        public string Path
        {
            get
            {
                return path;
            }
        }

        // Send a string message
        public void Send(string label, string body)
        {
            MsmqCOM.MsmqCOM_Send(ptrMsmqObjRef, label, body);
        }

        // Close the open queue
        public void Close()
        {
            // Check for a valid obj reference
            if(ptrMsmqObjRef != IntPtr.Zero)
                MsmqCOM.MsmqCOM_CloseQueue(ptrMsmqObjRef);
            ptrMsmqObjRef = IntPtr.Zero;
        }
    }

// Internal class wrapper for calling unmanaged MSMQ functions.
internal class MsmqCOM
{
    // DLL imports go here...
}
}
```

To use the MessageQueue class in the MsmqCE namespace within your application, you first need to reference the class library and import the library with the using MsmqCE; statement. The HelloWorld CF sample shows how to send a simple message from the contents of a text box. The complete VS.NET solution and source code can be found in the MSMQ_CF directory for this chapter.

```csharp
using System;
using System.Drawing;
using System.Collections;
using System.Windows.Forms;
using System.Data;
using MsmqCE;

namespace Hello_World_CF
{
    public class Form1 : System.Windows.Forms.Form
    {
        private System.Windows.Forms.TextBox textBox1;
        private System.Windows.Forms.Button Send;
        public Form1()
        {
            //
            // Required for Windows Form Designer support
            //
            InitializeComponent();
        }

        // Clean up any resources being used.
        protected override void Dispose( bool disposing )
        {
            base.Dispose(disposing);
        }

        #region Windows Form Designer generated code
        #endregion

        // The main entry point for the application.
        static void Main()
        {
            Application.Run(new Form1());
        }
```

```
private void Send_Click(object sender, System.EventArgs e)
{
    MessageQueue theQueue;
    string label, body;

    // Create and open the local message queue
    theQueue = MessageQueue.Create(".\\private$\\HelloWorldCF",
                                   MessageQueue.MQ_SEND_ACCESS);
    label = textBox1.Text;
    body = "Body: " + textBox1.Text;

    // Send a message with a string body
    theQueue.Send(label, body);
}
}
}
```

The click event handler for the Send button performs all the work. The Create() static method of the MessageQueue class is overloaded so it not only creates the queue, but also opens it with send access. The returned MessageQueue instance references the local queue and is subsequently used to send a message with a label and a string for its body. The wrapper class MessageQueue provides only a thin layer on top of the unmanaged functions in C++ that does the actual job of accessing the MSMQ APIs. Figure 8-5 shows the simple user interface of our managed code MSMQ sample.

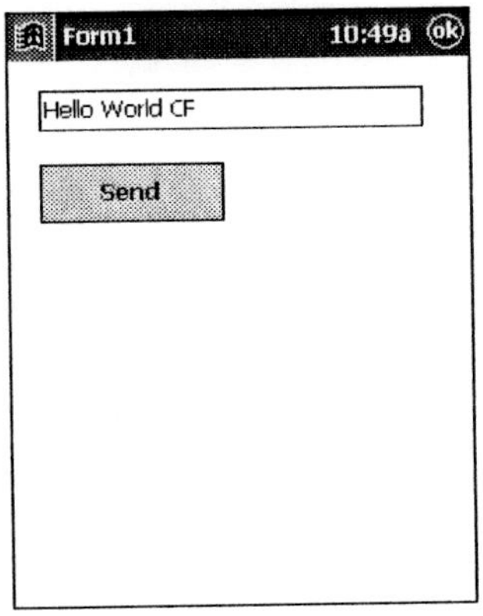

Figure 8-5. A managed code MSMQ application on Pocket PC using the .NET Compact Framework

Message Sending Options

We have seen the basic operation of sending a simple text message. Let's take a look at other sending options available under MSMQ and see how they affect the delivery and processing of messages. We'll look at these examples using eVB, but the same concepts can be used in C++ or C# applications.

Sending to Remote Queues

Sending a message to a queue on another computer is as simple as just designating that computer in the PathName of the MSMQQueueInfo object. We can send a "HelloWorld" message to our development workstation. First we need to create a HelloWorld queue on the desktop Windows 2000/XP computer. Use the Computer Management Console or Visual Studio .NET Server Explorer to create a new HelloWorld queue by drilling down to the Private Queues folder. Name the queue HelloWorld and make sure the Make queue transactional check box is cleared, as shown in Figure 8-6.

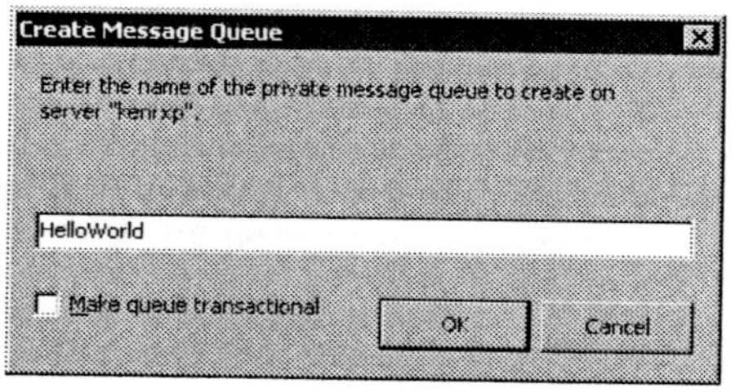

Figure 8-6. Creating a new transactional queue on a server

The Send Remote button in the HelloWorld eVB sample has the following click handler:

```
Private Sub SendRemote_Click()

    Dim qinfo As MSMQQueueInfo
    Dim q As MSMQQueue
    Dim m As MSMQMessage

    ' Create objects
    Set qinfo = CreateObject("CE_MSMQ.MSMQQueueInfo")
    Set m = CreateObject("CE_MSMQ.MSMQMessage")
```

```
' Open the queue for sending
qinfo.PathName = strRemoteComputer & "\private$\HelloWorld"
Set q = qinfo.Open(MQ_SEND_ACCESS, MQ_DENY_NONE)

' Send message
m.Label = Text1.Text
m.Body = Text1.Text
m.Send q

' Close queue
q.Close
```

End Sub

This function differs from our original Send_Click() method in that we are no longer creating a local queue. Recall that MSMQ on the Pocket PC can only create local private queues. We had to create our Windows XP queue using the Computer Management Console. The name of my Windows XP computer happens to be kenrxp, the value of strRemoteComputer, so to send messages from my Pocket PC to kenrxp, I need to set the PathName for the queue to kenrxp\private$\ HelloWorld. The queue could also be a public queue, in which case the PathName would be simply kenrxp\HelloWorld.

When the Open method is called for this queue, MSMQ knows from the path that this is a remote queue, and it will create a local outbound queue to hold the messages locally until they can be delivered to the kenrxp computer.

Sending messages from a Windows XP computer to the Pocket PC requires a special trick. Since the HelloWorld queue on the Pocket PC is local and private, a Windows XP VB application needs to know the FormatName of the Pocket PC queue. Setting the PathName for a remote private queue is not allowed on the desktop version of the MSMQ COM objects, and therefore to open the remote Pocket PC queue, the direct format name of the queue needs to be used. The name of the Pocket PC device I'm using is Kenr_Pocket PC. To send messages to the HelloWorld queue on that device, I need to set the FormatName of an MSMQQueueInfo object in my desktop application to DIRECT=OS:Kenr_Pocket PC\private$\HelloWorld. The Windows XP system needs to be able to resolve the IP address of the Pocket PC using its computer name. DNS, WINS, or a hosts file provides this information to MSMQ.

Delivery Options

There are several other optional properties a message may have that affect how MSMQ processes and delivers that message. Messages that are sent by an application can be transactional, journaled, recoverable, and given time-to-live values. To demonstrate how to set these parameters and what effect they have on messages, let's look at the Send Options button click handler in the eVB HelloWorld sample:

```
Option Explicit
Const strRemoteComputer As String = "kenrxp"

Private Sub SendOptions_Click()

    Dim qinfo, qadmin, qresp As MSMQQueueInfo
    Dim q As MSMQQueue
    Dim m As MSMQMessage

    ' Create objects
    Set qinfo = CreateObject("CE_MSMQ.MSMQQueueInfo")
    Set qadmin = CreateObject("CE_MSMQ.MSMQQueueInfo")
    Set qresp = CreateObject("CE_MSMQ.MSMQQueueInfo")
    Set m = CreateObject("CE_MSMQ.MSMQMessage")

    ' Open the queue for sending
    If Transactional = 1 Then
        qinfo.PathName = strRemoteComputer & _
                        "\private$\HelloWorldTrans;XACTONLY"
    Else
        qinfo.PathName = strRemoteComputer & "\private$\HelloWorld"
    End If

    Set q = qinfo.Open(MQ_SEND_ACCESS, MQ_DENY_NONE)

    ' Create a local admin queue
    qadmin.PathName = ".\private$\HelloWorldAdmin"
    qadmin.Create

    ' Create a local response queue
    qresp.PathName = ".\private$\HelloWorldResp"
    qresp.Create

    ' Send message with options
    m.Label = Text1.Text
    m.Body = Text1.Text

    m.Ack = MQMSG_ACKNOWLEDGMENT_FULL_REACH_QUEUE Or _
            MQMSG_ACKNOWLEDGMENT_FULL_RECEIVE
```

```
    m.Journal = MQMSG_JOURNAL
    m.Delivery = MQMSG_DELIVERY_RECOVERABLE
    m.MaxTimeToReachQueue = 15
    m.MaxTimeToReceive = 30

    Set m.AdminQueueInfo = qadmin
    Set m.ResponseQueueInfo = qresp

    ' Send as a transaction if requested
    If Transactional = 1 Then
        m.Send q, MQ_SINGLE_MESSAGE
    Else
        m.Send q, MQ_NO_TRANSACTION
    End If

    ' Close queue
    q.Close

End Sub
```

This sample is used to send another simple message to the HelloWorld queue on a computer called kenrxp. However, we have stipulated some extra delivery options for the message. The first is setting the Ack property. This property is used to tell MSMQ that the sending application wishes to receive some sort of acknowledgment with regard to the delivery status of the message. The type of status is determined by the application. In our sample, we have requested the Full Reach Queue acknowledgment, which lets our application know whether the sent message reached the destination queue. Other acknowledgments include Full Receive (for information on whether the destination application actually received the message out of its receive queue), and negative acknowledgments (which notify the sending application only if the sent message was not received or did not reach the destination queue). The Ack property can also have the Full Reach Queue and Full Receive settings OR'd together to get comprehensive data on the status of a message.

MSMQ notifies the sending application of this status by sending a message to an administrative queue specified by the message's AdminQueueInfo property. The message contains some of the original contents of the sent message. The most important information in the status message is the CorrelationId and Class. The CorrelationId property of the acknowledgment message will match the Id property of the sent message (the Id is generated automatically by MSMQ after it is sent to the queue). The Class property of the acknowledgment message will contain a code indicating the status of the delivery. A normal delivery would be indicated by a Class property equal to MQMSG_CLASS_ACK_REACH_QUEUE.

Acknowledgment messages are useful for tracking message delivery problems or for auditing message processing by the receiver.

The `Journal` property of a message being sent tells MSMQ to make a copy of the sent message and save it in the machine's journal queue. Each MSMQ computer has exactly one journal queue for storing all messages sent with the `Journal` property set to `MQMSG_JOURNAL`. The message is saved only in the system journal when it leaves the computer. The `Journal` property can also be set to `MQMSG_DEADLETTER`. This setting is used to tell MSMQ to place the message in the system dead-letter queue if the message cannot be delivered. The `Journal` property can have both settings for a message by `OR`'ing the two values together. Journaling is useful for keeping a copy of every message sent by the device. Unlike acknowledgement messages, journal messages contain the entire contents of the sent message. The dead-letter queue is useful for keeping track of any messages that were not delivered. Undelivered messages occur when the time-to-live for a message expires without successful delivery.

The last property that we set in our example is the `MaxTimeToReceive` property. This property allows the sending application to specify how long in seconds the message can live within the MSMQ system. The receiving application must read the message from the queue prior to this timeout expiring, or MSMQ will delete it. If the `Ack` property is set to `MQMSG_ACKNOWLEDGMENT_FULL_RECEIVE` and the message expires, a negative acknowledgment message will be sent to the specified administration queue. If you try sending a message to your Windows XP system with the `MaxTimeToReceive` property set to 30 seconds, you can watch the message appear on your MSMQ administration console. Wait 30 seconds and refresh the display, and you will see the message disappear. The message is purged from the receive queue automatically, because there was no application running that read that message out of the queue. As a result, MSMQ on Windows XP deleted the message and sent a message to your administrative queue with the `Class` property set to `MQMSG_CLASS_NACK_RECEIVE_TIMEOUT`.

Response Queues

The sender sets the response queue by specifying the `ResponseQueueInfo` property of the message:

```
Set m.ResponseQueueInfo = qrespinfo
```

The `qrespinfo` object is an `MSMQQueueInfo` object with the path name set to the location of the queue to be used by the receiving application to send responses to. To help the sending application match up message responses to corresponding original messages, the receiving application usually sets the `CorrelationId` property of the response message equal to the `Id` property of the message being responded to. Nothing prevents the sending and receiving applications from

using information within the message itself to correlate response messages, if
that is preferred.

Transactions

The last option we'll look at is sending a transactional message. MSMQ on the
Pocket PC has limited transactional support. A message can be sent from
the Pocket PC MSMQ system as a "single transaction." A single-transaction message
is one that uses the MSMQ internal ordering and transactional system and does not
require the use of an external distributed transaction coordinator (DTC). A single-
transaction message is guaranteed to be delivered exactly once to the destination
queue. Normally, MSMQ may send messages multiple times to a destination queue
when there are no transactions involved. Sending messages as a single transaction also implicitly sets the Delivery parameter to MQMSG_DELIVERY_RECOVERABLE.

To demonstrate the use of single-transaction messages, we will use the same
SendOptions handler function, but we'll add a check box called Transactional. We'll
use this check box to see if the message is to be transactional or not. This impacts
the opening of the queue, where the path must append the string :XACTONLY:

```
' Open the queue for sending
If Transactional = 1 Then
    qinfo.PathName = strRemoteComputer & _
                    "\private$\HelloWorldTrans;XACTONLY"
Else
    qinfo.PathName = strRemoteComputer & "\private$\HelloWorld"
End If
```

We also need to check in the Send method whether the message is a single-
transaction message by verifying whether the Transaction check box is ticked:

```
' Send as a transaction if requested
If Transactional = 1 Then
    m.Send q, MQ_SINGLE_MESSAGE
Else
    m.Send q, MQ_NO_TRANSACTION
End If
```

The Send method of the MSMQMessage class takes an optional Transaction
parameter. If the parameter is omitted, the default setting is MQ_NO_TRANSACTION.
Set the check box and send the message. You will see that the message does not
arrive in the HelloWorld queue. This is because the HelloWorld queue on our
Windows 2000 computer is not a transactional queue. To fix this, we need to
create a new transactional queue called HelloWorldTrans. Change the path of

the `SendOptions` function to point to this new queue and try sending the single-transaction message again. You should see the message appear this time.

Receiving Messages

Sending messages is just half of the MSMQ story. We'll focus now on receiving messages from queues. MSMQ on the Pocket PC is restricted to receiving messages from local private queues on the device. Reading messages from remote queues is not supported. The HelloWorld eVB sample has a Receive button to complement its Send button. The click handler is as follows:

```
Private Sub Receive_Click()

    Dim qinfo As MSMQQueueInfo
    Dim q As MSMQQueue
    Dim m As MSMQMessage

    ' Create objects
    Set qinfo = CreateObject("CE_MSMQ.MSMQQueueInfo")

    ' Create a destination queue
    qinfo.PathName = ".\private$\HelloWorld"
    qinfo.Create

    ' Open destination queue for retrieving messages.
    Set q = qinfo.Open(MQ_RECEIVE_ACCESS, MQ_DENY_NONE)

    ' Retrieve messages from the queue.
    On Error Resume Next
    Set m = q.Receive(, , , 1000)

    If m Is Nothing Then
        MsgBox "There are no messages in the queue"
    Else
        MsgBox "The first message in the queue was removed." +_
                Chr(13) + "Label: " + m.Label
    End If

    ' Close queue.
    q.Close
End Sub
```

The first several lines of this function are similar to the Send method. The objects are declared, an instance of the MSMQQueueInfo class is created, and the HelloWorld queue is created. Remember that if the queue already exists, the Create method will do nothing.

The queue is opened for receiving by calling the Open method:

```
' Open destination queue for retrieving messages.
Set q = qinfo.Open(MQ_RECEIVE_ACCESS, MQ_DENY_NONE)
```

The access parameter of the call is different. We are using MQ_RECEIVE_ACCESS to indicate to MSMQ that we want an MSMQQueue object that can read messages from the queue. The deny parameter can be MQ_DENY_NONE (which would allow other processes to open the queue for reading also) or MQ_DENY_RECEIVE_SHARE. Denying access to the queue to other processes means that only one process will be able to open the queue for reading. Any other process that tries to open the same queue will fail. Processes that share reading a queue are not guaranteed to get all the messages sent to that queue. A message can be read from a queue only once, so it is up to the MSMQ runtime which process will get the next message in the shared queue. However, only one application will access a queue for processing the messages received in that queue.

The next few lines actually read the message in the queue:

```
' Retrieve messages from the queue.
On Error Resume Next
Set m = q.Receive(, , , 1000)

If m Is Nothing Then
    MsgBox "There are no messages in the queue"
Else
    MsgBox "The first message in the queue was removed." + _
           Chr(13) + "Label: " + m.Label
End If
```

The Receive method is used to retrieve the first message in the queue. An application can call this method as Set m = q.Receive and use only the default values for all the parameters. The parameters for the Receive method mimic those found in the desktop version: Boolean Transaction (doesn't apply to CE receive queues), Boolean WantDestinationQueue (to get the destination queue for the received message), Boolean WantBody (defaults to True to receive the body contents of the message), and Long Timeout. However, the Receive method called in this way blocks until a message is sent to the queue. To prevent our application from hanging and waiting for a message to arrive, let's use a timeout of 1000 milliseconds (1 second). The Receive method will return immediately if there is a message in the queue, or wait up to one second for one to arrive. We are in effect polling the queue synchronously to see if there is a message ready to be read. If there is a message in the queue, the Receive method removes it and returns the message to the application. Error handling is needed because if the timeout period elapses with no message read, an error is returned by the Receive method. The On Error Resume Next line of code ensures that the program continues if this error occurs.

Once the Receive method returns, we need to check if we actually got a message or the timeout expired. If the timeout expired and no message was read from the queue, the message object returned will be Nothing. If there was a message in the queue and we read it out, then the MSMQMessage object is allocated and contains the attributes of the message. Our program displays the message's Label property in a MsgBox, or notifies us that the queue contains no messages. The last line of the function closes the queue, and all the objects are destroyed automatically when they go out of scope.

Try sending several messages with different text messages and receiving them with this application. Then, try reading the queue when it contains no messages. These few lines of code form the basis for any MSMQ messaging application. We can now build on this foundation and take a look at some of the more advanced capabilities of MSMQ and the MSMQ COM objects.

Accessing Messages with Peeking and Cursors

Calling the Receive method of an MSMQQueue object retrieves and removes the first message in a queue. While this is the main function for receiving messages, there are several other mechanisms for accessing messages in a queue. The Peek method of MSMQQueue does exactly what it says: it can peek at the first message in a queue and return all of the properties of that message without removing the message from the queue. The Peek method has the same signature as the Receive method, including the ability to specify a timeout value.

Peek works only on the first message in a queue. Since Peek does not remove the message, calling it again will return the same first message. To look at other messages in the queue, you must use a cursor, which allows an application to scroll through the queue looking at messages. Cursors in MSMQ are forward-only, and there is only one cursor per MSMQQueue instance. You can reset a cursor to the beginning of a queue by calling the Reset method.

The MSMQ Admin C++ sample application uses peeking and cursors to get information about all the receive queues on the device. The CMsmqAdminView::GetMessage() method takes an MSMQQueueInfo object and scrolls through all the messages in that queue to get to the message at a specific index:

```
HRESULT CMsmqAdminView::GetMessage(IMSMQQueueInfo* qInfo,
                                   long lIndex, IMSMQMessage** pMsg)
{
    HRESULT                    hr;
    CComPtr<IMSMQQueue>        spQueue;
    CComPtr<IMSMQMessage>      spMessage;
    CComVariant                varTimeout(long(0)),
                               varWantDest(true),
                               varWantBody(true);

    // Open the queue for recv access
    hr = qInfo->Open(CE_MQ_RECEIVE_ACCESS, CE_MQ_DENY_NONE,
                     &spQueue);
    if (FAILED(hr))
        return hr;

    // Peek for the first message
    hr = spQueue->PeekCurrent(&varWantDest, &varWantBody,
                              &varTimeout, pMsg);
    if (FAILED(hr))
        return hr;

    // Peek at each message
    while (SUCCEEDED(hr) && lIndex--)
    {
        // Release the message
        (*pMsg)->Release();

        // Peek at the next message
        hr = spQueue->PeekNext(&varWantDest, &varWantBody,
                               &varTimeout, pMsg);
    }

    // Return status
    return hr;
}
```

We are peeking at the messages in the local queue referenced by the given qInfo interface. The cursor for the queue is implicitly contained within the MSMQQueue object and is accessed by calling the PeekCurrent() method. PeekCurrent() must be called to set up the cursor at the beginning of the queue. This method will return the first message in the queue (or it will return an empty object if the timeout expires). The loop just releases the message, then calls PeekNext() to get the next message in the queue. PeekNext() advances the cursor and either gets the message at that location or waits for the timeout period for a message to arrive. The loop continues to call PeekNext() until the end of the queue is reached or the lIndex variable reaches 0.

There is an additional receive method for the MSMQQueue object called ReceiveCurrent. This method supports receiving the message from the current cursor location and removing it from the queue. The method is useful when used in combination with the PeekCurrent and PeekNext methods to traverse the messages in a queue and remove only selected ones, as shown in Figure 8-7.

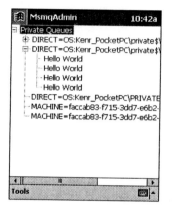

Figure 8-7. Viewing a list of queues and messages on a Pocket PC with the MsmqAdmin sample application

Queue Management

The final aspect of the MSMQ COM API we'll look at is not found in the MSMQ COM API present on the desktop. Although you can create queues and open them for both reading and writing, there is no facility for enumerating all the queues on a system. MSMQ has an undocumented set of APIs that provide access to the management of local queues. On a desktop system, these special APIs allow the MSMQ management console to list all of the queues on a system. These same APIs are supported on the CE version of MSMQ and are wrapped up in a new object called MSMQManagement.

The MSMQManagement object supports only a handful of properties and methods. The most important members of the object are the PrivateQueueCount property and the PrivateQueue method. Used together, they can retrieve every local queue, journal queue, and system queue on a Pocket PC quickly and efficiently.

The Management button in the HelloWorld eVB sample and the MSMQ Admin program both use the MSMQManagement object to iterate through all the queues on the device:

```
Dim mgmt As MSMQManagement
Dim i As Long
Dim qinfo As MSMQQueueInfo

' Create objects
Set mgmt = CreateObject("CE_MSMQ.MSMQManagement")

' Get each local queue
For i = 0 To mgmt.PrivateQueueCount - 1
    Set qinfo = mgmt.PrivateQueue(i)
    MsgBox "Queue " & CStr(i) & qinfo.FormatName
Next
```

This function creates the MSMQManagement object, gets the number of private queues that are on the device, and displays each queue's FormatName in a MsgBox. Only local queues created on the device are enumerated. Outbound queues that hold messages destined for remote queues are not accessible.

Network Configurations and Troubleshooting

MSMQ on CE uses the TCP/IP protocol exclusively. Unfortunately, you can't use ActiveSync between a Pocket PC and a desktop computer to deliver MSMQ messages. MSMQ will only deliver messages and can only receive messages when there is a TCP/IP network connection, either through a dial-up connection using Remote Access Service (RAS) or an Ethernet connection. One exception to that rule is with the Pocket PC 2002. Pocket PC 2002 supports tunneling of TCP/IP through ActiveSync; however, it shares the IP address with the ActiveSync host computer. This setup allows a Pocket PC 2002 device to send MSMQ messages but not receive them.

MSMQ on the Pocket PC only supports addressing remote queues using computer names. Path names or format names using TCP/IP addresses will not work. As a result, the Pocket PC requires the ability to resolve computer names to IP addresses using DNS, WINS, or a static host list. Other computers require the address of the Pocket PC, using the device's name, to send messages to a Pocket PC. This requirement forces all MSMQ-enabled Pocket PCs to have a unique computer name.

For static TCP/IP addressed networks that have no DNS or WINS name server available, MSMQ requires that all remote queues have their respective computers listed in the Pocket PC's Registry. The [HKEY_LOCAL_MACHINE\Drivers\TCPIP\hosts] key is used to maintain a host's list of remote computer names and their IP addresses. In this configuration, no NETREGD.DLL is needed on the Pocket PC.

Many corporate LANs and dial-up services use Dynamic Host Configuration Protocol (DHCP) to dynamically assign addresses to computers. A Pocket PC in this environment needs to register its name and assigned IP address to the network's name server so that other computers can locate the Pocket PC by name rather than by IP address. The NETREGD.DLL driver registers a Pocket PC on the network and notifies the name server of the device's name and its IP address. By registering with a name server, other computers can deliver MSMQ messages to that device using the device's unique computer name.

Problems with delivering messages with MSMQ almost always revolve around network addressing mistakes. Assuming that MSMQ is installed correctly on a Pocket PC and running, failure to exchange messages with another computer is usually due to incorrectly addressed remote queues or the inability of MSMQ to resolve remote computer names to a network address.

Troubleshooting message delivery problems requires a systematic approach to the problem. If you experience difficulties sending messages from your Pocket PC to another device or computer, try the following:

- Make sure your Pocket PC can resolve the name of the other computer. If the other computer happens to have a web server, use PocketIE to open an HTTP connection to that computer by name. If you cannot connect, try using a ping utility. Any failure to resolve the computer name to an address needs some network address debugging by a network administrator.

- If your Pocket PC can resolve the computer name, check that the remote computer actually has a queue with the same path you are trying (queue names are case-insensitive).

- Make sure that you are not trying to send a transactional message to a nontransactional queue, or vice versa.

- Be sure your message's time-to-live properties are not set too short.

If you have trouble receiving messages, try the following:

- Use ping.exe on your desktop to ensure that you can resolve the address of the Pocket PC by name. The MSMQ online help describes some useful tips for problems with NETREGD.DLL and name registering.

- Queues on a Pocket PC are always private, so be sure the path you are using includes the private$ keyword. For desktop MSMQ applications, you can only address a Pocket PC queue using the FormatName property with the direct syntax. Setting the PathName property to a private remote queue is not allowed on the desktop version of the MSMQ objects.

Summary

In this chapter, we've looked at how you can take advantage of MSMQ technology on CE devices, specifically Pocket PCs. The mobile nature of these devices and the often-disconnected state that they find themselves in are exactly the problems that MSMQ was designed to solve. We've examined the following:

- The capabilities and limitations of MSMQ on CE

- How to install and configure MSMQ on a Pocket PC

- How to program MSMQ in C++, eVB, and C#

- How to manage queues and messages on a device

- Troubleshooting hints for MSMQ on CE

The sample programs provided with this chapter will arm you with a wealth of tips and techniques to program MSMQ on CE, as well as provide some useful tools that will make your experience with developing a Pocket PC MSMQ application a successful one.

Index

A

Abort() method, using with transactions, 216–217

AboveNormal priority messages, description of, 130

"Access Denied" errors, troubleshooting, 207

ACID (atomicity, consistency, isolation, and durability), relationship to transactions, 212

AcknowledgeType property, description of, 91

acknowledgment messages, requesting, 130–133

Acknowledgment property of messages, description of, 34

ACLs (access control lists), enforcing security with, 189–191

actions
    performing on rules, 263
    relationship to triggers, 238–239

Active Directory Sites and Services snap-in, using on domain controllers, 139

Active Directory Users and Computers snap-in
    changing queue's properties with, 155–156
    creating and deleting queues with, 153–154
    creating distribution lists with, 354
    creating queue aliases with, 351
    finding queues with, 154
    managing messages with, 170
    opening, 152–153
    purging queues with, 156
    using on domain controllers, 139

Active Queues property, description of, 17

ActiveX objects, serializing and deserializing, 87

ActiveXMessageFormatter
    description of, 58, 75
    using, 87
    using with COM objects, 102

ActiveXSender.exe application, starting, 108

AD (Active Directory)
    description of, 42
    and MSMQ 2.0, 45

Add Counters dialog box, displaying, 181–182

AddRule request in TrigAdmin, description of, 266

AddTrigger request in TrigAdmin
    description of, 266
    example of, 267

admin_queue$ private system queue, description of, 24, 146

administration queues, features of, 20, 141

administration tools, using with Pocket PCs, 369–371

AdministrationQueue property
    description of, 92
    using with acknowledgments, 131–132

administrative information, obtaining from journal queues, 347

Administrative Tools, locating in Windows XP, 246

ADSI (Active Directory Service Interface), significance of, 14

ADSIEdit.msc MMC snap-in, finding GUIDs of distribution lists with, 356

AlertNextMessage() method, using with Server.exe, 327–328

APIs for Message Queuing, list of, 12

application queues
    administration queues, 141
    destination queues, 141
    report queues, 142–143
    response queues, 142

application queues, explanation of, 18

Application Specific property of messages, description of, 33

applications. *See also* decoupled applications; distributed applications; message-based applications
    interaction between, 7
    managing with Programmable Management COM interface, 339–342

forums.apress.com

FOR PROFESSIONALS BY PROFESSIONALS™

JOIN THE APRESS FORUMS AND BE PART OF OUR COMMUNITY. You'll find discussions that cover topics of interest to IT professionals, programmers, and enthusiasts just like you. If you post a query to one of our forums, you can expect that some of the best minds in the business—especially Apress authors, who all write with *The Expert's Voice™*—will chime in to help you. Why not aim to become one of our most valuable participants (MVPs) and win cool stuff? Here's a sampling of what you'll find:

DATABASES

Data drives everything.

Share information, exchange ideas, and discuss any database programming or administration issues.

INTERNET TECHNOLOGIES AND NETWORKING

Try living without plumbing (and eventually IPv6).

Talk about networking topics including protocols, design, administration, wireless, wired, storage, backup, certifications, trends, and new technologies.

JAVA

We've come a long way from the old Oak tree.

Hang out and discuss Java in whatever flavor you choose: J2SE, J2EE, J2ME, Jakarta, and so on.

MAC OS X

All about the Zen of OS X.

OS X is both the present and the future for Mac apps. Make suggestions, offer up ideas, or boast about your new hardware.

OPEN SOURCE

Source code is good; understanding (open) source is better.

Discuss open source technologies and related topics such as PHP, MySQL, Linux, Perl, Apache, Python, and more.

PROGRAMMING/BUSINESS

Unfortunately, it is.

Talk about the Apress line of books that cover software methodology, best practices, and how programmers interact with the "suits."

WEB DEVELOPMENT/DESIGN

Ugly doesn't cut it anymore, and CGI is absurd.

Help is in sight for your site. Find design solutions for your projects and get ideas for building an interactive Web site.

SECURITY

Lots of bad guys out there—the good guys need help.

Discuss computer and network security issues here. Just don't let anyone else know the answers!

TECHNOLOGY IN ACTION

Cool things. Fun things.

It's after hours. It's time to play. Whether you're into LEGO® MINDSTORMS™ or turning an old PC into a DVR, this is where technology turns into fun.

WINDOWS

No defenestration here.

Ask questions about all aspects of Windows programming, get help on Microsoft technologies covered in Apress books, or provide feedback on any Apress Windows book.

HOW TO PARTICIPATE:

Go to the Apress Forums site at **http://forums.apress.com/**.

Click the New User link.